SELF AND IDENTITY:
PSYCHOSOCIAL PERSPECTIVES

SELF AND IDENTITY: PSYCHOSOCIAL PERSPECTIVES

Edited by

KRYSIA YARDLEY

Mid-Glamorgan Health Authority and University College, Cardiff, U.K.

and

TERRY HONESS

University College, Cardiff, U.K.

JOHN WILEY & SONS

Chichester · New York · Brisbane · Toronto · Singapore

Library of Congress Cataloging-in-Publication Data:

Self and identity—psychosocial perspectives.
    Rev. and extended versions of the papers presented at the International Interdisciplinary Conference on Self and Identity held at University College, Cardiff, under the auspices of the Welsh Branch of the British Psychological Society.
    Bibliography: p.
    Includes index.
    1. Self—Congresses.   2. Identity (Psychology)—Congresses.   3. Self—Social aspects—Congresses.
4. Identity (Psychology)—Social aspects—Congresses.
5. Personality, Disorders of—Congresses.   I. Yardley, Krysia.   II. Honess, Terry.   III. International Interdisciplinary Conference on Self and Identity (1984: University College, Cardiff)
BF697.S424   1986   155.2   86-11059

ISBN 0 471 91125 9

British Library Cataloguing in Publication Data:

Self and identity: psychosocial perspectives.
    1. Self   2. Social psychology
    I. Yardley, Krysia   II. Honess, Terry
    155.2   BF697

ISBN 0 471 91125 9

Typeset by Acorn Bookwork, Salisbury, Wiltshire
Printed in Great Britain by St Edmundsbury Press Ltd,
Bury St Edmunds, Suffolk

DEDICATION

For Andréa and Keira

In the Mirror

In the mirror
On the wall,
There's a face
I always see;
Round and pink,
And rather small,
Looking back again
At me.

It is very
Rude to stare,
But she never
Thinks of that,
For her eyes are
Always there;
What can she be
Looking at?

Elizabeth Fleming

Contents

SECTION III: COGNITIVE, AFFECTIVE, AND CONTEXTUAL ASPECTS OF SELF

SECTION IV: DISORDERED AND PRECARIOUS SELVES

The Contributors

C. Norman Alexander, Jr. is a Professor of Sociology at the University of Illinois at Chicago. He has published widely on situated-identity theory and research. He is currently working to extend the theory to areas involving the Self and roles.

Susan M. Andersen is an Assistant Professor of Social-Personality Psychology at the University of California, Santa Barbara. She received her Ph.D. from Stanford University in 1981, where she also received clinical training. Her research has been concerned primarily with the sources of information about the self upon which people construct self-knowledge and with the 'subjective' nature of self-inferences. She has published numerous articles in psychological journals on this topic, and on social stereotypes, sex-role behaviours, and aspects of psychopathology as well. With a major grant from the National Institute of Mental Health, Dr Andersen is currently examining the psychiatric knowledge of mental illness stereotypes held by family physicians.

Robert M. Arkin is Professor of Psychology at the University of Missouri, Columbia. As an undergraduate at UCLA, he became interested in attribution processes (particularly concerning motivational biases). Coupled with an emphasis on processes of Impression Management during graduate school at Southern California, this interest led to his recent contributions to the literature on *self-handicapping* (which involves the management of one's public image through fairly sophisticated use of attributional principles). He has coauthored a textbook on *Human Motivation* and has contributed several chapters to edited volumes on attribution processes and the presentation of Self. Professor Arkin currently serves on the editorial boards of four journals in social psychology.

Norman K. Denzin received his Ph.D. in Sociology at the University of Iowa in 1966. He is Professor of Criticism, Interpretive Theory, and Sociology at the University of Illinois, Urbana-Champaign. He is the author of *The Research Act* (1970/1978), *Childhood Socialization* (1977), and *On Understanding Emotion* (1984). He is the series editor of *Studies in Symbolic Interaction: An Annual Review of Research*. His interests lie in the areas of critical theory, phenomenology, hermeneutics, biographical-narrative analysis, and the study of emotionality. He is currently completing a project on *The Recovering Alcoholic*, which is a social phenomenological analysis of the lived experiences of active and recovering alcoholics.

Thomas J. Figurski received his Ph.D. in Human Development from the University of Chicago in 1985. He is a trainer with the Focusing Institute in Chicago. Interested in the experience of the Self and its significance for interpersonal understanding, his current research focuses on the awareness of Self and others, particularly as it is related to changes in social context and emotional condition.

Kenneth J. Gergen is Professor in the Department of Psychology, Swarthmore College, Swarthmore, PA, in the United States. He received his B.A. at Yale University and his Ph.D. at Duke University. Before joining Swarthmore as Chairman of the Department he was at Harvard University. He is the recipient of fellowships from both the Guggenheim and the Fulbright Foundations. Among his most recent works are *Toward Transformation in Social Knowledge, Historical Social Psychology* (edited with Mary Gergen), and *The Social Construction of the Person* (edited with Keith Davis). Currently he is working on problems of metapsychology and on relational theories of human action.

Mary Glenn Wiley works in the faculty of the Department of Sociology at the University of Illinois at Chicago. Beginning with her first published research which concerned altercasting and stretching to the present chapter on self-attribution, her research reflects her persistent interest in the Self in social interaction. Her other current research involves the issues surrounding the relationship between social structure and attribution, particularly the impact of master statuses on the attribution of traits.

Jeff Greenberg is an Assistant Professor of Social Psychology at the University of Arizona. He received a B.A. degree from the University of Pennsylvania in 1976, an M.A. degree from Southern Methodist University in 1978, and a Ph.D. from the University of Kansas in 1981. Over the past several years he has collaborated extensively with Tom Pyszczynski on research concerning self-esteem maintenance and defence, depression, self-handicapping, and racial prejudice. He is currently continuing his research on the role of self-focused attention in depression and also pursuing projects concerned with the cognitive mechanisms through which motives influence inferential conclusions and the relationship between self-esteem and cultural world views and the anxiety-buffering function they both serve.

Rom Harré is University Lecturer in the Philosophy of Science, and Fellow of Linacre College, University of Oxford. He is also Adjunct Professor of Social and Behavioural Sciences at the State University of New York. He has been deeply involved in the critique and reconstruction of the theories and methods of social science. His books include *The Explanation of Social Behaviour*

(1972, with Paul Secord) and, more recently, his trilogy on *'Ways of Being'*: *Social Being* (1979), *Personal Being* (1983), and *Physical Being* (in preparation).

E. Tory Higgins is Professor of Psychology at New York University. He received his B.A. in Anthropology at McGill University, his M.A. at The London School of Economics and Political Science, and his Ph.D. at Columbia University. He has been on the faculty at Princeton University and University of Western Ontario, and has been a visiting Professor at University of Chicago, University of Michigan, Clarke Institute of Psychiatry, York University, and McQuarie University. He co-founded the Ontario Symposium on Personality and Social Psychology and is currently Associate Editor of *Social Cognition*. He has co-edited four volumes on social cognition, most recently the *Handbook of Motivation and Cognition* (with Richard Sorrentino). His current research focuses on people's use of standards to evaluate self and others and its relation to emotional vulnerability.

Terry Honess is a lecturer in Social Psychology at University College, Cardiff, Wales, U.K., where his prime interests are in the longitudinal study of adolescent identity (project currently supported by the Economic and Social Research Council), and in research methods and theory appropriate for eliciting and interpreting qualitative interview material. His interest in both developmental and social psychology stems from his doctoral work on children's personal constructions of their social worlds (awarded 1977, University of Exeter, Devon, U.K.). His journal publications reflect both his earlier 'personal constructs' work, but primarily his concern with 'self' and 'identity'. He is currently an Associate Editor of the *British Journal of Psychology*.

Ruth L. Klein received her B.A. from Barnard College in 1982 and is currently a doctoral student in both the clinical and social/personality psychology programmes at New York University. She is presently working on her dissertation which will attempt to understand the factors predisposing childhood and adolescent social ostracism.

Richard D. Logan has a background in anthropology and developmental psychology. He is Professor of Human Development, an inter-disciplinary life-span programme at the University of Wisconsin-Green Bay, where he teaches courses in personality theory and cross-cultural perspectives on human development. He has published several articles on Eriksonian theory and on the concept of identity, and has become interested in both historical and cross-cultural comparisons in self-definition, as well as having looked at the sense of Self in extreme situations such as solitary ordeals. He spent the 1984/85 academic year on sabbatical in England, studying among other things the changing Self in Western history.

Ivana Markova obtained her degree in philosophy and psychology at Charles University, Prague. Since 1967 she has worked in the United Kingdom. She is currently Professor of Psychology at the University of Stirling. Her theoretical research is concerned with conceptual and philosophical issues in social psychology, in particular in language, communication, and consciousness. She has published papers in these subjects, and a book on *Paradigms, Thought, and Language*, exploring the Cartesian and Hegelian frameworks for the study of language and thought. She also carries out research concerned with the social and psychological aspects of genetic disorders such as haemophilia and mental handicap.

Hazel Markus received her Ph.D. in Social Psychology from the University of Michigan in 1975. She is now an Associate Professor of Psychology at the University of Michigan. Professor Markus has worked in a range of areas including adult development, social facilitation, and birth order but she has been primarily concerned with issues of self-concept structure and function. The goal of her research has been to implicate the self-concept as one of the significant regulators of action. In 1984, she was the recipient of a John Simon Guggenheim Fellowship to develop some of these ideas.

Phil Mollon is Regional Psychologist in Psychotherapy, Tyne and Wear U.K. He is a qualified clinical psychologist and has a qualification in psychoanalytic psychotherapy from Tavistock Clinic. His research interests focus upon the clinical exploration of disturbances in the experience of the Self. A related conceptual interest is the exploration of the relevance of Kohutian self psychology to the approaches to psychoanalysis more prevalent in Britain. He is also concerned with furthering the availability of psychotherapy within the National Health Service.

George J. McCall obtained his Ph.D. in Social Psychology from Harvard University and currently holds the Chair of Sociology and Professor of Public Policy Administration at the University of Missouri, St. Louis. His 1966 book with J. L. Simmons, *Identities and Interactions*, was the earliest full-length formulation of the role-identity theory of Self. His involvement in the continuing development of that social structural approach to Self may be seen, not only in the 1978 revised edition of that book, but also in his *Social Relationships* (1970) and *Social Psychology: A Sociological Approach* (1982, again with Simmons), as well as a variety of journal articles and contributed chapters. McCall currently serves as Associate Editor (for Sociology) of the *Journal of Social and Personal Relationships*.

Paula Nurius received her Ph.D. in Social Work and Social Psychology from the University of Michigan in 1984. Currently she is an Assistant Professor in the School of Social Work at the University of Washington. Her interest in the self-concept and identity grew out of doctoral dissertation work which was an exploration of those aspects of the self-concept that are particularly sensitive to variations in the social environment. She has published widely on many aspects of mental health and has been particularly concerned with the translation of self-concept theory into practice.

Anand Chintaman Paranjpe obtained his Ph.D. in Psychology from the University of Puna, India, and did post-doctoral research with Professor Erik H. Erikson at Harvard University while on a Smith-Mundt scholarship and a Fulbright grant in 1966/67. He has been teaching and doing research at the Psychology Department of Simon Fraser University, in Burnaby, British Columbia, Canada since 1967. His publications include *Caste, Prejudice and the Individual* (1970, Lalvani, Bombay), *In Search of Identity* (1975, Macmillan, New Delhi, and Halsted/Wiley, New York), and *Theoretical Psychology: The Meeting of East and West* (1984, Plenum, New York).

Tom Pyszczynski is a lecturer in Social Psychology at the University of North Carolina at Chapel Hill. He received a B.A. degree from the University of Wisconsin-Milwaukee in 1976, and an M.A. and Ph.D. from the University of Kansas in 1979 and 1980, respectively. Over the past several years, he has collaborated extensively with Jeff Greenberg on research concerning self-esteem maintenance and defence, depression, self-handicapping, and racial prejudice. He is currently continuing his research on the role of self-focused attention in depression and also pursuing projects concerned with the cognitive mechanisms through which motives influence inferential conclusions and the relationship between self-esteem and cultural world views and the anxiety-buffering function they both serve.

Robert D. Romanyshyn is Professor of Psychology at the University of Dallas and Visiting Professor of Philosophy at the University of Texas at Dallas, 1985/86. He is the author of *Psychological Life: From Science to Metaphor* and has published numerous articles and chapters in the areas of clinical psychology and the interdisciplinary connection between psychology and art, literature, and philosophy. Currently he is working on a book concerned with the psychology of technology. In recent years he has been an invited lecturer and visiting Professor at many universities in the United States, Europe, and Africa.

Timothy J. Strauman is a doctoral candidate in clinical and in social/personality psychology at New York University. His theoretical interests include the integration of social-cognitive and psychodynamic perspectives on personality, as well as on emotional and psychosomatic disorders. Along with his work with E. Tory Higgins, his current research involves psychological and physiological aspects of anxiety disorders, including an investigation of the role of self-evaluative standards in social phobia.

Sheldon Stryker is Distinguished Professor of Sociology, Indiana University at Bloomington. He is currently Editor of the *American Sociological Review*, and is a past Editor of the Arnold and Caroline Rose Monograph Series of the American Sociological Association and of *Sociometry*. His long-term theoretical and research interests have been in examining and developing symbolic interactionist thought, especially through a greater appreciation for the ways in which social structures constrain the social psychological processes on which symbolic interactionism has traditionally focused, as well as through the elaboration of identity theory. Among recent publications exemplifying these efforts are the present chapter, a chapter with Anne Statham entitled 'Symbolic Interactionism and Role Theory' in the third edition of the Lindzey and Aronson *Handbook of Social Psychology*, and his *Symbolic Interactionism: A Social Structural Approach*.

Ralph Turner is Professor of Sociology at the University of California, Los Angeles. He received his doctorate from the University of Chicago. He is a former President of the American Sociological Association and a former Vice-President of the International Sociological Association. He has published extensively and is the author of *Collective Behaviour* (1957, 1972) with L. Killian, *Family Interaction* (1970) and *Waiting for Disaster* (1986) with J. Negg and D. H. Paz, and is co-editor (with M. Rosenberg) of *Social Psychology: Sociological Perspectives* (1981).

Ernest S. Wolf, M.D., is on the faculty and a training analyst at the Chicago Institute for Psychoanalysis, and an Assistant Professor of Psychiatry in the Department of Psychiatry of the Northwestern University Medical School. He was closely associated with Heinz Kohut in the development of the psychoanalytic psychology of the self. He has published widely on clinical and theoretical issues in self psychology as well as on psychoanalysis and literature. Other publications include essays on the development of Freud's thought and on the psychology of adolescence. Dr Wolf is preparing a study of the therapeutic process in clinical self psychology.

Krysia Yardley is a clinical psychologist working for Mid-Glamorgan Health Authority and an Honorary Research Fellow at University College, Cardiff. She is principally interested in methodological problems in social and clinical psychology especially those that bear on the development of qualitative research. She has researched and published in the areas of role play methodology (she is also trained as a psychodramatist) and social skills therapy. Her interest in Self arises both from her epistemological interests and from her practice of psychotherapy. She received her doctorate in psychology from the University of Wales in 1984.

Preface

There has been of late a re-emergence of 'self' as a focus of academic concern in the social sciences and related disciplines. Its recent history reveals only patchy interest from academics; for the most part the 'self' and its counterpart 'identity' have been virtually ignored or treated with mild derogation, particularly by psychologists, as being too mentalistic or elusive. Consequently, where there has been interest in 'self' this has predominantly existed within the narrow focus of 'self-presentation' and above all in the shape of 'self-esteem'. Such work continues to be important, and is indeed represented in this volume, but the reduction of self to the purportedly operationalizable and accessible is itself a symptom of the profound ambivalence with which researchers have viewed 'self'.

Current research occurs in a much wider and richer vein of exploration and is vigorously pursued by psychologists, psychoanalysts, sociologists, anthropologists and philosophers. These disciplines rarely 'speak' to each other and this is even true of sub-branches of individual disciplines. Yet frequently scholars of different disciplines, and of different theoretical persuasions, draw on the same rich historical resources and unwittingly share a community of ideas and concerns. This book is an attempt to foster cross-fertilization and communality, to re-establish the past and to establish the present and future community of ideas that emerge from leading authorities and innovative contributors to the field. Such an overriding purpose was also at the heart of the International Interdisciplinary Conference on Self and Identity held in Cardiff, 1984, under the auspices of the Welsh Branch of the British Psychological Society from whence the preliminary work for the chapters in this book first took shape. In order further to facilitate such debate, the editors have introduced four overview and discussion chapters and authors have familiarized themselves with the work of other contributors.

The issues that characterize the 'self' and 'identity' literature bring together a number of concerns that are echoed in the broader social science arena. Thus our 'metatheoretical' and 'self and social structure' sections explore the relation between individual and society, and include extensive discussion of social constructionism. The cognitive emphasis that characterizes much of psychology is reflected in the third of our four sections, which, however, moves beyond treating 'self' simply as a key information processing structure by the necessary inclusion of affect and the consideration of interactional context. The final section, which deals with 'clinical' issues, includes the most exciting of recent psychoanalytic developments, i.e. 'self psychology', which provides a way out of the intrapsychic and biological strait-jacket of classical Freudian theory.

We are today in the social sciences at a point where theoretical and epistemological sophistication is outstripping our familiar methodologies. One recurrent and important theme in this book is the extent to which research has relied upon inadequate methodologies such as reactive techniques and the isolation of aspects of 'self' and 'identity' on the basis of ill-conceived assumption. Many of the writers here attempt to redress the balance, particularly in favour of the experiencing subject. It is not the case however that this book takes on board the very notion of 'self' without allowing critical debate. Several writers challenge the very usefulness of 'self' and also challenge its validity as a phenomenon of a 'natural kind'. Above all then, we intend in this book to open up the debate, and further to facilitate an interchange between disciplines, and theorists of different persuasions, in the firm belief that all have something to say, and above all, in the context of scholarly development, all have something to say to each other.

Acknowledgements

Special thanks are due to those who helped shape and plan the 1984 Conference from which the stimulus for this book grew; in particular, the steering group, which consisted of Ken Gergen, Rom Harré, Ray Holland, Paul Heelas, William McGuire, Malcolm Pines, Joseph Rychlak, John Shotter and Ralph Turner. The Welsh Branch of the BPS also provided continuous support, and the early encouragement of Tony Chapman and Dave Müller is gratefully acknowledged. Finally, we wish to thank the Department of Psychology, University College, Cardiff, for significant support throughout the planning and execution of the whole enterprise.

Thanks are extended to Miss Alison Fleming for permission to quote 'In the Mirror' by the late Elizabeth Fleming.

Section I
Metatheoretical Commentaries

1

Metatheoretical Commentaries: An Introductory Review

Krysia Yardley and Terry Honess

Generations of learned and unlearned since the Reformation have scoffed at the medieval theologians who were concerned with arguing the number of angels who could dance on a pinhead. Some commentaries concerning the existence of self, particularly when viewed as a transcendental object, have taken on a similar superciliousness. Yet the persistence and constant re-emergence of diverse arguments and theories concerning the self demonstrate its continuing salience, and suggest it will remain a key concept for understanding personhood. The first section of this book deals with some of the arguments challenging the employment of the concept of self, and therefore provides an interesting and important counterpoint for the explicit acceptance of the centrality and importance of the concept by the contributors in the remainder of this book.

In the first contribution, Logan asks us to take a more cross-cultural and transhistorical view of the Self. He offers a set of hypotheses concerning the changes in 'sense of self' in Post-Classical Western European society up until the present time. Although he generally uses secondary sources upon which to base his arguments, he provides an intriguing description of the emergence of self that finds echoes in Erikson's (e.g., 1968) analysis of the life cycle. For example, Logan has pointed out that the current concern of Western Europe's 'social elite' with 'existential identity vs. meaningfulness' and the 'masses' concern with 'instrumental identity vs. identity confusion' echoes the Eriksonian individual 'psychosocial stage' of 'intimacy vs. isolation'. However, it is the broader socio-historical perspective that is the concern of the current contribution. Readers interested in an explicit treatment of the parallel with Erikson are referred to Logan (1981).

Logan's central proposition is that the individual's sense of self inevitably and necessarily reflects the general world views prevailing in a given era. (A similar analysis is provided by Romanyshyn (1982), in his *Psychological Life: From Science to Metaphor*; see also his contribution to this volume.) Moreover it is this mutual defining of self and society that leads Gergen (this volume) to argue that 'theories of self are no less than theories of what it is to be human'. Although, there is broadly implicit in Gergen's argument the suggestion that such theories also offer *no more* than an analysis of what it is to be human. Indeed, Logan does go further than Gergen in explicitly suggesting that the source of subsequent cultural development can be seen to be 'caused' by the currently prevailing sense of self.

Logan suggests, after Morris (1972), that self was 'discovered' in the Middle Ages having appeared disjunctively from a prior merging of the individual in group life. Logan characterizes this as 'the era of the self as newly autonomous subject in the world'. However, uniqueness is not emphasized, any personal element is seen 'to serve the typical and the general', and there is little concern with the inner life. The Renaissance is seen as implicating the 'assertive self', where the individual is as principally interested in his or her (although Logan acknowledges that the analyses upon which he draws almost invariably feature the male elite) effects on the world. Logan argues that here there is, once again, little concern with the 'drama of inner life', or the nature of self. However, there is some ambiguity here in that the Renaissance individual was also apparently 'not very clear what he wants to make of himself', a concern that partly characterizes the state of feeling of the 'post-modern', objectively aware individual, for implicit here is the idea that the self is 'makeable'.

The seventeenth and eighteenth centuries are characterized by the 'self as a competent subject' (a 'detached standpoint' for the 'I'). The later eighteenth century and the nineteenth century are posited as the time for the emergence of a 'brooding introspectionism', associated with the discovery of the Self 'as an observed object'—itself a reflection of the 'modern world' view: 'how does the world affect me? (An interesting factor here may be related to the explicit writing of novels *for* women, and the emergence of women writers.) Finally, in Logan's view, we are led to the 'post-modern' culture, 'the era of self as an alienated object', experiences that are vividly documented by Denzin (see the 'Disordered Selves' section).

In pursuing this general line of argument, Logan, at the very least, challenges the reader to consider that different societies, at different times, facilitate different views of what it is to be a person, which, in turn, circumscribe the form and content of individual experience. However, it is arguably the case that a too close adherence to the developmental progression advanced by Logan may lead to a distorted reading of the culture in which the sense of self is embedded. For example, let us consider the Middle Ages as a case in point. Logan argues that there was little concern with the inner life or individual identity and that self was not viewed as an 'object'. However, Logan and the commentators that he cites draw largely from literary works taken from highly specific contexts.

The following points suggest caution in the interpretation of literary, particularly prose works. For the vast majority of folk, the oral tradition was the only expressive medium and the only vernacular based tradition. (For example, in England, few could read or write in English, let alone Latin or

French.) Where the 'romance tradition' of the court intersects with this oral tradition, literature becomes more directly personalized and concerned with inner feelings (as occurred within the works of the troubadour and trouvères). Other literary romance work was arguably constrained by the context of public performance, non-vernacular language, and the treatment of feeling through the extensive use of allegory which typifies medieval art forms. Such use of allegory further inhibits our understanding of the nuance of intended emotional meaning. Moreover, prose (including the limited number of biographies that existed) occurred within a didactic and moralistic tradition at the hands of the clergy.

Chaucer and Dante wrote in the romantic tradition but they also significantly broke with the former tradition of writing in French or Latin by writing in, or developing, the vernacular. It is possible that their arguably great sensitivity to individual experience is associated with this use of the vernacular and the closeness it afforded them to ordinary lives and experiences. Moreover, Dante (1265–1321) persistently acknowledged the difference between 'inner' and 'outer' worlds:

> Were I a pane of leaded glass, I could not
> summon your outward look more instantly
> into myself, than I do your inner thought.
>
> (*The Inferno*, Canto XXXIII, ls. 22–24)

Indeed, Dante's work, particularly as regards the Commedia, is arguably pervaded by the poet's sense of self and his own subjectivity (which runs parallel to his more theological purposes), and is characterized by great psychological sophistication in describing others. His earlier and semi-autobiographical *Vita Nuova* (written in 1292) is, according to MacAllister (1953), 'a delicate and sensitive analysis of the emotions', a work also profoundly influenced by Dante's love for Beatrice Portinari.

Chaucer (1340–1400), is also a writer who can be seen to express both the general and particular with consummate skill. In writing his prologue to the *Canterbury Tales*, he frequently expresses the highly individuated and personal nature of his characters through the irony with which he juxtaposes their idealized roles and the actual manner in which these characters demonstrate individual flaws and eccentricities. This is precisely how twentieth century role theorists discuss notions of style, and even personality characteristics (see Stryker, this volume, for example). Finally, we might note that the denial of the self as object in the Middle Ages is also a contentious matter. In contrast to Logan, Harré (1983) cites the allegorical morality plays as an example of the high level of individuation in the Middle Ages and, in particular, as an example of the I/Me stance adopted by such writers as G. H. Mead. This is particularly significant as the morality plays in themselves constitute a highly restrictive expressive form. They are essentially and primarily didactic, constructed by a clergy wary of the perceived profanity of the earlier mystery plays.

Notwithstanding our last comments, it should be reiterated that Logan provides generally compelling arguments that the predominant modes of self reference do shift across time and between cultures (see Heelas and Lock, 1981, for more on the latter). However, this might lead us along two very different paths. First, that self is only a social construction, and that selves as such simply do not exist or, second, that selves do exist, subjectively and objectively thoughout history, since they are a necessary constituent of personhood, but that they attract different emphases at different times. This is a debate to which we will turn again in this review.

Whilst Logan principally takes a historical perspective, Paranjpe, the next contributor to this section, although drawing on a long historical tradition, takes an essentially cross-cultural view. Drawing on his considerable knowledge and experience of both Eastern and Western cultures, and his familiarity with the major philosophical works of both, he seeks to affirm the existence of the transcendental self, and its key position for both analytic and experiential understanding. Paranjpe argues that Western psychology has largely ignored 3000 years of Indian psychology, which throughout its history has been consistently and intimately concerned with questions pertaining to the nature and existence of self, its stability, and the relationship between the objective and the subjective self. Paranjpe draws on the Vedanta and Yoga systems and argues that the Vedanta system, in particular, is able to avoid the dualism of Kant, and overcome polarities that are held to be incompatible in the West: objective vs. subjective, analytic vs. existential, determined vs. willed, and value free vs. moral positioning.

Vedanta describes the self as having several dynamic modes which are transcended by the mode of self as unchanging passive witness, which overcomes the narrowness and bias implicated in being wedded to a particular position. The dynamic 'ego-involved modes' are 'self as knower', 'self as enjoyer/sufferer', and 'self as agent'. Paranjpe argues that this conceptualization deals with the difficulty of identifying the self with both permanence and impermanence, and the self as both subject and object. Moreover, the transcendental self is given a base that is realizable in experience (contrast Kant) and clearly articulated procedural steps are provided as to how to achieve this state. Thus far, examination of the witness mode is compatible with the canons of classical science. However, the final 'proof' lies not with publicly communicable data, but individual experience of the mode in question.

Despite Paranjpe's cogent criticisms of Western psychological research, there are, nevertheless, two important ways in which this analysis finds echoes in current Western research and practice. First, even within the relatively short span of Western psychology, there has been in some quarters a positive valuing of the subjective (e.g., Bakan, 1967), which is now reasserting itself in psychodynamic perspectives (see the last section of this volume). Second, moral imperatives, which are avowed in the work described by Paranjpe, are also involved in the analyses of Gergen and Harré (this section) who see an understanding of social relations as firmly rooted in the 'moral order'.

Quite unlike Paranjpe, however, Harré disputes self as having a transcendent reality but argues that self is a 'mode of personal organization' which exists through the grammatical properties of language games. This mode is refuted to be distinctly personal in the sense that it is not seen as internal, subjective, or belonging to an individual order, but is seen as a property of the social and moral order. In an earlier work (*Personal Being*, 1983), which the present contribution seeks to extend, he takes Strawson's (1959) ego/person distinction as fundamental 'The concept of pure individual consciousness . . . cannot exist as a primary concept in terms of which the concept of a person can be explained or analysed. It can exist, if at all, as a secondary non-primitive concept, which itself is to be explained, analysed in terms of the concept of the person' (1959, p. 102). This allows Harré to develop his constructivist thesis by positing 'persons' as being located in the primary structure (Strawson's 'primitive concept') of society, embodied as publicly identifiable and socially accountable. Self is the secondary concept, 'the inner unity to which all personal experience belongs as attributes of a subject' (this volume).

Now, for any society (moral order) to exist all of its functioning members are, by definition, persons; personhood is then, for Harré, a cultural universal. Now, it is precisely because Harré wishes to argue that the form and structure of our self understanding (our more or less inner unity) is patterned on the 'grammar' of the primary person relationships (which are, of course, embedded in particular cultures), that he is able to say that selves are 'socially constructed' (he might also have said 'linguistically constructed'). A bald statement of his thesis then, is that 'the organization of mind is a cultural artefact based on the learning of a local concept of self'.

Harré is at pains to emphasize that selves (unlike persons) do not exist in the sense of having immediately observable properties, rather, he supposes that self is a theoretical concept, 'the heart of a theory learnt by each' person. Harré suggests that invoking the concept of self should not trouble us since 'transcendental' realities are commonly invoked in physics and certainly are exploited in organizing our patterning of the physical world, e.g., through the concept of gravity. Parenthetically, we should note that Harré's use of the 'concept of self' is not to be confused with the more traditional 'self-concept', that is a person's beliefs about themselves, e.g., in response to the question 'Who are you?', but is close to Logan's 'sense of self'. It is surprising perhaps that Harré elsewhere (1983) acknowledges a link with Yoga, which it is suggested prescribes ways to discover a self without content, but here the similarity with Paranjpe's transcendentalism ends. The 'passive witness mode' is, unlike a theory, realizable in experience, and it cannot therefore be a parasitic concept.

How then does our reflexive self-discourse come to be modelled on public speech practices? (the 'Special Theory', significantly influenced by Vygotsky and Wittgenstein). Harré makes much of the distinction between the first person statements incorporating psychological predicates such as 'I am tired' which he sees as essentially authentic or inauthentic, which are contrasted with the use of psychological predicates in the third person (e.g., 'she is tired') for which he argues there will be criteria for their use. We have some difficulty with this particular point in that both assertions can be analysed from different positions. Thus, Figurski (this volume), for example, distinguishes inside/outside, coupled with self/other to generate four orders of self awareness, which can be seen to implicate, in various degrees, conditions of both authenticity and truth value. For example, the statement 'he believes he is right' may not be a matter of assessing the available public criteria or the actarial likelihood of implicated outcomes. Rather, the speaker's statement is first grounded in their own position (including their intentions, generally embedded in their own thoughts and feelings, to which they have privileged access) and there is often a recognition that the other has a similar 'privileged' position, which the speaker may attempt to empathically relate to, or project into. Moreover, the avowal 'I believe I am right' may not merely be a matter of dubiety, but a reflexive and evaluative statement referring to the speaker's privileged awareness of the various conflicting or complementary cognitive steps undertaken, situated within a gestalt of affectively experienced confidence or anxiety, in order to assess the object of belief.

Notwithstanding the above, Harré can still claim that first person avowals locate the position of the person who is the speaker, and that the concept of self does not need to be invoked for such appraisals. However, for Harré, the crucial case is that of second order avowals which involve an assessment of our first order avowals, e.g., 'I believe that I am tired' (compare Taylor, 1977, who sees 'second order evaluations' as the key feature of agency, but it leads him to talk of deeply rooted personal values). For Harré, the embedded 'I' (the concept of self has been invoked) has a logical grammar patterned on that of the third person statements which are located in the primary level of social accountability. Hence, selves, in everyday discourse, are evaluated as if they were third person statements. But are these second order avowals a cultural universal? Harré must acknowledge that 'real human beings are not mere localisations, they are internally complex, this internal complexity I call the secondary structure' (1983). This suggests that personhood necessarily involves, as a universal principle, a secondary structure, which is why he must say that although self is a theoretical concept, 'it is the heart of a theory learnt by *each* human being' (italics ours).

Furthermore, with respect to the status of the existence of the self, and indeed of thought itself, it appears difficult to us to sustain the idea that either are mere cultural artefacts since humans are more than creatures of a social and moral order, they are also creatures of a biological and phylogenetic order (an analysis pursued by Luckman, 1979). Although the importance of such may be the subject of dispute, it is difficult to conceive that the seemingly inherited organization of behaviour that occurs lower in the phylogenetic scale does not enter into the structure of the organization of the mind. Indeed, Harré in *Personal Being* (p. 92) acknowledges 'a preprogramming of actions that provoke from the mother the kind of performances and displays that are "just right" ', and here there are strong parallels with the position of some of the new dynamic school (Wolf, Mollon, this volume). Furthermore, neuro-psychological studies point to an intrinsic patterning in brain functioning—see Rychlak (1986) for extensive discussion on the neuropsychologically based patterned propositionality of thought. It is perhaps Harré's emphasis on language that may bias the case against other constitutive contenders for self. Much of human behaviour and experience is non-linguistically mediated or accomplished. Dreams, images, music, and dance are part of another symbolic order which may be seen to have only loose and oblique relations to everyday social transactions. Moreover, all the above have strong connections with sensory modes other than those normally implicated in language, such as the relationship between kinaesthesis and dance. The Vedantic 'seer' presumably exists experientially in this preconceptual realm.

Harré's suggestions for research practice follow closely his linguisitic analysis. Thus he encourages researchers to examine social practices and the language games of communities. From our perspective, such injunctions do seem to be of great importance, although subjective, especially non-verbal experience is pushed to the background, and is seen at best as a means of gaining insight into the collective. This is especially unfortunate given the only recent and precarious re-entry of the subjective as admissible in 'reputable' research. However, irrespective of the above, and irrespective of the degree to which self structures are necessarily involved in the concept of a person, Harré's analysis provides a powerful set of conceptual tools which allow self structure, not just content, to be seen as significantly socially constructed and, moreover, he allows a challenging and sensitive analysis of the social practices implicated in the use of self referent language.

In the next contribution, Gergen, whose conceptual position has so much in common with that of Harré, provides an overview of trends in psychological research. Gergen describes what he sees as the need for self to be understood in relational, not individualistic, terms. In addition, he is particularly concerned with moral questions since our rendering of self 'informs society as to what persons can and cannot do'. He cites as examples, the definitions of self implicated in the U.S. civil rights movements for blacks and women, abortion reform, and litigation in terms of insanity. All these depend on particular views of the person, ideas concerning the 'dignity of self', 'self-esteem', and the ownership, the inviolability of 'self'. Implicit in this part of his overview is that such views of 'self' were of significant value in promoting positive social change, but that this is no longer the case, since, in stressing individualism, the egocentric, selfish, and competitive order is increasingly encouraged.

This commentary on the moral state of our culture is underpinned by Gergen's conceptual analysis which emphasizes the communal, not individually generated, basis for the construction of 'individual minds'. Thus, Gergen (like Harré on self as a cultural artefact) talks of knowledge as an 'artefact of social collectivity'. He gives special consideration to the work of Schachter (1964) which allows a definition of the emotions which can also be seen to be parallel to the way in which Gergen understands 'self': '(it) . . . emerges from the co-operative and historically situated attempts of communities to render their constituents intelligible'. As Gergen himself notes, there are a number of criticisms of Schachter's work; McClure (1984), for example, presents an interesting set of counter-arguments which focus on the peculiarly ambiguous set-up of the social environment of Schachter's experiment and the fallaciousness of deducing that the emotional attributions made could be compared with mundane emotional attributing.

A key aspect of Gergen's thesis is that changes in self study have been part of broader shifts in our understanding of the social order. In particular, Gergen argues that our faith in the empirical basis of knowledge has been eroded and, with regard to selves, so has the assumption that persons should seek 'self-knowledge' through 'becoming appraised of the kind of mental events that they harbour'. Here, Gergen appears to completely equate the validity of the concept of self-knowledge (and thus self) with the validity of the empiricist based location of knowledge in external observation and with the validity of the argument of natural kinds. However, in rejecting the latter two arguments it seems that he has disallowed internal observation (subjectivity?) as a positive alternative to behaviourist claims to knowledge. Moreover, in arguing that persons generally only have access to the products of their mental processes, and little access to the process, he asserts that the individual route to understanding is severely limited. This argument is consistent with the arguments made by attribution theorists (e.g., see collection edited by Antaki, 1981), yet is one that arguably draws an unnecessary dichotomy between process and product, an issue pursued by Markova (this volume). Indeed, Gergen also acknowledges that the 'social process is carried out by self directing agents'. This suggests that Gergen too requires a 'secondary structure' (see Harré) to understand personhood, which we have suggested universally implicates self-reflexive discourse. But, as Markova comments, there is no analysis here yet of what constitutes agency, nor is there any concern with individual experience.

Gergen's location of the dynamic and constructive within the collective, but not explicitly within the individual, is of particular fascination since he acknowledges the influence of the interactionist tradition, yet he appears to be diametrically opposed to the increasingly individualistic aspects of interactionist writings of contemporary microsociologists (see Self and Social Structure section). For such authors, 'thingness' and stasis have become identified with the social and collective representation of interaction, and theorists have felt it necessary to reassert the importance of cognitive strategies and individual interpretations of meaning in order to account for social *action*.

Moreover, Gergen's position appears to be more radical than that of Harré in that the former appears to disallow (or is silent on) that which Harré would allow, i.e., that although the self may not exist as any thing, it can be interpreted as an organizing, structuring process to which we can ascribe properties, and which has real consequences. These issues are further pursued in the final contribution to this section where Markova seeks to show how process and structure are not polar opposites, and how process can be identified with 'self', without equating self with 'thingness'. Gergen, like Harré, concludes with the demand that we look more carefully at social practices and the nature of our attributions, moreover his rhetorical ending on the auspicious question of whether we can replace individualistic theories of self bespeaks a great concern for the moral values and actions of society. Conceptually he is beginning to map out a position that appears to demand a new vocabulary, and new metaphors to help with the task of explicating 'the discourse of relationships (which) represents a vastly unarticulated subtext upon which rests the text of individual selves'.

Lastly, in this section, Markova clearly espouses an individualistic model of self and self-knowledge in terms of there being a clear agent who is processing and structuring, someone who is 'doing the knowing'. However, a very important part of her model is interactional. Markova takes up Hamlyn's thesis (1977) that knowledge about self cannot be equated with knowledge of self, and agrees with his position and that of Hegel that knowledge of self occurs in action and interaction, through a practical involvement. Where she significantly departs from Hamlyn is over his repudiation of any tendency to stand back from one's own actions as inimical to self-knowledge proper. For Hamlyn, the sort of knowledge implicated in reflexivity leads to debilitating self-consciousness and anxiety that interferes with the process of knowing oneself (see also Mollon, this volume). Markova argues that Mead's three-step process of gaining self knowledge is a good deal more sophisticated than Hamlyn perceives and that the model handles both spontaneous action and knowing through the rapidity of the engagement of its phases. For Mead, action and reflection are but two phases of one and the same process; I and me constantly alternate positions and knowledge is constantly transformed through this process.

Markova agrees with Hamlyn, after Hegel, that there is no thing to be known with respect to self, but unlike Hamlyn she does not view reflection as reification of all objects. She views concepts and objects as only transitorily stable until revised because of changing dynamics. Again this is commensurate with Mead's model as she reads it and it helps her to get out of the trap the social constructionists may be in danger of falling into (see discussion of Harré and Gergen in this chapter) of dichotomizing the social as process, and the individual and internal as reification.

A possible difficulty that emerges in her work is her treatment of emotion. Although she is adamant that emotion should not be viewed as a disruptive phenomena, and must be conceptualized as part of the process of knowing, it is not altogether clear how this is to be the case. Mead's position on reflexivity appears very cerebral and there does not appear to be a clear place in the model for the biological substratum of behaviour. Are emotions to be treated as part of the creative spontaneous 'I'? And if they were so treated, to what extent are they modified by the 'me'? In contrast, for Hamlyn, knowing through action implicates emotion in a manner quite distinct from mere information gathering about oneself, rather he stresses involvement and commitment to oneself as a necessary condition for self knowledge. Would Markova give emotions a primordial status within her evolutionary epistemology? And, could this be extended to explain more profoundly the process of self deception? After all, Fingarette's model of self deception, as presented by Markova, suggests only a conscious, volitional turning away from knowledge of self despite the fact that Markova clearly suggests an unconscious factor in such 'turning away'. Indeed, we shall see that this last point is explicitly picked up in the dynamic contributions of the clinical section.

ACKNOWLEDGEMENTS

We are grateful to Prof. F. Jones and Dr G. Bedani, Dept. of Italian, U.C.C., for helpful conversations.

REFERENCES

Antaki, C. (1981). *The Psychology of Ordinary Explanations of Social Behaviour*, Academic Press, London.
Bakan, D. (1967). *On Methodology*, Jossey-Bass Inc., San Francisco.
Dante (1953). *The Inferno* (transl. J. Ciardi), Mentor, New York.
Erikson, E. (1968). *Identity: Youth and Crisis*, Faber, London.
Hamlyn, D. (1977). 'Self-knowledge.' In T. Mischel (Ed.), *The Self: Psychological and Philosophical Issues*, Blackwell, Oxford.
Harré, R. (1983). *Personal Being*, Blackwell, Oxford.
Heelas, P. and Lock, A. (1981). *Indigenous Psychologies*, Academic Press, London.
Logan, R. (1981). 'An Eriksonian model for the development of the self through history.' *International Psychohistorical Association*, New York.
Luckman, T. (1979). 'Personal identity as an evolutionary and historical problem. In M. Von Cranach *et al.* (Eds), *Human Ethology*, Cambridge University Press, Cambridge.
MacAllister, A. (1953). 'Introduction to the inferno.' In *The Inferno* (transl. and Ed. J. Ciardi), Mentor, New York.
McClure, J. (1984). 'Attributions of intent and motive.' *International Conference on Self and Identity*, Cardiff.
Morris, C. (1972). *The Discovery of the Individual 1050–1200*, Harper and Row, New York.
Romanyshyn, R. (1982). *Psychological Life: From Science to Metaphor*, Open University Press, Milton Keynes.
Rychlak, J. (1986) 'The logic of consciousness.' *British Journal of Psychology*, 77, 257–268.
Schachter, S. (1964). 'The interactions of cognitive and physiological determinants of emotional state. In L. Berkowitz (Ed.), *Advances in Experimental Social Psychology*, vol. 1, Academic Press, New York.
Strawson, P. F. (1959). *Individuals*, Methuen, London.
Taylor, C. (1977). 'What is human agency?'. In T. Mischel (Ed.), *The Self: Psychological and Philosophical Issues*, Blackwell, Oxford.

Self and Identity: Psychosocial Perspectives
Edited by K. Yardley and T. Honess
© 1987 John Wiley & Sons Ltd

2

Historical Change in Prevailing Sense of Self

Richard D. Logan

This contribution proposes that those who stress the influence of socio-economic context as a factor in influencing theory construction might do well also to consider that a major component of the broad cultural context for theorizing is the prevailing sense of self of members of that culture and that era, and that prevailing sense of self may be a 'cause' of subsequent cultural change. The paper proposes that sense of self be viewed as central in historical and cultural change, and goes on to argue that the sense of self has developed through Post-Classical Western European history (from an autonomous 'I' in the Middle Ages to an existential 'me' in modern times) in a way that strikingly parallels differing world views and orientations to experience in different eras.

INTRODUCTION

As the field of psychology has grown, it has become self-reflective about its own underpinnings and interested in the effects of surrounding *context* as a shaper of both theories and research agendas. Many propositions have been advanced of late from a sociology of knowledge stance that maintains that theories are but another form of social construction (e.g., Berger and Luckmann, 1967), having their origins in historical and socio-cultural conditions (Buck-Morss, 1975; Gergen, 1973; Sampson, 1977). Following these propositions have come calls to 'form a serious scholarly alliance with sociology and social history' (Youniss, 1983) in order to get at those factors that shape our theories and their biases. Sampson (1977) maintains, for example, that a prevailing cultural value of 'individualism' is one contextual factor that has had a major influence on contemporary Piagetian theory's view of the individual as a competent knower. I would suggest here that Sampson puts his finger on not just another of a set of contextual factors, but indeed a major one that should hold a special significance for psychologists. What might be termed 'prevailing orientation of self' in cultures and eras is a key factor of both natural topical interest to psychologists and of special significance in a time of concern about socio-cultural context. This proposition is a form of 'psychology as history' (cf. Gergen, 1973).

I also wonder why social constructivist critics of contemporary theory have not turned more to the work of those who might well be considered experts in the study of socio-cultural contexts of human undertakings—the anthropologists. I am myself influenced here by two anthropologists regarded by some as intellectual leaders of mid-twentieth century anthropology: Robert Redfield and A. Irving Hallowell. Redfield, for example, discussing differences in *world view*, says: '[E]very world view *starts* from the man who is the viewer and includes the idea of a self . . .' (Redfield, 1953, p. 19). Hallowell makes a similar statement:

> Just as different people entertain various beliefs about the nature of the universe, they likewise differ in their ideas about the nature of the self. And just as we have discovered that notions about the nature of beings and powers existent in the universe involve assumptions that are directly relevant to an understanding of the behavior of the individual in a given society, we must likewise assume that the individual's self-image *and his interpretation of his own experience* cannot be divorced from the concept of self that is characteristic of his society (Hallowell, 1955, p. 76; author's italics).

Strauss (1979) and Crapanzano (1979) make similar points.

The point here is that the above are not just statements about differences in the sense of self of 'people' (i.e., of those whom we social/behavioural scientists study), but of the sense of self (and therefore theoretical 'interpretation of experience') of social/behavioural theorists as well. Thus when Sampson (1977) mentions a bias toward 'individualism' in current Western psychology, he is referring not only to a possible prevailing Western sense of self as unique, self-contained individualities, but also to a tendency among theorists to see the self as a discrete *object* in—and shaped by—the world. Geertz (1974) is à propos here:

> The Western conception of the person as a bounded, unique, more or less integrated motivational and cognitive universe . . . set contrastively both against other such wholes and against its social and natural background, is, however incorrigible it may seem to us, a rather peculiar idea within the context of the world's cultures (Geertz, 1974, p. 31).

I am not equipped to do a cross-cultural comparison of varieties of self-definition, but I have looked at different eras within the history of Post-Classical Western European civilization. My proposition generally is that we consider change in the stance of the self as a beholding 'I' as central in historical change, i.e., change in the basic orientation and relationship of the person to the world and in the basic parameters of experience. Further, other cultural developments can be seen as predicated *upon* different prevailing senses of self, as will be briefly suggested. The argument in this paper is not, however, that change in sense of self is entirely 'cause' in historical and cultural change (although such a viewpoint used to be taken in the old Culture and Personality debates).

The evidence for my proposition comes from a variety of works that discuss changes in 'human consciousness' over history (e.g., Heller, 1982; Kahler, 1973), and, more importantly, from the arguments of a variety of authorities who see the emergence of the self occurring at different times in Post-Classical Western European history. I would maintain that they are all correct since each has found a significant 'stage' in the gradual emergence of individuality.

I recognize the vast range of conceptions and theories of self, and its essential nature, that is extant. By 'self' for the purposes of this contribution, I am relying simply on the dualistic conception of the self-as-subject (Knower) and self-as-object (Known)—G. H. Mead's (1943) 'I' and 'me'—and on the extent to which prevailing sense of self in various (historical) contexts tends toward one or the other of these two orientations. For example, if a person functions in the world as an independent beholding entity but is not beholding itself, that person exists as 'I'; on the other hand, a self ('I') highly concerned *with* itself has a strong sense of 'me'. This I–me conception of self is widely adhered to (Damon and Hart, 1982; Glicksberg, 1963; Macmurray, 1933; Paranjpe, this volume).

The problems of the development of self in Western history has been addressed by a small number of other writers. (I am here limiting myself to covering the Post-Classical world—what historians used to call the 'second great cycle' in the history of civilization.) Marc Bloch (1961), Colin Morris (1972), and Huizinga (1959), for example, see the self emerging in the Middle Ages, some time before 1200. On the other hand, it has been commonplace for years for historians to describe the Renaissance/Reformation era as 'the era of the rise of the individual' (cf. Burckhardt, 1867/1960; Macmurray, 1933; Williams, 1961). Smith (1952) and Rée (1975) imply that the self emerged at the time of DesCartes' famous *Cogito ergo Sum* in the 'Age of Reason', while Marshall Berman (1970) sees it arise with Montesquieu in the early eighteenth century. Other authorities (Foucault, 1970; Perkins, 1969; Lyons, 1978; Kauffman, 1980) maintain that the self was invented (Lyons' term) in the later eighteenth century, during the late Enlightenment/early Romanticism period. While at least four different periods have been put forth as the time of origin of the self, it is apparent from voluminous evidence that the 'self' described is different for each era and also fundamentally unlike the 'self' of people in the modern age of 'Existentialism' and self-conscious concern with 'Identity'. A progression from something closer to a group identity (in very early times) to an emergence of 'individualism' (at some point ranging from the later Middle Ages through the Renaissance to Romanticism, depending on whom one reads) to a relatively intense concern with self (in the contemporary era) can be discerned.

THE LATER MIDDLE AGES: THE ERA OF THE SELF AS NEWLY AUTONOMOUS SUBJECT IN THE WORLD

Colin Morris (1972) argues that the self is 'discovered' (his term) around 1050 to 1200 during the Middle Ages. (He argues that it appears not by increment, but more or less full-blown from preceding group-life.) Interestingly, many historians (e.g., Brinton, 1953) describe the Middle Ages in retrospect as one of struggle between 'individualism' and organization (e.g., the Church). Feudalism may have been a transition vehicle aiding the emergence of an autonomous 'self', since it involved more 'one-to-one' relationships between master and serf (Bloch, 1961; Morris, 1972). Ullman (1966) claims that in the thirteenth century the individual emerged out of the Corporate and Ecclesiological structures of society as a citizen.

Indeed, writings from the later Middle Ages did reactivate the Classical exhortation 'Know yourself', and Morris (1972, p. 65) maintains that '[S]elf-knowledge was one of the dominant themes of the age.' Yet, to the extent that the self *was* contemplated or 'known', it seems not to have been conceived yet as a unique 'me'. The prevalent theory that the mind of everyone consisted of four elemental moral virtues (prudence, temperance, fortitude, and justice) does not sound very individualized. Similarly, medieval biographies were generally descriptions of archetypal moral virtues rather than unique personalities (Kahler, 1973; Lyons, 1978). 'The personal element had to serve the typical and the general' (Weintraub, 1978, p. 58). (Indeed, according to Williams (1961), the term 'individual' meant 'inseparable' or 'member of a group' through most of the Medieval period.) The even rarer *auto*biographies seldom dealt with 'inner life', but instead recounted activities. Rosenthal (1971, p. 159) sums up the medieval ego as 'scantily concerned with individual sentiments'. Thus, the exhortation to 'know yourself' was perhaps more of a desired goal than a realizable fact. The emphasis may have been on the self-as-subject's *seeking* to know, i.e., '*know* yourself' as opposed to today's 'know your*self*'.

I would hypothesize that the primary (but not exclusive) self-sense of the Middle Ages was the emergence out of the corporate and the ecclesiological of the non-self-conscious sense of 'I' (I will, I choose, I observe). This is supported, for instance, by the painting of Giotto, generally regarded as a major innovative figure in the history of art (Janson, 1962). The fact that Giotto originated the use of *linear perspective* in painting shows that he was aware that he viewed the world not according to convention and tradition but from his individual *viewpoint*. He had a sense of where 'I (subject) stand' as a (newly) autonomous being in relation to the world. I would put it that Chaucer had a similar stance, seeing his characters more 'in depth' from a newly autonomous viewpoint. In fact, this sense of individual standpoint—oriented to the world rather than reflected back on itself—is virtually a definition of what it means to *be* an 'I'. Little sense of awareness *of* self entered in, however, and Giotto still painted subject matter dictated by group convention and tradition, and Chaucer wrote within conventional story frames and his 'individual' characters also represented corporate categories.

It seems only logical (as well as suggested by the evidence) that the very first experience of a 'self' could only be the individual's awareness of separateness from the larger whole, that is, 'I', with little awareness *of* self as unique individuality. In keeping with this beginning sense of self, philosophers of the time wrestled with the new discovery of their individual wills versus the Will of God, but still sought to use their new autonomous viewpoint and autonomous reasoning to arrive at a strengthened faith in the larger Corporate Being. Awareness of self was essentially of one's separateness as an autonomous being which seems to have been a matter of sensing 'Being Seen' by Others and God, as witness the writings of Abelard and his sense of shame. 'Being Seen' is a theme in chivalric romance literature as well (cf. Goldin, 1967; Hanning, 1977; Medcalf, 1980).

THE RENAISSANCE AND REFORMATION: THE SELF AS ASSERTIVE SUBJECT

The Renaissance seems to have been a time of increased independent action, self-assertion, and 'intrusion' of the individual self into the world. In the Renaissance, individuals (particularly elite male individuals) got 'into everything'. Men of the Renaissance spent their time 'advertising their own excellence and quarrelling over trifles' (Easton, 1966, p. 312). Having the foundation of the institutionalized historical legacy of Autonomy, the 'I' could now try to have *effects* on the new world it beheld. The individual of the elite asserted his/her desire to have effects and make a difference through the exercise of imagination, as revealed in the flowering of the arts, the pursuit of learning for its own sake, ambitious individual enterprise, and in the seeking of power by which to manipulate others (cf. Machiavelli's theorizing 'I certainly think that it is better to be *impetuous* than cautious, for fortune is a woman, and it is necessary . . . to conquer her by force'). Individual ambition was of course embodied in Calvinist thought and the emerging Protestant Ethic (Dillenberger, 1971), and McClelland (1961) has traced the origin of individualistic achievement motivation and Capitalism to the rise of Protestantism. Consider also in terms of individual assertiveness the words of Pico della Mirandola: '*Restrained by no narrow bonds*, according to thine own *free will* in thou, thine own *maker* and *molder*, mayest fashion thyself in whatever manner thou likest best' (Easton, 1966, p. 313). The Borgias, Rabelais, Henry VIII, Martin Luther, and Cervantes also seem to be archetypal self-assertive individuals of the sort that led Santillana (1956) to label this era 'The Age of Adventure'.

'[The Renaissance] humanist is a great individualist—he wants to be himself. But he is not very clear what he wants to make of himself [as an object]' (Brinton, p. 24). Individualists of the Renaissance were still remarkably (by today's standards) non-reflective and un-self-conscious:

One of the major characteristics of the Renaissance remarked on by all historians is the emphasis placed on individualism . . . [But this individualism] invariably stopped short of an interest in the drama of an idiosyncratic inner life . . . For [Florentine sculptor] Cellini or a Montaigne, as different as they were, the details of life are treated as the integers that add up to a sum. Still, the total is not so much themselves as it is what is typical of their time and place. What makes their accounts seem so modern is that they are specific and secular, but their inner life is a blank or a contrivance . . . (Lyons, 1978, pp. 70–71).

The Renaissance individualist asserted individuality but did not reflect on that fact; instead one identified with one's effects on the world and society, and autobiographies consisted of a narrative recounting of such activities rather than self-reflection (Weintraub, 1978). Self-awareness appears to have been most saliently a matter of beholding one's *actions* and *effects* on the world, and beholding others' *re*-actions to same (cf. Markova, this volume). The 'I' was in the stance of *agent*-in-the-world (cf. Paranjpe, this volume). The prevailing sense of self was as an assertive subject ('I') who affected society rather than being shaped *by* society, the opposite of the more contemporary view:

Such a self-conscious [not in the 'modern' sense] person will not find the self, the state, or the society, as finished givens of nature; he will perceive these as *human creations*, as works of art, or as artifices . . . The notion of a society composed of willful individuals responds better to the new individual consciousness than the [Middle Ages] notion of a traditional community in which the individual finds, ready-made, his organic function (Weintraub, 1978, p. 95).

The emphasis seen by many Renaissance historians on self-expression seems consistent with the characterization of the Renaissance as the era of the self as assertive subject, and the philosophies of such as Calvin, Luther, Machiavelli, and the writings of such as Cellini and Montaigne seem predicated on that type of stance of self as 'I'.

THE SEVENTEENTH AND EIGHTEENTH CENTURIES: THE SELF AS COMPETENT SUBJECT

For the elite at least, the seventeenth century 'Age of Reason' with its Rationalism (DesCartes, Leibniz, Spinoza) seems to have embodied another major change in the stance of the representative 'I' and its relation to the world it beheld. Close after came the eighteenth century 'Enlightenment', and the likes of Locke and Hume, with their faith that science and its empirical method would lead to a thoroughgoing understanding of both nature and man. Two major themes seem closely allied in these eras. One was the belief, widely held by rationalists and empiricists alike, that truth was a knowable single system of natural laws and material things, and that the universe was arranged according to a stable 'natural order', and second, the great beginning exercise of building (at least for the male elite) a new more 'democratic' order in the Western world, based on 'individualism' as then understood. Mauss (1979) sees the 'self' emerging with seventeenth century movements such as Puritanism. Others (cf. Rée, 1975) see a new emergence of self in DesCartes' broadly suggestive 'Cogito, ergo sum'. Berman (1970) also sees the origin of some kind of new self in the seventeenth century, linked with the writings of Montesquieu and Pascal.

What kind of 'self' are the above thinkers addressing and/or (more importantly) revealing? It is somewhat difficult to critique the evidence they cite as there has not been the concentrated focus on and voluminous argumentation for this era as for the Late Middle Ages and Renaissance as the time of the 'origin of the self'. The claim that the American Revolution was a significant beginning of a new kind of individual existence has frequently been more of a political claim than the tracing of the phenomenon of individuality to its roots, which probably in this case were in preceding Puritanism. DesCartes' *Cogito* might readily be taken as a self-evident datum of a new awareness of self, and it certainly must be predicated on *some kind* of self-awareness, but how thoroughgoing is not easily determined. Besides, DesCartes' emphasis in the *Cogito* was more a logical than a psychological one. However, the intriguing question remains of where DesCartes 'stood' as a beholding 'I' such that he would come to utter that statement. The rise of Rationalism in the seventeenth century (and its cohorts, logic and mathematics) and of Empiricism (and its ally science) so dominate these centuries that one must look to them to find the status of the elite 'I' in this age and its relation to the world. Self appears limited in its self-consciousness by virtue of being still more oriented to the 'outer' world than to its own 'inner' character (cf. Macmurray, 1933). I would propose the following model for self in this age:

Upon a cultural foundation of institutionalized individual instrumentality/ agency, which was a legacy of the Renaissance's 'adventurous overreaching' and the Protestant Reformation's success in affecting the religious order, and which had 'cleared away' many traditional forms of knowing the world, a typical elite 'I' of the post-Renaissance beheld a 'cleared world space' in need of re-conceptualization. The fact of the historical legacy (passed on through families via socialization, education, and modelled example) of individual autonomy and individual instrumentality meant that (elite) individuals were already prepared to believe that they could 'make a difference'. With that as given, the next step was a further realization of inherent agency potential in the form of having *constructive* effects on the world. It was now up to the individual mind as never before in history to *itself* be the source of an ordered model of its world. (I mean this as a statement of the general task for that age, but also as the task facing *individual* minds as they beheld their particular corners of the new world.) Both Rationalism and Empiricism are predicated upon a *Competent* construing, 'I', capable of initiating and conducting well-reasoned thought and systematic observation (and learning from same), respectively. The 'I' now relates to the world via 'constructive' effects on the world. The Newtonian model of the naturally lawful universe, the new practical technologies (e.g., Jefferson, Franklin), and the efforts to construct a new social order are all similarly predicated. The Puritan idea of American democracy, for all of its emphasis on individual liberty (read as 'institutionalized autonomy') and the 'pursuit of happiness' (reflecting institutionalized individual initiative?) seems less self-consciously but no less directly to have been predicated upon the *competent individual*, at least at the elite level, capable of the reasoned judgment necessary for participating in governance and economic life. It is the *individual competence* to reason, know, and choose (e.g. one's own government) that is the added element to the idea of individual liberty in this age. Only a *detached* 'I' could conceive of such systems of thought, or of Empiricism as well. The comprehensiveness, internal consistency, clear-cut elegance, and *certainty* of the new scientific (Newtonian, etc.) models of the world (theoretical, practical, and political) and the methods for reasoning (logic, mathematics) and for knowing the world (empirical science) indicate not just that the Beholding Entity is now a 'competent' detached observer but that the 'I' which lately moved through and bumped against the world must now (in order to *be* competent) have come into a *stabilized standpoint* as a detached observer standing apart from the traditional, corporate, and ecclesiastical structures as well as from nature and the world it beheld.

This leads to the question of how 'I' apprehended itself in this age (and how *individually* 'I's' beheld themselves), following on from having beheld oneself in one's *effects* on the world and on others in the Renaissance. Essentially, one beheld oneself in one's *constructive* effects on and in the world, and in one's skills, constructions, and ideas in dealing with the world. The self then is *beginning* to be apprehended as something 'inner', something 'personal', and as object, but the self is primarily as *mind*, or as reasoning process and it is the *mind* as the entity that is object (cf. Locke's *tabula rasa*), not so much the self in the sense prevailing today.

THE 'MODERN' WORLD: THE ERA OF THE SELF AS OBSERVED OBJECT

The nineteenth century seems to see the full tilt of the balance toward the self as object, and the kind of awareness of self ('me') that most today take as a simple and obvious given in their phenomenal worlds. The period known as Romanticism in the late eighteenth century may represent the transition point from a 'Competence' stage of the self-as-subject to a 'Self-Reflective' stage. Perhaps Rousseau, in his *Confessions*, represents this transition in the sense of self:

> This idea of 'living one's own life', and of the value of 'being one's self', of developing one's own individuality, is a very modern one. Before Rousseau, *hardly any one seems to have had this modern sense of personality and of its value*. That was partly because in the ancient world every one regarded himself and other people primarily not as individuals but as members of classes (Woolf, 1933, p. 103; author's italics).

Interestingly, Perkins (1969) and especially Lyons (1978) both also maintain that the late eighteenth century period of Romanticism is the time of the invention of the self altogether. Their analyses, however, make quite clear that it is the discovery of self as *object* of which they speak. Lyon says, for example:

> [The] difference between the assertive ego, often seen in writers of the Renaissance, and the *brooding introspection* of Romantic writers, is not always seen when their actual words are placed side by side, but it is a difference which results in other meanings . . . [Renaissance] individuality was based on respect for talent, or property and legal rights, but invariably stopped short of an interest in the drama of an *idiosyncratic inner life* [exhibited by Romantic writers] (Lyons, 1978, p. 70; author's italics).

Perkins (1969) describes in great detail the explorations of 'idiosyncratic inner life' of both Rousseau and Diderot in the later eighteenth century. Perkins observes further: 'Rousseau has clearly reached *a new concept of personality*, one which ingeniously combines the simple Cartesian sense of self-identification [self-as-subject] with the post-Lockean empirical development of self [as object]' (Perkins, p. 115). Kauffman (1980) and Weintraub (1978) see Goethe rather than Rousseau as reflective of the new personality concept.

On the heels of an era that had lionized rationalism, reason, systematic empirical observation, and the like (all reflecting the self as subject relating competently to the world) came the Romantics, for whom the self had clearly become the *object* of their interest. At the same time, in philosophy, 'In the field of self, Kant [in the late eighteenth century] was the first to clearly distinguish the two aspects of the self, the *I* [subject] and the *me* [object] which DesCartes had so conveniently merged in his *Cogito*' (Perkins, p. 38). This underlines the fuller emergence of the self as object, 'inner', and in a 'personal space' in the late eighteenth century, and a shift away from the dominance of self as subject. Authors began explicitly to write not just of recognizable individual characters as in previous eras but to personify them-*selves* in their writings. Romantic writers were 'deeply interested in themselves, their *reactions* to the world, the effect of the world on *them*, and their innermost feelings, which they were willing to bare to the world' (Easton, p. 631). Thus a concern with 'personality' as it is understood today began to emerge. The focus had begun to make an historic shift from 'How do I (subject) reason about and observe the world?', to 'How does the world make me (object) feel?', and 'What has experience made of me?'

Shortly thereafter, the major philosophers of the nineteenth century, Marx particularly (and Darwin and Spencer, of course), were revealing this prevailing sense of self by addressing precisely the phenomena suggested above: theorizing about the impact of history, evolution, social structure, social change, economic systems (mostly man-made products of the earlier 'I' stages), on the individual as *recipient* of world happenings rather than as instrumental *cause* (i.e., on how past history and experience had instrumentally created the self). By this stage predecessors would have 'built' enough of a legacy of cultural accomplishments for the focus to shift from how 'I' influence the world to how the world influences and has influenced 'me'. The focus of this era, then, was one of reflection on oneself and on *how one got here*, that is, on what the past, experience, the world, have made of 'me'. Thus, nineteenth century explorers scoured the world in search of 'sources' and 'origins'. Following a long period of the gradual emergence of self-awareness, a point began to be reached where the most important object of concern to the self *was* the self. Thus people began to sense themselves as unique individualities in and shaped by the world. This is the virtual opposite of the Renaissance view described earlier. Marx, for instance, wrote on the impact of the economic system on man. He also declared: 'In labor is the creation of the self [as object].' From God as the source, to individual as the worldly source, to individual as the worldly *product*, seems to be the historical progression.

In terms of an increasing awareness of self as prime object of its own interest, the rapid rise of the field of psychology in the twentieth century is itself a major case in point. (The rise of the social sciences also reflects a shift to seeing humans as socially *created* rather than the Renaissance view of creators (cf. Gergen, this volume).) Structuralist theory in psychology at the turn of the century focused explicitly on the introspective observation of oneself. Psychoanalysis stressed the intensive probing in depth of the psyche as an *object* of study (indeed, it used the term 'object' itself). Erikson's neo-Freudian concept of *identity* made the self even more explicitly the *object* of study. Behaviourism is particularly illuminating in view of the thesis of this paper. In the concept of operant conditioning, behaviourism recognizes that one operates as subject or agent upon the environment, but it focuses explicitly on the *consequences* of one's actions and on the effects of those 'reinforcements' back on the person as a recipient object. (Respondent conditioning, the other category of behaviour, is even more oriented to the effects of experience on the person.)

The European Piaget, imbued with still more classical notions, explicitly preserves the self as active knower and subject in his concept of 'assimilation', but even here assimilation is only half of the picture, balanced by accommodation, in which the mind/self is influenced as object by experience. Further, many (cf. Habermas, 1971) see Piaget as essentially a symbolic interactionist, for whom social interaction with others (accommodation) precedes the construing of and empathizing with (assimilation) others.

Skinner is explicit in stating that there is no 'free will' (no autonomy), no 'prime mover' (no self-assertion), and no 'creativity' (no competence) within the person. The self as 'I' or subject has thus not just been down-played in his scheme, it has *ceased to exist altogether*. (Skinner, of course, does not use 'self' language at all, so he would only agree that he has the human *organism* as an object of study, not the self. But then Skinner is consistent, and he implies a key and correct point: If there is no 'I' to behold it, no 'me' can exist either. Is this a statement presaging a still greater future identity crisis?

'POST-MODERN' CULTURE: THE ERA OF THE SELF AS EXISTENTIAL/ALIENATED OBJECT

In still more recent times, and perhaps more in the intellectual upper middle-class, a still further change in prevailing sense of self seems to have occurred. It is reflected in the rise of Existentialist philosophy and much of so-called humanistic psychology, especially that of the 'pop' variety. With a more complete removal from group, from the products of one's labour, and from past history, and with a life devoted to the present, the self as subject ceases to have much of a *created* 'me' to behold. ('I' becomes further 'alienated' from 'me'.) The self as 'I' must then undertake an effort to 'find' a self or to 'make' one in the here-and-now of existence with no major help from others or from the past. Thus, in the 'post-affluent' era, the social elite begin to seek their own individual destinies, in their individual ways, by their own efforts. They try to 'get in touch' with their selves—to find the 'real inner me'; that is, the self as object so long sought now becomes a kind of '*lost object*', so much has it become deeply 'inner' and so deeply is it held to be, not a *created* object, but an essence that is existentially 'there'.

Some of the most articulate proponents of the orientation that I have labelled self-as-existential/alienated objects are students of modern literature. Glicksberg (1963) is especially à propos:

> Dwelling in a universe that seems to him alien and hostile, man today retreats within the fastness of the self, only to discover that he does not know himself [as object]; but the curse or the glory of being human is that he must at all costs strive to know. He cannot endure existence without some light, however uncertain, of self-knowledge. Engaged in an interminable monologue, he develops the habit of introspection to such a degree that he comes to feel entirely alone, cut off from communication with others (Glicksberg, 1963, p. xi).

Glicksberg continues by addressing the other side of the state of the self—the erosion of that sense of definite standpoint or perspective that *is* the 'I' and which I have suggested *was* the core of the sense of self in previous centuries:

> He cleaves to his negations; he can embrace no certitudes, no existential faith born of subjective immediacy. He is an absence, a self stripped of ontological truth. He cannot say 'I' with any measure of spontaneous conviction. In how many curiously different ways the self as object is conceived by the self as subject—'the "me" by the "I" '. The hero of our time cannot accept or act on the vital principle: I am that I am . . . The grammatical fiction 'I' persists, but it is only a semantic phantom. The self as doer is as ghostlike as the self as subject . . . *Modern man cannot pause in his journey for ego-identification and say confidently: 'This is I.'* (Glicksberg, 1963, p. xi).

The 'real' self has become 'me', not 'I'. The self as subject has by now become merely the *tool* of the search for self ('know your *self*'), whereas in the Middle Ages what mattered was the search itself, i.e., the subjective self was what mattered *because* it searched. The time has long since passed for an individual to feel whole by realizing simply 'I am'. Now one is bound to seek to be able to say 'I am *me*' (or 'I've got to *find* me' . . . or '*be* me'). Modern psychology theory both reflects and must contend with this new orientation. Thus although modern humanistic psychology extols 'subjective experience', the focus is still on attaining and knowing the 'me', expressed for example as my 'gut feelings', my 'body', my 'head', my 'parent/adult/child', also expressed in the feeling that one's self is under constant observation, and in the emphasis on the self as one's 'best friend', self as consumer, self as victim of the world, and self as beneficiary or *object* of contemplation, stimulation, pleasure, and of affection in our narcissistic age. In Existential psychology, the self as subject is important mostly to *create* or discover a 'me'. Rogerian psychology, from the mainstream of Humanistic psychology, reveals that the essential core of our being today (the organismic self) is something we are alienated from and must get in touch with. It is explicitly *not* the self-as-seeker that is central, but the self-as-*sought-object*.

CONCLUSION

I have attempted to indicate some relationships between prevailing sense of self and types of undertakings and paradigms for understanding in different eras. Thus the world was seen anew by the Autonomous Self in the Middle Ages, moved and shaken by the Assertive Self in the Renaissance, re-made and scrutinized by the Competent Self of the Age of Reason, and the Self itself became the object in more recent times. I would point out, for example, that the contemporary view that sociocultural context determines our paradigms—and that culture has shaped human character—is *itself* a paradigm which can be seen as based on the contemporary sense that self (whether of 'theorist' or 'person') is *created object* in and of the world.

In terms of contemporary humanistic psychology, on the other hand, the difficulty with the claim that it is based on the self as *subject*, lies simply in our current self-conscious *awareness* of what existentialists term the core fact of existence—that 'I am'. I submit that the 'I' of the medieval individual was not the same as the asserted valuing of the subjective 'I' in humanistic psychology today. The medieval 'I' *was the new fact of autonomy itself*, and it was not reflected back on itself—it was simply a *standpoint* from which, as an individual beholder, to see anew the world, for the first time to make individual choices, etc. Today, we simply cannot escape the fact that our selves are objects in and of our awareness, and therefore also objects in and of (or alienated from) the world.

REFERENCES

Berger, P. and Luckmann, T. (1967). *The Social Construction of Reality*, Doubleday, New York.
Berman, M. (1970). *The Politics of Authenticity*, Atheneum, New York.
Bloch, M. (1961). *Feudal Society*, University of Chicago Press, Chicago.
Brinton, C. (1953). *The Shaping of the Modern Mind*, Mentor, New York.

Buck-Morss, S. (1975). 'Socio-economic bias in Piaget's theory and its implications for cross-culture studies.' *Human Development*, **18**, 35–49.

Burckhardt, J. C. (1867/1960). *Civilization of the Renaissance of Italy*, Mentor, New York.

Crapanzano, V. (1979). 'The self, the third, and desire.' In B. Lee (Ed.), *Psychosocial Theories of the Self*, Plenum, New York.

Damon, W. and Hart, D. (1982). The development of self-understanding from infancy through adolescence. *Child Development*, **53**, 841–864.

Dillenberger, J. (1971). *John Calvin: Selections From His Writings*, Anchor, New York.

Easton, S. (1966). *The Western Heritage*, Holt, Rinehart and Winston, New York.

Foucault, M. (1970). *The Order of Things*, Tavistock, London.

Geertz, C. (1974). From the natives' point of view. *Bulletin, American Academy of Arts and Sciences, XXVIII*, 1, 26–43.

Gergen, K. (1973). 'Social psychology as history.' *Journal of Personality and Social Psychology*, **26**, 309–320.

Glicksberg, C. (1963). *The Self in Modern Literature*, State University Press, Pennsylvania.

Goldin, F. (1967). *The Mirror of Narcissus in the Courtly Love Lyric*, Cornell, Ithaca, New York.

Habermas, J. (1971). *Knowledge and Human Interests*, Beacon, Boston.

Hallowell, A. I. (1955). *Culture and Experience*, University of Pennsylvania Press, Philadelphia.

Hanning, R. (1977). *The Individual in Twelfth Century Romance*, Yale, New Haven.

Heller, A. (1982). *A Theory of History*, Routledge and Kegan Paul, London.

Huizinga, J. (1959). *Men and Ideas*, Meridian, New York.

Janson, H. W. (1962). *The History of Art*, Prentice-Hall, New York.

Kahler, E. (1973). *The Inward Turn of Narrative*, Princeton, New Jersey.

Kauffman, W. (1980). *Discovering the Mind*, McGraw-Hill, New York.

Lyons, J. O. (1978). *The Invention of the Self*, Southern Illinois University Press, Carbondale, Illinois.

McClelland, D. C. (1961). *The Achieving Society*, Van Nostrand, Princeton, New Jersey.

Macmurray, J. (Ed.) (1933). *Some Makers of the Modern Spirit*, Methuen, London.

Mauss, M. (1979). *Sociology and Psychology*, Routledge and Kegan Paul, London.

Mead, G. H. (1934). *Mind, Self, and Society*, University of Chicago Press, Chicago.

Medcalf, S. (1980). *The Later Middle Ages*, Methuen, London.

Morris, C. (1972). *The Discovery of the Individual 1050–1200*, Harper and Row, New York.

Perkins, J. (1969). *The Concept of the Self in the French Enlightenment*, Librairie Droz, Geneva.

Redfield, R. (1953). *The Primitive World and its Transformations*, Cornell University Press, Ithaca.

Rée, J. (1975). *DesCartes*, Pica Press, New York.

Riegel, K. (1978). 'The influence of economic and political ideologies on the development of developmental psychology.' *Psychological Bulletin*, **78**, 129–141.

Rosenthal, B. (1971). *The Images of Man*, Basic Books, New York.

Sampson, E. (1977). 'Psychology and the American ideal.' *Journal of Personality and Social Psychology*, **35**, 767–782.

Santillana, G. de. (1956). *The Age of Adventure: The Renaissance Philosophers*, Mentor, New York.

Smith, N. K. (1952). *New Studies in the Philosophy of DesCartes*, Macmillan, London.

Strauss, A. S. (1979). 'The structure of the self in Northern Cheyenne culture.' In B. Lee (Ed.), *Psychosocial Theories of the Self*, Plenum, New York.

Ullman, W. (1966). *The Individual and Society in the Middle Ages*, Johns Hopkins Press, Baltimore.
Weintraub, K. J. (1978). *The Value of the Individual*, University of Chicago Press, Chicago.
Williams, R. (1961). *The Long Revolution*, Columbia University Press, New York.
Woolf, L. (1933). 'Rousseau'. In J. Macmurray (Ed.), *Some Makers of the Modern Spirit*, Methuen, London.
Youniss, J. (1983). 'Beyond ideology to the universals of development.' In D. Kuhn and J. Meacham (Eds), *On the Development of Developmental Psychology*, Karger, Basel.

Self and Identity: Psychosocial Perspectives
Edited by K. Yardley & T. Honess
© 1987 John Wiley & Sons Ltd

3

The Self Beyond Cognition, Action, Pain, and Pleasure: An Eastern Perspective

Anand C. Paranjpe

In the ancient intellectual tradition of India the self has been conceptualized as a passive witness or a centre of awareness which transcends the three active aspects of selfhood, namely the self as knower, enjoyer/sufferer and agent. This trilogy parallels the three parts of the soul conceptualized by Plato, and designates the self as the experiential centre of cognition, volition, and affect. In the present paper it is argued that this Indian conceptualization is comparable to Kantian transcendentalism, except that it escapes some major drawbacks of Kantianism noted by William James: its ambiguity, non-verifiability, and its barrenness with respect to useful outcomes.

Although the concepts of self and identity have moved only recently to the centre of the mainstream of psychological research, they have long been central and prominent topics in the Eastern as well as Western intellectual traditions. While the European legacy of 2000 years of studies in this field is not unknown to contemporary psychologists, the equally rich and varied contributions of the Indian subcontinent are little known. The purpose of this essay is to point out certain parallels in the views of self and identity from the Indian and Western intellectual traditions. The focus will be on certain distinctive Indian contributions which would complement and enrich the parallel trends of thought in contemporary psychology.

In the Indian subcontinent serious inquiry into the nature of the self dates back to the early *Upaniṣads*, about a dozen or so philosophical treatises composed probably around 1500 to 500 B.C. In an early Upaniṣad called the *Bṛhadāraṇyaka Upaniṣad* (2.4.5), the sage Yājñavalkya urges his wives to seriously meditate on the nature of the self. This appeal parallels the well-known Greek exhortation 'know thyself'. Thinkers in the East and the West have traditionally distinguished between self as subject and object (dṛk/dṛśya), and between self and identity. Identity refers to the unity and sameness in selfhood as opposed to the multiplicity and change in its various manifestations. In the non-dualistic Vedānta (which is one of the most prominent systems of thought of the Upaniṣadic origin), it is considered extremely important to make a 'wise discrimination between the permanent and the impermanent (nitya-anitya viveka)' in regard to the self. A focus on the permanent aspects of the self obviously refers to its self-sameness, i.e., its identity. It is necessary to add that the term identity as used here refers to that which ultimately accounts for the sameness of selfhood, and not to personal or social identities which it refers to in common usage.

Two rather different reasons for the importance of the identity issue may be pointed out. First, from an analytical and impersonal viewpoint, the question '*what* remains unchanged in the selfhood of a person?' is an intriguing puzzle that has challenged philosophers for centuries. Second, from an existential viewpoint, it is important to clarify the unchanging aspects of one's selfhood to be able to meaningfully answer the vexing and deeply personal question 'Who am I?' Analysis of the identity issue has been done from both these viewpoints in the Indian as well as Western traditions.

Indian and Western conceptualizations also distinguish three aspects of the self, namely, the self as knower, enjoyer or sufferer, and as agent. The Upaniṣads clearly conceptualize the self in these terms. The *Bṛhadāraṇyaka* (2.4.14) and *Kaṭha* (3.13) Upaniṣads, for instance, discuss the nature of the self as knower ('jñātṛ', or jñāna ātman); the *Kaṭha* (3.4) and *Śvetāśvatara* (1.8.12) Upaniṣads refer to the self as enjoyer/sufferer ('bhoktṛ'); while the self as agent ('kartṛ') is discussed in the *Praśna Upaniṣad* (4.9). (For an English translation of the more important Upaniṣads, see Hume, 1931.) The discussion of these concepts is followed up in the *Bhagavad-Gītā*, which is a widely known and influential compendium of the major schools of thought originating from the Upaniṣads. In the *Bhagavad-Gītā*, the discussion of these three aspects of the self is spread through several sections. Plato's three parts of the soul mirror this trilogy of concepts, and it has persisted in modern Anglo-American psychology as some variant of cognition, conation, and affect. The balance of this essay will focus on the Indian conceptualization of the self as knower, enjoyer/sufferer, and agent with the hope of bringing traditional insights into the mainstream of modern psychology. Within the limited scope of this essay it would not be possible to outline the basic concepts of the Upaniṣads, or of the major schools of Indian thought. Authoritative accounts of these are available in English (e.g., Dasgupta, 1922; Radhakrishnan, 1929). In this essay, instead of outlining the typical Indian views of the self (ātman, puruṣa), I shall begin with a discussion of certain issues of common concern in their more familiar Western form, and introduce parallel or contrasting concepts of Indian origin wherever appropriate.

Before turning to such a discussion, certain important differences between the Indian and Western approaches to the self may be noted. It is my impression that in the West two rather distinct types of emphases are common: an emphasis on analytical, objectivistic, impersonal, generally deterministic and value-free stance on the one hand, and an emphasis on existential, subjectivistic, personal, indeterministic, and moralistic stance on the other. The characteristics in the first set just mentioned are generally mutually supportive and are found in a cluster, and the same is true of their polar opposites. Although these are matters of relative emphasis rather than an *either/or* choice, Western thinkers have been somewhat polarized along these lines when compared with their Indian counterparts. Several classical systems of Indian thought, such as Yoga and Vedānta, combine impersonal logical analysis of the nature of self with personal existential concerns, and go ahead to develop practical programmes aimed at self-realization.

SELF AS KNOWER: THE PSYCHOLOGY OF COGNITION

The history of Western thought has witnessed a rivalry between the empiricist epistemology of Locke and Hume on the one hand, and the rationalism of Leibniz and Kant on the other. The former group of thinkers has generally viewed knowledge as a reflection on the mind's blank slate of a reality which is 'out there' so to speak, while the latter has suggested that the mind actively constructs and continually reconstructs models of reality. Hume, true to his empiricist doctrine, turned to an examination of experience for knowledge of the self, and discovered this or that particular thought, but no selfsame 'thinker' of the myriad of ever changing thoughts (Hume, 1886/1964, vol. 1, p. 534). Kant, however, turned to reason for an answer regarding the nature of the self-as-knower. He argued that it is necessary to grant the continued existence of a selfsame 'I' as a condition for the very possibility of knowledge. For if the knower who acquires some initial experience were to be replaced by other knower(s) over a period of time, then there would be no *one* percipient to whom the different experiences accrue, and are available to be meaningfully related to one another (see Kant, 1781/1966, p. 269). Kant's arguments in this connection have proved to be quite persuasive as evidenced by their influence on the phenomenological tradition.

As shown by Rychlak (1968; 1981), modern personality theorists tend to follow either the 'Lockean' or the 'Kantian' model, or adopt a mixture of the two. The behaviourists, in general, are successors to Hume. They view human beings as little more than 'bundles' of stimuli and responses, and either deny a unitary and self-same 'I', or treat the identity issue as unworthy of further inquiry as Hume seemed to suggest. At the other end of the spectrum, George Kelly and Erik Erikson display a Kantian spirit. Thus, Kelly (1955) emphasizes the fact that human beings continually construct and reconstruct images of the self and the world. Erikson (1968, p. 135) explicitly recognizes that '[T]here is in fact in each individual an "I", an observing center of awareness and of volition which can *transcend* and must survive the psychosocial identity . . .' (emphasis altered).

It is possible to find many parallels to the Lockean and Kantian Models in traditional systems of Indian thought. The approach of the Vedānta and Yoga systems to self and identity, for instance, is more like Kant's than Hume's. Regardless of many irreconcilable doctrinal differences between them on other matters, both systems postulate a selfsame 'I'. Yoga in particular provides arguments to justify the selfsameness of something beyond the self-as-knower to account for the possibility of knowledge in much the same way as Kant does (Paranjpe, 1984, p. 270). Vedānta as well as Yoga postulate a transcendental self, or 'seer' (draṣṭr), although they differ radically on matters such as the unity or multiplicity of the Self (ātman, puruṣa) and the nature of its relationship with the world.

In this essay I propose to focus only on certain similarities and differences between the transcendentalism of Kant on one hand and that of Vedānta and Yoga on the other, and point them out in the light of William James's critique of Kant.

(i) As noted by James (1890/1950, pp. 360–373), the Kantian view of the transcendental ego is ambiguous since it implies that the self-as-knower is simultaneously an active organizer of experience, as well as a (passive) element in it. The Eriksonian view of identity, which follows the Kantian model in recognizing a transcendental centre of awareness, does not escape the ambiguity inherent in the Kantian view. Note, for instance, that according to Erikson, the 'I' is simultaneously a centre of awareness and of volition. As a centre of *awareness*, the 'I' is suggested as being a passive and unchanging percipient, but as a centre of *volition* it must be viewed as active and changing, for anything fixed and inactive could never exercise its will. I am not sure how other psychologists in the Kantian tradition escape such ambiguity in their formulations, but for the purpose of this essay it should be sufficient to deal with Erikson alone since his work on identity is perhaps the most well known.

Vedānta escapes the ambiguity inherent in the Kantian variety of transcendentalism by separating the active element in the process of knowing from its passive and unchanging backdrop. The active element is conceptualized as the self-as-knower ('jñātr'), and is associated with the ego (ahaṃkāra) and its instruments of knowing (such as the senses and the intellect or 'buddhi'). A separate concept called the self-as-witness (sākṣin) designates the unchanging and passive centre of awareness. It is a centre of the whole universe of experience that provides a common reference point for knowing and unknowing, pleasure and pain, action as well as its repudiation. This passive percipient is said to reflect the drama of life without participating in it, unlike the self-as-knower which is actively engaged in making judgements of true or false, right or wrong, on an ongoing basis. The separation of the active element of knowledge from its unchanging backdrop is not a mere quibble. As we shall shortly note, it has important existential implications. With reference to such implications the Vedāntists have developed systematic methods for anchoring one's selfhood firmly in the witness mode, so as to overcome cognitive bias, narrowness, and similar other problems of an ego that may be overly attached to a particular psychosocial self-definition.

(ii) The Kantian transcendental ego is a mere logical postulate designed to escape the absurdity of its denial. As noted by James (1890/1950, pp. 363–367), it is not verifiable, and therefore leads to solipsism. In sharp contrast, the transcendental self or the 'seer' (draṣṭr or dṛk) of Yoga and Vedānta is verifiable. Patañjali's Yoga, for instance, specifies eight steps to be taken to help experience the 'seer': (1) a prescribed set of behavioural restraints and (2) observances, (3) postures, (4) breathing exercises, (5) 'withdrawing senses from their objects', (6) concentration, (7) contemplation, and (8) an altered state of consciousness called 'samādhi' in which the subject-object split characteristic of the 'ordinary' states of consciousness is said to disappear, thus leading to a direct experience of the 'seer'.

The yogic method is sometimes called the method of concentrative meditation (Goleman, 1977). Its basic strategy is to systematically slow down the activity of the thinker or the self-as-knower to a point at which it stops generating new thoughts or ideas. The stream of thoughts is gradually attenuated until the mind is cleared of its 'contents'. Thus the veil of thoughts which ordinarily covers the inner core of subjectivity is removed and the tabula rasa on which varied thoughts appear and disappear is laid bare. The result is a direct experience of the transcendental basis of the self-as-knower. The Vedānta system offers a different but equally effective method (sometimes called 'mindful meditation') for the experiential verification of the self-as-witness. (For a detailed account of the Yogic and Vedāntic methods see Paranjpe, 1984.)

The Yogic and Vedāntic claims regarding the nature of the transcendental self as 'seer' or 'witness' are not justified by a call to faith. Nor are they vouched as secret doctrines accessible only to the insiders of a cult. Instead, they are warranted on the basis of a long tradition in which the steps to such experience are clearly specified, and the training on how to take these steps is as openly available as training in any science. Anyone who desires to know the nature of the 'seer' can undergo the necessary training and follow the prescribed steps so as to either confirm or disconfirm its proclaimed properties. In other words, propositions regarding the nature of the self-as-witness or 'seer' are in principle falsifiable, to use a Popperian term. (For a detailed discussion of this issue see Paranjpe, 1984.)

The falsifiability of their propositions place Yoga and Vedānta on an epistemological footing comparable to that of science. Both are basically empiricistic insofar as they rely more on experience than on reason in validating propositions. However, they are radically different from science as it is generally practised in terms of the *kind* of experience that is admitted as evidence. Since the mandate of science is to deal with the *objects* of experience, it can afford to restrict itself to the kind of experience which is open to public verification. When one switches to the *experience* of objects as a domain of inquiry, however, one can no longer rely on the public verifiability criterion; many subjective experiences—such as those of pain or pleasure— lie within the strictly private realm accessible to the experiencer alone. If one wishes to investigate the innermost regions of the self, such as the very centre of awareness or the 'seer', it is necessary to go beyond the 'ordinary' wakeful states with which sciences can make do. The study of the self cannot be a part of a 'state-specific science' which restricts itself to a particular state of consciousness such as the ordinary wakeful state. It must include altered states of consciousness as part of its epistemological terms of reference (Tart, 1975). William James was well aware of the altered states of consciousness, including those of samādhi which Yoga and Vedānta talk about. But that was the James (1902/1958) of *The Varieties of Religious Experience*, not the James (1890/1950) of *Principles*, who was committed to the natural science model.

(iii) In his *Principles* James criticized Kant saying that 'By Kant's confession, the transcendental Ego has no properties, and from it nothing can be deduced' (James, 1890/1950, p. 364). Then he went on to add that 'The Ego is simply *nothing*: as ineffectual and windy an abortion as Philosophy can show' (James, 1890/1950, p. 365). This is obviously a strong indictment, and I do not wish to justify it. Instead, I would make a simple observation. What James was complaining about, I think, is the barrenness of the Kantian postulation of the transcendental ego. Regardless of its strong appeal to reason, it leads to nothing substantial in either theoretical or practical terms. A similar criticism may be levelled against psychologists like Erikson who display the Kantian spirit. Although Erikson points to a centre of awareness which, he claims, 'transcends' psychosocial identity, such a pointer leads to no further developments in the Eriksonian model of psychological theory or practice.

As noted, the Vedāntic model parallels the Kantian and Eriksonian models in accepting a transcendentalist approach to self and identity. It also complements them by suggesting some existential implications of the experience of the transcendental basis of selfhood (namely the self-as-witness), and by providing ways to make some substantial gains therefrom. The existential implications arise from the fact that one often identifies oneself strongly with particular beliefs and values which arise in the stream of thought at a given time, only to repudiate them later. If the repudiated beliefs and values happen to be the basic tenets of one's ideology, the result is a radical switch in one's psychosocial self-definition, as in the case of a staunch communist converting to Catholicism or Islam, for instance. In such a case, how can the self, as 'knower', claim with confidence that the world is like such-and-such when in fact the opposite seemed equally true just a while earlier? How could the 'I' switch from one cognitive framework to a vastly different one and still claim to be the *same* knower?

The hypothetical case just mentioned is but an extreme instance of the daily cognitive changes which may not be very radical or abrupt. The problem is that one often tends to hold on to one's current opinions so dearly and strongly that they appear to be the final truth—and this despite the recognition of their in-principle changeable character. Greenwald (1980) has marshalled converging evidence to demonstrate the 'totalitarian' nature of the ego's cognitive functioning, which resists change in beliefs even when warranted by new data or argument. Cognitive conservatism of the ego is much more pervasive than is generally recognized. The Vedāntic tradition has been implicitly concerned about this aspect of the ego; ever since the Upaniṣadic period it has explicitly emphasized that the same truth can often be alternatively construed—thus encouraging open as opposed to totalitarian belief structures.

The Vedāntic discussion of sameness and change (nitya-anitya viveka) in relation to the self focuses on the existential and personal implications of the changing perceptions of the self, in addition to minding its logic. In order to properly express the existential and personal implications of this issue, it would be useful to temporarily suspend the usual impersonal stance of the third person format, and switch to the first person singular.

Vedānta asks me to carefully examine my own past. If I am honest with myself, I would recognize that very often I have been proved to be dead wrong about things which I thought I knew for sure. As such, I must not allow myself to be permanently wedded to particular opinions, or unduly insist on their validity, since there is always a chance that I might be wrong again. The true 'I' has the potential for identifying itself with any and all shades of opinion, and, as such, it must lie beyond them all. Certainly it is necessary for me to often make conscientious judgments on all kinds of issues in practical life, and I have to be quite firm about them. However, I must remember that any perspective on the world, however convincing at a given time, must be considered only provisional and not final or absolute. All theories of science are tentative and forever revisable. If I am truly convinced about this, I would develop healthy skepticism and genuine tolerance. (For a more detailed discussion of this issue see Paranjpe, in press.)

The tone of the above paragraph is too personal and moralistic to fit the impersonal and value free stance popular in contemporary psychology. As such, it was perhaps appropriate to set it off from the rest of the text, regardless of its relevance to the issues on hand. Such separation of personal from impersonal considerations seems necessary only in academic psychology, but not in a T-group or an encounter group situation in which one is often asked to be 'here and now' or 'authentic'. I do not wish to question the need to suspend personal and value considerations from the scientific enterprise of collecting data and interpreting them. The Humean dichotomy of 'is *versus* ought' is well entrenched in Western thought, and for good reasons. The dangers involved in mixing matters of fact with those of value should be quite clear. First, there is the fear of the 'party line' beclouding the search for truth, as the history of the relationship between science and the Church (as well as the 'Party') has painfully shown us. Second, there is the danger of seeing the data the way we would like to see it ('experimenter bias'). Third, it also makes sense to keep personal concerns and ideological preferences out of the largely publicly funded institutions of academia in democratic societies. Such considerations make the impersonal and value free stance understandable and desirable within the context of psychological inquiry. But does this mean that as psychologists we must avoid at all costs any consideration of the personal, existential, and moral implications of issues on hand? I think not.

Against the background of the foregoing it may be noted that a sharp separation of the impersonal and analytical from personal and existential stances is not characteristic of Yoga and Vedānta. This does not mean that they hopelessly fuse epistemological and moral issues; just that they do not shy away from moral implications, and even go ahead to develop methods for translating them into one's own life. In essence, the result is the development of a strategy for 'self-realization', i.e., for the discovery of the ultimate basis of selfhood, and for the manifestation of such a discovery in daily life. The thrust of this strategy may be roughly paraphrased in contemporary psychological terms as follows.

The key to the Vedāntic strategy for self-realization is a tireless self-examination in which one is required to think through the various manifestations of the self. Such thinking is to be guided by a simple rule of the thumb, namely that the true self is that within oneself which remains always unchanged. Thus one must realize that one's body and possessions, social selves or roles, as well as beliefs and values do not constitute the true self, since all of these are subject to continual change. To put it in Jamesian terms, no aspect of the self-as-object (dṛśya) including the material, social and 'spiritual' selves, accounts for the true self; only the self-as-subject (dṛk) does.

Repeated thinking or contemplation (manana, nididhyāsana) about 'Who am I?' and 'What am I in relation to the world?' affects the entire thought process. In a manner comparable to the Husserlian 'epoché, all assumptions about the nature of the world—even the most fundamental axioms about space and time—are questioned (Husserl, 1913/1931, pp. 110–111). As a result, repeated questioning of this sort 'loosens' the entire cognitive framework from its foundations. Since the Vedāntic meditation involves repeated critical examination of one's worldview, it is somewhat like the critical examination of theories done by sociologists of knowledge. The result is that one does not take any worldview to be absolute. Like a Mannheimian sociologist of knowledge, one stays only 'loosely anchored' in a socially constructed reality, moves in and out of alternative perspectives and examines them, using those that have the maximum functional value in a given situation (Mannheim, 1929/1936). In a somewhat similar sense, a self-realized person adopts cognitive frameworks that allow him or her to function appropriately in socially constructed realities, but he or she remains firmly anchored in the true self which is beyond all thoughts and beliefs.

SELF AS ENJOYER/SUFFERER

Self-realization cannot be achieved by engaging in merely cognitive activities such as critical thinking, questioning, arguing, theory building, and so on. No amount of clarity in arguments, sophistication of beliefs, or elegance of theories can attain that which lies beyond thought. In order to experience the transcognitive basis of selfhood it is necessary to loosen, and temporarily dislodge, all kinds of beliefs and other cognitive structures. Cognitive structures are difficult to dislodge. This is because they are products of cognitive processes which are usually guided, sometimes misguided, and eventually entrenched through positive and negative experiences of pleasure and pain. The effect of emotion on cognition is extensively explored and documented in various branches of modern psychology, such as psychoanalysis, experimental psychology (Zajonc, 1980), and the more recent research in attribution theory. Attribution theorists, in particular, recognize the prevalence of a self-serving bias in cognitive processes arising from the ego's investment of affect in various issues. (For a brief review of attribution research in this field, see Schlenker, 1980, pp. 110–119.) Since deep-seated emotions and motives tend to entrench particular beliefs, one cannot expect to dislodge them without effectively dealing with one's emotional life.

Vedānta and Yoga consider the individual's investment of affect in objects and ideas—or ego-involvements—the most important obstacle to self-realization. Dealing with the affective aspect of life is a major concern of most of the traditional systems of Indian thought. However, there are major differences in perspective, in theory as well as practice. At the theoretical level, the focus in Indian thought is not on emotions as such, but on the 'one who enjoys or suffers' (bhoktṛ). At the practical level, the focus is on being able to deal with one's *own* emotional life, rather than helping someone *else* in dealing with his or her anxieties, as in most Western models of psychotherapy.

The typical Indian approach to a theory of the affective aspect of life is illustrated by the concept of 'suffering pertaining to the self' (ādhyātmika duhkha, which is found in the Sāṅkhya system and the *Bhagavad-Gītā*, among other sources. For an original source of the Sāṅkhya concepts and their English translation, see Raja, 1963.). What this concept means, I think, is that at least part of human suffering arises from self-chosen (and often misconceived) notions of the ego. If I create in myself an interest in collecting stamps, choose to be surrounded by fellow philatelists, and allow myself to be judged by their standards, I may feel happy with the prospect of buying a rare stamp, or feel angry and jealous about a rival who snatches that deal. Thus, at least part of my affective life depends on my acquired self-image as a stamp collector. The same is true about most of my self-definitions, which together account for my psychosocial identity. In Vedānta, this situation is described by a simple metaphor: a person lives in a world of his or her own creation—like a moth in its cocoon. (See Śaṅkara's *Vivekacūḍāmaṇi*, 1948, Verse No. 137.) The implication of this metaphor is that, to understand the basis of one's joys and sorrows, it is necessary to step out of one's shell and see what one has made of oneself. As long as we find ourselves completely wrapped up in this or that socially constructed reality, the signs of bad weather in this mini-world look like omens of doomsday. As a way of dealing with this problem, Yoga, Vedānta, and other similar systems recommend the systematic cultivation of a detached outlook on life. It is claimed that with the successful cultivation of a sense of dispassionateness, one transcends ordinary joys and sorrows typical of successes or failures in the practical world.

Pleasure and pain are largely a matter of a relationship between two entities: objects and events such as prizes and races on the one hand, and an ego interested in pursuing them on the other. Thus there is an object pole of the relationship, namely the objects of pleasure, and a subject pole which is the involved ego that feels elated or depressed with the win or loss of those objects. In the drama of life not only are the objects of pleasure subject to creation and destruction, but the ego also changes its position *vis-à-vis* such objects in a radical way. One may be totally infatuated with a particular person as long as one has construed oneself as a contender, but things must change radically the moment one turns to a different paramour. Sometimes a sudden transformation of the ego may turn an object of hate or fear into an object of love and adoration. As the well-known story goes, Jesus was once an object of intense hatred for Saul, but became an object of worship when Saul saw the light and converted himself into Paul.

While the points just made are commonplace, their implications for the nature of the self as enjoyer/sufferer are not. The 'I', the experiencing subject, must survive not only the changing fortunes of life in which objects of love and hate are gained and lost, but also the numerous reincarnations of the ego. The 'I' must therefore lie beyond both the subject and object poles of the pleasure/pain experience. There is, in other words, a transcendental basis for selfhood which lies beyond both the outer world of objects as well as the inner world of meanings attached to them. The Yogis and the Vedāntists claim that it is in fact possible to directly experience the unchanging basis of selfhood which transcends the ego.

In Vedānta it is claimed that the experience of the transcendental 'I' is positive without being so in an oppositional sense, like the pleasure of success as opposed to the pain of defeat for instance. It is claimed to be *qualitatively* different from the ordinary pleasures of life. Being independent of changing fortunes of the world 'out there', it provides an inexhaustible source of inner peace and tranquility. This claim, again, need not be accepted on faith. As in the case of claims regarding the transcognitive 'I', it is in principle verifiable with the help of the same means, such as concentrative or mindful meditation described before.

SELF AS AGENT: THE PSYCHOLOGY OF ACTION

The transcendentalism described so far suggests turning to an inner world. This would appear to be an autistic escape from the condition of 'thrownness' in the actual world, from which there is no real escape. Moreover, as finite particular individuals, humans are products of events which are governed by the laws of nature (umwelt) and society (mitwelt). Granted that individuals constitute themselves into unique worlds of their individuality (eigenwelt), is anyone's selfhood free from the constraints imposed by the laws of nature and society?

Freedom *versus* determinism is a complex issue hotly debated in the Indian as well as Western intellectual traditions for centuries, and no clear resolution of the dilemma is in sight. (For a discussion of this issue in the context of the Indian intellectual tradition see Tilak, 1915/1971.) Nevertheless, a 'hard' or 100% determinism does not make sense, since it leads to a fatalist view of the world in which scientists could not meaningfully choose truth from falsehood, let alone hope to control or direct the course of events. (For arguments supporting this position see Taylor, 1967.) While an unbridled 'free will' is equally unacceptable, a 'soft' determinism which allows for some degrees of freedom is a position acceptable to many (Popper, 1966; Taylor, 1967). The psychologist Rychlak (1979) has suggested that the exercise of a 'free will' is based on the human brain's capacity for dialectical reasoning (or generating logical opposites such as 'nothing' versus 'everything'), and for arbitrarily assigning meanings to the alternatives thus reasoned.

Whatever the resolution of the freedom-determinism dilemma, granting a latitude of choice to the human will does not imply accepting the possibility of interfering with, or violating, the laws of nature. Readers acquainted with Yoga might think that yogis who acquire special powers such as levitation or becoming invisible are capable of violating natural laws. However, the philosophy of Yoga is based on an axiomatic belief in the 'Law of Karma', which implies a thoroughly determinist view of cause and effect. Yogis do not view the special powers as divine or supernatural interventions, but as lawful events not easily accounted for by knowledge based on ordinary conscious experience. (For a further discussion of this issue see Paranjpe, 1985.) With regard to a discussion of human agency, it is not crucial to examine whether laws of nature may be violated by the exercise of free will, because we are not here talking about levitating in direct violation of law of gravity and so on. Let us grant—as yogis, behaviourists as well as other psychologists do—that human behaviour is determined by the history of its antecedents. Within such a determinist framework, it is important to see whether and how it would be possible to effectively deal with the consequences of past experience and behaviour which normally determine future behaviour.

The 'Law of Karma' is a widely accepted principle among classical systems of Indian thought (O'Flaherty, 1980). According to this law, all events are causally determined, tendencies to seek pleasure and to avoid pain are common determinants of the behaviour of organisms, and past experiences and behaviours determine later behaviours. Since these ideas are clearly accepted in Pantañjali's Yoga, and since the same ideas are found in (and are equally central to) behaviourism, Yoga and behaviourism lend themselves to a meaningful comparison despite vast differences in their socio-historic backgrounds. (For an English translation of Patañjali's Yoga aphorisms and its principal commentaries, see Woods, 1914/1972, and, for a more detailed comparison of Yogic concepts with those of modern psychology, see

Paranjpe, 1984. A quick look at some aspects of contrasts between them would be pertinent to the present discussion.

While both behaviourism and Yoga grant that present behaviour is determined by the past, Yoga implicitly emphasizes self-regulation of behaviour rather than environmental control, and seeks to emancipate the individual from the burden of the past. In behaviourist psychology it is implicitly assumed that the experimenter is somehow free to alter the course of future behaviours, but in classical behaviourism the focus has been, by and large, on controlling someone else's behaviour rather than one's own. More recently, however, issues such as the concept of agency and self-control are being brought into the purview of a behaviouristically oriented psychology (Mischel and Mischel, 1977). Nevertheless, the issue of self-control is neither central to behaviouristic psychology, nor is it approached from an existential and personal viewpoint as it is in Yoga. Indeed the impersonal stance is so strong in behaviourism that it has not only neglected the self, but has also led to a psychology which is predominantly a 'psychology of the other-one'. (See Meyer, 1922; Paranjpe, 1984.)

For behaviouristically oriented psychologists, the concept of agency has been a reminder of a homunculus, or a 'ghost in the machine', and is therefore unacceptable. As well, the role of cognitive and anticipatory factors as determinants of behaviour were often denied in behaviourist psychology except by the likes of Tolman. This trend is changing, though, as indicated in the work of Bandura (1977, 1982) who recognizes expectations of future outcomes as an important determiner of behaviour, and even attempts to account for human agency. It should not be surprising that this new interest in agency is combined with the recognition of the anticipatory determinants of behaviour at the same time. For, after all, without an awareness of the future consequences, behaviour would involve only blind and mechanical processes, rather than acts of will.

Karma Yoga, a form of spiritual self-discipline which aims at self-realization through transcending the agentic character of the ego, focuses on the expectations about future outcomes (Tilak, 1915/1971). The main argument is that as long as one is ego-involved in specific gains for the future, one is 'bound' to a specific course of action which is expected to lead to them, and must face the actual consequences of that course of action, good or bad. However, if one does not hanker for specific desirable outcomes, and is also not scared of unpleasant consequences, one is essentially exempt from the lure of rewards and the threat of punishments. In other words, by changing the meanings attached to future outcomes, one can be freed from the 'contingencies of reinforcement', rather than becoming a prisoner of self-appointed expectations. This can be done by adopting a stance such that the 'I', grounded in the witness mode, becomes a participant observer in the drama of life without being egoistically elated by successes and depressed by failures. This way one can effectively deal with the fears, as well as hopes, arising from the anticipation of what Hazel Markus calls 'possible selves' elsewhere in this volume.

It should be clear from the foregoing discussion that the Yogic and Vedāntic approaches adopt a transcendentalist approach to self and identity which goes a step beyond the Kantian transcendentalism familiar to the West. Instead of merely offering arguments to support a transcendental basis for selfhood, these Eastern approaches provide a verifiable experiential basis for it and thus avoid the solipsism and emptiness of the Kantian transcendentalism. From the perspective of Yoga and Vedānta, the unity and sameness of a human being ultimately depends on a centre of experience which lies beyond knowing, enjoying/suffering, and acting. It is onto this centre of the universe of experience that the processes of cognition, volition, and emotion converge. Yoga and Vedānta offer their own specialized methods for experiencing this transcendental centre of awareness. Such experience is said to lead to certain existential and personal benefits. It allows a person to realize that an ultimate and firm basis for selfhood cannot be found in an ego attached to continually changing beliefs, emotions, and action plans. Those who realize this remain firmly anchored in a transcendental basis for their selfhood and thereby attain freedom from the commonly pervasive self-serving cognitive bias, remain unruffled by gains or losses in practical life, and can freely participate in an active life without becoming prisoners of a self-made world.

ACKNOWLEDGEMENTS

I am grateful to Krysia Yardley, Terry Honess, and Ross Powell for their useful comments on a previous draft of this contribution.

REFERENCES

Bandura, A. (1977). *Social Learning Theory*, Prentice-Hall, Englewood Cliffs, New York.

Bandura, A. (1982). 'Self and mechanisms of agency.' In J. Suls (Ed.), *Psychological Perspectives on the Self*, vol. 1, Erlbaum, Hillside, New Jersey.

Bhagavad-Gītā. (undated/1973). (transl. and Ed. S. Radhakrishnan), Harper and Row, New York.

Dasgupta, S. N. (1922). *A History of Indian Philosophy*, 2 vols, Cambridge University Press, Cambridge.

Erikson, E. H. (1968). *Identity, Youth and Crisis*, Norton, New York.

Goleman, D. (1977). *Varieties of Meditative Experience*, E. P. Dutton, New York.

Greenwald, A. G. (1980). 'The totalitarian ego: Fabrication and revision of personal history.' *American Psychologist*, **35**, 603–618.

Hume, D. (1886/1964). 'A treatise of human nature.' In T. H. Greene and T. H. Grose (Eds), *David Hume: The Philosophical Works*, 4 vols, Scientia Verlag, Aalen, Germany.

Hume, R. E. (trans.) (1931) *The Thirteen Principal Upanishads*, 2nd edn, Oxford University Press, London.

Husserl, E. (1913/1931). *Ideas: General Introduction to Pure Phenomenology* (transl. W. R. Boyce Gibson), Humanities Press, New York.

James, W. (1890/1950). *Principles of Psychology*, vol. 1, Holt, New York.

James, W. (1902/1958). *The Varieties of Religious Experience*, New American Library, New York.

Kant, E. (1781/1966). *Critique of Pure Reason* (transl. F. Max Müller), Doubleday Anchor Books, Garden City, New York.

Kelly, G. A. (1955). *The Psychology of Personal Constructs*, Norton, New York.

Mannheim, K. (1929/1936). *Ideology and Utopia: an Introduction to the Sociology of Knowledge* (transl. L. Wirth and E. Shils), Harcourt, Brace and World, New York.

Meyer, M. (1922). *Psychology of the Other-one*, 2nd edn, Missouri Book Company, Columbia, Missouri.

Mischel, W. and Mischel, H. N. (1977). 'Self-control and the self.' In T. Mischel (Ed.), *The Self: Psychological and Philosophical Issues*, Basil Blackwell, Oxford, pp. 31–64.

O'Flaherty, W. (1980). *Karma and Rebirth in Classical Indian Traditions*, University of California, Berkeley, California.

Paranjpe, A. C. (1984). *Theoretical Psychology: The Meeting of East and West*, Plenum, New York.

Paranjpe, A. C. (1985). 'Parapsychology and Patañjali's Yoga.' *International Conference of the Parapsychological Association*, Waltair, India.

Popper, K. R. (1966). *Of Clouds and Clocks: an Approach to the Rationality and Freedom of Man*, Washington University Press, St. Louis.

Radhakrishnan, S. (1929). *Indian Philosophy*, 2nd edn, 2 vols, George Allen and Unwin, London.

Raja, C. K. (1963). *The Sāṅkhya Kārikā of Īśvarakṛṣṇa: a Philosopher's Exposition*, Kavyalaya Publishers, Hoshiyarpur, India.

Rychlak, J. F. (1968). *A Philosophy of Science for Personality Theory*, Houghton Mifflin, Boston.

Rychlak, J. F. (1979). *Discovering Free Will and Personal Responsibility*, Oxford University Press, New York.

Rychlak, J. F. (1981). *Introduction to Personality Theory and Psychotherapy*, 2nd edn, Houghton Mifflin, Boston.

Śaṅkara (1978). *Vivekacūḍāmaṇi*, (transl. and Ed. S. Madhavananda), Advaita Ashrama, Calcutta. (Original work dated early 9th century A.D.)

Schlenker, B. R. (1980). *Impression Management: The Self-concept, Social Identity, and Interpersonal Relations*, Brooks/Cole, Monterey, California.

Tart, C. (Ed.) (1975). *Transpersonal Psychologies*, Harper & Row, New York.

Taylor, R. (1967). 'Determinism.' In P. Edwards (Ed.), *The Encyclopedia of Philosophy*, vol. 2, Macmillan and Free Press, New York, pp. 359–373.

Tilak, B. G. (1915/1971). *Śrīmadbhagavadgītārahasya or karmayogaśāstra* (transl. B. S. Sukthankar), 3rd edn, Tilak Brothers, Pune, India.

Woods, J. H. (1914/1972). *The Yoga-system of Patañjali*, Motilal Banarsidass, New Delhi.

Zajonc, R. B. (1980). 'Feeling and thinking: Preferences need no inferences.' *American Psychologist*, **35**, 151–175.

Self and Identity: Psychosocial Perspectives
Edited by K. Yardley and T. Honess
© 1987 John Wiley & Sons Ltd

4

The Social Construction of Selves

Rom Harré

The basic Vygotskyean hypothesis that the mind is the result of the imposition of form, derived from the practices of the social-collective world, on inchoate material is sharpened into a specific theory about selfhood. The language games through which the grammatical models of self appear as a mode of personal organization are identified. These ways of speaking are argued to have a particular place in the moral order.

THE GENERAL THEORY

The Vygotskyean approach to personal psychology

The Vygotskyean position is based on a distinction between the 'material' of mind, fragmentary thoughts, feelings and so on, and the structure or order of that material as a mind. According to Vygotsky (1962), the organization we call 'the mind' is the result of the imposition of form on inchoate material. The forms from which mental organization derives are originally to be found in the practices of the social-collective world. If we notice some striking organizational feature of human mentation the Vygotskyean approach bids us look for its origin in the social world, and particularly in the structure of language. I believe that the 'inner centredness' we call 'the self' is an organizational feature of experience, imposed through the power of certain grammatical models. There is no 'entity' at the centre of our experience of ourselves. But there are standard ways in which we express our comments upon our own mentation.

In the course of his investigations into philosophical psychology, Wittgenstein developed a kind of linguistic realism which I believe is complementary to the Vygotskyean approach. Ways of speaking cluster into 'language games', linguistically imbued social practices which can serve the Vygotskyean role as bearers of organizational properties of mind and action. But language games are embedded in 'forms of life', coherent bodies of practices which, with a hierarchy of moral orders, make up local cultures. My task in this contribution is to identify the language games through the grammatical models of which the self appears as a mode of personal organization. These ways of speaking have a particular place in the moral orders which invoke such language games. I shall not concern myself with the process by which features of the social order and its constituent practices are manifested in an individual mind as a characteristic mode of organization, the process Vygotsky called appropriation. (For a detailed discussion see Harré's (1983) *Personal Being* and Shotter's (1984) *Social Accountability and Selfhood*.)

Person and self distinguished

The uses of the words 'person' and 'self' in ordinary and technical English form a complex network of applications, with some measure of overlap. Much as Mead reworked the pronouns 'I' and 'Me' to suit his expository purposes, I want to tidy up the usage of 'person' and 'self' to suit mine. By 'person' I will mean a human being as a social individual embodied and publicly identifiable, while by 'self' I will mean that inner unity to which all personal experience belongs, as attributes of a subject. There could be persons who did not have selves. This way of putting the matter reflects a traditional and apparently problematic way of dealing with the singularity of each person.

This way of talking about 'selves' is part of a larger picture. People are thought of as enclosed and embodied minds, tentatively extending mental 'pseudopodia' in the hope of making (problematic) contact with another of their kind, and striking up a conversation. I want to replace this picture with another, in most respects its negative. A mind, according to the alternative picture, is a partially fenced off area of the vast prairie of human conversation, an area in which a little individual farming goes on, with a few animals taken from the vast herds that roam the prairie.

The first picture leads to the familiar Cartesian impasses. We can free ourselves from it by looking for its source in certain characteristic misunderstandings of common forms of speech. By revealing the 'deep grammar' of self-ascriptive statements the temptation to think in terms of the first picture can be resisted.

Psychologists have not made things easier for themselves by introducing a curious term, 'self-concept'. Its appearance on the linguistic scene as a working concept has to be tolerated. Of course, it does not mean 'concept of self', but rather the set of beliefs that a person has about him or herself, a personal history, beliefs about dispositions, aspirations, appearance in the eyes of others, and so on. To have a 'self-concept' one must have mastered some version of the concept of 'person'. But no concept of 'self', as the inexperiencable subject of all experience, the hidden centre of the ego-structured organization of experience, need be invoked.

Why is there a problem about the 'self'?

The spatio-temporal centre of experience seems to be neatly located at the person, the very same embodied being whose interactions with others, in particular whose contributions to the human conversation, locate him or her not only in time and space but also in whatever local moral orders are relevant. For all the predications to persons within their cluster of language games the logical grammar of first person talk requires only indexical reference. But an 'inner centre' of which all experience is predicated as this or that mental attribute seems to be required too. However, as philosophers from Hume through Kant and Ryle have reiterated, whatever is at that centre can never be an object of experience. It is 'systematically elusive'. Its presence, somehow, in the person has been thought by many to be a necessary condition for the possibility of human experience taking the form it does, for example including the exercise of the capacity of choice. But it can never be studied empirically, in itself, so to speak. According to Kant, transcendental objects can have only transcendental properties. The 'self' as a necessary condition for the possibility of experience could not be studied empirically. The Vygotskyean approach suggests that though transcendental objects can not be studied in themselves, and in this case have no immediately observable psychological properties (only powers or dispositions to create order) they may have *social* properties. They may even turn out to be social entities.

To take this insight further a solution is needed to the empirical status of the 'self'.

THE SPECIAL THEORY

We must now sharpen up the general Vygotskyean hypothesis into a specific theory about selfhood as it is manifested in the mental organization of Western European people. Such a theory is based on the claim that public interpersonal speech practices serve as grammatical models for the general forms of reflexive discourse. This scarcely seems too radical a hypothesis. Couple it with Vygotsky's thesis that these reflexive speech forms are the very agents by which the unities of mind are accomplished and we have a very daring claim indeed. It is just this claim that I want to recommend as a potent source of empirical and theoretical hypotheses.

First person talk

To understand the logical grammar of first person talk we need to use two major distinctions, that between avowals and descriptions and that between indexical reference and denotative reference. We owe to Wittgenstein (1953) the realization that first and third person statements incorporating psychological predicates are radically different.

We should not interpret statements of the form 'I am in pain', 'I am sure the key is in the house', 'I wish he would come', as descriptions of the state of mind of the speaker. In particular, it would be wrong, in many cases, to treat such statements as true or false assertions of fact based upon evidence. For instance, 'I wish he would come' is not a hypothesis which might turn out to be mistaken. The readiness to produce such psychological assertions is, in many cases, part of what it is to be in the state or condition in question. 'My God, that hurts' functions more like a groan than like a description of an inner state annexed to myself. Wittgenstein arrives at this analysis partly from a careful look at how people actually use psychological predicates in first person utterances, and partly from the observation that, unlike descriptive statements proper, these utterances lack criteria. The idea of there being a sensory criterion for my being in pain, about which I could, in principle, be mistaken, makes no sense. We could call verbal expressions of intention, of wishing, of feeling, 'avowals'. As part of a public performance they may, of course, be so contrived as to lead the listener astray. This does not make them false descriptions of inner states, but insincere public acts. A person may insincerely avow an intention without there being a conscious counter-intention which he or she keeps to themselves.

However, when psychological predicates are used in the third person they are being used to describe that state, performance, etc. of the person being referred to, and there will be criteria for their use. Second person talk is much more tricky to assess, since an utterance like 'You *said* you would wait' is perhaps both an accusation of bad faith *and* a true or false description of meaningful performance or a mental condition; compare with 'You *said* you loved me!'

An example of how the Wittgensteinean theory of avowals clears up a viper's nest of problems is the case of intentions and other performatives of commitment. According to the avowals theory it is not that a public declaration of intention describes (accurately or inaccurately) a private state of intending. Rather, there are both public and private declarations of intention, the latter mimicking the logical grammar of the former. In both cases the psychologist is presented with the *same* problem, namely how do actors realize declarations in action? They might as well study the problem in the public domain. (I believe this is the right way to interpret the 'telesponding' of Rychlak, 1984, and the suggestion by Warner and Williams, 1984, that action, intention, and circumstances mutually define each other.) It follows from this approach that the laws of thought are not the laws of physiology, nor the laws of logic, but the conventions of conversation (and hence we can account for the dialectical character of 'real thought', cf. Rychlak, 1984).

We judge the sincerity of an avowal, not by trying to estimate how accurately the sentence uttered describes an 'inner state', but by how sincere we take the speaker to be, for instance with regard to his or her attitude (for instance degree of commitment) to the sustaining of the content of the avowal, perhaps in some future action. Just the same analysis applies of course to the concept of 'attitude'.

The same point can be made about the psychology of motives. As Kenneth Burke (1969) and C. Wright Mills (1959) long ago pointed out, we have a vocabulary of motives, the rhetorical force of which is to present ourselves, according to the conventions of our society, in the best possible light relative to some project of self-presentation (which may or may not include displaying ourselves as agents). We *do* what makes sense in the circumstances, and what we do makes sense of the circumstances. We, or others, provide the motives, sometimes by a mere shrug of the shoulders or perhaps a narrow smile, as a self-presentational scaffolding. And of course we can engage in *sotto voce* motive talk. The question whether there *are* intentions or *are* motives which we might try to study as a puzzling class of hidden objects is simply bypassed. Questions about these entities are ill-conceived. They are formulated by reason of a misunderstanding of a language-game. No wonder they seem to pose intractable difficulties.

Thus 'criterionless avowals', which take their meaning as part of the psychological state or process they express, are to be assessed within a moral order, on the basis of such judgements as sincere or insincere, boastful or modest, and so on. It is an echo of the above misunderstanding to try to assess them within an epistemic order that is with respect to their truth or falsity as descriptions. Failure to act in accordance with an intention, whether expressed as a public or private avowal, is to be explained, not by mistakes about one's real intentions, but by reference to weakness of character, dishonesty, etc.; that is as a matter of moral appraisal.

Paralleling the distinction between avowals and descriptions is that between indexical and denotative reference. Compare 'Put the cup here' with 'Put the pencil in the red rack'. The latter could be complied with by anyone who could pick out red racks. There would be no need to know where the order had been spoken. But to know which place is meant by 'here', a listener would need to know where the command was spoken. Indexical expressions are referring terms whose meaning is completed by the interlocutor knowing when, where, and by whom the statement was made. An indexical expression could be thought of as labelling a speech act with the occasion of its utterance. A sentence like 'I don't care what you do!' is indeterminate in meaning unless we, the listeners, know who said it. That information is not contained in the sentence itself. But 'Jim doesn't care what you do' is, relative to a pretty broad context of shared knowledge, meaningful relatively independently of time, place, and person of utterance.

The indexical pronouns of first person psychological avowals can be understood as labels, serving to locate the avowal in question, and the psychological complex of which it is a part, at the person who is the speaker. It follows that the indexical uses of 'I' can be explained without recourse to an inner being of which the psychological states are predicated as properties. Only the concept of 'person' as a public and social being is required. In analyzing a statement like 'I hope to pick up the photos tomorrow' the ascription of referential force to 'I' as denoting an inner subject of psychological states (say of hoping) is gratuitous. If these forms were the only kind of reflexive speech, the concept of 'self' would gain no purchase in the description of our mental organization.

But these simple forms are not the only grammatical models for speech-acts of self-address. There are more complex forms to be found in self-appraising discourse.

Avowals of epistemic quality

The first person talk so far analysed assumes only a metaphysics of public embodied persons and indexical uses of pronouns. Our public speech is shot through with another kind of avowal. It is that kind of avowal by which we express our assessment of our own first order avowals. Second order avowals take such forms as 'I believe I . . .', 'I am not quite sure but I think I . . .', and so on. The embedded sentence has, I believe, a logical grammar modelled on that of third person psychological statements. I assess the quality of my own avowals as I would assess yours. If that is so, to what being are the psychological states mentioned in the embedded sentences ascribed? It could have been the public person, the very same being which is indexed by the outermost 'I' which locates the second order avowal of belief, doubt, etc. in the array of persons. But I believe that in our culture the embedded 'I', behaving like 'He' or 'She', is taken to denote the unobservable centre of our experience, that which I have called the 'self'. Second order avowals make a 'space', so to speak, for a theory of our 'selves' to get a purchase on our psychology, and so on our mental structure. The grammatical forms of higher order avowals have just the right kind of structure for aligning the public concept of the 'person' with the gap in our conceptual scheme which comes from our selfconscious struggle to locate our 'inner selves'. The gap is filled with the theoretical concept of 'self' which appears in our grammar as the logical subject of all ascriptions of psychological states to ourselves on the model of third person ascriptions, *and* as the organizing principle of the synthetic unities of experience.

Why do we have the language-game of iterated self-ascription? One plausible theory could be that it allows us to avow our attitudes to the moral and epistemic quality of our first-order avowals, that is to their honesty, their worthiness to be believed, their trustworthiness to be acted upon in a practical context, and so on. But to express these attitudes we must embed first-order avowals in a context which allows us to treat them as if they were descriptions, that is as if they were true or false ascriptions of states or processes of thought to *somebody*. For such ascriptions there should be criteria. We treat ourselves as and with 'third persons'. So within one species of criterionless avowal are embedded ascriptions of psychological and action predicates to persons, for which on a denotative reading of the embedded 'I' there ought to be criteria.

The question 'How do you know this is your attitude to the reliability of your perception?' asked with respect to an avowal like 'I am not quite sure that what I saw was a tarantula' is as misplaced as 'How do you know you are in pain?' addressed to someone who complains of toothache. To be ready to make the above avowal is part of what it is not to be sure. There need be no 'inner state' of dubeity which *must* accompany the remark and with respect to which it is a true description. There may be such a state, but it too is part of what it is to be in doubt.

Because the embedded sentences mimic the logical grammar of third person descriptions, that is are statements about something (a person) we slip into thinking that they must be descriptive of another something (a 'self' perhaps). This illusion is quite essential to the 'centred' organization of thought and feeling as it presents itself to each of us. In my view it is a straightforward consequence of the logical grammar of the discourses of self-appraisal. It is the self-centredness of predication, and it matches the person-centredness of perception. Taken seriously, it not only tempts us into a hippogryph hunt, but also into trying to find criteria for our original criterionless avowal of this or that emotion, plea, motive, and so on. Revealed as the shadow of a grammatical form it should lose its power to mislead.

Much of the philosophy of the physical sciences is based on a polar opposition between empirical and theoretical concepts, between observable and hypothetical entities, properties, and processes. Though the poles are distinct, we now recognize a continuum of cases between. With what concepts in the physical sciences should 'self' be compared? The tradition forbids us treating it as an empirical concept. Suppose it is a theoretical concept, the heart of a theory which is learned by each human being (a theory which may have culturally diverse versions) in terms of which that *person* organizes their experience, providing the kind of structures that Kant called syntheses, by which complementary unifications of perceptual experience and thought and feeling are avowals in the manifolds of 'outer' and 'inner' sense. The physical sciences are full of such concepts, including those expressed in terms for unobservable things, properties, processes, and even dispositions such as those we call 'fields' and 'potentials'. I am *not* suggesting that the 'self' is some kind of mental field, rather that the philosophical logic of the way the concept 'self' behaves might usefully be compared to the way the concept 'gravity' or of 'charge' behaves. The study of the Kantian syntheses and of the way the 'self' is involved in them is an independent area of study. To understand theoretical concepts in the physical sciences we look to the source analogies from which their logical grammar is derived, and so much of their meaning determined. If the 'self' is such a concept from what empirical concept is it derived? I believe its source is in analogy with the social concept of human individuality, the 'person'.

The genesis of theoretical concepts

Theoretical concepts often appear in the physical sciences to describe processes and entities which are held responsible for patterns found in observation and experiment, but which are beyond existing observational techniques. Since these concepts cannot acquire their meaning by an ostensive act to that which they describe, it being unobservable, we must look elsewhere for the source of our understanding of their force. In many cases this is a source analogue. The theoretical concept 'molecule' is based on an analogy with 'Newtonian material thing'; 'natural selection' is based on an analogy with 'domestic selection', and so on. In the physical sciences theoretical concepts are in equilibrium between two analogy relations. A swarm of molecules must *behave like* a real gas behaves, while a molecule must *be like* a Newtonian particle. Just how like in each case is a matter for skilled judgement.

If the concept of 'self' is a theoretical concept then our understanding of its logical grammar can be advanced by subjecting it to the same kind of analysis we would use to reveal the logical grammar of a similarly placed concept in the natural sciences. From whence are the rules for its use derived? Or to put this question in more traditional philosophical language, how do we decide of what natural kind it is?

How did Darwin fix the rules for the use of the term 'natural selection'? He describes his procedure in some detail. It depends on setting up a parallel between the formula 'Domestic novelties (new breeds, etc) are created by differentially encouraging Domestic variations by acts of Domestic selection' and the formula 'Natural novelties (new species) comes about by differential encouragement of Natural variations by a process of Natural selection' (the rules for its use *in the language game of evolutionary biology*, but not necessarily in other contexts) by analogy with the concept 'Domestic selection'. 'Domestic selection' is a source-model for 'Natural selection'. Darwin is careful to point out the ways in which the concept 'Natural selection' differs from its analogue 'Domestic selection'. The logical grammar of the former concept is analogous to the domestic concept, not identical to it.

In accordance with the General Theory my social constructionist thesis of selfhood can be stated quite simply; my hypothesis is that the organization of mind is a cultural artefact based on the learning of a local concept of 'self'. This concept is related to the public-social concept of the 'person' in just the same sort of way that 'Natural selection' is related to 'Domestic selection'. We do not find out how to use the concept by studying the entity to which it refers. In neither case, though for different reasons, is this possible. In both cases we *create* the concept out of an existing concept by making various changes in the rules of use. We do this because there is some job for the new concept, and we tailor-make a concept to do it. The concept of 'person' provides a source-model for the concept of 'self'. Since we know how to use the concept of a person it offers a coherent body of rules from which we can construct the grammar of our new concept. Thus 'the self' is used in such a way as to be compatible with the entity to which it seems to refer (if there is one), which is supposed to persist in time, to be continuous in its passage through space, to be the subject of a variety of predications, including not only psychological states and powers but also ascriptions of responsibilities and rights, and various kinds of praise and blame.

The term 'self' is a term of art introduced by me to name the concept which I believe is tacitly involved in the actual logical grammar of the apparently denotative (as contrasted with indexical) uses of 'I'. That logical grammar arises, I have argued, in the same way as the logical grammar of novel concepts in the activity we call 'theorizing' in the natural sciences.

If I must hold such a theory about myself to become a being capable of the sort of higher order self-ascription provided for by the language, it seems likely that I would apply the same theory to other people who use those language forms and share my form of life. Thus 'He' and 'She' too take on the double aspect of person location and self denotation that I have argued is characteristic of the way we use 'I'.

The embedded 'I' of the sentence forms by which we comment on our own avowals has referential *force*, but we can be quite agnostic about whether it actually 'hits' anything, to use Aronson's vivid metaphor (Aronson, 1984). The most economical way of explaining all that I have pointed out about our reflexive language games is to suppose that the 'self' is not a thing but exists only as a concept. It is the central concept of a theory, which the persons who hold it use to impose order upon their thoughts, feelings, and actions. In this way we can help ourselves to the logical grammar of the theoretical terms of the physical sciences to make clear how this concept works. And that is the justification of the talk about source-models, behavioural and material analogies and so on.

Thus the deployment of the concept of 'self' produces a structure which can be represented as

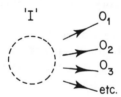

where O_1, O_2, O_3, etc. are intentional objects of various kinds. If I am right in thinking that the concept 'person' serves as a source-analogue for the concept of 'self', one way of understanding that relation would be in terms of an isomorphism between the above structure as it appears phenomenologically in the organization of perception and memory with respect to a space-time geometry in which 'Here', 'Now', and 'I' as embodied person are co-indexical and that which mimics it, the structure of predication. The structure can exist whether or not there is any being at the 'centre' to which the concept of 'self' refers, since it is a reflection of the structure of a form of talk, a commentary on the quality of one's own avowals. As I have argued above, the embedded 'I' can be a common subject of predication in just the way a theoretical term in physics can. In this way the 'self' is a concept very like the concept of 'gravity', which serves to organize our experience with respect to structured and centred fields, while we can remain quite agnostic as to whether there is anything substantial occupying the 'centres of gravity' of the dispositional array we call the gravitational field of a material body.

WHY HAVE WE BUILT UP A DUALITY OF PERSONAL UNITIES?

Moral orders

We need to supplement this analysis of the grammar of reflexive talk with an ethnography of speakers. (Such an ethnography as has been sketched, for instance, by Julian Jaynes (1979) in his *Origin of consciousness in the breakdown of the bicameral mind*, in those sections where he discusses social disorder in the Ancient World, the beginnings of writing and the like.) A clue to this ethnography can be found by contrasting socio-linguistic practices of a culture without our concept of 'self'. The Eskimo language, Intuit, admits only of indexical reference to persons, a pronominal suffix, directing attention towards or away from the speaker. And the ethnography reveals a complementary doctrine of collective moral responsibility, a theory of art in which the craftsman is merely a passive releaser of the potency of the material, and so on. To return to the Vygotskyean–Wittgensteinean features of the General Theory once again, we would be guided by these ethnographic considerations to go beyond grammatical models to the moral orders and material practices characteristic of forms of life, and our form of life in particular, to find the origins of the theory by which persons organize a 'centred' discourse of self-ascription. Perhaps the theory and the discourse of self-appraisal have the same origin.

One obvious candidate for that origin might be the rise of the concept of individual responsibility and moral agency. We all have to live within moralities of choice. But there are moral orders in which the idea that someone could have done something different from that which he or she did do, in the sense of could have made a different choice amongst alternatives, plays no serious part. The morality outlined by Socrates involves only the problem of knowing what is good, not of choosing it once known. Islamic moral psychology, like that of Ancient Greece, finds moral failing not so much in choosing the worst, but in akrasia, weakness of will, lack of resolution, stick-to-itiveness, and so on. Allah has already written the life course of a man—the residual moral question is only whether he will have the resolution to accomplish it. Unlike Elizabethan women, the wives and mothers of the Sons of the Prophet were not expected to display moral qualities other than obedience.

If we think of our moral lives, whatever may be the reality of the matter, as based upon choice, even choice in the face of equal inclinations, it is not surprising that the fact that we do do things should have been routinely explained by the introduction of an 'elusive self' into our working ontology to provide a location for this amazing feat. But there are no inner selves—

merely the shadows cast by grammatical models which constrain the forms of talk by which the current cluster of moral orders are managed.

Tying in the 'unities'

The problem for a psychology of selfhood is posed by the need to analyse and account for the unity or unities that make for individual minds and thus for personal being. The problem is tantalizing by reason of the way that there is, so to speak, a natural and a cultural strand to the kind of personal being we find displayed by modern people.

There is the unity of embodiment: our experience as centres of spatio-temporal spheroids of perception (and action). This is the unity of our physical being. Person as the public individual is not differentiated from self. The point of view to which the indexicality of pronouns and other first person devices ties down avowals is a point of view defined by reference to our embodiment in a space–time world of things.

But there is also the unity of predication. I have argued in this paper that to understand the unity of personal being of persons of our sort we need to recognize a differentiation of concepts, called by me for convenience the 'person' and the 'self'. These concepts are differentiated by grammar, in the wider Wittgensteinean sense. The grammar of the person concept is exhausted by that of indexical reference in public avowals. The grammar of the self is more complex, since it arises, I believe, by a complex interweaving of a theory about the nature of ourselves and the appearance of a grammar of iterative and reflexive self predications.

It follows that the self is not a being, but a concept; a concept which plays an essential role in the way people of our sort organize our experience, because I believe we organize our experience in such a way that that experience can be reported, commented on, etc. within the linguistic resources we possess, themselves adjusted to the expression and maintenance of our local moral order. How could the constructivist position be tested? Traditional experimental psychology will not help much because any studies of that kind will of necessity be carried out within the very framework of linguistic and other practices upon which we wish to comment. We shall have to be more subtle and energetic in our procedures. Testing can proceed in two ways:

1. Scrutinizing the coherence and trying out the power of the analysis of the socio-linguistic practices of self description, disclosure, and comment, by which one hopes to have revealed the deep grammatical rules for the use of the concepts of person and self in our community of speakers.
2. Demonstrating the existence of alternative forms of life, through anthropological and historical research into the discourses and even the material practices of other cultures. We can study their methods of

creating works of art, their moral practices and so on, with the help of which the general theory of the social construction of the self can be established.

REFERENCES

Aronson, J. (1984). *A Realist Philosophy of Science*, Macmillan, London.
Burke, K. (1969). *A Grammar of Motives*, California University Press, Berkeley and Los Angeles.
Harré, R. (1983). *Personal Being*, Blackwell, Oxford.
Jaynes, J. (1979). *The Origin of Consciousness in the Breakdown of the Bicameral Mind*, Allen Lane, London.
Rychlak, J. (1984). 'Telosponsivity, dialectical reasoning, and the concept of self.' *Conference on Self and Identity*, Cardiff, Wales.
Shotter, J. (1984). *Social Accountability and Selfhood*, Blackwell, Oxford.
Vygotsky, L. (1962). *Thought and Language*, MIT Press, Cambridge, Massachusetts.
Warner, C. T. and Williams, R. (1984). 'The self and its freedoms: four versions of a radical approach.' *Conference on Self and Identity*, Cardiff, Wales.
Wittgenstein, L. (1953) *Philosophical Investigations*, Blackwell, Oxford.
Wright-Mills, C. (1959) *The Sociological Imagination*, Oxford University Press, New York.

Self and Identity: Psychosocial Perspectives
Edited by K. Yardley and T. Honess
© 1987 John Wiley & Sons Ltd

5

Toward Self as Relationship

Kenneth J. Gergen

*One of the most significant trends in recent inquiry into self has been towards
social constructionism. As is increasingly evidenced, what have traditionally
been viewed as both mental and behavioural events are now held to be
historically situated constructions emerging from social process. Increasing
emphasis on human agency and on persons (as opposed to structure) have
fortified this movement. When the implications of constructionism are extended
we find ourselves on the frontier of a new and challenging conception of self,
one that shifts the locus of understanding from individual selves to the relationships in which selves are made possible.*

There is a sense in which the present era finds us at a critical point of balance.
On the one side, we now have over 2000 years of accumulated thought on the
self at our disposal. We share with Plato the concept of abstract ideas (now
termed prototypes), with Aristotle the concept of logical forms (now cognitive
heuristics), with Machiavelli conceptions of social strategy (now impression
management), with Augustine, Hobbes, and Pascal the concept of self-love
(now self-esteem), and with Locke a concept of the empirical basis of abstract
ideas (now called self-knowledge). These, along with numerous other
significant distinctions, represent a legacy of symbolic resources—resources
that richly inform our contemporary colloquy. Indeed, contemporary inquiry
into the self represents the continuation of a finely honed scholarly tradition
of which these concepts are but a few important artefacts. In our present
dialogue our forbears stand as silent interlocutors.

On the one side of the balance thus stands the work of many gifted thinkers
whose work is dispersed over the past 25 centuries. On the other side is the
contemporary research community, composed of thousands, and which represents the most conceptually advanced, methodologically sophisticated, and
politically and economically unencumbered group of scholars ever to engage
in concentrated consideration of the self. While scholars of earlier centuries
were scattered historically and geographically, often ignorant of each other's
work, the contemporary research community is in continuous communication,
cutting across geographic, ethnic, religious, and political domains. One may

be justifiably awed at the intellectual power brought to the contemporary study of self. And one might be damned curious over the accomplishments.

The consequences of such investigation could be considerable. Theories of the self are, after all, nothing less than definitions of what it is to be human. Such theories inform the society as to what the individual can or cannot do, what limits may be placed over human functioning, and what hopes may be nurtured for future change. Further, they inform society as to rights and duties, designate those activities to be viewed with suspicion or approbation, and indicate who or what is to be held responsible for our present condition. To define the self is thus to sit in implicit judgment of society. It is in this sense that we may understand the execution of Socrates as an attempt by the Athenians to rid themselves of one whose construction of the human being placed abstract truth at the centre of human functioning. Conventional virtues of the time, such as filiality and piety, were placed in jeopardy. In 1600 Giordano Bruno was burned at the stake for attacking faith and revelation as grounding components of human makeup. Much like Socrates, Bruno wished to place reason at the centre of optimal human functioning.

Today we largely accept abstract truth and reason as central to human existence, and none of us would probably be subjected to hemlock or torch for our conceptual work. Yet, conceptions of the self have played and continue to play an immensely important role in human affairs. Within the present century, for example, the concept of self-deception has been enormously influential in sustaining the insanity defence in courts of law. Many individuals virtually owe their lives to this conceptual implement. Similarly, the legalization of abortion depended strongly on the elaboration of the concept of 'mental suffering' for the female, and the deterioration of 'motherhood' as the basis of women's self-conception. The concept of self-esteem was pivotal in American civil rights legislation. To vilify the segregationist position, it was necessary to construct the individual as one who possesses self-esteem, and for whom level of self-esteem lies central to personal existence. In the hands of behavioural scientists depleted self-esteem has been tantamount to neurotic illness. These manoeuvres in the game of competing intelligibilities are of no small consequence.

Yet, how are we to understand the present intensification of concern with self? In earlier years self inquiry in psychology, sociology, anthropology, philosophy, and related areas was a spasmodic affair. Fashions were sometime affairs that occurred in one or another domain, but briefly and without significant reverberation. At present, concern with self is substantial, persevering, and pervasive. But why? How are we to account for such a movement. A number of answers could be provided. I would like to elaborate on one of these. In particular, there is good reason to believe that such active and concentrated pursuit is the result of a more general evolution in understanding. For over a century now the Western intellectual tradition has been strongly committed to an empiricist conception of knowledge. The empiricist view has been an optimistic one, for on its account we may anticipate the accumulation of properly warranted knowledge. As it is proposed, such warrants are furnished by systematic observation. In this light self-understanding or self-knowledge was not only possible but essential for effective adaptation. One could and must employ observational skills to develop an accurate, reliable, and adaptive representation of the self.

Yet, the past several decades have witnessed a continuous erosion of confidence in the empiricist version of knowledge. Feyerabend, Hanson, Habermas, Kuhn, Popper, Quine, Taylor, and Winch are only a few of those who have been centrally responsible in philosophy for the demise of empiricist foundationalism. As it is said, we are now in a 'post empiricist' phase. What is most apparent about this phase is that the concept of knowledge has been bereft of secure foundations. No longer is there justification for employing observation as the firm basis for conceptual systems. As it is said, theories are radically underdetermined by the nature of evidence. Most important, as the foundations of empiricism drop away, so does the justification for the traditional assumption of self-knowledge. It is precisely in this domain that one may understand the emergence of contemporary concern. If the empirical basis of self-knowledge is torn away, what is to be made of the concept of self-knowledge? If the empirical coordinates for defining self are lost, what is to be made of the concept of self or identity? What are the sources of what we take to be self-definition? What implications are to be drawn from a reoriented view of self-knowledge for the science of human behaviour and for the society more generally? Such issues send reverberating ripples throughout the social sciences and humanities.

In this light it is interesting to consider the recent history of self-study. In important respects this history recapitulates the demise of empiricist assumptions at the more general level. In effect, the study of the self has played out many of the important themes within more general colloquy over the nature of knowledge. More importantly, however, inquiry into self has furnished an *alternative* view of knowledge, one that could well form the basis for a new concept of knowledge at the more general level. It will be useful to consider the future implications of the emerging view of self. If we begin to unpack more fully the implications of recent work, we find that we may be on the threshold of an entirely new vocabulary for understanding the self. In effect, we may be balanced on the edge of an historical disjunction, a disjunction that would distinguish contemporary work from its historical predecessors. Let us consider then (although briefly) several converging strands of recent history along with future implications.

FROM SELF-KNOWLEDGE TO COMMUNAL CONSTRUCTION

The Delphic inscription 'Know Thyself' has long served as an intellectual emblem in Western culture. The underlying rationale for such an injunction is readily appreciated. As often reasoned, the inner world of motives, thoughts, and feelings is an ambiguous one, and the correct identification can often be critical to one's well-being. If such psychological wellsprings are disregarded, or mistakes are made in their identification, then one's behaviour may often militate against one's true interests. In knowing oneself, it is said, it is also essential that one be able to identify properly one's overt behaviour—to 'see it for what it is'. If one fails to realize that her actions are callous and cruel, for example, she will be debilitated in her interactions with others. It is important that one not be deluded about the true character of one's activities.

Belief in self-knowledge is also wedded to the companionate assumption of 'natural kinds'. This view, amply illustrated in early scientific work, holds that the world is made up of classes of particulars, such as various species of animal, chemical elements, racial groupings, and the like. Knowledge commences when one begins to isolate and develop a taxonomy of the various kinds. In the case of self-knowledge this means that people should properly be apprised of the kinds of mental events that they harbour—their motives, emotions, intentions, and so on—and should be conscious of the kinds of behaviour in which they are engaged (thus knowing, for example, that they are being friendly as opposed to flirtatious, seriously discussing as opposed to playing at oneupsmanship). Recent inquiry into self poses a major threat *both* to the assumptions of self knowledge and to that of natural kinds.

THE SOCIAL CONSTRUCTION OF MENTAL STATES

Let us first consider the unfolding of research on identifying mental states. For many of us the breakthrough of singular significance was embodied in the 1964 publication of Schachter's two-factor theory of emotion. From an historical perspective, this theory accomplished two important ends. First, it proposed a fundamental alteration in the character of the 'things to be known'. Reinforced by a belief in 'natural kinds' it was traditionally believed that emotion terms stand in rough correspondence to an array of independent physiological states. The major problem was to determine how many states exist and to develop an appropriate set of measures for them. Schachter's work threw this line of thinking into sharp question. To what entities of physiological states did the widely variegated vocabulary of emotions refer? With no convincing answer available to this question, the conclusion seemed inescapable that the linguistic variations were not 'mirrors' of physiological states but were products of social convention. Over time the emotional language had become reified. In place of these reifications Schachter proposed that there was only a single 'entity', a generalized, and amorphous state of arousal. Suddenly the hoary problem of emotional identification was dissolved; there was no set of entities to be identified.

Schachter's second accomplishment was that of lodging the process of psychological knowledge within the social sphere. Traditionally, it was believed that the individual alone had access to his or her private states, and as a result, it was the individual who was left with the problem of accurate identification. In this sense one could properly know oneself. From Schachter's perspective the individual-centred tradition is found wanting. It is no longer the individual who is at the centre of 'knowledge' production, but the social group. The individual's act of labelling is but a by-product of social interchange. It is the social group that furnishes the vocabulary with which emotional 'identification' is to proceed, along with the semantic rules for proper usage.

Although this early work was sketchy and incomplete, and although amply criticized, the concept of emotion as a social construction has continued to capture the intellectual imagination. It has fired researchers to reconceptualize the nature of love, pain, depression, anger, and so on. Such terms no longer stand—as they have for almost 2000 years—as designators of natural kinds, that is, mankind's basic emotional makeup. Rather, they emerge from the cooperative and historically situated attempt of communities to render their constituents intelligible.

Concomitant with the erosion of belief in emotional knowledge has been a progressive socialization in what is taken as knowledge of cognitive process. With strong support garnered from the domain of cognitive study, it is argued that people are aware of the products of their mental processes but generally have little if any access to the processes giving rise to these products. There is considerable debate over the evidence in support of this view. And well there should be if, indeed, evidence is itself a product of social negotiation. The case can be more effectively made on conceptual rather than empirical grounds. For example, how is one to justify the assumption that people can recognize their own mental states: their ideas, intentions, beliefs, attitudes, and the like? What is the object of knowledge in this case that it can be separated from the subject? What concept of mind are we forced to accept if we agree that consciousness can perceive itself, that it can simultaneously function as the perceiving agent and the thing perceived? And, if one can perform the theoretical circumlocution necessary to justify this sort of mental dualism, what safeguards could ever be placed over misperception of mental states? Why are processes of internal perception not biased by the very entities (i.e., memories, hopes, intentions) one wishes to discover? And if one agrees with Freud that just such biases are the prevailing feature of mental life, on what grounds or by what criteria could the 'true' state of mind be ascertained? There are further problems of infinite regress: the knower of mental states must be able to recognize when accuracy has been achieved, that is, one must be aware of one's process of evaluation. Yet to be aware of one's evaluation entails judging its proper functioning, thus requiring yet another level of self-awareness, and so on to infinity. As we see the concept of self-knowledge, whether in terms of emotions, cognitions, or other psychological states, is fraught with conceptual difficulty.

THE SOCIAL NEGOTIATION OF BEHAVIOURAL EVENTS

The attempt to relocate psychological knowledge in the social sphere has played a robust and catalytic role in self theory of recent decades. A similar shift may be discerned in the case of knowledge of one's behaviour. That is, inquiry has begun to question the assumption of 'natural kinds' of behaviour, and the concomitant belief that a person can be accurate or inaccurate, biased, or self-deceived when reporting on his or her activities. However, developments in this realm have proceeded at a slower pace than in the preceding instance, possibly because a successful relocation of behavioural knowledge within the social sphere would pose a lethal threat to the traditional view of behavioural science as 'truth teller'. If the identification of human action is socially embedded, then the attempt to generate secure knowledge by reference to empirical coordinates is also vitally threatened.

The seeds for a social constructionist view of behavioural knowledge have long been latent within symbolic interactionist theory. As argued by both Mead and Cooley, one's understanding of his or her actions is principally dependent on the views communicated to him or her by significant others. This view leaves the individual's knowledge of self fully dependent on the social surrounds. Yet, when this view is extended to its logical outcome, one is led to the conclusion that there is no behavioural knowledge outside of social opinion. That is, if each individual is dependent on others to decide when an action is 'aggressive', 'intelligent', 'cautious', and the like, then what is the source of truth in such matters? On what grounds could any individual be singled out as furnishing an accurate or privileged portrayal rather than a reflection of social opinion? Symbolic interactionist accounts have generally remained silent on this question.

A similar message lies implicit in the continuing line of research on social comparison. As Festinger initially proposed, people frequently lack objective information with which to evaluate their various capacities and attributes. As a result, they often compare themselves with others to reach an *adequate* self-definition. However, when the theory is pressed we find that 'adequacy' in this case is more appropriately viewed as a normative concept rather than a surrogate for objectivity. That is, one makes inferences that are acceptable within the immediate social milieu. However, such inferences are not thus rendered the more accurate. This conclusion has been made with increasing clarity by much subsequent research on scanning strategies in social comparison. As researchers have tried to demonstrate, the conclusions of social comparison depend importantly on the target chosen for comparison. Thus, depending on one's strategies of target selection, virtually any conclusion may be drawn regarding one's attributes. In this context, who is to designate which comparison group would yield a correct understanding of the self?

Wide ranging research programmes have since emerged which share with this early work a concern with the effects of various cognitive sets on people's conclusions about their objective characteristics. For example, in the study of self-attribution it was once reasoned that people could be accurate or inaccurate regarding their attributions of causality. Many investigators believed that it was possible to locate the causal source of human action either within the person or the environment. Others set out to demonstrate that actors furnish more correct views of the cause of their actions than observers. However, such assumptions of accuracy in attribution have since been eroded. Demonstrations have been arranged to show that both actors and observers may direct their attention in many different ways (internally, situationally, historically, etc.). The conclusions reached about the causal source of one's actions are largely a function of which scanning strategy is employed. Similarly, as a given action slips into the historical past, one may come to see the action increasingly as a result of the situation; as its effects become known, attributions may change again. When the implications of this work are extended, the assumption of accuracy in self-attribution is placed in severe jeopardy.

This latter view becomes more fully articulated among investigators sensitive to the presentational function of self-attribution. In this domain attribution is often viewed as a form of 'social accounting'. To say that one has or has not been responsible for a given action is not thus a report of a 'mental event' or a 'reading of the world'. Rather, on this account it is an attempt to gain social ends. For example, self-accounts may be used to silence questions of various kinds, to avoid blame, to gain others' regard or respect, or otherwise manage one's social trajectory.

In its most recent metamorphosis the replacement of objective knowledge by socially constructed knowledge is represented in wide-ranging inquiry into self-maintenance, that is, how people manage to maintain a given image of self, or retain a given level of self-esteem. As it has been proposed, people review information or seek feedback in such a way as to confirm existing hypotheses. It is thus one's perspective on the evidence that creates the taken for granted world, not the brute facts themselves. When this view is extended to its logical conclusion, one must ask, 'how else could it be?' Can behavioural observations ever be free of the perspectives we bring to them? Can there be 'facts of behaviour' independent of the perspectives we use to understand what constitutes a fact? Again we find ourselves at the brink of social subjectivity in the concept of self-knowledge.

AGENCY, PROCESS, AND SCIENCE

Thus far I have tried to argue that much self-inquiry over the past several decades has increasingly removed the locus of self-knowledge from objective entities and placed it within the community. I am not suggesting that this thereby represents an increment in objective knowledge. My sympathies are sufficiently with Kuhn, Feyerabend, and the sociologists of knowledge not to mistake change for accretion. Rather, one may consider these various movements a form of intellectual growth which enhance the symbolic resources of the culture.

We may briefly note two other major trends in self-inquiry over the past 20 years which are consistent with and related to this major evolution toward social constructionism. Of particular importance has been the deterioration of mechanistic theories of self-conception and a re-awakening of concern with self-agency. The behaviourist orientation, long adopted by psychologists more generally, strongly militated against the view of self as origin of action. With it programmatic aim of developing laws or principles relating environmental antecedents to behavioural consequences, the behaviourist orientation twice impugnes the concept of human agency. It does so, first, in its location of the causal force for human activity: from the behaviourist perspective the cause of behaviour is removed from the person and placed within the environment. Psychological constructs such as the self concept function as mere integers in a three-step (S-O-R) process in which the stimulus retains the function of 'first cause'. The behaviourist orientation also threatens the concept of agency in its committed search for laws and principles, a search suggesting that human actions are, like the movement of the planets or the tides, subject to inexorable determination. To the extent that the research focus is on the lawful relationship among observables, the concept of intention is obscured.

Yet the concept of a stable structure of conceptions that simply reflects environmental inputs and gives direction to behaviour has never proven fully satisfying for most self-psychologists. Concepts of self as agent were deeply woven into early theories of self. In large measure the way for this return has been presaged by the generalized deterioration in the romance with neobehaviourism. This deterioration has raised widespread questions regarding the intellectual, empirical, and ethical outcomes of research in the S-O-R paradigm. Its outcomes are most apparent in theories of self-presentation, rule–role formulations, ethogenics, and telic theories. In part the return to agency has also resulted from the cognitive revolution, and its emphasis on internal bases of action. This shift toward the internal has essentially given a rebirth to the possibility of self as opposed to environmentally originated action. This rebirth is witnessed in the neobehaviourist concern with self-control and with self-sustaining mechanisms. It is also discovered in the attempt at cognitive theorists to develop 'top-down' conceptions of information processing.

A second important evolution is from theories of self-structure to process. Slowly withering are theories that conceive of stabilized structures of the mind. Increasing attention is being given to ongoing, interactive processes where persons are actively engaged with their ecological surrounds. This shift in concern is also manifested in neobehaviourist theories of person- by situation-interaction. It is more clearly apparent in dramaturgical theories, dialectic theory, lifespan developmental formulations, and the ethno-methodology of the self.

Both the movements toward agency and process are intimately linked with the constructionist trend. If knowledge is not 'data driven' as the behaviourist tradition suggests, but is constructed by interacting individuals, then one is inclined to grant to the individual a certain power of agency. The individual is liberated within this perspective, from mechanistic dependency on environmental inputs, as he or she masters and/or contributes to the rules of understanding within the social sphere. With respect to the shift away from structure, we find the very concept of internal mechanism may be viewed as a social construction. Thus the psychological mechanism as a 'thing to be explored' ceases to be compelling. If psychological mechanisms are considered social constructions, and the social process is carried out by self-directing agents, then the concept of internal machinery plays little explanatory role. Rather, one's attention shifts to social processes unfolding over time. Social life is no longer a juxtaposition of disconnected S-O-R sequences, but a process in continuous and coherent emergence. The metaphor of the *machine* is replaced by the metaphor of the *dialogue*, the *dance* or the *game*, as it is these latter endeavours in which voluntary agents are united in an ongoing, interdependent process.

Earlier it was pointed out that social psychological research on the self posed a dramatic challenge to the 2000 year old belief in self-knowledge. As is also apparent, if the current trends in self-inquiry are extended and proliferated, the discipline of psychology (and related disciplines) may undergo a substantial evolution. For, as the present work suggests, that which is taken to be psychological knowledge is more properly to be viewed as a product of social interchange. From this perspective an understanding of social life is not to be derived from knowledge of psychological principles. Rather, what are taken to be psychological principles are derivative from the ongoing process of negotiation and conflict among persons. Thus, understanding community is prior to and establishes the grounds from which psychological construals are achieved. The mechanistically oriented, individual centred, law producing investments of the discipline would thus give way to a communitarian perspective. Forms of social process, their potentials and their failings would become focal concerns of the discipline. The outcomes of research would not be laws for putative purposes of prediction and control, but rendered understandings that might stimulate the social process which is science and challenge the common conventions of the society more generally.

BEYOND INDIVIDUALISM: SELF AS RELATIONAL

As we see, recent history in self-inquiry reflects in important respects the general deterioration of confidence in objective knowledge. Such inquiry also reveals an alternative framework for understanding knowledge, to whit, knowledge is an artefact of social collectivity. The implications of such a conclusion are far reaching, both for the sciences and the culture alike. However, rather than pursue these implications more deeply at this junction I wish to extend the present analysis in one final direction, namely toward the future shape of self enquiry. For, as indicated earlier, if we unpack the assumptions underlying the present trends we find ourselves pressing the edges of understanding—moving significantly beyond the conceptual framework we have inherited from the past. For over two thousand years the prevailing form of understanding in Western culture has been individualist. It is the individual person who stands as the subject of inquiry, and the attributes of the person consistently figure in explanations of human nature. Yet, as we have seen so far, we are now moving to the point in our understanding of knowledge where the individual is being replaced by social process. The auspicious question is whether we can replace individualized theories of self with relational theories. Rather than viewing individuals as making up relationships, we can shift our conceptual lens and view selves as manifestations of relationship. Such a direction is presaged in John Shotter's concept of 'joint action': it is also implicit in Harré's work on the social construction of selves. How is such thinking to reach full articulation?

Let us consider the possibility more directly. We speak of persons as having motives, beliefs, understandings, plans and so on, as if these are properties of individual selves. However, if my arm is positioned above my head there is little that may be said about me as an individual. I am merely a spatio-temporal configuration. In contrast, if another person were before me, crouching and grimacing, suddenly it is possible to speak of me as aggressive, oppressive, or ruthless. In contrast, if the other person were a child standing on tiptoes, arms outstretched, his ball lodged in a tree above my head, it would be possible to characterize me as helpful or paternal. Additional configurations of the other might yield the conclusion that I was playful, obedient, protective, proud, and so on. Note that my action is the same in all circumstances: yet, there is little that may be said of me—to characterize myself—until the relational context is articulated. Similarly, the other person's movements have little bearing on our language of understanding until they are seen within the context of my own. In effect, what we acquire as individualized characteristics—our aggressiveness, playfulness, altruism and the like—are primarily products of the joint configuration. They are derivatives of the whole.

There is a sense in which this discussion is preceded by Hegel's conception of *Folkgeist*—literally spirit of the people. For Hegel this overarching spirit of community was fundamental to the human condition; the individual was a secondary derivative. As Hegel argues, 'The individual *is* an individual in this substance (which characterizes a community) . . . No individual can step beyond [it].' Or again, '. . . for the single individual as such, is true only as a universal multiplicity of single individuals. Cut off from the multiplicity, the solitary self is, in fact, an unreal, impotent self.' Walt Whitman similarly captures the flavour of self as relationship in his 'Song of Myself'.

> I celebrate myself, and sing myself
> And what I assume you shall assume
> For every atom belonging to me
> As good belongs to you

Both Hegel and Whitman's words border on the mystical, and I am not at all proposing to replace the pragmatic business of generating theoretical understanding with mysterious impalpables.

However, we do find that the discourse of relationship represents a 'vastly unarticulated subtext' upon which rests the text of individual selves. The pragmatic question is whether we can articulate this subtext. Can we bring into the foreground that which has remained in the penumbra of intelligibility? It is as if we have at our disposal a rich language for characterizing rooks, pawns, and bishops but have yet to discover the game of chess. The present question is thus whether we can redefine qualities of self in such a way that their derivation from the whole is made clear? Can we develop a language of understanding in which there are not powerful, helpful, intelligent or depressed selves for example, but in which these characterizations are derivatives from more essential forms of relationship? Can we define the games in which the characteristics of self are rooted? It is my belief that we can forge the necessary language of understanding. It will not be easy, as we are not in the same position as twentieth century psychology, that is, drawing heavily from the commonplace conceptions of the culture. We must press beyond existing understanding in this case and therein lies the major hurdle. In order to make the conceptual leap new metaphors are required. It is my suspicion that the most useful metaphor may prove to be that of the text. In the same way that individual words cannot be understood outside of a linguistic context, the understanding of individuals requires comprehension of social context. Text comprehension may thus stand parallel to comprehension of the more wholistic units of which individuals are localized manifestations.

There is good reason to press on toward a language of relationships. We confront the possibility, for one, of writing an entirely new chapter in the history of self-inquiry. In this sense we confront the possibility of adding significantly to the 2000 year accumulation of symbolic resources. Rather than elaborating and extending the past—as much of our work tends to do—we could realize a new form of intelligibility. More important, perhaps, there is widespread criticism of the ideological and practical implications of the prevailing commitment to individual centred explanation. Many contend that explanations of human activities in terms of individual selves—motives, mechanisms, drives, structures, and the like—help to sustain institutions in which competition, alienation, and isolation are central features. Worse still, as the individual centred metaphor enters into our consideration of political affairs, we are led to differentiate ourselves from other selves, to cast the world in terms of us versus them. The implications could now be catastrophic. So we stand at a point of balance. There is much reason to be excited by our prospects.

Self and Identity: Psychosocial Perspectives
Edited by K. Yardley and T. Honess
© 1987 John Wiley & Sons Ltd

6

Knowledge of the Self through Interaction

Ivana Markova

It is argued that self-knowledge develops by the individual's practical involvement with the world and his or her interpretation of information about himself or herself obtained from other people. The self is both structure and process, these two being relative to each other. The study of self-knowledge is inseparable from that of self-deception just as cognition is inseparable from emotion.

In his chapter 'Towards self as relationship', Gergen (this volume) points out that in the last few decades the focus of the study of self-knowledge has been shifting from a search for objective self-knowledge towards self-knowledge as a social construction. The objective approach to self-knowledge is based on the belief that systematic observation in empirical studies can furnish one with the grounds for precise definitions and concepts employing the metaphors of *self-as-machine* and *self-as-structure*. In contrast, the social constructivist approach argues that the idea of *objective* knowledge is founded on a misconception as to what it means to know. Following Hanson (1958), Kuhn (1962), and many others, the social constructivist approach maintains that there is no knowledge on its own but, instead, that all knowledge is laden with existing societal presuppositions and beliefs, indeed, that knowledge is 'an artefact of collectivity' (Gergen, this volume). Psychological principles are also products of social interaction, and thus there is no independent self; the self has risen out of a relationship between the individual and his or her social environment. Moreover, while the objective knowledge approach defines the self as a *machine* and a *structure*, the constructivist approach adopts the view that the self is an *agent* and a *process* (Gergen, this volume).

However, although there has been a considerable shift in the assumptions as to what the self and self-knowledge are, concepts such as *self-as-agent* and *self-as-process*, employed in the constructivist approach, still need to be clarified. The concept of self-knowledge is itself replete with difficulties (Toulmin, 1977) and the underlying assumptions of the constructivist approach are prone to different interpretations. For example, while Gergen (1977, 1984, and this volume) argues that the social constructivist approach is closely linked with agency, the nature of this link remains to be shown. Thus, Hamlyn (1977) challenged the constructivist approach precisely because agency was missing from it. On the issue as to whether the self is a structure *or* process, here again the question of the nature of the relevant concepts still has to be answered.

SELF KNOWLEDGE: SOCIAL CONSTRUCTION OR SELF-INVOLVEMENT?

I   In his paper on *Self-knowledge* Hamlyn (1977) criticized the social constructivist approach, according to which an individual's self-knowledge is gained through interpretation of information about the individual received from other people. This approach Hamlyn maintains, is derived from the view of George H. Mead that

> [an individual] becomes an object to himself only by taking the attitudes of other individuals towards himself within a social environment or context of experience and behavior in which both he and they are involved (Mead, 1934, p. 138).

Hamlyn argues that beliefs about oneself, although they may be true, are, nevertheless, only beliefs and therefore on no account can they be identified with knowledge proper. In addition, preoccupation with information about oneself might lead, not to a deeper insight about one's increasing self-knowledge, but, instead, to the inhibition of one's activity. Although it is important to know what one means to others, one cannot become a real self if one is constantly looking over one's shoulder to see how one is being regarded by others. Instead of being committed to what one is doing one would simply become self-conscious in the ordinary sense of being anxious about one's appearance and performance and thus become detached from one's activities, and so alienated. Self-consciousness would be antithetical to self-knowledge because the essential condition of self-knowledge proper, i.e. involvement, would be missing (Hamlyn, 1977, pp. 173–4). The essential difference between our knowledge of others and our knowledge of ourselves is that we can, at least to a limited degree, control our own futures by making decisions about the course of our actions. We cannot decide about the futures of others in the same way. Decision-making about our futures 'is vital to any view of self-knowledge that we can form' (Hamlyn, 1977, p. 196). Moreover, new decision-making often leads to a reinterpretation of our past decisions and life events, and thus it may completely alter our understanding of ourselves. Our future decisions, therefore, may give a new sense to our past: things that only yesterday might have seemed marginal, in the view of a new decision may be seen in a different light, and consequently be reinterpreted as essential. Finally, Hamlyn claims:

> A person is not a static thing. If there are some constant things about us (there *is* such a thing as personal identity, and some constant about us may be genetically determined), we are also changing entities with both a history and a possible future. For this reason alone there can be no complete story about what has to

be known for adequate self-knowledge. Indeed it might be said that a central fact about self-knowledge is that there is no *thing* to be known (Hamlyn, 1977, p. 196).

To sum up, Hamlyn is saying that although concerns about interpersonal interaction and relationships are an important precondition for gaining knowledge *about* oneself, one has to be *practically* involved to gain genuine self-knowledge. In other words, it is through doing and making decisions that one gains self-knowledge. Therefore, it is false that 'self-knowledge can properly be viewed as a social construction, even if social factors enter in an important way into its content' (Hamlyn, 1977, p. 199).

II It is interesting that the ideas of both the social construction of self-knowledge by focusing on recognition of oneself by others, and Hamlyn's emphasis on practical involvement, originate in Hegel's theory of self-knowledge in which these two ideas are built into a coherent theory. Thus, it was Hegel who, in modern philosophy, pointed to the importance of practical activity for knowledge and self-knowledge, and it was Hegel who first emphasized the importance of recognition by others in gaining self-knowledge.

Hegel (1807) maintains that it is through practical activity that people acquire their own minds. In the process of practical involvement people not only transform things but also change themselves and gain self-knowledge. This happens in the following way: by altering external things people impress the seal of their own being upon the world; by being acted upon, external objects acquire characteristics of the moulders themselves. As Hegel puts it:

> Man does this in order, as a free subject, to strip the external world of its inflexible foreignness and to enjoy in the shape of things only an external realization of himself. Even a child's first impulse involves this practical altera-tion of external things; a boy throws stones into the river and now marvels at the circles drawn in the water as an effect in which he gains an intuition of something that is his own doing (Hegel, 1842, p. 31).

The more people shape things with their own ideas, the more they achieve mastery over them. The more people see objects as their own doing, the more they project and understand themselves in terms of their products and creations. In other words, people humanize things. The things are no longer alien to them but have the purpose of their creators stamped into them.

People do not, however, live only in the world of physical objects. They live in a social world and thus they also struggle to impress the seal of their own being upon social objects. However, the people who are the objects of this social world all operate with powers such as perception, cognition, emotions, and the freedom of decision-making. Therefore, the seal of a person's being cannot be impressed upon others by means of physical manipulation as in the case of physical objects. Instead, human beings can be brought voluntarily to recognize each other as equals in their social, emotional, and intellectual powers. By mutually recognizing themselves as mutually recognizing one another, human beings acquire self-consciousness, and the ability to take the attitudes of each other. By doing so the one recognizes how the other participant feels, thinks, and what he or she intends, and the one knows that the other participant knows these things about the knower himself or herself. It would be wrong, however, to view self-consciousness as just the mirroring of the others' attitudes onto oneself. In becoming a human, one is working to become human, indeed, one has to struggle for it, as Hegel made clear. Everything a human being achieves comes from active practical involvement rather than from sheer acceptance of information and attitudes.

To sum up, just as people find themselves in the products of their own action, so they find themselves in the products of their interactions with other people. Interpersonal interaction *is* a kind of action and any claims concerning an acting agent must also be applicable to an interacting agent. Just as people gain self-knowledge through practical involvement in their action in general, so they gain self-knowledge through practical involvement in their interaction with others. In this sense, involvement with both physical objects and with other people appears to be important for self-knowledge. The question that remains to be answered is what kind of relationship there is between practical involvement with physical and social objects on the one hand, and self-consciousness and reflexion on the other. I shall try to answer this question by considering in some detail the above two claims by Hamlyn about self-knowledge: first, the claim that since a person is not static there can be no complete story about what has to be known for adequate self-knowledge, indeed, 'a central fact about self-knowledge is that there is no *thing* to be known'. Secondly, his claim that self-consciousness and 'concentration on making explicit the reasons for our actions must inevitably involve a kind of detachment from oneself' (Hamlyn, 1977, p. 192) and, therefore, that self-consciousness is not conducive to self-knowledge.

III   Let us consider the first claim. The idea that persons recognize themselves gradually through their active experience and interference with the external world is not new. Kosik (1963) has drawn attention to the fact that the idea of 'odyssea', that is, picturing human beings as wanderers who, on their journey in the world, and through their own active transformation of the world, eventually recognize themselves, was quite common in nineteenth century German literature, philosophy, and social science. The essence of this motif is that subjects who return from their journey after wandering in the world are different from what they were at the beginning of the journey. The world itself is different because of the wanderer's activities affecting it. Moreover, the world also appears to be different to the wanderers after completion of their journey because they themselves have changed: their experience and perception of the world is now different.

This idea is best elaborated by Hegel in his *Phenomenology of Mind*.

Self-knowledge, just like knowledge in general, is gained through a process of active education of the mind, in which indeed 'there is no *thing* to be known' because the process of knowing is never ending and inexhaustible.

In a rather simplified form Hegel's argument is as follows. Traditional Cartesian epistemology postulated the existence of the world as it is, on the one hand, and of the cognizing subject, on the other. The problem that this division created was how the cognizing subject can know that what is cognized is true, i.e., that the world cognized is the world in itself. Traditional epistemology could give no satisfactory answer to this question since it could not provide any proper standards by which to judge one's knowledge of the world.

For Hegel the whole problem is incoherent because what the knowing subject has access to is not the world as it is but the world as it is for the knower. Knowing the world is a process in which the knower and the object of his or her knowledge both undergo transformation. The object is the standard against which knowledge is measured; it is the testing criterion of knowledge. Since the object can only be the object that is perceived or cognized, the object that is the standard lies within the knower rather than in the outside world. Further, because one's knowledge of an object in part determines one's cognition of the object, the standard against which knowledge is measured itself changes as knowledge of it progresses. If the knower's concept of the object satisfies the testing criterion, there is no need for a change in either the knower of the object or in the object of his or her knowledge. Such satisfaction, however, is usually only temporary. Once knowers increase their involvement they find that what appeared to be coherent on the surface suffers from internal contradictions, and therefore a solution of such contradictions is required. By being able to solve the contradictions between their temporary concepts and testing criteria, the knowers understand not only about the objects of their knowledge but also about themselves. In addition, they are now more free because they can better control the objects, knowing them better, and they can also make more meaningful decisions about the objects, and therefore about their own course of action. Thus, in Hegel's conception, knowledge in general is gained through self-knowledge, because as knowledge in general becomes more adequate so self-knowledge becomes more adequate.

This theme of the constant transformation of the knower and the object of his or her knowledge has influenced Mead's theory of the development of mind. According to this theory, mind arises from communication, or, as Mead put it, from a conversation of gestures. This theory is a miniature of a truly evolutionary and interactive approach, although overlooked by social construction theory. One participant in interaction makes a gesture, let us call it gesture A_1, and it serves as a stimulus for the other participant in interaction who adjusts his or her own gesture, let us call it gesture B_1, to that of the first participant. This gesture in turn becomes a stimulus for the first participant to adjust appropriately his or her own gesture to the gesture of the second participant, A_2, and so on. Thus arises 'a conversation of gestures, a reciprocal shifting of the . . . positions and attitudes' (Mead, 1934, p. 63). The important feature of this rather simple scheme is that the minimum meaningful unit of interaction has three steps, corresponding to a Hegelian dialectical triad. The first step is the gesture, A_1, of the first participant which leads to the second step, a gesture B_1, of the other participant: finally, the triad is completed with a gesture A_2 of the first participant which incorporates both A_1 and B_1. The third step, A_2, means that A_1B_1 have come, so to speak, into the first actor's mind. First, the knower acts, second, the other participant responds, and finally, the knower reflects upon his or her own act and the other participant's response. Or the knower acts upon an object, the form and qualities of the object changes, and as a result the knower reflects upon the reasons of his or her action and the change in the object. It is important that while most theories of communication and interpersonal interaction are based on a two-way process, from A to B and from B to A, it is essential that a Hegelian and also a Meadian process are three-step processes. This is what makes continuity and development possible: A to B, B to A, and finally AB, that is, a transformation of A and B through reflexion. This triad is also the minimum unit of the well-known hermeneutical circle. Mead unfortunately talks in this context only in terms of adjustment and shifting of positions and attitudes which makes his position sound rather mechanistic. However, it is clear from Mead's overall conception of mind that, while interacting with each other, participants progress to more complex levels of their awareness as creative and reflexive individuals.

IV   Hamlyn's second important claim is that self-consciousness and 'concentration on making explicit the reasons for our actions must inevitably involve a kind of detachment from oneself' (Hamlyn, 1977, p. 192). Any tendency to stand back, Hamlyn maintains (p. 194), mitigates against the possibility of genuine self-knowledge.

However, Hegel's and Mead's theories do not imply a constant looking over one's shoulder and a constant searching for reasons of action. Self-consciousness and reflexion by the Me are only one side of, or one stage in, the process of self-knowledge, while agency, or the I, is the other stage. In Mead (1934), such a process is to be understood as follows. The I is the experiencer, the agent. While actually experiencing and being involved in the world, the I is unable to reflect and evaluate. It is when the act has passed that one looks at it and interprets it. In other words, the I becomes Me. As Mead puts it:

> We can go back directly a few moments in our experience and then we are dependent upon memory images for the rest. So that the 'I' in memory is the spokesman of the self of the second, or minute, or day ago. As given, it is a 'me' which was the 'I' at the earlier time (Mead, 1934, p. 174).

For example, a child may be trying to find out how loudly he or she can shout. The child does it as *an agent*, as the I. Just a minute later the child realizes that granny is lying in bed with a bad headache and that shouting has obviously made granny worse. The I becomes Me as the child reflects upon his or her activity. Action and reflexion are two phases of one and the same process, and I and Me constantly alternate their positions and one changes into the other, or one is relative to the other.

If we now return to the three-step theory of knowledge and self-knowledge, it is obvious that while step A_1 is an active step in which the knower is practically involved with the object of his or her knowledge, step A_2 is a reflexive step based on a mental transformation of A_1 and B_1. Only after A_2 has taken place can it become the first step in the next triad, i.e., can A_2 become a new activity involving decision-making. Thus, a stage of spontaneous activity is followed by a stage of reflexion and evaluation. Recognizing oneself in one's own action is necessarily reflexive and evaluating. But this kind of reflexion and evaluation, rather than leading to alienation, is simply a stage in the developmental process of self-knowledge. Working on something, the knower first separates himself or herself from it and then unites himself or herself with it again, so that a new separation can follow. Thus, involvement necessarily posits itself against non-involvement and in order for development (or progress in knowledge) to take place, non-involvement must be a part of that process. It is in this way that practical and theoretical activity work together as two aspects of conscious activity.

For something to count as *knowledge*, it should in principle be possible for everybody using the same procedure to arrive at the same conclusion. In the sciences, repeatability of experiments or events under the condition that all the variables remain stable counts as a criterion as to whether something is knowledge or not.

We have established that gaining knowledge is a two-way relationship between the knower and the object of his or her knowledge. Moreover, it is an intimate relationship. For example, the way I learn about growing roses is something totally unique between me, as the knower, and the roses, as the known. Thus, the object of my knowledge is always to some extent different for me than it is for others, and consequently the concept I form of that object is to some extent different from that of others (Markova, 1982). However, since people operate within the same conceptual frameworks or paradigms, both their objects of knowledge and the concepts they form overlap considerably so that they can communicate about them. The more substantial the social and psychological characteristics among knowers sharing the same conceptual frameworks or paradigms, and the deeper the levels of their involvement with the objects of knowledge, the greater the overlap between the knowledge they obtain and concepts they form.

Just as with knowledge in general, for self-knowledge to count as knowledge, it should be possible, in principle, for *others* to share it. However, how can others have access to my self-knowledge, something that is special to me that I acquire on the basis of my own involvement with the world around me and through my private reflexion? In raising this issue I do not wish to initiate a discussion as to whether others have access to my mental states and processes (cf. Descartes, 1641; Wittgenstein, 1953), but rather to point to the similarity between gaining knowledge in general, and self-knowledge. Just as there is an idiosyncratic relationship between the knower and object of his or her knowledge, e.g. between the knower and roses, so there is a totally unique relationship between I as the knower and the Me, as the known: the more similar knowers are with respect to their social and psychological characteristics and the more closely they are involved with each other, the more mutual the knowledge of each other one would expect them to have.

THE SELF: STRUCTURE OR PROCESS?

I   In the work of Mead, the self is both the I and the Me, the agent acting and the agent reflecting, the knower and the known, alternating their positions in the process of self-knowledge. One can say that the acting agent is associated with the process while the reflecting agent is associated with the structure: the acting agent is *becoming* while the reflecting agent *is*. For many psychologists, however, it has been difficult to maintain both aspects of the self, process, and structure, in the centre of their attention, and definitions usually state that the self is either process, or that it is structure, with the more or less explicit or implicit indication that it also, of course, involves the other, the unstated aspect of the self. Thus those who focus on its cognitive aspects, such as Kelly (1955), Rogers (1951), and Gordon (1968), tend to describe the self as a structure, while those focusing on its social characteristics, such as Horrocks and Jackson (1972), Crook (1980), and McCall (1977), tend to describe the self as a process. Gergen (1971), wishing to play down the controversy between the two approaches, maintains that they 'need not be seen as mutually exclusive, but rather as complementary ways of approaching the same subject matter' (Gergen, 1971, pp. 18–19).

The distinction between structure, which refers to the relatively stable nature of the self, and process, which refers to the changing nature of the self, is an important one and should not be swept under the carpet because the two approaches are in some ways complementary, or because of the increasing tendency to view the self as process (Gergen, this volume).

Why should it be so difficult to maintain both structure and process in the centre of attention when theorizing about the self? The answer to this question is that on the whole it is held that if something is a process, then it is not a structure, just as if something is black then it is not white. In other words such pairs are held against each other as opposite and mutually exclusive entities. Yet, we have seen that in Mead's theory of the self the opposites, I and Me, are not held against each other as mutually exclusive entities, but the I transforms into Me and the Me transforms into I, in other words, *becoming* alters into *is*, and *is* alters into *becoming*. The difference between the two positions is that, in the former the self is treated as a *static here-and-now*, while in the latter it is *dynamic and developing*.

The problem of how to conceptualize phenomena resulting from the complementary contributions of two mutually opposing factors, in this case structure and process, is a common one (Markova, 1987). It arises whenever the researcher attempts to explain characteristics related to self-organizing natural phenomena that are in constant development and change. Consider how natural self-organizing phenomena and their opposites come into existence: it is by polarization from what was originally undifferentiated. For example, one can talk about individuals only insofar as they can be differentiated from, or opposed to, their environment; there is the I only insofar as it can be distinguished from the Me; in the same vein, one can talk about the structure of something only insofar as it can be distinguished from its opposite, i.e. process. Thus, the meaningfulness of the one phenomenon is dependent upon the meaningfulness of its counterpart. Polarization of the phenomenon and its counterpart is the result of an internal tension produced by opposing forces, or by contradictions, to use Hegel's (1830) term. For Hegel, if any movement and development is to take place, a resolution of tension between opposite forces must occur. Contradiction, Hegel says, 'is the very moving principle of the world and it is ridiculous to say that contradiction is unthinkable' (Hegel, 1830, p. 223). As Solomon (1983, pp. 316–317) maintains, Hegel's concept of contradiction was often objected to as a matter of intellectual perversity and was often ridiculed. For Hegel, however, a contradiction is an internal dilemma of consciousness which has to be practically resolved so that knowledge can progress. Thus, contradictions are practical dilemmas that demand resolution, rather than logical incoherencies.

Just as self-organizing phenomena are defined by their oppositions to their counterparts, so concepts referring to self-organizing phenomena must be considered in relation to their counter-concepts. In general, we learn at the same time both what a thing is and what it is not, and consequently every concept makes sense only in the context of its counter-concept. Just like the phenomena to which they refer, so the relevant concepts and their counter-concepts arise together from the undifferentiated and fall back together into the undifferentiated should they at any time become redundant. Since the self is both itself and yet undergoing development, in its explanation we should make use of both concepts and their oppositions, i.e. what I have termed counter-concepts, in our case, structure and process.

II   Recently, structure and process have been conceptualized in a much more related manner. Thus, Piaget (1971) maintains that structures are both *structuring* and *structured* (p. 10) and that 'all known structures—from mathematical groups to kinship systems—are, without exception, systems of transformation' (p. 11). In Piaget's account all kinds of structures have basically the same characteristics: they are organic wholes rather than aggregates, they are systems of transformation rather than static complexes; finally, they are self-regulating systems entailing both self-maintenance and closure. Self-maintenance and closure mean that the transformations of a structure never lead beyond the system itself and that the boundaries of the structure are preserved despite the emergence of new elements in such a structure. Piaget uses an example from mathematics to demonstrate the closure of a structure by pointing out that adding and subtracting any two whole numbers only lead to other whole numbers.

Markus and Sentis (1982) in their study on the 'Self in Social Information Processing' conceptualize the self as a 'system of *self-schemata*', these being 'knowledge structures developed by individuals to understand and explain their own social experience' (p. 45). Systems of self-schemata consist of memories or beliefs about the self. Schemata may be restructured, and can be activated by appropriate stimuli. Thus, Markus and Sentis say that a schema is 'at once a structure and a process'.

It seems to me, however, that although Piaget, and Marcus and Sentis, conceptualize structure and process together, at least two problems still remain. The first problem is that *interaction* is missing from both models. At the beginning of their history, whether biological or social, the individuals and their environment jointly arose from the undifferentiated and jointly defined their mutual boundaries: from their very origin they have affected each other, and they continue to affect each other in their future structuring and process of development. In Piaget's case, however, structure is self-contained. The structuring process proceeds within the structure itself, from its own elements, as in Piaget's own example of adding and subtracting just mentioned. Thus, transformations of structure are based on the unfolding of what is contained in the structure already. In Marcus and Sentis's model the information for restructuring comes from the individual's social experience and is processed in the system of self-schemata.

The second problem with both models is that *agency* is missing from them. While physical objects interact with their environment according to the laws of physics, an agent, in contrast to a mechanism, dominates its environment. In the case of the self the agent not only processes information while interacting with its environment, but also makes decisions about its future, evaluates its decisions and takes responsibilities for its actions. In other words, for the self to be an agent, it must develop both through *interaction* with the physical and social world and through *reflexion* on and evaluation of its actions.

Making a distinction between the I and Me, or process and structure, William James (1892) thought that the I would be difficult to explore empirically because of its unpredictable and spontaneous nature. Indeed, reviews of studies on the self (Wylie, 1979; Damon and Hart, 1982) have shown that the majority of empirical studies have been concerned with one aspect of the self only, with the Me, that is, with structure, although theoretically such studies subscribe both to process and structure. Wylie points out that such studies have mainly explored self-evaluation, that is, people's positive and negative feelings about themselves, their beliefs about themselves, and how others consider them.

In sum, although it is important to conceptualize the self as a process, it is also essential to acknowledge that a process can be understood properly only in relationship to a structure, just as in the study of self-knowledge agency is to be understood in the context of reflexion.

SELF-KNOWLEDGE AND EMOTION

When one talks about knowledge one generally assumes that to know is to use the available facts and information in a rational way and to employ one's cognitive faculties to do the job. Similarly, when one talks about self-knowledge, one assumes that the self-knower absorbs relevant information and reflects upon it employing cognition. In accordance with this assumption psychological theories and empirical studies concerning self-awareness and self-knowledge are cognitively or socio-cognitively based. For example, according to Selman (1980), as children in their development progress from one socio-cognitive stage of self-awareness to a more complex one they become increasingly able to understand and control the thoughts and feelings of themselves and others. Subjects such as morality and agency, too, are usually treated on cognitive assumptions. In both the Piagetian and Heiderian frameworks morality has been explored in the context of cognitive development, with moral judgment and moral reasoning in the child unfolding alongside changes in the structure of knowledge (e.g. Piaget, 1926; Kohlberg, 1968; Heider, 1958; Shaw and Sulzer, 1964). Emotions, on the other hand, have been viewed as disruptive, interfering with the child's operational thinking, and causing him or her to focus on irrelevant aspects of situations (Lickona, 1976). Similarly, the dramaturgical approach to the study of human action, favoured now by many of those concerned with agency and self, also disregard emotions, since, as Harré (1979) maintains, they are not admissible as causes of actions. The role of emotions in psychology in general has traditionally been relegated to the realm of disruptive behaviour, to be treated by therapy or controlled by the individual who suffers it. Indeed, psychotherapists, for example those of the attributional, cognitive, and Gestalt schools, often explain emotions cognitively to the patients to enable them to get better.

Yet neither our involvement with the physical and social world, nor the knowledge we acquire about ourselves, is ever based on neutral 'facts'. Most often, when we are involved in activities and acquire knowledge about ourselves, there is much emotional content both in the involvement and in the knowledge acquired. Thus, information is perceived as threatening or as promising something good; it is evaluative and has consequences for the individual and his or her social relationships. Consider the following example from genetic counselling. One generally accepted principle in genetic counselling is the neutrality of the counsellor in providing the counsellee with information as to his or her involvement with the genetic disorder in question, and information as to the lines of action available to the counsellee. The counsellor provides information but does not give advice as to which lines of action the counsellee should adopt. Having been given the facts, and only facts, the counsellee should make up his or her mind without any influence. However, in two research studies concerning the content and availability of genetic counselling in haemophilia, a sex-linked genetic disorder of blood clotting, carried out in different countries of the world (Markova *et al.*, 1984; Markova *et al.*, 1986) it was found that only a small proportion of people perceived the information given to them as just information; what the counsellor intended as information, the counsellee perceived as advice towards a particular course of action, most often as advice *not* to have children. One Canadian patient expressed his views as follows:

> Doctors are too biased to be counsellors. They are good only for giving medical and biological information. They look at people as physical objects which should be 'pure'. Having haemophilia is thus a defect from the 'pure' object wanted by the doctors and thus best to get rid of these by not having children.

It is, therefore, quite natural that people try to protect themselves from damaging information. What is perceived as damaging information is often socially induced in the sense that we are socialized as to what is and what is not threatening to one's self. For example, mental handicap in our present culture is associated with having difficulties with some skills, such as arithmetic, reading and writing, but not with others, such as painting, playing musical instruments or singing.

Traditionally, preventing oneself from becoming aware of something that is damaging to the self, has been called self-deception. However, in contrast to self-knowledge, self-deception has rarely been the subject of psychological theorizing and, even less, of empirical studies. There is, of course, Freud's theory of self-deception or defence. Freud's (1955, Freud, A., 1941) theory of defence is concerned to explain the person's conflict between conscious and unconscious belief and the ego's struggle against undesirable affects by repressing them from conscious thought, such defence mechanisms having psychopathological consequences for the sufferer, who requires treatment. In philosophy, on the other hand, the subject of self-deception has been discussed more often. Self-deception has been most often treated as the paradox of holding two contradictory beliefs at the same time, i.e. believing and not believing that something is the case. In contrast to general philosophical efforts to characterize self-deception in terms of a kind of cognition or perception, Fingarette (1969) offers a volition-action account of self-deception. He argues that notions such as 'to be aware of', 'to know', or 'to be conscious of' are readily associated with a passive metaphor, with information coming to the individual from the outside and the individual accepting it and becoming aware of it. However, consciousness is not a matter of passive receiving but of actively doing: it is an exercising of the skill of expressing our engagement with the world (Fingarette, 1969, p. 62). Thus, Fingarette proposes a model according to which people are active rather than passive, doers rather than thinkers, and in which to become explicitly conscious means to exercise a particular skill. A self-deceiver is someone who, for some reason, does not spell out his or her engagement in the world, that is, although having the skill of spelling it out, he or she has particular reasons for not doing so and for avoiding becoming explicitly conscious that he or she is avoiding it (Fingarette, p. 43). Referring to Sartre's comparison of getting into bad faith with getting to sleep, Fingarette maintains that 'in going to sleep we to some extent do something, but we are unable to reflect upon what we are doing, for to reflect upon the fact that one is waiting for sleep is to hinder its coming' (Fingarette, ibid., p. 99). Getting to sleep means avoiding reflexion because in reflexion the mind is active and does not let one get to sleep.

Fingarette's approach to self-deception is thus in some ways similar to the three-step approach to self-knowledge discussed earlier in this chapter. A self-deceiver, just like a person obtaining true self-knowledge, is engaged in some kind of action. The two differ, however, with respect to reflexion. The self-deceiver, unlike the self-knower, does not let reflexion occur so that the process of self-knowledge really does not come off. It is important in Fingarette's analysis of self-deception that the self-deceiver has the skill of spelling out her or his engagement with the world but does not do so because spelling out threatens the self.

If, however, the individual's information about her or himself, and her or his involvement with the physical and social world, is usually loaded with emotions just as it is with cognitions, what consequences are there for the study of self-knowledge? Can one indeed study the phenomenon of self-knowledge without also being involved in the study of self-deception? I would like to suggest that, just as one cannot separate the phenomenon of cognition from that of emotion, so one cannot separate the phenomenon of self-knowledge from that of self-deception. For most of us, in most situations, pure self-knowledge or pure self-deception rarely exist. For this reason the concepts of self-knowledge and self-deception should also involve both cognition and emotion.

CONCLUSION

In this chapter I have tried to show that self-knowledge is not based on self-involvement alone, or on construction out of information received from others alone. Instead, both self-involvement and construction (or reflexion), i.e. the I and the Me, are stages in the development of self-knowledge. Mead (1936) in his *Movements of Thoughts in the Nineteenth Century* maintained that the process of transformation of the I and the Me as we conceptualize them today was discovered only by the Romanticism of the nineteenth century (Markova, 1982). Jaynes (1976), who analysed the origin of human awareness in history, claimed that the people of the Mycean culture had no awareness of subjective states, either of their own or those of other people. According to him the Homeric heroes did not have subjectivity as we have it today; they had no awareness of their awareness of the world; they did not introspect. Stone (1977) in his study of the history of the family in Britain also provides ample evidence that before the sixteenth century people's relationships with each other were different from those of today; people were more aware of their position as members of a family within the community rather than of their own uniqueness or personalities. Only after the seventeenth century did individuals become increasingly orientated towards one another as independent, autonomous agents, and concepts of personal identity gradually emerge. Luria (1976), who in the 1930s studied the self-awareness of Russian peasants, whose living conditions have not changed for centuries, found that they were unable to describe themselves in terms of any psychological characteristics. Logan (this volume) offers insight into the development of the self by presenting a historical survey of such a development and showing, as Mead did, that the conceptualization of the I and the Me has emerged in a particular socio-historical context.

Earlier in this chapter we discussed the emergence of phenomena by polarization from the undifferentiated. As Logan shows in his chapter, the Cartesian Cogito can be interpreted as the undifferentiated from which the polarity of the I and Me eventually emerged. The Cartesian I, although we use the same word for it, is thus qualitatively different from the I in the dyad I and Me, just as Cartesian reflection is different from the Hegelian and Meadian reflexion (Markova, 1982). Moreover, even within the cultural conditions of a particular era one may still, in various contexts and at various levels of analysis, form different oppositions at different hierarchical levels. Thus, at one level I may be opposed to Me, as done in the context of this chapter, while at another level both I and Me, that is, the self, may be opposed to society, forming the dyad I and Society rather than the I and Me. For example, the self's creative view of the world may stand in opposition to the conventional and established societal view.

According to Hegel (1830) all universals undergo transformation in the end. Logan suggests that the concept of the self as an interaction of the I and the Me may already be changing in certain new directions.

REFERENCES

Crook, J. M. (1980). *The Evolution of Human Consciousness*, Clarendon Press, Oxford.

Damon, W. and Hart, D. (1982). 'The development of self-understanding from infancy through adolescence.' *Child Development*, **53**, 841–64.

Descartes, R. (1641). Meditations on first philosophy. In E. S. Haldane and R. T. Ross (transl. and Eds), *The Philosophical Works of Descartes*, vol. 1, Cambridge University Press, London and New York, 1911.

Fingarette, H. (1969). *Self-deception*, Routledge and Kegan Paul, London.
Freud, A. (1941). *The Ego and the Mechanisms of Defence* (transl. C. Baines), Hogarth Press, London.
Freud, S. (1955). *Complete Psychological Works*, Standard edn, Hogarth Press, London.
Gergen, K. J. (1971). *The Concept of Self*, Holt, Rinehart and Winston, New York and London.
Gergen, K. J. (1977). The social construction of self-knowledge, in T. Mischel (Ed.), *The Self: Psychological and Philosophical Issues*, Blackwell, Oxford.
Gergen, K. J. (1984). Theory of the self: impasse and evolution. *Advances in Experimental Social Psychology*, **17**, 49–115.
Gergen, G. J. (1986). 'Toward self as relationship.' In K. M. Yardley and T. M. Honess (Eds), *Self and Identity*, Wiley, Chichester and New York.
Gordon, C. (1968). 'Self-conceptions: configurations of content.' In C. Gordon and K. Gergen (Eds), *The Self in Social Interaction*, Wiley, New York and London.
Hamlyn, D. (1977). 'Self-knowledge.' In T. Mischel (Ed.), *The Self: Psychological and Philosophical Issues*, Blackwell, Oxford.
Hanson, N. R. (1958). *Patterns of Discovery*, Cambridge University Press, Cambridge.
Harré, R. (1979). *Social Being*, Blackwell, Oxford.
Hegel, G. W. F. (1807). *Phenomenology of Spirit* (transl. A. V. Miller), Clarendon Press, Oxford, 1977.
Hegel, G. W. F. (1830). *The Encyclopedia of the Philosophical Sciences*, part I, *The Science of Logic*. In W. Wallace (transl.). *The Logic of Hegel*, Oxford University Press, London, 1873.
Hegel, G. W. F. (1842). *Aesthetics: Lectures on Fine Art*, vol. 1 (transl. T. M. Knox), Clarendon Press, Oxford. 1975.
Heider, F. (1958). *The Psychology of Interpersonal Relations*, Wiley, New York.
Horrocks, J. E. and Jackson, D. W. (1972). *Self and Role: A Theory of Self-process and Role Behaviour*, Houghton Mifflin, Boston.
James, W. (1892). *Psychology: the Briefer-Course*, Harper, New York.
Jaynes, J. (1976). *The Origin of Consciousness in the Breakdown of the Bicameral Mind*, Allen Lane, London.
Kelly, G. A. (1955). *The Psychology of Personal Constructs*, vol. I, Norton, New York.
Kohlberg, L. (1968). *Stages in the Development of Moral Thought and Action*, Holt, Rinehart and Winston, New York.
Kosik, K. (1963). *Dialektika konkretniho (Dialectics of the Concrete)*, Nakladatelstvi Ceskoslovenske Akademie Ved, Prague.
Kuhn, T. S. (1962). *The Structure of Scientific Revolution*, Chicago University Press, Chicago.
Lickona, T. (Ed.) (1976). *Moral Development and Behavior*, Holt, Rinehart and Winston, New York.
Logan, R. D. (1986). 'Historical change in prevailing sense of self,' in K. M. Yardley, and T. M. Honess (Eds), *Self and Identity*, Wiley, Chichester and New York.
Luria, A. R. (1976). *Cognitive Development: Its Cultural and Social Foundations* (transl. M. Lopez-Morillas and L. Solotaroff) Cambridge, Harvard University Press, Cambridge Massachusetts and London.
McCall, G. J. (1977). 'The social looking-glass: a sociological perspective on self-development.' In T. Mischel (Ed.), *The Self: Psychological and Philosophical Issues*, Blackwell, Oxford.
Markova, I. (1982). *Paradigms, Thought, and Language*, Wiley, Chichester and New York.
Markova, I. (1987). 'On the genetic nature of social psychology'. In Butterworth, G. and Bryant, P. E. (Eds), *Causes of Development: Interdisciplinary Perspectives* (in preparation).

Markova, I., Forbes, C. D. and Inwood, M. (1984). 'The consumers' views of genetic counselling in hemophilia.' *American Journal of Medical Genetics*, **17**, 741–752.

Markova, I., Forbes, C. D., Aledort, L. M., Inwood, M., Mandalaki, T., Miller, C. H. and Pittadaki, J. (1986). 'A comparison of the availability and content of genetic counseling as perceived by hemophilic men and carriers in the U.S.A., Canada, Scotland, and Greece.' *American Journal of Medical Genetics*, **24**, 7–21.

Markus, H. and Sentis, K. (1982). 'The self in social information processing.' In J. Suls (Ed.), *Psychological Perspectives on the Self*, vol. 1, Lawrence Erlbaum, Hillsdale, New Jersey.

Mead, G. H. (1934), *Mind, Self, and Society*, University of Chicago Press, Chicago and London.

Mead, G. H. (1936). *Movements of Thought in the Nineteenth Century*, University of Chicago Press, Chicago and London.

Piaget, J. (1926). *The Language and Thought of the Child*, Routledge and Kegan Paul, London.

Piaget, J. (1971). *Structuralism* (transl. and Ed. C. Maschler), Routledge and Kegan Paul, London.

Rogers, C. R. (1951), *Client-centered Therapy: its Current Practice*, Implications and Theory, Houghton Mifflin, Boston.

Selman, R. L. (1980). *The Growth of Interpersonal Understanding*, Academic Press, New York and London.

Shaw, M. E. and Sulzer, J. L. (1964). 'An empirical test of Heider's levels in attribution of responsibility.' *Journal of Abnormal and Social Psychology*, **69**, 39–46.

Solomon, R. C. (1983). *In the Spirit of Hegel*, Oxford University Press, New York and Oxford.

Stone, L. (1977). *The Family, Sex and Marriage*, Weidenfeld and Nicolson, New York.

Toulmin, S. E. (1977). 'Self-knowledge and knowledge of the "self".' In T. Mischel (Ed.), *The Self: Psychological and Philosophical Issues*, Blackwell, Oxford.

Wittgenstein, L. (1953). *Philosophical Investigations*, Blackwell, Oxford.

Wylie, R. C. (1979). *The Self Concept: Theory and Research on Selected Topics*, revised edn, vol. 2, University of Nebraska Press, Lincoln.

Section II
Self and Social Structure

Self and Identity: Psychosocial Perspectives
Edited by K. Yardley and T. Honess
© 1987 John Wiley & Sons Ltd

7

Self and Social Structure: An Introductory Review

Terry Honess and Krysia Yardley

The contributors to the Self and Social Structure section address a central question for all social scientists, i.e., the status of the relationship between individual and society, and use 'self' as the key analytic concept. The issues that emerge here are reminiscent of the free will/determinism debate. Fingarette's (1983) comments on this general issue are helpful; '. . . the endless attempts to do away with the dilemma have continued to be unsuccessful for the simple reason that the horns of the dilemma are both real . . .'. This leads Fingarette to argue that agency (where one's experience dictates that, at times, one is the 'real mover and shaper of events') is found within the relatively narrow frames of everyday life. Here a knowledge of the 'larger context' is simply not relevant to the significance of what is within the frame for the individual concerned. It is likely that a similar position is implicit in the ostensibly vapid, but oft repeated, assertion that 'we must take account of the social contexts of behaviour', since the form that this accounting will take will simply be a matter of where one enters the argument. Nevertheless, having selected a position from which to enter the argument, the need to explicate the individual/society relationship from that position remains.

The most important tradition that bears on the work presented in this section is that which Blumer in 1937 (see Blumer, 1969) termed 'symbolic interactionism' which is profoundly influenced by the work of G. H. Mead (1934). Consider two of Mead's key propositions which carry different emphases for the position at which one enters the individual/society debate. First, that self is a reflected entity and mind a social product which implies a form of social determinism. However, second, Mead's writings also stress that self implicates a dynamic, self-reflexive process, evinced in the dialectic between the 'I' and the 'me'. (Markova, this volume, discusses this second proposition in detail.) Stryker, the first contributor to this section, has, in the past, sought to examine the broad constraints that operate on individuals in developing his 'Identity Theory', a 'structural symbolic interactionism', which can be seen to reflect an emphasis on the first proposition introduced above.

In this chapter, however, he specifically addresses the criticism of his earlier work that his own structural position is overly deterministic. He argues that 'There is nothing illogical about viewing human social behaviour as importantly the consequences of constraining and sometimes coercive processes while recognizing that, in principle, those processes are open to denial, rejection or modification' and 'Structure merely represents a recognition that the probability is high that extant lines of differentiation in a society affect particular people as opposed to other sets of persons' (see also Markova, this volume, on self as both structure and process). In sum, Stryker asserts that the proper question for research is not whether behaviour is either constrained or constructed, but under what circumstances will it be relatively constrained or constructed, a position that is consistent with our formulation of the individual/society problem.

For Stryker, structural features are understood in terms of peoples' involvement in particular social networks which 'embed' them in particular identities. Such constraints are most clearly asserted in his definition of identities as 'internalized role designations corresponding to the social location of persons'. Individual identities comprising the self are seen to be organized hierarchically by the probability of their invocation. These salience hierachies are seen to be significantly influenced by an individual's 'commitment' to particular role identities. Commitment is defined by the costs to the person, in terms of the number and intensity of relationships implicated, should a particular role identity be lost. In the present contribution, Stryker introduces self-esteem into the debate, in considering how our performance itself impacts upon salience, which is an emphasis more consistent with the process focus of interactionism since it entails consideration of self and significant other evaluations.

It is, therefore, important to reiterate that Stryker does not see his lack of consideration of the traditional interactionism foci of process and emergent meaning as antithetical to his own work. Rather, he urges the recognition of constraints, and that different outcomes are not equiprobable; 'probabilities differ for various structural elements entering the construction, and for various outcomes of the constructed process'. Stryker's treatment of 'master statuses' is a good example of this: such statuses (e.g., race or gender) are pervasive features of social stratification since they do not determine the form of particular networks but, rather, enter into them. Hence, the salience of a particular role identity might be enhanced insofar as it is concordant with the meaning of a master status (Stryker does not specify whether this meaning is that appropriated by the individual or that 'given by society').

Stryker further seeks to develop his analysis of the constructed rather than constrained aspects of social conduct through the general argument that new meanings are likely to emerge when there is a breakdown of the working consensus (designed to meet individuals' needs) underlying social interaction. (Although it might be observed that the psychological evidence about groups who are under threat suggests they are less likely to tolerate dissensus, e.g., Breakwell, 1983.) More closely within the interactionist tradition he also argues that persons seek out situations that allow the operation of salient identities. There are clear parallels here with the strategic interaction litera- ture (especially the work of Goffman), as well as the widely researched social psychological focus on impression management (e.g., see Arkin, and Pysz- czynski and Greenberg, this volume). In this regard, Stryker's position suggests a relatively conscious Machiavellian actor, whereas we shall see that Turner (this section) suggests that 'in many cases who I am is little more than where I fit. I think we are often misled into overloading self-conception with intense value implications'.

Finally we should note that Stryker now argues for the need to incorporate personality characteristics (one's pervasive styles of relating) in future con- ceptual and theoretical developments of 'Identity Theory'. This is also in order to help re-establish what he calls the 'processual thrust' of interaction- ism, since such characteristics are also 'thoroughly interactional in source and expression'. Turning to methodology, it is perhaps significant that Stryker largely draws on survey work and, statistically, on factor analysis, procedures which certainly give general support for the key propositions of 'Identity Theory'. However, in order to examine the meanings appropriated by indi- viduals, and the process of meaning emerging between individuals, different methods may be more appropriate for a concern to re-establish a 'processual thrust'.

The work of Wiley and Alexander is also firmly within the interactionist tradition and shares key assumptions with that of Stryker. In their words 'the social person is shaped by interaction and social structure determines the possibilities for action.' They do, however, argue that their conceptual posi- tion is different to that of Stryker insofar as they explicitly eschew the introduction of 'personal traits' into the argument since they reject the role versus traits dichotomy in explaining self. There is some ambiguity here, for, despite the rejection of this specific dichotomy, they do in their closing words insist upon the conceptual need to sustain self and role as separate concepts and apparently leave an open door for traits in stating that 'Self consists of dispositional schema *regardless* of their source or their degree of connection with social structure.' Nevertheless, and notwithstanding the very important dynamic aspects of their theory, Wiley and Alexander are primarily interested in the impact of structural features on the self; hence, their title: '*From situated activity to self attribution* . . .'. Their definition of 'situated activity' clearly implicates a 'reflected self' (see our comments on Mead): '. . . conduct anchored outside self, constrained by actor's belief that it is being moni- tored . . .'. This relates to a key proposition of Alexander and Wiley's (1981) 'situated identity theory': 'we define the phenomenon of social action in terms of the dispositional attributes that flow from the perspectives of given perceivers of the event field'. Wiley and Alexander further maintain that settings and actors evoke typified combinations of dispositional dimensions which result in 'situated identities'. It is important to note therefore that situated identities are not attributes of the person or the environment but summarize the relationship between them at a given point in time, which allows a more dynamic interpretation of the mirror metaphor (see Honess, 1986, for a complementary analysis of the way in which the mirror metaphor can accommodate emotional life).

As particular actors repeatedly engage in certain role-related activities, they become typified as the sorts of persons (appropriated as 'myself') who do these sorts of things. In essence, therefore, Wiley and Alexander see selves as being significantly constituted and modified by situated identities that are generated by social action. In this sense, then, their work is certainly consistent with Stryker's earlier formulation of his 'Identity Theory', and resonates with the classic Park (1926) formulation that the content of self comprises sets of role identities which reflect the role structure of society. Hence the second half of Wiley and Alexander's title '. . . the impact *of* social structural schemata', reflects a different focus to the new extensions of Stryker's theory. Nevertheless, Wiley and Alexander's considerable exploitation of the cognitive literature does suggest a more individualistic stance. Thus, the concept of 'schema' is used for understanding the key concepts of 'self', 'role', and 'situated identity', where schema, following Markus and Sentis (1982) and Markus (this volume) is defined as 'memory structures of conceptually related elements that guide the processing of information'.

The next contribution, that of Turner, raises a number of problems with a too ready acceptance of the argument that selves are simply appropriated social identities. First, he suggests that any such appropriation should not be taken to imply a high degree of self awareness: 'in many cases who I am is little more than where I fit, I think we are often misled into overloading self-conception with intense value implications'. Turner appears to be arguing here that the concept of self might best be employed when how people see themselves is relatively highly articulated. Second, when individuals are asked for an occasion when 'action or feelings served to express their true selves', they rarely point to an institutionalized context, rather, the real self is typically situated in casual and personal conversation. Similar findings are reported by Yardley (this volume). Third, Turner argues that a significant part of people's learning to orient themselves involves 'self-affirmation', '. . . an effort to construct a particular kind of self, in contrast to the more passive act of self discovery'.

Indeed, Turner amongst the sociological contributors here, affirms most strongly a concern with the individual experience of selfhood. For him, self is the concept which eludes mechanistic determinism and is the very vehicle for conceptualizing a balance between structural determinacy and individual creativity. He states '. . . without a concept of self, individual behaviour is either simply role determined or determined by some force between social role and biology. Self as a folk concept conveys the idea of autonomy but not social disengagement. The idea of self conveys an image of autonomy in engagement with society'. (See Wilshire, 1982, for an extended analysis of this point from a phenomenological perspective.) Moreover, Turner argues that this 'balance' is not fixed: thus, in contrast to Kuhn's (1964) findings with the twenty statements test (Who Am I?), he notes that Zurcher's (1977) more recent work reveals that students answered the T.S.T. with relatively few role designations, but predominantly with personality and mood characteristics. Turner interprets this shift as related to individual's altered conceptions of reality stemming from changed opportunity and reward structures.

It is, however, the case that despite Turner's focus on individual experience as demonstrated in his empirical work, he does not involve subjects as reflexive negotiating informants about the situated meanings of their own responses to 'Who are You' type questions (cf. Yardley, this volume). His reasons may relate to his findings that people do not necessarily have well-formulated and readily communicable self concepts (see above comments on 'who I am is often little more than where I fit'). Notwithstanding his detailed consideration of experiential aspects of self-conceptualization, even at times appearing to accept an essentialist position with regard to self, there is a contradictory sense in which Turner is prepared to view the self-concept as merely a social construction. In talking of the affirmation and observation modes of self-discovery, he states 'If people should learn early in life to orient themselves as if they possess and should govern their own behaviour through a self, their perception of the characteristics of that self derives from both affirmation and observation.' In introducing the 'as if' into this posited ontogenic process, Turner appears to come very close to the arguments presented elsewhere in this volume by Harré and Gergen.

The final chapter in this section is that of McCall who provides us with an innovative integrative overview of sociological interpretations of how the organization of society may be seen in the content, structure, and dynamics of self. These constituents of self are discussed in terms of societal organization understood in each of three closely related ways: as 'a network of organizations', 'a network of social relationships', and as 'a network of social roles'. The last of these receives most attention not only because McCall has long been associated with role-identity theory (viz., the seminal McCall and Simmons, 1966) but also because the other two conceptions of society can be seen to derive from the network of social roles. Indeed, McCall's analysis of how the content and structure of self reflects the organization of society, seen as a network of social roles, is also taken to encompass the other two conceptions of society.

On the other hand, in addressing the dynamics of the self, the mutual shaping and reciprocity between self and society, in which McCall is most interested, the conception of society that is adopted determines a particular locus for identity negotiation. First, with respect to society seen as a network of social roles, McCall observes that much of this work can be characterized in terms of the individual trying to live up to a single role identity through both intra-individual processes (cognitive restructuring strategies) and interpersonal processes (especially impression formation). McCall observes that the more significant problem is, however, striving to live up to one's structured set of identities, i.e., managing multiple roles. With respect to the second conception of society seen as a 'network of social relationships', McCall notes, in a similar vein, that the dynamics of multiple relationships are more difficult to manage than those for a single relationship: '. . . one's network, then, represents a 'personal economy' of relationships to be managed more or less effectively'. Third, there is society viewed 'as a network of organizations', the key dynamic is, like 'social relationships', one that relates to 'logistics', the balancing and managing of one's entire network of organizational links. A key theme then is the importance of multiple sets of bargaining, and the persistent concern with negotiation which can be seen to reassert the dynamic roots of interactionism in order to more clearly articulate the self and social structure relationship.

REFERENCES

Alexander, C. and Wiley, M. (1981). 'Situated activity and identity formation', in *Social Psychology: Sociological Perspectives* (Eds M. Rosenberg and R. Turner), Basic Books, New York.

Blumer, H. (1969). *Symbolic Interactionism: Perspectives and Methods*, Prentice-Hall, New Jersey.

Breakwell, G. (Ed.) (1983). *Threatened Identities*, Wiley, Chichester.

Fingarette, H. (1983). 'Framing, and the meaningfulness of human agency,' *Unpublished Ms.*, Santa Barbara, California.

Honess, T. (1986). 'Mirroring and social metacognition,' in *Mental Mirrors*, (Eds C. Antaki and A. Lewis), Sage, London.

Kuhn, M. (1964). 'Self and self-conception,' in *A Dictionary of the Social Sciences*, (Eds J. Gould and W. Kolb), The Free Press, New York.

Markus, H. and Sentis, K. (1982). 'The self in social information processing.' In J. Suls (Ed.) *Psychological Perspectives on the Self*, vol. 1, Erlbaum, New Jersey.

Mead, G. (1934). *Mind, Self and Society*, University of Chicago Press, Chicago.

McCall, G. and Simmons, J. (1966). *Identities and Interactions*, The Free Press, New York.

Park, R. (1926). 'Behind our masks.' *Survey*, **56**, 135–139.

Wilshire, B. (1982). *Role Playing and Identity*, Indiana U.P., Bloomington.

Zurcher, L. (1977). *The Mutable Self*, Sage, Beverley Hills, California.

8

Identity Theory: Developments and Extensions

Sheldon Stryker

Identity theory takes as its central proposition that commitment structures identity structures role performance. That 'formula' emerges from an attempt to develop the traditional symbolic interactionist framework by introducing into that framework a viable conception of interactional structure compatible with its premises, by finding ways of conceptualizing the impact of large-scale societal structures on interactional structures again in ways compatible with its premises, and by finding ways to state its propositions to permit reasonably rigorous tests. Such an attempt responds to major criticisms of the symbolic interactionist framework appearing over the years in the literature.

INTRODUCTION

The central proposition of identity theory (Stryker, 1968; 1980) asserts that commitment impacts identity salience impacts role performance. Implicit in an emergent structural symbolic interactionist framework (Stryker, 1980) from which the theory derives, is the further argument that the social psychological processes described by that proposition take place in and are critically affected by larger social structural phenomena (e.g., community organization, class structure), which are presumed to operate essentially through commitment. Thus, an expanded formulation of the central proposition of identity theory is that 'large-scale' social structures affect commitment affects identity salience affects role performance. This formulation attempts to restate the traditional symbolic interactionist framework, which argues that self is the product of society and is in turn the prime determinant of social behaviour, in a manner that permits reasonably rigorous empirical test. It conceptualizes the self as made up of identities or internalized role designations. It specifies that the important aspects of society in relation to self are the interactional networks premised on given identities in which networks persons are embedded, and that the important dimension of self in relation to social behaviour is the way in which individual identities comprising the self are organized hierarchically by the probability of their invocation in or across social situations.

Thus, identity theory, beginning with the symbolic interactionist dictum that self is an emergent from society and organizes social behaviour, conceptualizes the self as a structure of identities organized in a hierarchy of salience. It defines identities as internalized sets of role expectations, with the person having as many identities as roles played in distinct sets of social relationships. The salience hierarchy is conceived as an ordering of these identities by their differentiated probabilities of coming into play within or across situations. Recognizing that persons enter many more or less distinct sets of social relationships, and defining commitment as the costs to the person in the form of relationships foregone were she/he no longer to have a given identity and play a role based on that identity in a social network, the theory predicts that the distribution of identities in the salience hierarchy will reflect the varying levels of commitment to the roles underlying the identities. Commitments, in turn, are seen to depend importantly on the 'larger' structure of society, social organizational principles (e.g., class, age, etc.) that either facilitate or impede the entry of persons into and the exit of persons from social relationships. That is, the larger institutional, organizational, and stratification features of society enter the theory by influencing the formation, maintenance, and dissolution of social networks. Finally, the theory predicts that choices among behaviours reflecting alternative roles, when such choice is realistically possible, will reflect the differential location in the identity salience hierarchy of identities related to those alternatives.

Identity theory, those familiar with the literature of symbolic interactionism will recognize, attempts to respond to major criticisms of the symbolic interactionist framework that have been made over the years.

From the standpoint of many symbolic interactionists, as well as others who may or may not be sympathetic with its aspirations, the attempt has not succeeded. A major criticism is that the introduction of social structural conceptualizations, both the structure of the immediate interactive situation and the 'larger' social structure, in the form envisaged by identity theory emasculates the fundamental processual thrust of the symbolic interactionist framework and its capacity to see human behaviour as emergent and constructed. The argument is that what is most valuable about the symbolic interactionist framework, its capacity for analysing the unfolding character of social interactional processes, and the creative, 'non-determined' aspects of social life, is lost in an ill-advised return to a structural emphasis better left abandoned. Such criticism, obviously, argues the wrong-headedness of identity theory.

Identity theory is open to a variety of criticisms from other standpoints that accept rather than deny its basic legitimacy. One observes that the symbolic interactionist framework postulates the reciprocal relation of self and society, and that identity theory as formulated undercuts that reciprocity by concentrating on the directional influence of interactional structure on self and of self on role performance, leaving relatively untreated the influence of role performance on self and of self on social structure. A second is that the processes by which self impacts on role performance—the 'mechanisms' of that linkage—remain relatively unelucidated and therefore essentially mysterious, implying that theoretical progress requires a more satisfactory specification of how the hierarchical structures of identities comprising the self work to produce given behavioural 'outcomes'.

The foregoing two criticisms accept the central identity theory proposition with which this discussion began. A third criticism argues the insufficiency of that formula, and is undoubtedly correct. Identity theory developed with a 'minimalist' theoretical strategy in mind: i.e., a simplifying strategy was adopted emphasizing one theoretically important aspect of self (identity salience), one theoretically important aspect of structure (involvement in networks of social relationships premised on given identities), and examining relationships between these and role performances. From the beginning it was recognized that additional variables would have to be incorporated into the theory to increase its ecological validity and its predictive potential, but the argument was made that such extensions should (ideally) respond to the impetus of research findings. That recognition has not yet extended to systematic examination of such variables and incorporating them into the structure of identity theory.

This chapter has multiple goals. It seeks to develop and extend identity theory by addressing issues of concern to those who hold to a traditional symbolic interactionism, issues posed by the apparent contrast between structural and processual perspectives. It also seeks to extend identity theory by giving substance to its ostensible concern with how self affects social structure, going beyond current discussions by beginning to specify how identity salience influences role performances, and by extending identity theory, however rudimentary the fashion, to accommodate affect as well as to accommodate the impact of other self-relevant variables.

STRUCTURE AND PROCESS, CONSTRAINT AND CONSTRUCTION

The first issue to be discussed is meta-theoretical, arising from a consideration of the structural symbolic interaction frame, rather than from a direct consideration of identity theory *per se*.

The issue is also parochial, although not entirely so. It is parochial in that the validity or invalidity of introducing structural concepts into accounts of human behaviour is of most intense concern within the family of symbolic interactionist adherents. The issue in that circle is: what if any place is there for the concept of social structure within a framework that historically has been appreciated for being radically processual? The issue is not entirely parochial, however; the concept of structure, whose usual referent is the (at least) relative stability in the systematic patterning of parts made up of action systems, appears to be equivalently suspect among social scientists who are not identified with symbolic interactionism but who emphasize comparable themes, in particular the theme that social 'reality' is no more than an imposition by actors on inchoate experience (Gergen, 1982) rather than underlying or organizing that experience, and the correlate of this theme, namely, that social structure is a fiction derived from linguistic usage rather than a representation of underlying reality.

The source of the antipathy toward the concept of social structure, then, is reasonably clear. The concept disturbs traditional symbolic interactionists and others because it appears to deny the fluidity and constructed character of social experience, and because it seems to impose limits on human freedom and creativity by asserting the obdurate character of social patternings. Traditional symbolic interactionism (cf. Blumer, 1969) has located the ultimate sources of interactional outcomes in interpretive, definitional processes of virtually limitless potential with respect to the range and character of those outcomes. Given that *a priori*, a concept of structure that appears to deny that potential, that imposes (variable) limits on the degree to which definitional processes can modify or transform patterns of social life, is indeed objectionable. The outlook and aspiration of many traditional symbolic interactionists is humanistic, with that outlook and aspiration being defined largely in contradistinction to a scientific outlook and aspiration. The opposition, so conceived, is the scientist's emphasis on the ways in which human social behaviour is constrained and the humanist's emphasis on the autonomy and the creativity of the human being.

The foregoing suggests that, at an extreme, the argument around the introduction of structural concepts into symbolic interactionist framework will not be resolved. There cannot be at the same time an acceptance of social behaviour as free and creative without constraint and an acceptance of the deterministic impact of social structure. The former requires the rejection of structural concepts, the latter recognition of limits on human freedom and creativity in practice if not in principle.

However, the argument need not be formulated at an extreme. Using concepts of social structure does not imply acceptance of a total deterministic outlook, no more than accepting the possibility of freedom and creativity requires believing that real constraints do not exist on freedom and creativity. There is nothing illogical about viewing human social behaviour as importantly the consequences of constraining and sometimes coercive processes while recognizing that in principle those processes are open to denial, rejection, or modification. We can see social behaviour as constructed, at the same time recognizing that probabilities differ for various structural elements entering the construction and for various outcomes of the constructive process. We can understand that in particular situations all possible interactional sequences and all possible outcomes of those interactional sequences are not equiprobable. That is all conceptions of social structure require, and all that is required as underpinning for a structural symbolic interactionism.

Illustratively, we can understand that it is possible for students in our classes to usurp the prerogatives of the instructor in violation of extant patterns and norms of classroom interaction while recognizing that this possibility is heavily constrained by way of participants' prior experiences, self conceptions, conceptions of the situation, permissible and possible ways of defining situations, resources for altering or maintaining the extant patterns of relationships, and the organizations of power within which the classroom is embedded. We can also recognize that the possibility is heavily constrained because the larger social structure will have worked to bring particular kinds of persons to this interactive situation while operating to exclude others. Who is brought together with what previous experience, what range of definitions, what resources, etc., may not determine interactional outcomes but surely will make some outcomes more or less probable than alternatives.

The concept of social structure has been variously defined, and there is little utility in reviewing those definitions. But a reasonable usage is that implicated in what has just been said: structure 'merely' represents a recognition that the probability is high that extant lines of differentiation in a society affect particular people as opposed to other sets of persons, that some persons rather than others get together in particular situations to interact over particular issues with particular interactional skills and resources. That is the meaning for a structural symbolic interactionism of the concept of social class, or power structure, or age structure. That is the meaning of structural concepts in general for identity theory.

If some such conception did not enter analyses of social processes, we would in effect be asserting that interactional possibilities are unconstrained, that any process or outcome of a process is equiprobable. Such a view defies simple common sense and common observation. It also defeats efforts at building general social science theory *a priori*, denying warrant for believing that commonalities across interactive sequences or episodes exist.

The proper question is not whether human social behaviour is constrained or constructed; it is both. The proper question is under what circumstances will that behaviour be more or less heavily constrained, more or less open to creative constructions. A start has been made in developing a response to that 'proper' question (Powers, 1980; Stryker and Statham, 1985). Very briefly, the key element in understanding constraint on or construction of social behaviour, role imposition or role improvization, lies in the stability or breakdown of the working consensus underlying social interaction. The working consensus will be stable when existing patterns of social organization appear to actors to meet their needs and goals. The working consensus will break down, making situations problematic, when conditions draw attention to inadequacies of existing patterns of social organization. When structures in which roles are embedded meet needs, constraints will be heavy and roles will be imposed; when they do not, construction will become possible and role improvisation will occur. This topic will be pursued no further here, in order to turn to a consideration of identity theory itself.

THE IDENTITY SALIENCE-ROLE BEHAVIOUR RELATIONSHIP

One set of issues that arise in considering identity theory concern the relationship of identity salience to role behaviour. Two particular issues will be considered:

1. How is the impact of identity salience on role behaviour, insofar as that impact exists, to be understood? What are the processes that underwrite that linkage?
2. While an underlying supposition of the theory has been that the relationship between identity salience and role behaviour is reciprocal, the emphasis clearly has been on the directional effect of salience on performance, with that linkage warranted through a consideration of the writings of classical symbolic interactionists (Mead, 1934; Cooley, 1902; Thomas and Thomas, 1928), as well as more contemporary theorists (Stryker, 1980; Turner, 1962; McCall and Simmons, 1978).

What of the impact of role performance on identity salience? Why, theoretically, would that impact be expected? Does it exist in appreciable degree? To the extent that it does, what are the processes through which it flows?

With respect to the expected impact of identity salience on role performance, the claim of identity theory is clear: a major determinant of variation in behaviours-in-role is expected to be the location of the identity(ies) reflecting that role in the identity salience hierarchy. There is some evidence available on this claim (Stryker and Serpe, 1982; Serpe, 1985; Hoelter, 1983) which is supportive although revealing the need to make explicit a scope condition of the theory: the expectation holds in the degree that persons are 'free' to exercise and act upon choice. (This condition makes exceedingly clear the requirement that structural elements be incorporated into the theory on some level, for it is social structure that will either foreclose importantly or open up choice possibilities.)

Thus, for example, we can draw on evidence from a sample survey of a general population in an urban area in the United States, which survey contained measures of commitment (as previously defined), identity salience, and a particular indicator of role performance, namely, time spent in role-related activities, as well as a measure of how much time subjects would choose to spend in activities related to particular roles if they were free to allocate their time as they wished. The evidence is that:

Identity salience better predicts preferred allocation of time than time actually allocated.
Identity salience predicts reasonably well time allocated to each of the roles studied—work, spousing, parenting, and religion.
Identity salience predicts time allocated to religious activities best, then spousing, parenting, and work, in that order.

Identity salience predicts the time allocated to work better for working females than for males (the sample includes mostly blue and white collar workers, and relatively few managers, professionals, etc.);
Identity salience predicts time allocated to parenting better for males than for females.

We can, then, reasonably conclude that the empirical linkage between identity salience and role performance subject to choice exists, and ask: what underlies that linkage? The generalized answer to such questions derives from the assumption that identities seek validation, i.e., that identities motivate interactional performances whose function it is to reaffirm in interaction that one is the kind of person defined by the identities. But can that generalized answer be specified, at least in degree?

It is likely that the more salient an identity, the more sensitive one is to opportunities for behaviour that could confirm the identity. Also, the more salient an identity, the more likely is a behavioural opportunity to be used to perform behaviours associated with the role on which the identity is based. There is much current theorizing and research in social psychology that supports these assertions, in particular work on impression management (Goffman, 1959, 1961; Schlenker, 1980) and on scripts and cognitive schema (Abelson, 1976). Within the latter, work on self-schema is most directly pertinent. Markus (1977) has demonstrated that self-cognitions constituting self-schema sensitize persons to environmental cues according with those self-cognitions; and that the more elements of self cohere, the greater that sensitization. The mechanism being discussed helps to clarify how self-fulfilling prophecies operate. The high salience of an identity increases sensitivity to environmental evidence pertinent to that identity. Identities attached to age may incorporate the expectation that if one is old, one is infirm, leading one to be closely attentive to aches and pains that might otherwise be regarded more neutrally and less meaning-laden with respect to one's identification as old.

Identity salience, then, increases motivation to seek opportunities to perform in terms appropriate to identities, and increases the likelihood of visualizing a particular situation as an opportunity to perform in such terms by increasing sensitivity to cues calling for the performance of roles attached to highly salient identities.

High identity salience likely also increases the number of 'real' or 'objective' opportunities to perform role behaviours. In interaction with others, we produce cues that serve to cue those with whom we interact to produce cues that enable us to act in terms of a salient identity. The mechanism here is a straightforward restatement of the altercasting process identified by Weinstein and Deutschberger (1963).

The foregoing enables a better understanding of how salience impacts role performance, but is not yet sufficient to lead to a thorough understanding. The question of just what behaviours are selected out to perform from the range of behaviours associated with any given role when an opportunity arises has thus far been begged. Alternatively and more simply phrased, the question becomes: what does it mean to say that a behaviour confirms an identity? While the answer to this question cannot yet be detailed, Burke (Burke and Reitzes, 1981) has provided a key element in a prospective answer in the commonality of 'meaning' of identity and behaviour. A basic premise of the framework from which identity theory develops is that social behaviour is symbolic behaviour, that symbols 'mean' the set of activities cued by that which they symbolize. 'Things' in the world become 'objects' by taking on meanings in this sense. The self—and by extension the identities that comprise the self—is an object whose meaning can be defined in semantic space. Particular behaviours can be thought of as having meanings also locatable in semantic space. Burke's argument then follows: people will select from behaviours it is possible to perform those whose meaning is located in semantic space most closely to the meaning attached to a salient identity. This theoretically pregnant and powerful argument has yet to be tested empirically, and it should be.

Turning now to the impact of role performance on identity salience, the general nature of that impact is reasonably clear. Bem (1972) long ago pointed out that we use what we do as the basis for drawing inferences about who and what we are; that is, our self-conceptions derive, in important part, from self-attributions made on the basis of observations of our own behaviour: I score well on tests, therefore I must be a good student. While only part of the larger picture, this behaviouristic account of self-formation is part of the picture, and is not incompatible with the frame on which identity theory draws. That persons are both actors and observers of their own action, both subjects and objects of action, is a long-standing part of the tradition of that frame. The 'we observe what we do to learn who we are' argument can be extended to the assertion that our observations of how we behave in situations leads to inferences about how salient particular identities are to us: one takes out pictures of a grandchild in the most unlikely situations, and that evidence informs one of the high salience of an identity as a grandparent. A slight extension of this assertion is that we obtain information about the relative salience of identities from the choices made in situations in which activation of alternative identities is possible. The mechanism by which this linkage is forged is presumably the same mechanism of commonality of meanings discussed previously.

What has been shown is only that we recognize ourselves as particular kinds of people from our actions; it is not yet clear why or how the salience of identities (as differentiated from the perception of the salience of identities) are impacted by our role performances. That gap can be closed by invoking a concept not yet introduced systematically into identity theory but closely related to its central concepts: self-esteem. Role performances are subject to self-evaluations by the performer, and subject to evaluations by others in conjunction with whom the performance is played out as well as by significant others external to the performance (the student evaluates his/her school performances as do other students and teacher and as do parents acting as an audience for the performances). These evaluational processes are reflected in the person's role-specific self-esteem; and role-specific self-esteem is reflected in identity salience in accord with the principle that the higher the role-specific self-esteem attached to a role, the more salient the identity based on that role. Incidently, but to make the important point that there are affinities between identity theory and attribution theory (Stryker and Gottlieb, 1981), we can expect that the success or failure of our role performances will be of varying importance to identity salience.

THE COMMITMENT–IDENTITY SALIENCE RELATIONSHIP

In keeping with the dictum that self reflects society, the focus of identity theory has been on identity salience as the consequence of commitment. The evidence (Stryker and Serpe, 1982; Serpe, 1980; Hoelter, 1983) is that this impact occurs and is reasonably strong. Yet that evidence is not entirely unproblematic.

To indicate the problem and therefore what requires theoretical clarification, it is necessary to go back to the conception of commitment. As defined in the earliest statements of identity theory (Stryker, 1968), commitment referred to the degree to which an individual's relationships to particular others depended upon his or her being a given kind of person, i.e., occupying a particular position in a network of relationships, playing a particular role, and having a particular identity. The person, given this definition, is committed to a role to the extent that extensive and intensive social relationships are built upon that role; and the measurement of commitment can be seen to be a matter of estimating the loss of social relationships in general and 'important' relationships in particular, were the person no longer to play a given role. Measurement strategies developed to operationalize the concept in the first empirical test of identity theory (Stryker and Serpe, 1982) involved questions about the numbers of persons known by subjects as a consequence of occupying particular positions and playing particular roles, and also asking how important to subjects were particular others with whom they interacted through given roles.

Factor analyses showed that the 'extensiveness' (numbers) and the 'intensiveness' (importance) of network relationships did not belong in the same measure: the two ostensible dimensions of commitment clearly were not intrinsically linked to one another. Subsequent work has used largely the extensiveness and a related overlap dimension (the degree to which networks premised on different identities incorporate the same persons, e.g., the number of persons known through work who are also known through one's religious activities) to map commitment, largely leaving the intensiveness dimension aside. Yet, the latter must have consequences for the salience of identities, at least of certain types and under certain conditions. For example, one would expect the impact of the threatened or real loss of important and irreplaceable relationships on identity salience to be considerable, whereas the loss of important relationships for whom substitutions are available might be expected to be less consequential. It makes sense in developing identity theory to retain both the embeddedness of persons in social networks and the subjective import of the others to whom one relates in those networks as concepts within the theory, but to recognize the potential independence of the two.

Suppose, then, commitment is conceptualized as being of two types: interactional commitment, referring to the extensiveness of relationships that would be foregone where one to no longer play a given role; and affective commitment, or the emotional costs attached to departure from a given role. (The 'intensiveness' dimension of commitment as previously conceptualized, emphasizing the subjective import of others with whom one interacts, is represented in such emotional costs.) If Homans (1950) is correct concerning the relation of interaction to liking, then other things equal, interactional and affective commitment will be positively related; and we would expect that if persons are reasonably free to exercise choices that would alter their inter-actional partners, over time that relationships would strengthen. When other things are not equal, the two could well be independent of one another or even negatively related. As an instance of the latter, consider the person locked into a job or into a marriage that she/he detests or who must deal with persons she/he hates as a consequence of being locked into a job or marriage by structural constraints of one sort or another (e.g., living in a depressed economic area without resources to move, or a religious identification that militates against divorce).

The relation of interactional commitment and affective commitment is clearly complicated, and is worthy of theoretical development and investigation in its own right. Here, however, speculation will be limited to how interactional commitment and affective commitment may together or separately relate to identity salience. When the two reinforce one another, when both are high or both are low, their joint impact on identity salience may be particularly strong. Indeed, it may be that either high interactional commitment or high affective commitment, perhaps within the limits of a particular range of the other, is sufficient to 'cause' high salience. Whether or not one likes people one must deal with, frequent interactions means that behaviours associated with a particular identity will be more or less continuously cued and that one is hard put to avoid behaving in terms of that identity; such interaction would be expected to increase the salience of that identity. Should one be strongly and positively attracted to others to whom one might relate on the basis of a given identity, even if interactional opportunities are blocked, we could again reasonably expect the salience of that identity to be high at least so long as one can remain optimistic about the possibility of developing relationships and entering networks.

The preceding discussion appears to hold when commitment of one of the two types is high and commitment of the other type is either in a neutral range or benign (low interactional commitment but optimism about the chances of developing relationships would illustrate the latter). What about the case when the values of one type are very high, the values of the other very low? The suggestion has already been made that high positive affective commitment and low interactional commitment may lead to high identity salience, at least so long as persons do not see the chances for higher rates of interaction to be blocked (an interesting question is whether it makes a difference whether the blockage is structural or the product of rejection, i.e., the exercise of choice by others). The opposite case, high but negative affective commitment and high interactional commitment, it might be surmized, would dampen identity salience, and lead—unless structural conditions interfered —to withdrawal from relationships and consequently to lower salience of the identity on which the relationships are premised.

What about the reciprocal impact of identity salience on commitment? Recent analyses of data tracing the relationships over their first semester in residence of freshman students leaving home to enter a university (Serpe, 1985), at least tentatively indicate that the impact of commitment at a given point in time on identity salience at a succeeding point in time is stronger than the impact of identity salience at that second point in time on commitment at a still later point. The finding makes sense: there are structural constraints on at least the interactional type of commitment that do not operate on identity salience; therefore, salience will be less determinative of commitment than will commitment be of salience. To illustrate, there are limits on the degree to which one can avoid work and the contacts that come through work, no matter how low in salience an identity associated with work.

How is the link that does exist forged? What are the mechanisms by which identity salience works its effects on commitment? Again, it is useful to separate affective commitment from interactional commitment. With respect to the former, the relationship seems relatively easy to understand theoretically: a highly salient identity, on the assumption that identities 'seek' confirmation, will lead people to value and invest positive affect in those persons who permit the expression of that identity through the playing out of a role to which the identity is attached.

The link between identity salience and interactional commitment seems both less clear and is almost certainly less direct. It is likely that the motivational potential of identities again operates here. High salience likely will lead to efforts to join with others in settings in which the highly salient identity can be behaviourally enacted, or to increase the frequency of interactions in networks of which one is already a member. High salience can also be expected to lead persons to involve others with whom they interact in one arena of their lives in still other arenas of their lives, thus increasing the degree to which networks overlap. An illustration: we invite a person known through marriage to join a poker group, thus potentially increasing the interactional costs of leaving the marital role. Again, it should be clear that the relation of identity salience to interactional commitment is subject to structural constraints to which the relation of salience to affective commitment is not.

EMOTIONS, MASTER STATUSES, AND PERSONAL TRAITS

The final topic of this chapter is the expansion of identity theory to incorporate conceptions not yet in, or not explicitly in, the theory. The need for such expansion is clear, even without sufficient research on the basic relationships postulated in the theory. Models relating the original theory to empirical data have provided reasonable fits to those data, but these fits can be improved. While variance explained is not the goal of theoretical work, ecological validity and utility of work is enhanced in the degree that 'complete' explanation is provided. Thus, the question arises: what next by way of additional conceptualization of identity theory?

Using such informal or formal appraisals of identity theory or the symbolic interactionist framework from which identity theory stems as the grounds for so asserting, there are three prominent conceptual candidates for incorporation into the theory: emotion, master statuses, and personal traits (Stryker and Statham, 1985).

The first of these, emotion, has been dealt with in the discussion of how self-esteem may enter the relations among commitment, identity salience, and role performance, and as well in the discussion that argued the disaggregation of the original conception of commitment into interactional and affective commitments. At this point, only the obvious can be added: there must certainly be other ways in which emotion enters the relations among the variables of the theory. One likely possibility is the way in which affect enters the meaning of social objects, including self and others. As Heise (1979) demonstrates, social objects as well as behaviours linking them are invested with affective value; and he argues that disparities in the affective values attached to self, other, and behaviour linking the two introduces a motivational dynamic in social interactions.

'Master status' refers to the structurally-based attributes like sex, age, race, social class that (a) derive from pervasive features of the social structure, particularly stratification features, in which role relationships are embedded; (b) do not in themselves provide the grounds for specific networks of social interaction; but (c) enter the formation and interactional content of many of the specific networks of interaction in which persons play a role. Virtually by definition, then, master statuses must be implicated in the processes by which identities form and change and the processes by which identities impact behaviour.

This is also true for personal characteristics or what have been called 'traits' in the literature of personality psychology. Personal characteristics, the more or less pervasive styles of relating to the external world, surely affect patterns of relationships to others, the particular behaviours played from a range of alternative possible behaviours, and may affect directly the salience of various identities. More fundamentally, these—like master statuses—may enter the very structure of self.

The focus of identity theory, like the focus of the symbolic interactionist frame, has been on role-linked aspects of self and so on the situated networks of interaction in which roles are made and played out. Such a focus can downplay the existence and import of situation-transcending elements in the structure of self. Symbolic interactionists have tended to define their position in specific opposition to trans-situational conceptualizations, whether the stratification concepts of a functionalist sociology or the trait concepts of a person-centred psychology, arguing that neither meet the criterion of being interactional in conception.

A trans-situational emphasis is not absent from identity theory; the point of the concept of identity salience is precisely to account for behaviour that occurs across situations. Nothing in the theory or in the frame from which it derives requires that self-concepts be limited to role-linked identities. The processes by which self develops can and sometimes do result in self-concepts organized around either master statuses, personal traits or some combination of the two: black, Jew, worker, honest woman, shy person, stuffed shirt, etc., represent possible self-concepts none of which is intrinsically tied to particular interactive situations. As Rosenberg (1979) instructs us, the domain of the self is highly differentiated, incorporating master statuses and personal traits. Self generally is the product of relations with others, and both master statuses and personal traits can be viewed as thoroughly interactional in source and expression: they become part of the self and they enter interaction in the same ways as do role-based identities.

The theoretical question, from the point of view of identity theory, is how master statuses and personal traits enter the processes described by the relations among commitment(s), identity salience, and role performance. There may be differences between the two in how they enter that process. A master status is perhaps as much or more defined by the responses of others not incorporated into our interactional networks as by those who are or as by our own 'identification with' processes. Personal characteristics likely become part of the self through the inferential processes by which what we do affects how we view ourselves. (Both, it seems reasonable to assert, become stabilized as part of self through confirmatory responses of those with whom we do interact in networks of relationships.)

Nevertheless, both can be usefully viewed as operating primarily through impacting role-defined identities and behaviours, by modifying the salience and the interactional meanings of role-linked identities. Master statuses are likely to impact commitments directly, either by facilitating or deterring the formation of particular kinds of interactional networks. That is, apart from the structural impact of, say, age, in moving persons of differing ages in different directions, or to different social locations, and so tending to keep them apart, comparable consequences flow from one age group defining another as inappropriate interactional partners. Master statuses, especially insofar as they are both reflections of the kinds of exclusionary tactics just noted and positive identification as well, will enhance the salience of those identities calling for behaviours that are open to master status-related modifications. If, for example, one's positive identification is as a Black, if one is barred or discouraged from contacts with others because one is black, and if the role content of, say, being a lawyer is open to specification in terms of the meaning of being black, the salience of the lawyer identity is likely to be strengthened relative to identities for which blackness is less relevant. The salience of a role identity, it is suggested, is enhanced insofar as that role identity is infused with the meaning of a master status.

It is hardly novel to suggest that most roles permit considerable leeway in how they are played, and that how they are in fact played out depends in part on the personal styles of those playing them out; this is the basis of the distinction, sometimes drawn, between social roles and personal roles. It may be more novel, and is perhaps theoretically fruitful, to suggest that personal traits supply significant parts of the content or meanings of both roles and role-based identities. This is one implication of work by Heise (1979) in which the meanings of the elements that enter interaction—self, other, the activity that joins the two, and the setting—are provided by the semantic domains of affect, potency, and activity which among them incorporate most if not all the stylistic tendencies to which the label 'trait' has been assigned. Insofar as identities are defined in terms that incorporate the meanings connoted by personal traits and insofar as behaviours can also be defined in these terms, it may be that it is the trait dimension of self that heightens the salience of the identity and that brings identity and particular behaviour together.

CODA

That is about as far matters can be pushed at this juncture. Clearly, there are many ways in which identity theory can be modified and extended. On the assumption that the basic theory is sound, it is worth examining in terms that will in fact require its further development.

REFERENCES

Abelson, R. P. (1976). 'Script processing in attitude formation and decision making.' In J. S. Carroll and J. W. Payne (Eds), *Cognition and Social Behavior*, Erlbaum, Hillsdale, New Jersey, pp. 35–45.

Bem, D. (1972). 'Self-perception theory.' In L. Berkowitz (Ed.), *Advances in Experimental Social Psychology*, vol. 6, Academic Press, New York, pp. 1–62.

Blumer, H. (1969). *Symbolic Interactionism: Perspective and Method*, Prentice-Hall, Englewood Cliffs, New Jersey.

Cooley, C. H. (1902). *Human Nature and the Social Order*, Scribner's, New York.

Gergen, K. G. (1982). *Toward Transformation in Social Knowledge*, Springer-Verlag, New York.

Goffman, E. (1959). *The Presentation of Self in Everyday Life*, Doubleday, New York.
Goffman, E. (1961). *Encounters*, Bobbs-Merrill, Indianapolis.
Heise, D. R. (1979). *Understanding Events*, Cambridge University, Cambridge.
Hoelter, J. (1983). 'The effects of role evaluation and commitment on identity salience.' *Social Psychology Quarterly*, **46**, 140–147.
Homans, G. C. (1950). *The Human Group*, Harcourt, Brace, New York.
McCall, G. and Simmons, J. L. (1978). *Identities and Interaction*, Free Press, New York.
Markus, H. (1977). 'Self-schemas and processing information about the self.' *Journal of Personality and Social Psychology*, **35**, 63–78.
Mead, G. H. (1934). *Mind, Self, and Society*, University of Chicago, Chicago.
Powers, C. (1980). Role-imposition or role-improvisation: some theoretical principles. Annual Meeting of the Pacific Sociological Association.
Rosenberg, M. (1979). *Conceiving the Self*, Basic Books, New York.
Schlenker, B. R. (1980). *Impression Management: The Self-Concept, Social Identity, and Interpersonal Relations*, Brooks-Cole, Monterey, California.
Serpe, R. T. (1980). 'Placing social psychological analysis in a structural context: commitment, identity salience, and role behavior.' *Annual Meeting of the American Sociological Association*.
Serpe, R. T. (1985). *Identity Salience and Commitment: Measurement and Longitudinal Analysis*, Unpublished Ph.D. Dissertation, Indiana University.
Stryker, S. (1968). 'Identity Salience and role performance.' *Journal of Marriage and the Family*, **30**, 558–564.
Stryker, S. (1980). *Symbolic Interactionism; A Social Structural Version*, Benjamin/Cummings, Menlo Park, California.
Stryker, S. and Gottlieb, A. (1981). 'Attribution theory and symbolic interactionism: A comparison.' In J. Harvey, W. Ickes and R. Kidd (Eds), *New Directions in Attribution Research*, vol. 3, Erlbaum, Hillsdale, New Jersey, pp. 425–458.
Stryker, S. and Serpe, R. T. (1982). 'Commitment, identity salience, and role behavior: theory and research example.' In W. Ickes and E. S. Knowles (Eds), *Personality, Roles, and Social Behaviour*, Springer-Verlag, New York, pp. 199–218.
Stryker, S. and Statham, A. (1985). 'Symbolic interaction and role theory.' In G. Lindzey and E. Aronson (Eds), *Handbook of Social Psychology*, 3rd edn, Random House, New York, pp. 311–378.
Thomas, W. I. and Thomas, D. S. (1928). *The Child in American*, Knopf, New York.
Turner, R. H. (1962). 'Role-taking: process vs. conformity?' In A. M. Rose (Ed.), *Human Behavior and Social Processes*, Houghton-Mifflin, Boston.
Weinstein, E. A. and Deutschberger, P. (1963). 'Some dimensions of altercasting.' *Sociometry*, **26**, 454–466.

Self and Identity: Psychosocial Perspectives
Edited by K. Yardley and T. Honess
© 1987 John Wiley & Sons Ltd

9

From Situated Activity to Self Attribution: The Impact of Social Structural Schemata

Mary Glenn Wiley and C. Norman Alexander, Jr

We postulate that social action always produces situated identities, which are conceived as dispositional schemata associated with activities, settings, roles, and the Self. A given event may activate some portion of several schemata as well as interrelationships among them. Since the Self is seen as the primary anchorage for actions, its frequent evocation in conjunction with schemata associated with acts, settings, and roles is likely to establish patterns of relationship between the Self schema and these other schemata. Self attribution requires the actor to disentangle the situated implications of action from the trans-situational schemata associated with roles. We argue that these role schemata are accommodated or assimilated to the Self schemata, thereby linking Self and social action.

The central question of this section of the volume is how Self and social structure articulate. We believe that part of the answer lies in the way in which attributions of traits to the Self are affected by the combinations of traits associated with specific actions and in turn how these combinations of trait dimensions or schemata are inextricably tied to social structure. To investigate how social structure affects self attribution, we initially must focus on the process of social interaction in which an actor obtains information (not always accurate) about others' attributions of traits to him or her.

We begin our exploration of self attribution with the concept of situated activity. Situated activity is conduct that is anchored outside the Self; it is constrained by the actors' belief that it is being monitored. This means that actors construct the meaning of their own conduct on the basis of their understanding of the meaning given to their conduct by specific others or types of others. The context in which a monitored action occurs is also extremely important to defining the meanings of the action. As Garfinkel (1967) has demonstrated, not only is information about the setting necessary for an action to have a relatively unambiguous meaning, but information concerning the actors and their goals, the time sequence, and the audience is also crucial. Thus, action acquires its meaningfulness only in a context where the actor's identity and the nature of the situation are known.

THE DISPOSITIONAL STRUCTURE OF SITUATED ACTIVITY

Heider (1958) further specifies the way in which meaning is constructed. He maintains that we can only gain a sense of the orderliness and predictability of social events by focusing on dispositional qualities, i.e., by 'perceiving psychologically'. This perceptual focus on dispositional qualities permits us to construe the events we observe in terms of orderly causal processes. However, the dispositional qualities that organize our psychological perceptions cannot be either random or individualistic. If they were, social interaction as we know it would be impossible. Not only would we be unable to anticipate others' behaviour but we also would be incapable of predicting the responses of others to our actions. Dispositional qualities must be typified in some fashion to be useful in the interpretation and prediction of social action.

Situated identity theory proposes that 'we define the phenomenon of social action in terms of the dispositional attributes that flow from the perspectives of given perceivers of the event field (Alexander and Wiley, 1981, p. 274)'. It further argues that settings and actors evoke typified combinations of dispositional dimensions which result in situated identities. Situated identities are *not* attributes possessed by a particular individual or imposed by an environmental structure. Rather, situated identities summarize the relationship between actors and their environments at a given point in time. There are as many possible situated identities for a single actor in a specific situation as there are perspectives relevant to the events in that situation. However, current research and theory has been restricted to considerations of situations in which perspectives are similar rather than multiple and divergent.

To reiterate, situated identities are combinations of dispositional dimensions that are linked to specific action contexts. We call the unique combination of dimensions connected to a specific situated identity a schema. Schemata,* thus, consist of combinations of dispositional dimensions which vary in importance and salience and which are linked to each other in ways peculiar to a specific situated identity. For example, Alexander and Sagatun (1973) found ratings on the dispositional dimensions *warm, friendly, personal, casual, honest,* and *interesting* to be linked in the situated identities available to experimenters portrayed as administering high and low levels of shock to human subjects.

People organize and guide their own behaviour as well as their adjustments to others in terms of situated identities and use them to anticipate responses (Alexander and Rudd, 1984). Thus, actors come to structure social activity

* We follow Markus and Sentis' view of 'schemata as memory structures of conceptually related elements that guide the processing of information' and as 'conceptual frameworks for representing relationships among stimuli that are built up on the basis of experience with reality' (1982, p. 43).

sequences in terms of these momentary situated identities. However, these self images, as Turner (1968) calls them, are like snapshots that give a picture of reality at a single point in time. They are the basis for the self attributions that concern us in this chapter, but they do not directly correspond to the Self, merely to the situated identity of an actor at a given moment. A situated identity can be thought of as 'self-in-situation' because it is bounded by the context of the action which created the dispositional attributions. The Self with which we are concerned is a conception of who one 'really' is. This self conception is resistant to change and, thus, relatively stable over time.

How can we link social actions which produce self images of a fleeting and sometimes false nature to the Self which is 'true' and continuous? We begin with the sociological dictum that the social person is shaped by interaction and that social structure determines the possibilities for interaction. To this we add the idea that Selves are constituted and modified by the situated identities that are generated by social actions. Turner (1984) has stressed that discovery and recognition of one's Self occurs in the 'exploration of self-in-situation interactions'. Since the dispositional products of activity (i.e., self attributions) are situated, we need some framework that organizes them over time and across contexts. As Merton (1957) suggested, the complex relationship between social structure and social action can be explicated, in part, by the concept of role or more precisely role set. Social roles* can provide the principles that structure patterns of attribution and produce dispositional schemata to give actions their meaningful form. Although Turner has suggested this: 'social roles constitute the organizing framework for the self conception' (1968, p. 24), he has not provided a means by which roles operate cognitively to structure self conception. We believe that the way in which 'self images' or situated identities are constructed is the key. We argue that not only are self images structured as complex combinations of dispositional dimensions but so are roles and Selves. Thus, we conceive of both Selves and roles in the same way in which we conceive of situated identities, that is, as schemata consisting of dispositional dimensions.

The articulation between Self and social structure has been problematic previously because theorists and researchers have not described social structure in a way that was compatible with conceptions of the Self. As a result, theorists such as Stryker (this volume) have been led to view Self as consisting of both role identities and personal traits. Our conception avoids this dichotomy since Self consists of dispositional dimensions regardless of their source or the degree of connection with social structure.

Conceiving of roles as dispositional schemata also allows measurement of the relationship between roles and Selves. This conceptualization of role also frees it from the limitations imposed by conceiving of role, the way most role

---

* When we speak of a role, we are in fact envisioning a schemata that includes dispositional dimensions relevant to the entire role set (Merton, 1957). We do not restrict the concept of role to only one type of role relationship.

theorists do, that is as a set of specific behavioural expectations (Biddle and Thomas, 1966; Heiss, 1981). Rather, the combinations of trait dimensions which characterize a particular role can guide behaviour even in new situations. Actors do not have to be socialized to specific behaviours but to overriding principles concerning the 'identity' or set of traits an actor holding a particular position is expected to express. This conception is also compatible with Turner's more processual view of role and role-taking (Turner, 1962).

ROLES AS DISPOSITIONAL SCHEMATA

Why do roles become organized as dispositional schemata? It seems reasonable that role schemata develop to serve the same anticipatory purposes that prompt perception at a dispositional (rather than stimulus-specific) level in the first place (Heider, 1958). For purposes of both psychological preparedness and social control, we believe actors need to generate cognitive representations that abstract constant elements from the contextually embedded flow of events. Such schematic representations furnish a configuration of interrelated dispositional dimensions around which immediate perceptions are organized and to which they are assimilated. They are an important means by which the diversity and idiosyncrasy of any concrete interaction is reduced, so that the participants can concentrate on the central themes of the episode with a minimum of distraction.

Any particular role elicits specific salient attributional dimensions and prescribes their interrelationship. For example, the role of general practitioner elicits a specific set of dispositional dimensions that includes both those associated with competence and knowledge and those associated with empathic caring and concern for patients. Evaluation of role performance depends on all of these dimensions, not just caring or competence alone. This precise configuration would not be cued by other roles such as scientist or surgeon.

When we say that the content of a specific role (role set) is structured as a combination of dispositional dimensions or a schema, we mean that there are learned conceptions in each culture about what people who portray certain social roles are like. A role schema organizes the behaviour of the occupant of a particular position and the behaviour of others toward him or her, just as other language symbols organize behaviour toward the 'thing' expressed. The dispositions included result from the action choices that are suggested or made possible by incumbency in specific roles. As actors repeatedly engage in particular role-related activity, they become typified as the sorts of persons who do those sorts of things (Berger and Luckmann, 1967). They become routinely characterized in terms of a limited set of dispositional dimensions, which they carry with them across action sequences and situations. In addition to specific action choices, situations in which the role incumbent typically acts may contribute characterizing dimensions. Also, frequent role partners may altercast still other dispositions (Weinstein and Deutschberger, 1963), as when attorneys are characterized by the types of clients they represent. In short, variations in actions, situational factors, and role partners affect the salience and importance of particular dimensions in a specific role schema.

Attribution theories, which attempt to specify the rules by which people explain behaviour from its context, have largely ignored the socio-cultural elements in that context (Stryker and Gottlieb, 1981). Correspondent inference theory (Jones and Davis, 1965; Jones and McGillis, 1976), for example, uses expectations based on cultural or normative standards as a background against which information about the person may be gained primarily when behaviour contrasts with these expectations. Kelley's (1967) theory emphasizes departures from consensual behaviour as the critical basis for inferring personal rather than object attributes. These approaches assume that dispositions flow from the objective character of the act itself. Only recently (e.g., Cantor and Mischel, 1979) have cognitive psychologists addressed themselves to the organization of persons and events in terms of schemata, and even in these instances the impact of interactional contexts is treated minimally. These foci reflect the traditional emphasis on the isolated 'person', which began with studies in person perception and implicit personality theory (Asch, 1946; Bruner, *et al.*, 1958). Although later studies of this type did deal with schema-like trait intercorrelations, only rarely were the stimulus persons systematically considered in terms of social roles or contexts (e.g., Warr and Knapper, 1968).

The content of role schemata is socially shared and emerges through continued exposure to the situated identities generated by the recurrent social activities that role occupants perform. Just as children learn to distinguish cats from dogs, they also learn to distinguish social positions. The role schemata associated with social positions are comparable to the criteria used to categorize 'objects'. The number of criteria which a particular individual uses to categorize objects frequently varies with the exposure he or she has to the 'objects' to be categorized. In the case of role schemata, we expect that the greater the exposure an individual has both to the various situated identities which result from a particular status set and to the number of situations in which these relationships are enacted, the more numerous and complex will be the dispositional dimensions making up the particular role schema associated with the social position.

The structure of the society in which an individual is socialized affects the role schemata learned, and the salience and importance of the dispositional dimensions that comprise them, in the same way in which it affects other perceptions of the world (e.g., Mead, 1962; McCall and Simmons, 1966). This conception of role schemata does not imply that social structure is static. Role schemata can change in structure (i.e., meaning) over time in conjunction with changes in the social and physical environment. If new role partners are added, if former ones are substracted, or if the situations in which the role incumbent acts change, the role schemata also may change. For example, physicians at the turn of the century frequently treated patients in the patients' homes. Now the home setting is excluded from the settings in which physicians and patients enact their roles. With this change, the role schema associated with both the physician and the patient role has changed.

ROLE SCHEMATA AND THE SELF

Now we turn to the question of how role schemata composed of combinations of dispositional dimensions can affect the attribution of various dispositions to the Self. Previously Turner (1978) has suggested some individual determinants of what he terms the role-person merger. We have adapted the principles underlying his propositions to provide the following illustrations of the link between social action and the core or continuous Self.

First, those roles which are, in their entirety, highly valued would be most likely to generate a linkage to the core Self. Whatever the specific dimensions conveyed by activities in roles that are high in esteem, status, or power, the rewards to the occupant are likely to motivate embracement of the role. Furthermore, almost by definition, such roles embody the more important dispositional values of the society, which the occupant is likely to share. Virtually all significant others should similarly share these values, and they should respond to the occupant as if investment in the role were personally valuable and self-expressive.

Second, when one component of a particular role prescribes or permits action choices that lead to extremely rewarding identity attributions, the actor may choose to enact the entire role for the situated identities received from this component alone. An extreme example is the amateur athlete or performer who practices long hours for the relatively brief, crowning moments of the performance. Although the actor may dismiss those portions of a role that are regarded as undesirable necessities, it is perhaps more usual for these situated identities to take on positive value due to their association with other highly valued situated identities.

Third, when an individual performs multiple roles that express the same specific dispositional dimension(s), sheer consistency across roles, over time and across situations should lead to self attributions along the dimension(s) involved. A related principle of congruence may have the same effect when there is simultaneous enactment of roles, all of which portray the actor similarly along the same dimension(s).

Fourth, certain roles pervade all, or almost all, of one's social interactions. Examples include diffuse status characteristics (e.g., black or female), negative or stigmatized roles (e.g., criminal or cripple), and certain positive roles (e.g., monarch or minister). Since the actor is never out of this role and is always treated by others as if the role is the Self, or an essential portion of it, the most salient dispositions in the schema for this role are likely to be attributed to the core Self.

Fifth, although the actor makes action choices, certain roles constrain attributions by limiting the other roles one may enact and/or the people with whom one interacts. Action choices which elicit certain dispositional dimensions are unavailable to the actor because of these constraints, i.e., these action choices are associated with roles that conflict with current roles or require fellow actors who are not available to the actor due to social position. For example, if the actor is a man, he is proscribed from making certain action choices associated exclusively with the female role. Thus prevented from performing in ways that would lead to situated identities including such dimensions, he is unlikely to attribute certain dispositions to Self. On the other hand, constraints on available interactants also affect self attributions. For example, an actor who holds the status of monarch does not have access to poverty-stricken individuals for social interaction. Consequently, certain situated identities and their dispositional structures are unavailable and certain self attributions are not possible.

Finally, Sarbin's notion of organismic involvement provides another set of conditions under which role schemata may influence the core Self (Sarbin, 1966). Organismic involvement varies, according to Sarbin, in direct relation to the degree of affect and effort involved in the role performance. Based on this conception, we would predict that the components of role schemata would be more likely to be attributed to the core Self, the greater the organismic involvement required in acting in accord with the role schema. In other words, the more effort and affect involved in the production of actions expressive of the role schema, the more likely the dispositional dimensions in that role schema will be attributed to the 'real' Self.

UNINTENDED CONSEQUENCES FOR THE SELF

As noted earlier, the actor may attempt to confirm or deny certain attributions which might be generated by various situated identities. However, some action choices that are meant to confirm one conception of Self may also result in changes in the Self. How does this occur? Here again the notion that roles and situations are structured as schemata is helpful. In attempting to validate or confirm particular aspects of the Self, behavioural choices activate specific role and situational schemata. Although there may be a specific set of dispositions guiding the initial action choice, an entire schema is activated. Thus, action choices elicit attributions on dispositional dimensions included in the schema that did not inform the actor's choice. Although the individual may not initially 'buy' the entire set of dispositional dimensions cued by the action, continual choices which lead to these same configurations may result in the inclusion of these dispositions in the core Self.

Particular dispositions may also be cued and eventually attributed to the Self because the actor must play out roles within institutional contexts. Such contexts require actions and impose alters and audiences not directly connected with the actor's initial conception of the boundaries of the role schema. For example, the training of most graduate students for academic professions emphasizes scholarly and research abilities. Little emphasis may be placed on their pedagogical skills, and even less on the dispositions that are associated with the administrative aspects of a professor's role schema.

More profound changes in the Self may await the individual who finds that to maximize the positive identity attributions derived from a chosen role, a substantial change in the perceived content of the role itself is required. The researcher whose role evolves into one of grant entrepreneur or programme coordinator is a familiar example. In other words, the socialization process is limited frequently to only one or a few relationships within the role set.

In a somewhat different vein, conceptually, is the circumstance in which persons find that the occupancy of one role dramatically increases the salience of other, extraneous roles. An example is the increased salience of a woman's gender role when she is employed in a stereotypically male occupation. The performance or choice of one role may require dealing with dispositions associated with an entirely different role schema when there is no 'logical' connection between the two.

Finally, there are conditions under which the roles of significant others in one context determine one's interactions in quite another. The spouse of a business executive who finds that entertaining clients is a required role and the private person who is related to a public celebrity are examples of actors who receive unsolicited evaluations along personally irrelevant dispositional dimensions.

These unintended, unsought, often extraneous contexts for and constraints on interaction confront the individual with precisely the same situated identities and images from which the self conception has been forged and in which it is ultimately anchored. We conceive of these unintended but socially imposed dispositional attributions as having an impact on the Self if they occur in several roles, in several contexts, with several different audiences over time or with great frequency.

RESEARCHING SELF AND ROLE SCHEMATA

The conception of roles as configurations of dispositional schemata derived from the action choices associated with roles permits us to relate them to behaviours and to the Self in measurable terms. It seems helpful to contrast our views with recent attempts by Burke and his associates (Burke and Tully, 1977; Burke and Reitzes, 1981) to approach these operational problems from a similar theoretical orientation. Basically we agree with their conception of how identities are linked to role performances. However, we disagree with their treatment of roles in three critical respects.

First, Burke speaks of role/identities rather than roles. Role/identities are sets of meanings that 'characterize the self-in-role' (Burke and Reitzes, 1981, pp. 85). By looking only at identity in relation to a specific role, the important distinction between Self and role is obscured. We, like Burke, conceive of roles as consisting of sets of meanings. However, in our view the set of dispositional dimensions which is linked to a role is distinct from those formed by individual identities. This distinction between Self and role is extremely important to our perspective since we contend that investigation of the congruence between dispositional schema comprising situated identities, roles, and the Self will help to explain the relationship between social structure and an individual's self conception. If the role-person merger is taken as a given, what we believe is the key to unlocking this complex relationship will be eliminated.

Although Burke and his associates purport to be dealing with role/ identities, their operationalization in effect taps the social psychological aspects of roles. Our other points, therefore, will contrast their role/identity concept with our concept of role.

Burke and his associates define roles as unitary concepts, while we see them as derived from multiple situated identity schemata. We define a situation for an actor as '. . . the configuration of situated identities that is created by each of the perspectives that are salient for him or her' (Alexander and Wiley, 1981, p. 288). Thus, at a specific moment in interaction, we recognize that the perspectives of participants and audiences may differ. It is further the case that a role may involve several situational sequences that differ substantially in the situated identities they evoke and the schemata that organize them. We are familiar with aspects of the professor role that are primarily involved with counselling, teaching, research, or administrative duties; yet we recognize them all as component parts of the professor role. They are constructed from different activity sequences, take place in different settings, and involve different altars and audiences. The situated identities they evoke contribute to different components of the role schema.

In measuring roles from our perspective, we require first the measurement of the situated identities generated by typified actions from the presumed (or, in some cases, actual) perspectives of important alters or audiences. This will tell us how many dispositional components or situated identities constitute the role schemata. Actions and alters will be grouped together as equivalent to the extent that they evoke similar configurations of dispositional dimensions. Although the idea of having to measure multiple perspectives on normative conduct in activity sequences involving many settings may seem a staggering task, it may not be in practice. The actual number of substantially different schematic components that we employ to organize our constructions of role schemata may prove quite manageable. Where we do encounter discrepancies and dissensus among alters, we are also likely to identify those areas marked by structural change, role conflict, or institutional disorganization. It may be precisely in these areas where the behaviour of the individual is most influenced by definitions of Self that have emerged from role contexts, but are no longer governed by them.

Depending upon the level of analysis at which we wish to predict role-related phenomena, we can relax or restrict our criteria to include a narrow or broad range of actions and alters. For example, to assess the link between behaviour and the Self we would need to investigate all dispositional dimensions included in situated identities essential to general conceptions of the role itself. On the other hand, if we were interested only in specific aspects of a role such as relationships with particular role partners, we would look at only those dimensions which derive from the typified action sequences played out with those alters or audiences of interest.

Finally, Burke and associates define role/identities in terms of dimensional differentiation from other relevant roles or 'counter-identities'. Contrasts between a present career stage and its former or future stages or between a chosen role and other roles precluded by the choice (e.g., the college student role compared to high school student, graduate student, and working young adult roles) may indeed tap some relevant dimensions of the role in question. However, this definition of roles may limit the dispositional dimensions considered to those affecting the decision to adopt the role in question. In other words, this procedure measures components of the role that are believed by others to be most highly valued by those who opt to embrace it. It may be a useful way of indicating which, among a role's several dimensional aspects, are likely to be incorporated into the Self, just as we have hypothesized earlier, but it ignores components unrelated to role selection.

Contrasts between the role and those of primary alters (e.g., the college student and professors) leads to an equally biased sample of dispositional dimensions. It highlights those aspects of the role that differentiate the occupant's potential situated identities from those of role partners. The dimensions it emphasizes may arise from altercasting, as when alter emphasizes a dimension such as helplessness pressuring the actor to be helpful, or from the fact that they are used as 'diagnostic' attributes (Tversky, 1977), as in our example of the dispositional dimensions associated with the female gender role being highlighted when a woman enters a 'male' occupation. In any case, the dimensions involved are those that distinguish the occupant from the interpersonal context and focus attention upon its occupant's uniqueness. Again, this may increase the probability that the dimensions will be self-relevant, as we hypothesized, but it isolates a special segment of the role schemata and ignores important commonalities. Such a contrast can severely distort the dispositional content of certain role relationships. A lover is not the less affectionate and caring because the primary alter shares these characteristics, nor is a combatant any the less aggressive and competitive because the opponent is also. Two roles are similar if the schemata applied to organizing the behaviours of each are similar, but the particular situated identity configurations generated by their action sequences still guide and shape their respective behaviours.

In contrasting our perspective with Burke's, we have indicated that a schematic approach to research on the relation of roles to the Self needs to relate the dimensional structure of a particular role schema to the typified actions in the setting of empirical interest. Furthermore, this must take into account possible differences in participants' perspectives. However, the points made so far provide only a limited view of our empirical position. To test propositions concerning the relationship between Self, role, and action, we require four measures for each of these entities.

Specifically, we would need measures of relevance, importance, valuation, and placement. We conceive of a universe of dispositional dimensions, each of which is potentially relevant to schemata involving typified actions, roles or self-concepts. A given dimension can vary in its relevance to the schema of interest. We have previously used relevance to provide operational criteria for selecting dimensions to define situated identities, and there is every reason to apply the same procedure to the measurement of other schemata. In addition, the importance of these dimensions should be measured to determine if they are organized in schematic rather than aschematic fashion (Markus and Sentis, 1982). A third variable is the valuation of the dispositional quality with respect to the schema in question. It may be that some characteristics are valued similarly no matter what the context, but, at times, the context can and does influence value (Santee and Jackson, 1982). Finally, of course, we need to know how act, role, or Self are rated along each relevant and important dimension.

Once we have established the dispositional structure of the role schema, Self schema, and typified action of empirical interest, we need to employ some template-matching technique (e.g., Bem and Funder, 1978; Burke, 1980) to relate schemata at different levels of analysis. As research on situated identities has shown, this approach can permit rather precise empirical tests of exacting hypotheses.

Through the investigation of the dimensional structure of settings, actions, roles, and Selves, we can establish the impact that socialized patterns of dispositional attribution have on the acceptance or rejection of social roles and, ultimately, the specific elements of an individual's roles that become imputed to the Self. Further, we can look at the ways in which Self is altered over time through the enactment of various role identities in specific settings.

REFERENCES

Alexander, C. N. and Rudd, J. (1984). 'Predicting behaviors from situated identities.' *Social Psychology Quarterly*, **47**, 172–177.

Alexander, C. N. and Sagatun, I. (1973). 'An attributional analysis of experimental norms.' *Sociometry*, **36**, 127–142.

Alexander, C. N. and Wiley, M. G. (1981). 'Situated activity and identity formation.' In M. Rosenberg and R. Turner (Eds), *Social Psychology: Sociological Perspectives*, Basic Books, New York, pp. 269–289.

Asch, S. (1946). 'Forming impressions of personality.' *Journal of Abnormal and Social Psychology*, **41**, 258–290.

Bem, D. and Funder, D. (1978). 'Predicting more of the people more of the time: Assessing the personality of situations.' *Psychological Review*, **85**, 485–501.

Berger, P. and Luckmann, T. (1967). *The Social Construction of Reality*, Doubleday, New York.

Biddle, B. J. and Thomas, E. J. (Eds) (1966). *Role Theory: Concepts and Research*, Wiley, New York.

Bruner, J., Shapiro, D. and Tagiuri, R. (1958). 'The meaning of traits in isolation and in combination.' In R. Tagiuri and L. Petrullo (Eds), *Person Perception and Interpersonal Behavior*, Stanford University Press, Stanford, pp. 277–288.

Burke, P. (1980). 'The self: Measurement requirements from an interactionist perspective.' *Social Psychology Quarterly*, **43**, 18–29.

Burke, P. and Reitzes, D. (1981). 'The link between identity and role performance.' *Social Psychology Quarterly*, **44**, 83–92.

Burke, P. and Tully, J. (1977). 'The measurement of role identity.' *Social Forces*, **55**, 881–897.

Cantor, N. and Mischel, W. (1979). 'Prototypes in person perception.' In L. Berkowitz (Ed.), *Advances in Experimental Social Psychology*, vol. 12, Academic Press, New York, pp. 4–52.

Garfinkel, H. (1967). *Studies in Ethnomethodology*, Prentice Hall, Englewood Cliffs, New Jersey.

Heider, F. (1958). *The Psychology of Interpersonal Relations*, Wiley, New York.

Heiss, J. (1981). 'Social roles.' In M. Rosenberg and R. Turner (Eds), *Social Psychology: Sociological Perspectives*, Basic Books, New York, pp. 94–129.

Jones, E. and Davis, K. (1965). 'From acts to dispositions: The attribution process in person perception.' In L. Berkowitz (Ed.), *Advances in Experimental Social Psychology*, vol. 2, Academic Press, New York, pp. 219–266.

Jones, E. and McGillis, D. (1976). 'Correspondent inferences and the attribution cube: A comparative reappraisal.' In J. Harvey, W. Ickes, and R. Kidd (Eds), *New Directions in Attribution Research*, vol. 1, Erlbaum, Hillsdale, New Jersey, pp. 389–420.

Kelley, H. (1967). 'Attribution theory in social psychology.' In D. Levine (Ed.), *Nebraska Symposium on Motivation*, vol. 15, University of Nebraska Press, Lincoln, pp. 192–238.

McCall, G. J. and Simmons, J. L. (1966). *Identities and Interactions*, The Free Press, New York.

Markus, H. and Sentis, K. (1982). 'The self in social information processing.' In J. Suls (Ed.), *Psychological Perspectives on the Self*, vol. 1, Erlbaum, Hillsdale, New Jersey, pp. 41–70.

Mead, G. H. (1962). *Mind, Self, and Society*, University of Chicago Press, Chicago.

Merton, R. K. (1957). *Social Theory and Social Structure*, The Free Press, New York.

Santee, R. and Jackson, S. (1982). 'Identity implications of conformity: Sex differences in normative and attributional judgments.' *Social Psychology Quarterly*, **45**, 121–125.

Sarbin, T. R. (1966). 'Role enactment.' In B. J. Biddle and E. J. Thomas (Eds), *Role Theory: Concepts and Research*, Wiley, New York, pp. 195–200.

Stryker, S. and Gottleib, A. (1981). 'Attribution theory and symbolic interactionism: A comparison.' In J. Harvey, W. Ickes and R. Kidd (Eds), *New Directions in Attribution Research*, vol. 3, Erlbaum, Hillsdale, New Jersey, pp. 425–458.

Turner, R. (1962). 'Role-taking: process versus conformity.' In A. M. Rose (Ed.), *Human Behavior and Social Processes*, Houghton Mifflin, Boston, pp. 20–40.

Turner, R. (1968). 'The self-conception in social interaction.' In C. Gordon and K. Gergen (Eds), *The Self in Social Interaction*, Wiley, New York, pp. 93–106.

Turner, R. (1978). 'The role and the person.' *American Journal of Sociology*, **84**, 1–23.

Turner, R. (1984). 'Locating self in social structure.' *Conference on Self and Identity*, *British Psychological Society*, University College, Cardiff, Wales.

Tversky, A. (1977). 'Features of similarity.' *Psychological Review*, **84**, 327–352.

Warr, P. and Knapper, C. (1968). *The Perception of People and Events*, Wiley, London.
Weinstein, E. and Deutschberger, P. (1963). 'Some dimensions of altercasting.' *Sociometry*, **26**, 454–466.

Self and Identity: Psychosocial Perspectives
Edited by K. Yardley and T. Honess
© 1987 John Wiley & Sons Ltd

10

Articulating Self and Social Structure

Ralph H. Turner

In seeking to understand self as autonomy in engagement with society and to progress beyond hierarchy of identities theory, we suggest the importance of distinguishing between observational and affirmational modes of the self and recognizing a series of levels of self experience ranging from unarticulated contextual identities through milieus where we fit comfortably to valued identities and personal qualities.

For some behavioural scientists, the self-conception is no more than a kalaidescope of self-images. A recalcitrant male university student, when asked to describe an occasion when his actions or feelings seemed to express his true self better than at other times, asserted this view emphatically.

> This is a load of rubbish as it is impossible to comprehend what my true self is. When there are innumerable contradictions of actions and feelings, how is it possible to judge what is the true self? Today I might feel that I am an academic with plans to go a long way in this field, yet yesterday I may have felt like throwing everything in and becoming a factory worker with no responsibility. The day before that I may have felt like becoming a professional sportsman. How, then, can I judge what is 'my true self' if my character, actions and feelings all differ from day to day in an unstable manner?

The response of a different subject (male student) to a companion query, to recall an 'occasion when your actions or feelings contradicted your true self', illustrates how a competent role performance, evaluated positively by others, can nevertheless be experienced as inauthentic by ego, because of discrepancies between self-image and a more generalized self-conception (Turner, 1968).

> When I was at Tech College I went in for a Rag King competition in which I dressed up in drag and went on stage in front of thousands. I won the competition and during the Rag Week I was the main personality. This extrovert personality wasn't really me and I think this is the only time that I can say that I was inauthentic. I am basically a quiet person, I don't really like crowds, cliche sets and boozy parties. The title of Rag King made me into an extrovert extreme. I flirted with the girls when, really, I wasn't interested. I did it to show a group of friends that I was a good chap. Plenty of guts.

My interest in this contribution will be to examine the way in which a somewhat generalized self-conception has been interpreted as a mechanism for articulating person and social structure. A few illustrations of this use of self-conception can be mentioned. For several decades students of crime, delinquency, and other forms of social deviancy have seen the self-conception as predisposing or insulating the individual from deviancy (Wells, 1978). Super (1951) saw occupational choice as the effort to find an occupation within which the self-conception could find harmonious expression. The mechanism here is similar to that suggested by Ernest Burgess (Shaw, 1930, pp. 184–205) in showing how the delinquent 'jack roller' could establish a law abiding role for himself only when his occupational and living arrangements provided scope for behaviour consistent with his self-conception. In another and more explicit use of the concept of self-conception, Burgess (1954) tried to distinguish citizens who occasionally availed themselves of wartime black markets from 'real' criminals on the basis that the latter had distinguishing criminal conceptions of self.

AUTONOMY IN ENGAGEMENT WITH SOCIETY

Before proceeding we must ask: why study the self-conception? The answer of special relevance to this paper is that the concept of self permits us to deal with the balance of determinacy and indeterminacy in the relationship between person and social structure. Without a concept of self, individual behaviour is either simply role-determined or determined by some resolution of forces between social role and biology. Self as a folk concept conveys the idea of autonomy, but not social disengagement. When one acts incomprehensibly or displays uncontrollable emotion, we say one is out of one's mind or beside oneself. The idea of self conveys an image of *autonomy in engagement with society*. The concept of self is equally relevant in explaining the rebel and the conformist, and is critical in understanding the difference. We use the concept of self to help in answering the question of how we can be creatures of society without being mere castings from the moulds supplied by social structure.

To escape the trap of mechanistic determinism we must remember that the self-conception does not consist of simple tendencies to act, like the concept of attitude. The distinctive feature of the self-conception is to provide the lens through which perceived or anticipated self-images are examined and accepted or rejected, with appropriate behavioural adjustments. The self-conception cannot be understood apart from the reflexive self-process in which it is an essential element (Mead, 1934; Stone, 1962, p. 104).

SELF-CONCEPTION AS A HIERARCHY OF SOCIAL IDENTITIES

Building on ideas from William James, Charles Cooley, and Robert Park, Manford Kuhn developed the formulation and the method for studying personal articulation with social structure through the self-conception on which most sociologists and many social psychologists have based their work.

Central to an individual's conception of himself is his *identity*; that is, his generalized position in society deriving from his statuses in the groups of which he is a member, the roles which stem from these statuses, and the social categories that his group memberships lead him to assign himself (sex, age, class, race, etc.) (Kuhn 1964, pp. 630–631).

Based on the symbolic interactionist axiom that 'Persons must first make self-identifications before they can organize and direct their own activity' (Spitzer, *et al.* 1970, p. 9), Kuhn assumed that people should be able to formulate and communicate their self-conceptions to others. Hence he developed the well-known *twenty statements test* (TST), asking the subject:

Please write twenty answers to the simple question 'Who am I?' Answer as if you were giving the answers to yourself, not to somebody else.

Some confusion has arisen because of varied usages of the term *identity*, which is sometimes not distinguished from the self-conception. Many sociologists have accepted Gregory Stone's (1962, p. 93) formulation.

. . . identity establishes *what* and *where* the person is in social terms. It is not a substitute word for 'self'. Instead, when one has identity, he is situated—that is, cast in the shape of a social object by the acknowledgement of his participation or membership in social relations. One's identity is established when others *place* him as a social object by assigning him the same words of identity that he appropriates for himself or *announces*. It is in the coincidence of placements and announcements that identity becomes a meaning of the self . . .

Stone's usage of identity clearly anchors the person to social structure through the mutually defining exchange that is crucial in social interaction. But there is no implication that identities transcend situations or persist over time. This usage contrasts with that of Erik Erikson (1959) and even of Kuhn.

Stryker (1968) has probably expressed most clearly the view that was implicit in Kuhn's work, that the self-conception is indeed composed of social identities, but that identities are arrayed in a hierarchy of salience. My own work on role-person merger gives a more behavioural twist to this approach by emphasizing 'failure of role compartmentalization: a subject [continues] to play a role in situations where the role does not apply' (Turner, 1978, p. 3). One manifestation of class and ethnic consciousness is a reduced ability to tolerate roles or symbols that identify one with a different class or ethnic group.

Essentially two kinds of hypotheses have been derived from this view of the self-conception as a hierarchy of social identities. One type hypothesizes a relationship between the firmness with which self is anchored in recognized social statuses and memberships, and the conventionality and stability of behaviour. One of Kuhn's earliest distinctions was between *consensual* and *non-consensual* referents, the former including well-recognized statuses, groups, and classes, and the latter consisting of characterizations and ambiguous placements. Louis Zurcher's (1977) discussion of the mutable self and my contrast between institution and impulse as anchorage for the self-conception (Turner, 1976) are variations on this tradition. The other type relates the substance of identities mentioned to behavioural dispositions. For example, if some respondents mention their racial identities more often or earlier than other respondents, their behaviour should reflect their racial identities more intensely and consistently.

Several problems have emerged in the course of working within this tradition, however, whether the TST format or another procedure is used. First, correlations between coded self-conception responses and behavioural indicators have been disappointing.

Second, people discussing 'who I really am' often disavow areas of major behavioural investment and commitment as their real selves and give leisure or 'escape' identities as 'the real me'. Thus the business executive who finds little time to be with his family in real life may insist that he is his real self during those infrequent periods spent with his family, rather than in his office or the executive boardroom. Or a devoted scholar or scientist may claim to be most himself when away from the laboratory on a fishing trip. The hypothesis of a simple correspondence between the verbalized hierarchy of identities and behavioural commitment is oversimplified, if not altogether incorrect.

Third, the discovery by Louis Zurcher (1972, 1977) and others of an historical shift in the pattern of students' answers to the TST away from obviously social-structural identities and toward statements of dominant moods and dispositions renders less tenable the earlier assumption that the mature self-conception articulates self with social structure in a fairly direct and manifest fashion. Zurcher interprets the shift as a loosening of coupling between self and social structure that facilitates adaptation in a rapidly changing society, while I (Turner, 1976) have interpreted the shift more phenomenologically as an altered conception of reality stemming from changed opportunity and reward structures. Whatever the explanation, Snow (1982) presents evidence that the shift has persisted in fresh cohorts of university students beyond the period of upheaval in the 1960s and early 1970s.

Fourth, the approach has sometimes been employed with simplistic assumptions about the implications of role incumbencies and group memberships for behaviour. Early formulations of role theory referred to a collection of behavioural prescriptions, fairly mechanically translated into behaviour as a consequence of assuming the role. But few scholars still adhere to so simple a view of role dynamics (Turner, 1962; Handel, 1979).

Furthermore, it is easy to find illustrations of strong personal identification with a role leading to divergent ways of enacting it. Consider, on the one hand, the devoted pastor who carries out every aspect of church leadership, meeting all the responsibilities of office. Consider, by contrast, the pastor of a California church, outstanding in attracting parishioners through his preaching, who suddenly discontinued traditional church services and dissolved the established structure of church committees in order to find a pattern of worship more consistent with the spirit of the Christian religion. Both fulfilment and repudiation of the role as commonly understood were manifestations of deep personal identification with the pastorate.

Finally, in recent research we have discovered that the conception of self implied by circumstances leading to a sense of inauthenticity are often not counterparts to the circumstances leading to a sense of authenticity (Turner and Gordon, 1981). *Not self* is not necessarily a simple obverse of *self*.

CONSIDERATIONS TOWARD REFINING SELF-CONCEPTION THEORY

Among the many extensively discussed features of the self-conception and self process, I have selected a few that I think are crucial in working toward a more adequate view of the relationships among self-conception, behaviour, and social structure.

Self-conceiving 'as if'

Contrary to Manford Kuhn's assumption, experience with TST and other instruments abundantly demonstrates that people do not necessarily have well-formulated and communicable self-conceptions. Supplying answers to the TST is a difficult exercise for many people, who often disclaim their own replies as valid accounts of who they really are after completing the task (see also Yardley, this volume). But the important consideration is that people for the most part orient themselves *as if* they had discoverable and ultimately characterizable selves. Many people insist that they know themselves but can't put their insights into words that would be understood by others. People often reject any specific characterization as too limiting, too stereotypic, and by implication as demystifying. The availability in the culture of a folk concept of self is critical in allowing people to take for granted that there is some essence that constitutes their real selves (Turner, 1957; Blacking, 1984).

Self as milieu

While role and group membership identities are regularly named in response to the TST, there are striking disjunctions between the characteristics of such identities and folk concepts of selves. In the extreme, identity can be strictly expedient. Bargaining and negotiation are often key processes in establishing situational identities. More enduring identities are variously ascribed, adopted by default, negotiated, and retained because of social structural rather than personal commitment. Only for the fortunate few do even one's master identities evoke a vital sense of selfhood, and sometimes then only when these are threatened. These comments on how identities are acquired or retained are in strange contrast to the adjectives commonly applied to the self-conception, such as *internalized, natural,* and *real.* With such contrasting characterizations, how can identities form the core of the self-conception?

For clarification we look at a recurring antinomy within designations of both identity and self-conception. The process of establishing an identity in a particular interaction can be principally a matter of indicating topics for conversation and signalling the biases and interests that might contribute to disruption or facilitation of interaction. In this sense identities can be relatively value-neutral. One might say that they indicate potential *milieus* for interaction. To know whether one is talking to a man or to a woman, a child or an adult, to a retiree, a golfer, a Republican, a resident of the Pacific Palisades, is to evoke topics of interest and to signal regions where one must tread lightly. To identify oneself in a store as a customer or a salesperson merely signals the appropriate basis for interaction.

Alternatively the process can be guided by efforts to assert a valued identity and to bolster self-esteem. The university regent who prefaces comments to the Board with the words, 'As the regent with the longest period of service . . . ,' the professional who contrives to be addressed as 'doctor', the neighbourhood conversationalist who manoeuvres to bring his or her current hospital volunteership or office in the Parent Teachers Association into conversation, all illustrate this pattern.

We find a corresponding mixture of patterns in self-designations of self-conception. When social identities are mentioned, it is sometimes a matter of asserting prideful identities. One may be proud of being a mother, of being a scholarship student, of being a priest, of being an Olympic games medal winner. But many, and possibly most social structural self-designations simply identify *milieus* in which the individual feels comfortable and fulfilled.

Units of social structure such as consensual roles and group memberships may be incorporated into the self-conception primarily as *milieus* for action and not necessarily as intrinsically valued significations. There is, of course, a mixture in most experience. One's distinctive milieus tend to be viewed with a sense of possessiveness—the sense of *my* and *mine* that Cooley (1902) viewed as the root experience from which the sense of self develops. And one's personal possessions usually take on an increment of value. So one can take pride in having a special milieu that is distinctively one's own and attach an increment of prestige to that arena. This was clearly the case with the waiter in one of San Francisco's oldest restaurants who commented:

> Anybody can carry a plate from the kitchen to the table, but to be a waiter you have to give something of yourself, your knowledge, your personality. That's what makes a difference between this place and a shoe store (*Los Angeles Times*, October 28, 1984, part I, p. 1).

But, in many cases, who I am is little more than where I fit. I think we are often mislead into overloading self-conception with intense value implications in all its facets.

The same observation can be made about collective identities that may eventually be escalated into the basis for class and ethnic mobilizations. The roots of ethnic consciousness are often unspectacular. In a study of third generation Japanese American university students, Hosokawa (1978) found that the first ethnic consciousness arose for most of her subjects as a consequence of leaving the neighbourhood and encountering the vast and impersonal university campus. In their home neighbourhoods and neighbourhood-based primary and secondary schools, their race had not been an issue. It was not prejudice but anonymity and social isolation at the university that started the process that ended in ethnic consciousness. Ethnic commonality became the excuse for striking up acquaintances, leading to the formation of ethnic cliques within which ethnic consciousness blossomed. Milieus for interaction rather than values for commitment were the beginning of ethnic consciousness.

Affirmation and observation of the self

If people learn early in life to orient themselves as if they possess and should govern their own behaviour through a self, their perception of the characteristics of that self derives from both *observation* and *affirmation*. Elsewhere I have suggested that the mature and relatively stable self-conception 'consists of a selective organization of values and standards, edited to form a workable anchorage for social interaction' (Turner, 1968, p. 105). Initially affirmed as goals and guidelines for self-directed behaviour, conceptions of self are subject to revision as one is reflexively an object to oneself. But much of the time one can hold diverse and even conflicting conceptions of self which come to the fore when engaged at different moments in self-observation and self-affirmation.

Self-affirmation is an effort to construct a particular kind of self, in contrast to the more passive act of self-discovery. A little girl of 26 months surprised her mother by suddenly refusing to allow her mother to diaper her, saying, 'no pee: big girl!' Her mother reports that she was successful most of the time in living up to her new self-affirmation. This was clearly not a matter of passive discovery but of decision backed by will. Her mother also reports that on the rare occasions of incontinence she seemed quite disgusted with herself.

The more passive observation mode includes the continuous monitoring through which we come to recognize the milieus in which we fit best and a panoply of capabilities and dispositions. It also includes the more dramatic experiences of self-discovery. For example, one man reports self-discovery in the instant when he realized an automobile collision was inevitable. First, he was surprised that the ideas of pain, injury, or death did not cross his mind, but that he experienced an intense fear of being maimed. Thus, he was made aware of how important the integrity of his body was to his conception of self. Second, he was most distressed over the realization that nothing he could do or could reasonably have done could save him from the consequence of the other driver's erratic behaviour. He had not previously recognized the extent to which he thought of himself as capable of mastering any situation affecting him. In the same way, a worker may not discover how central his occupational identity is to his self-conception until retirement deprives him of the regular use of that identity. Moreover, the TST and similar procedures assume a high degree of self-awareness, consistent with the assumptions underlying self-presentation and self-disclosure theory. But the idea of self-discovery pre-sumes a set of tendencies that have been shaping behaviour and perspective before they entered into conscious awareness. In some instances self-discovery means discovering what one can do, like the student who was surprised and gratified at her success in handling a difficult family situation, or another who was shocked to realize how badly he could behave.

Separation of the affirmation and observation modes can lead to quite different conceptions of self, but the two modes are combined in much self-experience. Observation can supply confirmation for the affirmed self-conception, and some of the true-self experiences reported by students are of this character. Alternatively, a dramatic disconfirmation or a series of dis-confirming observations can lead to abandonment of the affirmed self-conception. A dramatic illustration of temporary disorientation when an affirmed and long-confirmed self-conception is confronted with potentially discordant self-discovery is supplied by remarks attributed to world top-seeded tennis player, Martina Navratilova, when she suffered a humiliating defeat in two sets at the hands of third-seeded Hana Mandlikova.

> 'I just couldn't believe I lost the first set after having so many chances,' Navratilova said. 'Of the six games she won to get to the tie-breaker, five went to deuce and four I had game points in. And my heart was not there in the second set, and I certainly have some soul-searching to do because that's not me.' (*Los Angeles Times*, March 9, 1985, part III, p. 10.)

Even the best players occasionally lose matches, but Navratilova expresses self-concern over her loss of motivation in the second set—a matter of more far-reaching concern than how well she played on a given day.

Affirmation can be self-limiting as well as expansive. Self-limiting affir-mations are characteristically announced to oneself and others as conclusions from self observation. One recognizes one's limitations and plans one's life accordingly. Alcoholics Anonymous socializes its members to make the self-limiting affirmation of once an alcoholic, always an alcoholic, as the grounds for total abstinence. In another culturally based form of self-limiting affirmation, people often learn to justify their unwillingness to repair personal shortcomings by the assertion, 'But that's just the kind of person I am!'

The discussion of milieus and of affirmation and observation underlines the variety of ways in which conceiving the self can be used, with the result that self-conceptions held or expressed in different contexts can be diverse in content and in their relations to behaviour.

True self and not self

We need, finally, to take account of the self sentiments of authenticity and inauthenticity. We are all familiar with such incidents as the dramatic resignation of a charismatic woman minister from her pulpit on Easter Sunday, 1985, with the declaration: 'I no longer want to be a television evangelist. I no longer want to be a religious leader. I want to be myself.' (*Los Angeles Times*, April 8, 1985, part II, p. 6.) And we have heard comments like those of the young people who like to attend rock concerts because there they can be themselves with their friends. Expressions such as these raise two important questions in developing a realistic understanding of the self-conception. First, what is the nature of relationships among expressions of true self, not self, and the self-conception in the Kuhn tradition? Second, what is the relationship between articulated and unarticulated identities?

Considering how we resent being misidentified by others, it is surprising that investigators have not more often complemented the TST and other self-instruments by asking, 'Who am I *not*?' The assumption of investigators often seems to be that people will feel genuine when behaviour corresponds to self-conception and inauthentic when it does not. Although this assumption has been implicit in much work on the self-conception, few investigators have tried to match up self-designations of self and not-self. In asking students to describe separately situations in which they were their true selves and situations in which they were not their true selves, we have been able to do this (Turner and Gordon, 1981). Comparably chosen samples from four universities in the United States, Great Britain, and Australia revealed a consistent pattern, with about two-thirds reporting a true self experience in the acknowledgement, release, active expression, or mutual exchange of institutionally untrammelled impulse. But in reporting experiences of inauthenticity—not my true-self—two-thirds described situations in which an institutionally anchored self-conception was violated. From this finding and examination of selected groups of protocols, we made two suggestions. First, there is not a single threshold between true-self and not-self experience, but rather an extended realm that we called the *customary self*. Second, true-self and spurious self could often not be seen as poles of a single dimension, but as belonging to different dimensions. Thus, the sense of not-me often came from disruption of underlying order in relations with social structure, while the true-self experience often reflected the luxury of disregarding or even flaunting institutional order.

Perhaps the *customary self* encompasses the realm of mood, impulse, behaviour, and relationships that can be taken for granted because a tolerable accommodation or harmony has developed between the individual and milieu and within the individual. If this generalization is valid, the lines between what pertains distinctively to self process and what is grounded in habit are blurred.

The tripartite distinction brings us back to the phenomenon of self-consciousness and our second question: the relationship between articulated and unarticulated identities. It is useful to remember Freud's (S. Freud, 1933; A. Freud, 1946) view of the ego as the seat of negotiation among contending forces within the psyche. If we avoid the simple dichotomy of an instinctual id opposed by a socio-cultural superego, we can agree with the dynamic features of this conceptualization. Articulation of a self-conception is instrumental in the negotiation process. But when it ceases to be relevant to ongoing negotiations it loses salience for articulating the self-conception. After administering the TST to a freshman university class, the instructor reviewed some common findings, such as a greater tendency for women than for men to mention their sex among their responses. After class a young woman student expressed concern to the instructor that she had not mentioned her sex among her TST responses, and was she therefore somehow lacking in femininity? It is a reasonable assumption that her sexual identity was not 'on her mind' because it had not been problematic for her recently. Nevertheless, it remained a vital component of her customary self, as demonstrated by how minor a jolt could make it salient.

One further observation from our investigation is relevant to this discussion. Respondents often described in quite vivid terms the circumstances under which their true selves were manifested or in which they felt unreal, but did so without conveying or implying any well-formulated and articulated account of who they really were. The largest number of respondents experienced the sense of really being themselves in the course of casual and personal conversation with one other person, in a purposeless encounter without sexual overtones. The grounds for self-feeling in many of these cases are more clearly articulated in terms of the social situation than in terms of a characterizable self-conception. A similar pattern is revealed by a junior high school boy who said simply that he felt most himself when he was all alone. We should be prepared to accept the inference that we often understand ourselves in terms of social relationships without individuating ourselves out from the situation.

This discussion of true self, not self, and customary self, and of the relationship between articulated and unarticulated self-conceptions, accentuates the conclusion from our earlier discussion that we cannot capture what is distinctive about self process by accumulating a simple unidimensional characterization that we call the self-conception, consisting merely of a hierarchy of identities, but must develop a more complex and dynamic paradigm.

CONCLUSIONS

It seems clear that the various manifestations to which we attach the label self-conception are not all of one kind, even when account is taken of their hierarchical organization. A realistic view of the organization and dynamics of self must take account of this complexity.

First, we must recognize a rough continuum in how people see themselves, from the relatively unarticulated and contextual to the highly articulated and personalized. At one pole of the continuum are the unarticulated hierarchies of social identities, styles and values. These may never have been committed to words, but more often they have been articulated at some stage of development, then made habitual and 'forgotten' when no longer problematic. We cannot rely on TST responses or other self-characterizations in identifying this subterranean level of self-conception because it includes much that the respondent will not think of in answering an open-ended question, and whose significance will not be recognized in responding to more directive questions. One might choose not to call these characterizations parts of the self-conception because they are not articulated. Nevertheless, they do serve as the frame of reference within which many decisions are made, and they are subject to self-recognition and self-discovery under appropriate circumstances.

If we cannot employ self-identifications as the guide to this subterranean self, how can we deal with it empirically? There are at least two ways of doing so. One way is to employ behavioural indicators such as the carry-over of role behaviour from one role to another, as suggested in my (Turner, 1978) discussion of role and person merger. Another way is to gather characterizations of relevant others and interactive settings. If we assume that pairs and larger sets of roles are linked in interactive reciprocity, how one conceives relevant others supplies powerful clues to how one conceives of oneself. Because we are generally more able and willing to delimit others than ourselves, we may discern unarticulated elements of the self-conception in this way.

A second level in the self-conception consists of incompletely articulated milieus and relationships in which sentiments of authenticity and inauthenticity are experienced. The self is articulated to the extent of describing the situation and what in the situation made one feel authentic or inauthentic, but no clearly personalized picture of how the respondent conceives himself or herself emerges. Thus, the boy who feels his real self when alone would not necessarily take the next step of identifying himself as a loner. Much self-awareness in real life is at this level, with knowing myself meaning knowing where I fit and do not fit. But reflexive self-process begins to operate to permit the individual to make self-conscious choices at this level.

A third level consists of personalized milieus. These are self-designations in which I am identified by the milieu in which I feel genuine or unreal, but without strong value implications. Identifying oneself as a student probably has this character for most university level students.

A fourth level consists of valued social identities. The self is still being identified in terms of a social structural setting and relationship, but that structural linkage is now fully personalized. One is proud to be known as the doctor, the son, or the veteran.

A fifth level consists of valued identity-personal quality combinations. Here the individual sees himself or herself as a certain *style* of professor, or mother. And a sixth level consists of identifications strictly in terms of personal qualities detached from specific roles or group settings.

Self-discovery and self-recognition can occur at all but the subterranean level. Self-affirmation becomes increasingly important at the fourth, fifth, and sixth levels. In each individual's repertoire of self-conceptions there are many discrepant pairs, seen through the contrasting lenses of the observation and affirmation modes. Often the self-conception that is called up incorporates the pair and makes the discrepancy salient.

For the purpose of analysing one type of self-conception protocol, we found it useful to partition the self-conception into true self, customary self, and not self, with the first and last being articulated and the customary self inferred. This classification cross-cuts the six levels, except that elements from the subterranean level are included only in the customary self. The tripartite breakdown, however, is situational rather than stable as a personality orientation. Many elements that in one interactional context are relegated to the customary self would conceivably be incorporated into true-self experiences under a different set of circumstances. And other customary-self boundaries could be infringed to evoke the sense of inauthenticity. This observation reminds us that an individual's reservoir of already articulated self-conceptions is peculiarly reflective of the kinds of social encounters that have highlighted the boundaries of the self.

The identification of levels in the self-conception underlines the importance of understanding the self as lodged in selected relationships with social structure and relevant others. We have allowed an unwitting individualistic bias to influence the way we conceptualize and describe the self-conception. Coupled with a bias toward disproportionately cognitive formulation, our prototype of the self-conception has been too much a sharply defined picture of an individual detached from social surroundings. I believe it is important that we highlight more strongly the social-relational aspects of self-designations, and supplement instruments in the TST tradition with systematic questions about occasions, settings, and relationships in which the sense of self is evoked.

The nature of social situations in which self identifications are evoked is the topic of research now underway, and I will not elaborate further on it at present (see Turner and Billings, 1984). But one other consideration should be incorporated into any meaningful scheme for understanding self-conceptions. This is the observation that people organize what they experience into meaningful objects by fitting them into the folk concepts available to them culturally and subculturally.

The concept of self is a folk concept whose general character changes historically and varies culturally and subculturally at any given time. Among other things, the folk concept sensitizes people to see certain evidence as indications of self and to discount other evidence (see also Andersen, this volume). The study of self-conceptions in individuals and categories of people should be paralleled by continuous monitoring of prevalent fold concepts of self, so that we can understand why the self-relevance of equivalent experiences can be different for different populations.

Any folk concept can be thought of as a resource that can be used to serve the purposes of the individual. Whenever identification of self is used purposively, the use contributes toward shaping the product. I have cited examples in which self-identification was used to claim credit or deny responsibility for actions, and there are other uses. Instruments for eliciting self-conceptions are generally 'purposeless'. We should systematically supplement protocols from these instruments by observing the various ways in which self-delineation is used, stressing those uses that lead the user to accept the useful self-conceptions as valid.

ACKNOWLEDGEMENT

This study was revised for presentation as the annual Katz-Newcomb Lecture in Social Psychology at the University of Michigan, April 26, 1985 and has benefited from helpful criticisms by Melvin Seeman.

REFERENCES

Blacking, J. (1984). 'The concept of identity and folk concepts of self: A Venda case study.' In A. Jacobson-Widding (Ed.) *Identity: Personal and Socio-Cultural*, Amqvist and Wiksell International, Stockholm.

Burgess, E. (1950). 'Concluding comment.' *American Journal of Sociology*, **56**, 34.

Cooley, C. H. (1902). *Human Nature and the Social Order*, Charles Scribners, New York.

Erikson, E. (1959). 'Identity and the life cycle.' *Psychological Issues*, **1**, 1–171.

Freud, A. (1946). *The Ego and the Mechanisms of Defense*, International Universities Press, New York.

Freud, S. (1933). *New Introductory Lectures on Psycho-analysis*, Hogarth Press, London.

Handel, W. (1979). 'Normative expectations and the emergence of meanings as solutions to problems: convergence of structural and interactionist views.' *American Journal of Sociology*, **84**, 855–81.

Hosokawa, F. (1978). *The Sansei: Social Interaction and Ethnic Identification among the Third Generation Japanese*, R & E Research Associates, Inc., San Francisco.

Kuhn, M. H. (1964). 'Self and self-conception.' In J. Gould and W. L. Kolb (Eds), *A Dictionary of the Social Sciences*, Free Press of Glencoe, New York.

Mead, G. H. (1934). *Mind, Self, and Society*, University of Chicago Press, Chicago.

Shaw, C. (1930). *The Jack Roller: A Delinquent Boy's Own Story*, University of Chicago Press, Chicago.

Snow, D. and Phillips, C. (1982). 'The changing self-orientations of college students: from institution to impulse.' *Social Science Quarterly*, **63**, 462–476.

Spitzer, S., Couch, C. C. and Stratton, J. R. (1970). *The Assessment of the Self*, Davenport, Iowa: Bawden Brothers.

Stone, G. (1962). 'Appearance and the self.' In A. M. Rose (Ed.), *Human Behavior and Social Processes*, Houghton Mifflin, Boston, pp. 86–118.

Stryker, S. (1968). 'Identity salience and role performance: The relevance of symbolic interaction theory for family research.' *Journal of Marriage and the Family*, **30**, 88–92.

Super, D. E. (1951). 'Vocational adjustment: implementing a self-concept.' *Occupations*, **30**, 88–92.

Turner, R. (1957). 'The normative coherence of folk concepts.' *Research Studies of the State College of Washington*, **25**, 127–136.

Turner, R. (1962). 'Role-taking: process versus conformity.' In A. M. Rose (Ed.) *Human Behavior and Social Processes*, Houghton Mifflin, Boston, pp. 20–40.

Turner, R. (1968). 'The self-conception in social interaction.' In C. Gordon and K. Gergen (Eds), *The Self in Social Interaction*, vol. I, Wiley, New York, pp. 93–106.

Turner, R. (1976). 'The real self: from institution to impulse.' *American Journal of Sociology*, **80**, 989–1016.

Turner, R. (1978). 'The role and the person.' *American Journal of Sociology*, **84**, 1–23.

Turner, R. and Gordon, L. (1981). 'The boundaries of the self: the relationship of authenticity to inauthenticity in the self conception.' In M. Lynch, A. Norem-Heibesen, and K. Gergen (Eds), *The Self Concept: Advances in Theory and Research*, Ballinger Press, Cambridge, Massachusetts, pp. 39–57.

Turner, R. and Billings, V. (1984). 'The social contexts of self-feeling.' *International Conference on Self and Identity*, B.P.S., Cardiff.

Wells, L. E. (1978). 'Theories of deviance and the self-concept.' *Social psychology Quarterly*, **41**, 189–204.

Zurcher, Jr., L. A. (1972). The mutable self: an adaptation to accelerated social change.' *Et al*, **3**, 3–15.

Zurcher, Jr., L. A. (1977). *The Mutable Self: A Self-concept for Social Change*, Sage Publishing, Beverly Hills.

Self and Identity: Psychosocial Perspectives
Edited by K. Yardley and T. Honess
© 1987 John Wiley & Sons Ltd

11

The Structure, Content, and Dynamics of Self: Continuities in the Study of Role-Identities

George J. McCall

Most theories of a social self posit some type of reciprocity between the organization of society and the organization of self. The role-identity theory of self has proved especially successful in detailing and demonstrating such reciprocity. A variety of recent theoretical and empirical work concerning role-identities is critically reviewed to further our understanding of how it is that the organization of society may be seen in, respectively, the structure, the content, and the dynamics of self. Studies of how the dynamics of self are connected with self-structure or with self-content are viewed as particularly significant advances. Greater attention is urged concerning the neglected but critical linkage between self-structure and the content of self.

Most theories of a social self posit some type of reciprocity between the organization of society and the organization of self. The role-identity theory of self, as it emerged through the writings of several American sociologists during the late 1960s, provided a particularly clear-cut and plausible analysis of this reciprocity. The past ten years, especially, have seen further development of the theory and, more importantly, a good deal of methodological and substantive research on role-identities that goes a long way towards empirically demonstrating this reciprocity. I draw heavily on this most recent work in attempting to make more explicit how it is that the organization of society may be seen in (1) the content, (2) the structure, and (3) the dynamics of self.

An immediate complication, of course, is the fact that scholars are not in unanimous agreement concerning what is meant by 'the organization of society'. Accordingly, my analysis here will need to take account of several perspectives on the organization of society. Let me begin with the notion—fundamental to the origins of the theory—that society may be viewed as a structured network of social roles (Heiss, 1981a).

SOCIETAL ORGANIZATION AS NETWORK OF SOCIAL ROLES

Content of self

Fundamental to role-identity theory is Robert E. Park's (1926, p. 137) claim that

> Everyone is always and everywhere, more or less consciously, playing a role . . .
> It is in these roles that we know each other; it is in these roles that we know
> ourselves.

Our conceptions of ourselves are therefore role-based conceptions: *role-identities*, defined as individuals' imaginative views of themselves as they like to think of themselves being and acting as the performers of particular roles. Theory has it that a person has such a role-identity for each social role that the person performs, has performed, aspires to perform, or has considered performing. The *content* of self comprises this set of role-identities and, thus, does reflect the role-structure of society.

The key development of the past decade in this respect is Peter Burke's (1980) conceptual refinement of the notion of role-identity, emphasizing that such identities are *meanings* (specifically, the meaning of self-in-a-role) and are *relational* (contrastive meanings relative to counter-roles or counter-identities). This view implies that self-in-a-role can be placed within a multidimensional semantic space, an implication which in turn suggests the applicability of complex scaling techniques for the quantitative measurement of role-identity (Burke, 1980; Burke and Tully, 1977). Several types of role-identities have already been empirically studied through these techniques. Burke and Tully (1977) examined sex role-identities, Reitzes and Burke (1980) studied the role-identity of college students, and Mutran and Reitzes (1981) studied the old-age role-identity.

Structure of self

A person's set of role-identities is not without its own internal structure, of course, and this *structure* of self also reflects the role-structure of society in several ways.

First of all, in societies distinguishing more roles, the average *size* of the identity set of individual members will be greater (Stryker, 1980; Sieber, 1974).

Second, the *composition* of a person's set of role-identities is never a random selection from the societal role-structure but instead reflects the differential clustering and cross-linkages among roles (McCall and Simmons, 1982). In the first place, some roles are dependent on other roles of the individual (Banton, 1965). 'Basic roles', such as the age-sex role, determine one's eligibility for a great many other roles; 'general roles', such as wife or policeman, restrict one from entering into certain specifically proscribed roles that are open to others who share the same basic roles. Second, cross-pressures within and between roles engender the interpenetration of roles. Katz (1976) shows how the content of one role may intrude itself into other roles in the form of 'riders', and how extent of participation in one role may cause other roles of the person to be redelineated. Interdependent and interpenetrating roles lead to 'nested identities' (Feldman, 1979). The intrusion of content from one role into another has major consequences for the composition of the role-identity set (Turner, 1978).

Finally, society's relative valuation of roles will tend to be reflected (somewhat loosely) in the individual's *hierarchical valuation* of role-identities as more or less central to self (Turner, 1978). The hierarchical organization of role-identities has become more widely appreciated during the past decade (Heiss, 1981b; Rosenberg, 1981; Zurcher, 1983). It is then surprising that, apart from Turner's (1978) influential analysis of how and why a person may come to 'merge' with a key social role, advances in conceptualizing and measuring the hierarchical structure of identity sets have been quite modest. Worth mentioning here, however, is the use of new measures of the salience of identities in a pair of empirical studies. Stryker and Serpe (1982) employed rankings of expected situational choices among identities, and Hoelter (1983) devised semantic differential ratings of personal importance or centrality of role-identities.

Dynamics of self

I turn now to the more complex aspect of the *dynamics* of self, again taking my text from Park (1927, p. 738):

> One thing that distinguishes man . . . is the fact that he has a conception of himself, and once he has defined his role he strives to live up to it. He not only acts, but he dresses the part, assumes quite spontaneously all the manners and attitudes that he conceives as proper to it. Often enough it happens that he is not fitted to the role which he chooses to play. In any case, it is an effort for any of us to maintain the attitudes which we assume; all the more difficult when the world refuses to take us at our own estimates of ourselves.

Identity is, then, something that must be *negotiated*. In the process, as noted by Eugene Weinstein and Paul Deutschberger (1964), the individual must strike two bargains: one with the world and one with herself/himself. It is in this key dynamic of identity negotiation, then, that reciprocity—not merely as mirroring but in the deeper sense of *mutual shaping*—is to be found between self and society.

From the beginnings of role-identity theory in the early 1960s, much of the work on identity negotiation has dealt with what Rom Harré (1983) has termed 'identity projects', that is, the individual's strivings to live up to a single role-identity, considered in isolation from the rest of that person's identity set. Some of this work treats mainly the *intra*personal processes of negotiation—the bargaining with oneself—in the form of cognitive restructuring tactics. Selective perception, biased judgment, and selective memory substantially bias one's views of self (Greenwald, 1980). Recent works detailing the dynamics of confirmatory biases include Wicklund and Gollwitzer (1982) on symbolic self-completion, Markus and Sentis (1982) on self-schemata in processing information about oneself, and Matlin and Stang (1978) on the bias toward favourable evaluation of information about oneself. *Inter*personal processes within 'identity projects' have tended to emphasize the tactics of impression management, that is to say, self-consciously strategic presentation of a temporary public image of self framed in response to situational pressures (Schlenker, 1980; Snyder, 1979; Tedeschi, 1981; Jones and Pittman, 1982). More comprehensive frameworks attempt to relate more even-handedly both the intra- and the interpersonal processes of identity negotiation. For example, the work of Swann (1983, 1985) on mechanisms of self-verification and that of Schlenker (1985) on the process of self-identification attempt to relate tactics of cognitive restructuring to the individual's efforts to construct a social environment supportive of identity claims.

However, the core problem of identity negotiation is seldom that of striving to live up to a single role-identity but is instead that of striving to live up to one's structured *set* of role-identities, of managing the role strain attendant upon playing multiple roles. Indeed, this problem of managing multiple roles has received considerable attention recently among sociologists more generally, as William Goode's (1960) rather pessimistic theory of role strain has been challenged by the claims of role accumulation theory (Sieber, 1974; Marks, 1977; Thoits, 1983) that multiple roles can enhance self-development and self-fulfilment.

Several strands of theory and research on the problem of multiple identities need to be distinguished here. To begin with, the tactics of identity negotiation depend heavily on the *timeframe of negotiations* (McCall and Simmons, 1982, pp. 429–433).

1. Within the framework of a day or a specific occasion, the multiple identity problem is a matter of *managing situations*. The Weinstein tradition of research on situational tactics of identity bargaining now appears to have topped out in the work of Philip Blumstein (1973, 1975), leaving this field almost exclusively to C. Norman Alexander's equally ingenious tradition of situated identity research (best reviewed in Alexander and Wiley, 1981). Current developments in that tradition (Wiley and Alexander, this volume) are especially exciting, in that they now offer some theoretical and methodological purchase on the longer-run, cumulative effects of situation-scale identity negotiations.

2. Within a framework of months or weeks, the multiple identity problem is a matter of *managing roles*, through such classical tactics as role segregation,

role scheduling, and role bargaining, as developed in the well-known role negotiation theory of Secord and Backman (1974). More recently, Robert Broadhead (1980) has developed a comprehensive theory of multiple-identity articulation that is particularly germane to role-scale negotiations. Multiple identities must be related to one another symbolically, as well as in behaviour, within situations, and across time. Relations among identities are not objectively given; we must discover the meanings that individuals themselves assign as making up the 'symbolic calculus' among their own identities. Broadhead notes several forms this calculus may take: an enblending calculus, where the perspectives of each identity are seen as virtually identical or as evidences of one another; a utilitarian calculus, where one identity is seen as a means of expressing other, relatively separate identities; a diversionary calculus, where one identity provides an escape or a respite from another identity; or a problematic calculus, where the relationship between identities is at best partial, tentative, and continuously shifting.

3. Within a framework measured in years, the multiple identity problem is a matter of *managing careers*, that is, the acquisition, long-term development and transformation, and perhaps the eventual phasing out of role-identities. Chad Gordon (1971, 1976) has done much to illuminate these long-run negotiations of identity, a tradition continued in John R. Kelly's (1983) work on leisure identities. Pertinent here too is Louis Zurcher's (1979, 1983) refurbishment of the theory of role selection, showing how a once dominant role-identity may come to be essentially replaced, yet continue to dictate selection of a variety of ancillary roles for years to come.

Linkages among dynamics, content, and structure

In theory, of course, the dynamics, content, and structure of self are viewed not in isolation but rather as interlinked aspects of self. Further, the role-identity theory of self quite consciously seeks to ground its talk about the self in the observable realities of concrete role performances. These two characteristics of the theory are nicely exemplified in, among others, Jerold Heiss's (1981b) rather comprehensive *Social Psychology of Interaction*.

Practically speaking, however, the most productive lines of new research tend to examine the aspects of self two at a time, *as these paired aspects relate to role performance*. At the role-scale timeframe of identity negotiation, for example, three lines of tightly integrated theoretical, methodological, and substantive research currently stand out, and each of these lines deals primarily with a different pairing of self aspects, grounded in role performance.

Dynamics/content/role performance

For example, Peter Burke and his students have concentrated on the linkages among dynamics, content, and role performance. Most notably, they view

(Burke, 1980) performance as the externalization of the content, in the sense that the meanings of the behaviours in the performance are the meanings of the self in the content. This approach is developed and applied (Burke and Reitzes, 1981) by empirically locating role-identities and role behaviours in the same semantic space; 'the link between identity and performance lies in the process of assessing each *on the same dimensions of meaning*' (p. 90). This linkage of content and role performance is so engagingly novel that the connection of each with the dynamics of identity negotiation—though clearly diagrammed in Burke's (1980) model—has been almost overlooked in many scholarly discussions.

Dynamics/structure/role performance

The group associated with Sheldon Stryker is most concerned with the links from dynamics to structure to role performance, as mapped out in Stryker (1980): 'commitment [that is, premising one's interpersonal relations upon an identity] leads to identity salience leads to role performance.' That hypothesized sequence of influences found substantial empirical support in a study of religious roles by Stryker and Serpe (1982). Peggy Thoits (1983) examined essentially the same pathway in her empirical research on multiple identities and well-being. The reverse influences, of role performance on structure and of structure on dynamics, receive discussion in Stryker (this volume). Hoelter (1983) empirically examined structure (identity salience) as a consequence of both dynamics (commitment) and role performance, finding that positive evaluation of role performance at least equalled the influence of network commitment.

Structure/content/role performance

The group associated with Ralph H. Turner is especially interested in the linkages among structure, content, and role performance. I have already noted Turner's (1978) continuing advances in identifying the effects of the composition and the hierarchical structure of the identity set upon (1) the content and (2) the performance of lower ranking role-identities. Although Turner has viewed the hierarchical structure of self as reflecting which roles seem to the individual to be more characteristic of herself, empirical data have led Turner (1976) and Zurcher (1977) to question the extent to which roles are in fact the anchors of the sense of self. Turner and Schutte (1981) developed measurement techniques suited to exploring this question of anchorage. Turner and Gordon (1981) review empirical results from these measurement techniques in considering variations in how individuals delineate the boundaries between authentic and spurious self anchorages. The current working views of this group are cogently set forth in Turner (this volume).

SOCIETAL ORGANIZATION AS NETWORK OF SOCIAL
RELATIONSHIPS

Obviously, not all students of society are content to equate societal organization to any network of social roles. What changes might be necessary in the
foregoing analysis of the reciprocities between self and society under some
alternative view of societal organization?

Suppose, for instance, we view the organization of society as a structured
network of social relationships (Holland and Leinhardt, 1979). Such a 'social
network' vision of society has rapidly gained ground among contemporary
students of social organization, in part because this view of social structure
facilitates application of formal techniques of analysis which require no
cultural or subjective data concerning role expectations.

Social roles give way, in this vision, to structural roles, defined by patterns
of interpersonal ties (White *et al.*, 1976). Many of these structural roles are
apparent and sensible to the individuals who perform them and, thus (quite
like social roles) provide a basis for self-identification, that is, for role-
identities. In just such a vein, Stryker (this volume) defines identities as
'internalized role designations corresponding to the social locations of persons
in their various networks of interaction'.

Conceptions of self thus remain role-based conceptions, despite the different sense of 'role'; the content of self therefore still reflects societal organization. The propositions mentioned above regarding the size, composition, and
hierarchical organization of a person's identity set continue to hold under the
revised sense of 'role'; thus the structure of self also may be said to reflect
societal organization.

It is, rather, the analysis of the dynamics of self that is affected by the
alternative vision of societal organization. How must we construe the negotiation of identity, if we now view society as a structured network of social
relationships?

Role-identity theory has, from the beginning, accorded close primary
relationships a unique influence in the formation and nurturance of role-
identities (compare Gergen, this volume). In fact, as Carl Backman (1983)
shows us, identities and a primary relationship are twin products of sustained
(role-scale, often even career-scale) identity negotiations between two persons. (Conversely, Duck and Lea, 1983, show how the breakdown of such a
relationship distinctively threatens these identities.) Drawing heavily upon
critical theory, Secord (1982) delineates a deep reciprocity between the
dynamics of dyadic negotiations of a role-identity and the macro-realities of
the institutional realm.

Yet, just as examination of multiple identities is more strategic than
examination of a single identity, so the dynamics of multiple relationships are
more strategic than those of any single relationship. That is to say, the
negotiations of identity take place between the individual and her entire
network of relationships (McCall, 1982, pp. 212–213):

As Simmel noted, the focal individual appears differently to—indeed, *is* different with—each of the persons in the network; the individual presents a somewhat different *persona* to each of these others. A personal relationship holds not between two persons but between two personas, and its nature (flowing from the fit between these personas) will therefore never be fully comprehended by any of the other persons in the network. Each of these persons serves as a differently distorted looking-glass, reflecting a somewhat different image of the focal individual . . . A person's self-conception then depends not only upon the character of each of his or her relationships but also upon the *social organization* of the personal network; that is, the organization of his or her various personas into an integrated self-conception mirrors the organization of the personal network . . .

[This in turn will] depend upon one's skill and efforts in *cultivating* this network. Passive exploitation of the fruits of the interpersonal environment rapidly depletes resources, while active cultivation—the skillful and caring investment of self in managing the demands and opportunities of the various relationships—may conserve, maintain, or even enrich these resources. One's network, then, represents a 'personal economy' of relationships to be managed more or less effectively.

However, it is in the works of Sheldon Stryker that the significance for self of such negotiations with the network of relationships is most sharply developed. Not only does he define identities in terms of these networks, but he also suggests (Stryker, 1980) that the place of a role-identity within the hierarchical structure of self is conditioned primarily by the extent to which one's existing network of relationships is premised on that particular identity. That proposition concerning the network-embeddedness of role-identities has received empirical support in the findings of Stryker and Serpe (1982) and, more complexly, in those of Hoelter (1983). More recently, Stryker (this volume) has reintroduced the 'intensiveness' (affective involvement) of network-embeddedness as a somewhat independent dimension of commitment affecting the place of an identity in the hierarchical structure of self.

SOCIETAL ORGANIZATION AS NETWORK OF ORGANIZATIONS

Another challenge to role-identity theory's analysis of the reciprocities of self and society is posed by yet a third view of societal organization, that society may be seen as a structured network of organizations (Aldrich, 1979). This view, too, is an increasingly popular one among contemporary students of social organization, as the topic of inter-organizational relations has assumed considerable centrality in the field. In fact, this third view can be considered (Aldrich, 1982) to incorporate, as a special case, everything in the second (network of social relationships) view, since (a) each dyadic relationship is itself an organization and (b) the network of relationships therefore amounts to the pattern of inter-organizational relations among the constituent dyads. An important advantage of the network of organizations view is that it applies to the inter-organizational relations not only of similar sized organizations but also those of greatly disparate organizations.

Similarly, the network of organizations view might even be said to subsume, also, most of what is contained in the first (network of social roles) view. To the extent that social roles are incorporated into an organizational setting, role differentiation tends to become grounded in organizational goals and tends to link roles to positions within the organization (Turner, 1968). That is to say, social roles then tend to become organizational roles.

Once again, then, a new sense of 'role' is entailed by a differing view of societal organization. Again also, this sense of 'role' is readily accommodated by role-identity theory, so that no real changes are necessitated in the analysis of how the content and the structure of self reflect the organization of society.

It is our understanding of the dynamics of self that is most affected by the shift of attention to 'organizational roles'. When social roles have become organizational roles, the negotiations of role-identity must take place principally between the individual and the organization.

The nature of the individual's organizational role is developed through the operation of certain organizational processes (McCall and Simmons, 1982). Recruitment and socialization jointly determine the individual's prescribed role, which in turn influences the interaction process that determines his or her performed role. Role performance always involves the individual in the innovation process, as a creative or deviant performer, and this process in turn involves him or her in the social control process, in which creativity is rewarded and deviance is punished. This role-making/career development system also exhibits a variety of complex feedback connections among these basic organizational processes, as one might anticipate.

A more important feature for present purposes is that the character of each of these processes is jointly affected by the character of the individual and that of the organization. The operation of such organizational processes could hardly be unaffected by the interests, resources, and tactics of the individuals and of the organization. How these negotiations are carried on differently within a very wide range of organizational sizes and types is detailed within the main text of McCall and Simmons (1982).

Once again, however, it is the problem of multiple identities that is most strategic for theory. If society is a loosely coupled, mildly hierarchical network of all sorts of organizations, for example, communities, associations, groups, polities, economies; then it is obvious that the individual plays some sort of manifest role with respect to quite a number of specific and concrete organizations. The concluding part of McCall and Simmons (1982) suggests that the individual negotiates identity with the entire *network* of organizations, through the dynamic process of 'logistics', that is, the balancing and creative managing of the interests and capacities of both individuals and organizations. Numerous organizations jockey and compete for the energies and compliance of the same individual, and the tactics of all concerned are constrained by the existing inter-organizational relations. This joint process of logistical bargaining thus shapes the individual's overall *pattern of roles*.

One's overall pattern of roles is, of course, a most powerful influence on both the structure and the content of one's set of role-identities. Less obvious, perhaps, is how these individual patterns of roles affect the shape of the inter-organizational network that is society. Just as individuals' roles within one particular organization (for example, a university) are constitutive of that social organization, so their respective overall patterns of roles are constitutive of the inter-organizational network. The deep reciprocity of influence— of mutual shaping—between self and society is thus to be found within the joint process of logistical bargaining over multiple organizational roles.

CONCLUSIONS

In this chapter, I have tried to explicate more sharply the reciprocity between the organization of society and the organization of self that is claimed by the role-identity theory of self. First, I have tried to make clear that there are two relevant senses of reciprocity here—reflection, and mutual shaping—both of which apply. Second, I have tried to specify each of these reciprocities, by distinguishing several aspects of self in which they may be seen. The content and the structure of self tend to reflect societal organization; it is in the dynamics of self (that is, negotiating identities) that the mutual shaping of self and society is to be observed. Finally, I have tried to examine how the form of these reciprocities may vary depending on one's conception of the organization of society. The three conceptions reviewed here each entail a variant sense of 'role', all of which senses can be accommodated by role-identity theory. The ways in which societal organization is reflected in the content and the structure of self are little affected by these alternative conceptions. The forms that mutual shaping takes are, however, more clearly dependent on choice of conception. Each sense of 'role' implies a different arena and a different focus of identity negotiation.

REFERENCES

Aldrich, H. E. (1979). *Organizations and Environments*, Prentice-Hall, Englewood Cliffs, New Jersey.

Aldrich, H. E. (1982). 'The origins and persistence of social networks: A comment.' In P. V. Marsden and N. Lin (Eds), *Social Structure and Network Analysis*, Sage Publications, Beverly Hills, California, pp. 281–293.

Alexander, C. N. and Wiley, M. G. (1981). 'Situated activity and identity formation.' In M. Rosenberg and R. H. Turner (Eds), *Social Psychology: Sociological Perspectives*, Basic Books, New York, pp. 269–289.

Backman, C. W. (1983). 'Toward an interdisciplinary social psychology.' *Advances in Experimental Social Psychology*, **16**, 220–261.

Banton, M. P. (1965). *Roles: An Introduction to the Study of Social Relations*, Basic Books, New York.

Blumstein, P. W. (1973). 'Audience, Machiavellianism, and tactics of identity bargaining.' *Sociometry*, **36**, 346–365.

Blumstein, P. W. (1975). 'Identity bargaining and self-conception.' *Social Forces*, **53**, 476–485.

Broadhead, R. S. (1980). 'Multiple identities and the process of their articulation: The case of medical students and their private lives,' *Studies in Symbolic Interaction*, 3, 171–191.

Burke, P. J. (1980). 'The self: Measurement implications from a symbolic interactionist perspective.' *Social Psychology Quarterly*, **43**, 18–29.

Burke, P. J. and Reitzes, D. C. (1981). 'The link between identity and role performance.' *Social Psychology Quarterly*, **44**, 83–92.

Burke, P. J. and Tully, J. (1977). 'The measurement of role identity.' *Social Forces*, **55**, 881–897.

Duck, S. and Lea, M. (1983). 'Breakdown of personal relationships and the threat to personal identity.' In G. Breakwell (Ed.), *Threatened Identities*, Wiley, New York, pp. 53–73.

Feldman, S. D. (1979). 'Nested identities.' *Studies in Symbolic Interaction*, 2, 399–418.

Goode, W. J. (1960). 'A theory of role strain.' *American Sociological Review*, **25**, 483–496.

Gordon, C. (1971). 'Role and value development across the life cycle.' In J. W. Jackson (Ed.), *Role*, Cambridge University Press, Cambridge, pp. 65–105.

Gordon, C. (1976). 'Development of evaluated role identities.' *Annual Review of Sociology*, 2, 405–433.

Greenwald, A. G. (1980). 'The totalitarian ego: Fabrication and revision of personal history.' *American Psychologist*, **35**, 603–618.

Harré, R. (1983). 'Identity projects.' In G. Breakwell (Ed.), *Threatened Identities*, Wiley, New York, pp. 31–51.

Heiss, J. (1981a). 'Social roles.' In M. Rosenberg and R. H. Turner (Eds), *Social Psychology: Sociological Perspectives*, Basic Books, New York, pp. 94–129.

Heiss, J. (1981b). *The Social Psychology of Interaction*, Prentice-Hall, Englewood Cliffs, New Jersey.

Hoelter, J. W. (1983). 'The effects of role evaluation and commitment on identity salience.' *Social Psychology Quarterly*, **46**, 140–147.

Holland, P. W. and Leinhardt, S. (1979). *Perspectives on Social Network Research*, Academic Press, New York.

Jones, E. E. and Pittman, T. S. (1982). 'Toward a general theory of strategic self-presentation.' In J. Suls (Ed.), *Psychological Perspectives on the Self*, vol. 1, Erlbaum, Hillsdale, New Jersey, pp. 231–262.

Katz, F. E. (1976). *Structuralism in Sociology*, State University of New York Press, Albany.

Kelly, J. R. (1983). *Leisure Identities and Interactions*, Allen and Unwin, London.

McCall, G. J. (1982). 'Becoming unrelated: The management of bond dissolution.' In S. Duck (Ed.), *Personal Relationships 4: Dissolving Personal Relationships*, Academic Press, New York, pp. 211–231.

McCall, G. J. and Simmons, J. L. (1982). *Social Psychology: A Sociological Approach*, Free Press, New York.

Marks, S. R. (1977). 'Multiple roles and role strain: Some notes on human energy, time and commitment.' *American Sociological Review*, **42**, 921–936.

Markus, H. and Sentis, K. (1982). 'The self in social information processing.' In J. Suls (Ed.), *Psychological Perspectives on the Self*, vol. 1, Erlbaum, Hillsdale, New Jersey, pp. 41–70.

Matlin, M. W. and Stang, D. J. (1978). *The Pollyanna Principle: Selectivity in Language, Memory, and Thought*, Schenkman, Cambridge, Massachusetts.

Mutran, E. and Reitzes, D. C. (1981). 'Retirement, identity and well-being: Realignment of role relationships.' *Journal of Gerontology*, **36**, 733–740.
Park, R. E. (1926). 'Behind our masks.' *Survey*, **56**, 135–139.
Park, R. E. (1927). 'Human nature and collective behaviour.' *American Journal of Sociology*, **32**, 733–741.
Reitzes, D. C. and Burke, P. J. (1980). 'College student identity: Measurement and implications.' *Pacific Sociological Review*, **23**, 46–66.
Rosenberg, M. (1981). 'The self-concept: Social product and social force.' In M. Rosenberg and R. H. Turner (Eds), *Social Psychology: Sociological Perspectives*, Basic Books, New York, pp. 593–624.
Schlenker, B. R. (1980). *Impression Management: The Self-Concept, Social Identity, and Interpersonal Relations*, Brooks/Cole, Monterey, California.
Schlenker, B. R. (1985). 'Identity and self-identification.' In B. R. Schlenker (Ed.), *The Self and Social Life*, McGraw-Hill, New York, pp. 65–99.
Secord, P. F. (1982). 'The origin and maintenance of social roles: the case of sex roles.' In W. Ickes and E. S. Knowles (Eds), *Personality, Roles, and Social Behaviour*, Springer-Verlag, New York, pp. 33–53.
Secord, P. F. and Backman, C. W. (1974). *Social Psychology*, 2nd edn, McGraw-Hill, New York.
Sieber, S. D. (1974). 'Toward a theory of role accumulation.' *American Sociological Review*, **39**, 567–578.
Snyder, M. (1979). 'Self-monitoring processes.' *Advances in Experimental Social Psychology*, **12**, 86–128.
Stryker, S. (1980). *Symbolic Interactionism: A Social Structural Version*, Benjamin/ Cummings, Menlo Park, California.
Stryker, S. and Serpe, R. T. (1982). 'Commitment, identity salience, and role behaviour: theory and research example.' In W. Ickes and E. S. Knowles (Eds), *Personality, Roles, and Social Behaviour*, Springer-Verlag, New York, pp. 199–218.
Swann, W. B., Jr. (1983). 'Self-verification: Bringing social reality into harmony with the self.' In J. Suls and A. G. Greenwald (Eds), *Perspectives on the Self*, vol. 2, Erlbaum, Hillsdale, New Jersey, pp. 199–218.
Swann, W. B., Jr. (1985). 'The self as architect of social reality.' In B. R. Schlenker (Ed.), *The Self and Social Life*, McGraw-Hill, New York, pp. 100–125.
Tedeschi, J. T. (1981). *Impression Management Theory and Social Psychological Research*, Academic Press, New York.
Thoits, P. A. (1983). 'Multiple identities and psychological well-being: a reformulation and test of the social isolation hypothesis.' *American Sociological Review*, **48**, 174–187.
Turner, R. H. (1968). 'Role: Sociological aspects.' In D. L. Sills, (Ed.), *International Encyclopedia of the Social Sciences*, Crowell Collier and Macmillan, New York, pp. 552–557.
Turner, R. H. (1976). 'The real self: From institution to impulse.' *American Journal of Sociology*, **81**, 989–1016.
Turner, R. H. (1978). 'The role and the person.' *American Journal of Sociology*, **84**, 1–23.
Turner, R. H. and Gordon, S. (1981). 'The boundaries of the self: The relationship of authenticity in the self-conception.' In M. D. Lynch, A. A. Norem-Hebeisen, and K. J. Gergen (Eds), *Self-Concept: Advances in Theory and Research*, Ballinger, Cambridge, Massachusetts, pp. 39–57.
Turner, R. H. and Schutte, J. (1981). 'The true-self method for studying the self-conception.' *Symbolic Interaction*, **4**, 1–20.
Weinstein, E. A., and Deutschberger, P. (1964). 'Tasks, bargains, and identities in social interaction.' *Social Forces*, **42**, 451–456.

White, H. C., Boorman, S. A. and Breiger, R. L. (1976). 'Social structure from multiple networks. I. Blockmodels of roles and positions.' *American Journal of Sociology*, **81**, 730–780.

Wicklund, R. A. and Gollwitzer, P. M. (1982). *Symbolic Self-Completion*, Erlbaum, Hillsdale, New Jersey.

Zurcher, L. A., Jr. (1977). *The Mutable Self*, Sage Publications, Beverly Hills, California.

Zurcher, L. A., Jr. (1979). 'Role selection: The influence of internalized vocabularies of motive.' *Symbolic Interaction*, **2**, 45–62.

Zurcher, L. A., Jr. (1983). *Social Roles*, Sage Publications, Beverly Hills, California.

Section III
Cognitive, Affective, and Contextual Aspects of Self

Self and Identity: Psychosocial Perspectives
Edited by K. Yardley and T. Honess
© 1987 John Wiley & Sons Ltd

12

Cognitive, Affective, and Contextual Aspects of Self: An Introductory Review

Terry Honess and Krysia Yardley

In recent years 'social cognition' has become a central feature of the study of social psychology, especially in North America and the United Kingdom. The key tenets of this approach are that the person must be seen as an active processor of information and that social behaviour is therefore largely the product of individual decision-making. This processing is seen to depend on one's prior expectations and standards of comparison, and to serve the function of guiding immediate and future courses of action. Thus, social cognitive psychologists are concerned with examining the different stages of a processing sequence, where affect might be seen to interfere with rational decision-making, but where bias is also acknowledged through the need of the person to simplify input and minimize inconsistencies (the introductory texts of Eiser, 1980, and Fiske and Taylor, 1985, provide an overview of this kind of work).

Within this broad tradition, there is a strong and active group of researchers who see the 'self' as far and away the most important information processing structure, or memory system, and have therefore developed concepts such as 'self schema', 'self monitoring', 'private vs public' self-awareness, and so on (examples are to be found in the edited text of Wegner and Vallacher, 1980). Several of the contributors to this section can be readily identified with this tradition, but they provide significant developments. First, Markus and Nurius discuss the importance of taking account of our often vivid and highly particular 'possible selves' in order to understand the motivation that relates to our current cognitive strategies. Second, Higgins, Klein, and Strauman sustain the well-established emphasis on the individual's discomfort with different self views, but importantly demonstrate quite different emotional outcomes for different types of inconsistency. Arkin, the third contributor, draws attention to the tension between the extensively researched 'self-serving bias' and the overriding need for some individuals to obscure feedback in order to avoid social disapproval.

Other contributors (Anderson, Yardley) address the dangers of decontextualizing the individual, in both the personal and cultural senses. Figurski and

Yardley provide details of important methods that allow empirical exploration of the oft repeated, but rarely realized, conceptual concern with the
process and experience of various self states. One constant theme of this
section, then, is the breaking away from the mechanism evident in an
exclusively 'information processing' perspective, and the related assumption
that affect cannot merely be seen as a disruptive phenomena that 'interferes'
with rational decision-making.

The primacy of emotion and motivation in these analyses brings researchers
must closer to the hitherto largely philosophical debate which is summarized
by Toulmin (1977) as 'not to speculate about concealed mechanisms, but
rather to elucidate confused motivations'. Before proceeding to a detailed
consideration of the different contributions to this section, it will be useful to
rehearse aspects of this philosophical debate. One important argument is that
the knowledge involved in knowing persons can be of a different kind to that
involved in knowing objects (see Hamlyn, 1974, for the general position and
Taylor, 1977, and Honess, 1986, for an elaboration of these arguments in the
context of self-knowledge). Thus, there is, on the one hand, a form of
knowledge that involves a concern with expectations *about* phenomena in
which predictions concerning the inanimate world ('that table is about to
collapse'), other persons ('she is about to collapse') or, indeed, ourselves ('I
am not about to collapse') are all accorded the same status. On the other
hand, we also think in terms of our expectations *of* others and ourselves.
Here, failure of a prediction is not mere falsification of a hypothesis but
involves disappointed hopes, e.g., 'letting oneself down', and betrayed trusts,
e.g., 'I tried so hard with her and look what happened'. Markus and Nurius
also make this point when they say that the self-concept is not just the
integration of past and present actions, but is a claim of *responsibility* for
future behaviour in a particular domain.

It is to Markus and Nurius that we now turn, and to their treatment of
possible selves, which are regarded as the cognitive manifestations of *enduring* aspirations and motives, they are 'the interface between motivation and
the self-concept'. Moreover, such 'selves' are not represented in abstract,
impersonal structures, but rather as vivid possibilities of what we hope and
fear. Where such possible selves involve high levels of commitment and
investment, they qualify as self-schemas (although more transient anticipated
selves could also be understood in terms of schemata as is the case with Wiley
and Alexander's 'situated identities'). Possible selves are therefore seen as
part of the system of self-schemas that make up the self-concept. There are
clear resonances here with the perspective of Stryker as well as that of Wiley
and Alexander (viz., our commentary on Gergen's paper noting the closeness
of current interactionist thinking to psychology's cognitive orientation). For
example, like Stryker, Markus and Nurius recognize structural constraints on
the possibilities for action, yet when choice is possible, people's possible
selves (see Stryker's salience hierarchies) operate as 'blueprints' for action.

Markus and Nurius stress that different aspects of the self-concept vary in the degree of their accessibility, thus at any given moment the 'working self-concept' depends on the contents of the antecedent self-concept and those cognitions that are activated by immediate circumstances. Here, they are close to Wiley and Alexander (this volume) on situated identities, but there are important differences. The latter stress the *situated* nature of action (constrained by the actor's belief that it is being monitored). Markus and Nurius have a different emphasis through the addition of a third component for the working self-concept: 'those self-conceptions that have been *wilfully* invoked by the person in response to current experience'. Here they bring to the fore an agentic dimension which fully implicates a responsibility that is individually located. Thus, when they say that 'significant behaviour is in the service of meeting and resolving . . . identity tasks', and 'the possible self that puts the self into action', they are close to philosophers such as Taylor (1977). The latter argues that 'a self decides and acts out certain fundamental evaluations', that is, identity is defined by certain evaluations which are inseparable from ourselves as agents.

Consistent with a broad cognitive perspective, Markus and Nurius note that they are only concerned with information about self that is available to consciousness or working memory, but do acknowledge the existence of unconscious desires. It is possible that future developments of their theory will need to include the latter to accommodate 'self-deception', and the reasons for acting in 'bad faith'. A more immediate problem may be their stress on 'wilful' acts, which is also consistent with the cognitivist's emphasis on decisions determining action. There are, for example, powerful arguments (e.g., Hamlyn, introduced in Markova's contribution to this volume) that self-knowledge does not necessarily develop by bringing more activities under intentional control (although this would certainly amplify our beliefs about ourselves). Thus, Hamlyn (1977) suggests that 'we can be said to know in the doing, we do not have to watch ourselves to get this kind of knowledge' (Markova, this volume, offers one solution to this problem).

In developing their important theoretical thesis, Markus and Nurius also provide a broad range of empirical support for their propositions. Both empirical and conceptual implications are nicely summarized in their observation that 'thoughts about what is possible allow the individual to develop a narrative of the self, to construct a self that is different from the present one' (cf. the similar perspective offered by G. H. Mead, again emphasizing the commonalities between interactionists and cognitive psychologists).

As noted above, Higgins, Klein, and Strauman are clearly within the cognitive tradition in that the person is seen to be motivated by perceived discrepancies in cognitions (the 'consistency seeker'). Moreover, they accept that affect follows the (cognitive) recognition and interpretation of such discrepancies which is also consistent with cognitivist assumptions. The important advance of 'self-discrepancy theory' is the recognition of the varieties of possible discrepancies concerning one's self-concept. In addition, Higgins, Klein, and Strauman provide generally compelling evidence that different affective consequences follow. However, an alternative interpretation to their cause-effect model might be noted, that is, that they offer conceptual clarification of the way in which we are taught to organize our emotions (cf. Gergen, this volume).

They distinguish three domains of self: perceptions of 'actual' attributes, 'ideal' attributes, and attributes that one 'ought' to possess. These domains are reflected upon from two different standpoints: one's own or that of particular others, this 3 × 2 array yielding six basic types of 'self-state representations'. Theoretically, discrepancies could presumably occur between any pair, or within any cluster of these self-state representations. However, Higgins, Klein, and Strauman identify three broad areas of potential discrepancy. First, between 'actual' attributes and external behavioural feedback from self (e.g., 'I'm honest, but acting deceitfully', which, incidentally, the subject might seek to overcome by invoking possible selves, see Markus and Nurius), or feedback from other ('she treats me as untrustworthy'). Although Higgins, Klein, and Strauman note that persons seek to obtain responses that verify their own position. Second, there are possible contradictions within the 'actual' domain (own or other standpoints) that would impede coherence. Third, there are potential discrepancies between 'actual' attributions and, on the one hand, 'ought' attributions, and on the other, 'ideal' attributions, and it is to this third group that Higgins, Klein, and Strauman give most attention.

Actual (own) vs Ideal (own or other) discrepancies are demonstrated to engender *dejection*-related emotions and Actual (own) vs Ideal (own or other) discrepancies are demonstrated to engender *agitation*-related emotions. Chronic discrepancies of either type may result in a clinically diagnosed disorder (cf. Arkin, this volume, on shyness; Pyszczynski and Greenberg, this volume, and their analysis of depression; and Mollon, this volume, on guilt and shame). The more common, transitory discrepancies (based on momentary evaluative feedback) are also considered by Higgins, Klein, and Strauman, and complement our preceeding discussion of 'situated identities'. The stimulating articulation of the complexity of this field provided by Higgins, Klein, and Strauman is given a further twist by Arkin, the next contributor to this section.

Arkin is one of a number of cognitive self psychologists who particularly focus on the process of strategic self-presentation, the establishment of identities through control of the various images of self that are made available to others (e.g., the review of Jones and Pittman, 1982). This orientation has much in common with the 'situated identities' argument of Wiley and Alexander, and the 'working self-concept' of Markus and Nurius. It also shares many of the assumptions of the work of Goffman (e.g., 1957), especially with regard to what is now called the 'acquisitive' self that seeks the most favourable image possible. However, Arkin argues that this is not a universal motivation, rather, that there are a significant number of us (the 'shy') for whom protectionism is paramount. For such people, 'disapproval must be a compelling experience; it would confirm self-doubts and damage an already precarious sense of self worth'. The individual is seen as actively engaged in this protective stance, e.g., through seeking out a publicly acknowledged handicap for a particular task in order to obscure the link between performance and evaluation.

The role of distorted or obscured feedback in his analysis is specially interesting since it readily allows an integration with the work of other contributors to this volume. For Markus and Nurius the chronically shy individual would be one dominated by negative possible selves that have become relatively impervious to change, and these authors describe various strategies for restructuring positive possible selves into the working self-concept. Similarly, the important role of evaluation (by self or other) in the various domains of self posited by Higgins *et al.*, would be severely limited in its potential as a positive motivator for change.

In briefly discussing the aetiology of relatively chronic self-doubt, Arkin hints at a developmental scenario that is entirely consistent with the 'self' psychoanalytic literature introduced in Section 2 of this volume. Another important clinical source is the work of Sullivan (1953), who, like Arkin, stresses the tension between positive development and the need to protect against anxiety through what Sullivan calls 'security operations'. Thus, the 'self-system' is 'the principle influence that stands in the way of unfavourable changes, yet it is the principle stumbling block to change'. In summary, then, Arkin has emphasized an important *dynamic* element in the Machiavallian picture of acquisitiveness, that is the need to protect, as well as to enhance one's self-system.

The next contribution to this section is that of Figurski who, like Higgins *et al.*, distinguishes different perspectives that are employed in attending to different targets. Figurski introduces the 'allocentric' perspective, either taking the (real or imagined) other's view on oneself, resulting in a focus on one's self image or, taking the other's view of the other's experience, resulting in an empathic identification. The 'allocentric' perspective then is 'outside' of self and is contrasted with the more familiar 'egocentric' perspective, which results in either a focus on one's own experiences or a focus on the image of the other. It can be seen that Figurski emphasizes the person's own interpretations more than Higgins *et al.*; the latter, as we have seen, are more concerned to distinguish different domains of self (actual, ideal, and ought) and, of course, the impact of discrepancies.

Figurski's concern with experience is translated into his using a technique designed to sample mundane, moment-to-moment levels of awareness and into his using questions that seek to minimize pre-empting the respondent's form of answering. This is important since much of the experimental literature in the general area of social cognition, including self studies, is dominated by simple questionnaire methods, notwithstanding the conceptual concern with process and experience. Although the overall levels of self and other awareness reported in his study may be inflated, as Figurski himself acknowledges, there are two important findings. First, persons appear to typically employ different perspectives, with different foci, at the same time. Hence to think of persons generally being enmeshed in one mode ('private' or 'public', for example) would not be a good representation of everyday life. However, second, Figurski reports interesting individual differences: some respondants appear to regularly use both the 'allocentric' and 'egocentric' modes. In contrast, other respondants primarily work in the 'egocentric' mode alone, i.e., by focusing only on 'self-experience' and 'other image'.

This second finding leads Figurski to speculate that the allocentric and the egocentric systems of awareness may develop independently. Moreover, that the capacity to take the other's perspective, allocentrism, involves the conjoint development of empathic identification (focus on other's experience) and objective self awareness (focus on one's own 'self-image'). Indirect, but fascinating support for this proposition comes from the psychoanalytic work described in this volume. Thus, Mollon (see also Price, in press, for a more detailed account) discusses how those especially prone to self-consciousness (viz., Figurski's 'objective self-awareness') have typically experienced a mothering one who required the child to function as an extension of herself, resulting in the child having too great a preoccupation with the *other's* experience. Mollon's suggestion that such a preoccupation may result in a pathological self-consciousness, ties the two 'allocentric' possibilities together, as postulated by Figurski.

Although Figurski seeks to explore respondant's mundane states of awareness, even with his technique, respondants are asked to break the flow of their ordinary activity, to reflect back upon an earlier activity, in order to answer the investigator's questions. They are being asked to provide what Shotter (1984) calls an 'account'. To give an account involves stepping out of the 'flow' of mundane activity to provide reasons, justifications, and commentaries on such activity. Shotter contrasts this with 'accounting', which keeps the person 'within' the flow of ordinary activity, that is, elucidating what has been done (and what is likely to happen next) by some further activity that is unlikely to implicate conscious reflection on the preceeding activity or, more concretely, would not stem from some preplanned experimenter intervention.

The methodological developments offered by Yardley, the next contributor to this section, suggest one solution to this problem through her use of role play, in which participants are imaginatively engaged, are re-situated, in different contexts. Thus, she reports that the most salient category of response to a 'Who Are You?' probe in an imaginatively involved situation, is 'self in experiential state/mode of being', e.g., 'I'm feeling desolate at this moment', suggesting a form of account*ing*. Indeed, the distinction between an account demanded (Who are you?) and accounting in flow (typically a description of 'ongoing events') becomes especially clear in that the W.A.Y.? demand was felt by some respondents to be intrusive and disruptive of flow.

The forgoing reflects Yardley's more general concern to see methodological developments keep pace with conceptual concerns, particularly as these relate to experimenters' wishes to explore and explain their participants' self-experiences. Her position is amply reinforced by her demonstration of the intimate connections between respondents' interpretations of the experimental situation, and the form and content of their responses. Consideration of researchers' use of the 'Who are You?' question allows a more general discussion of this issue. The conceptual and methodological roots of this probe lie with the more cognitive interpretations of the interactionist tradition, especially the work of Kuhn (see Self and Social Structure section, this volume). However, it is ironic, as Yardley notes, that one of the central tenets of interactionism (especially that encouraged by Blumer), i.e., meaning is an emergent quality and one that is highly context bound, was ignored for all practical purposes in this early work, and in its later derivatives.

Yardley's solution is to go 'inside' the interview, to accept that the 'self' is at least partly a situational construction (cf. Gergen, this volume), which requires that the interview itself must be assessed with respect to its status as a 'context of asking'. Thus, the necessarily situated nature of the 'self concept' can be properly taken into account. Consider, for example, Yardley's request that her respondents name a situation in which they 'feel most free to be themselves'. A substantial minority of respondents chose a situation with an intimate other. Such subjects appear to have elected to trust the interviewer as they would trust their friends or spouses. However, for others, the choice of say a family context held unforseen consequences in that the initial choice became increasingly uncomfortable as participants begin to detail what was actually going on within such groupings.

Finally, there was a significant group of respondents who selected contexts in which they were alone. One man chose playing the organ alone at night. He described this situation as so engrossing that thoughts were not possible, let alone words and answers. Indeed, this man felt the interview was like having an argument with his wife where he was asked to answer impossible questions. However, given the interactionist tenet stressing the 'situated' nature of identity (see Stryker, and Wiley and Alexander, this volume, and our comments, above, on the working self-concept of Markus and Nurius) one should not be surprised that detailing particular situations might 'call out' particular identities in which an individual feels, for example, distinctly trapped.

Whereas Yardley reminds us of the importance of the personal frame for interpreting self experience, Andersen, the final contributor of this section, asserts the importance of the cultural frame for understanding the form and content of our self experiences. In this sense, her position is similar to the social constructivist account introduced in the first section of this volume, however, her argument stems primarily from a consideration of experimental work in social cognition. She first notes an intriguing paradox, i.e., in spite of the high premium placed on rationality and intentional control in the West, those aspects of ourselves that are felt to be *beyond* our control are seen to be more accurate reflectors of our 'true' selves (a similar argument is advanced by Turner, this volume). It appears, therefore, that common-sense understanding of much of our public behaviour acknowledges the 'staged' aspects of such behaviour (cf. the social cognitivists use of the *Machiavellian* metaphor). Directly related to this (culturally grounded) understanding is the high value that we place on exclusivity, privacy, and the importance of distinctiveness from others.

Andersen's arguments are amply supported by reference to her own experimental work and that of other social cognition researchers. For example, she shows how even apparently public sources of information about the self are, in fact, privately appropriated. Thus it is the individual who selects and interprets available public information, selects others for comparison and, moreover, gives greater weight to his or her own covert reactions and feelings rather than his or her public behaviour. Thus, in the same way that we see other's 'off-guard' reactions as specially revealing, we, in the West, perceive our own thoughts and feelings as relatively distinctive in comparison to others. This is the case even though Andersen provides evidence to suggest that such covert reactions are not necessarily more distinctive that overt reactions. In essence, then, her thesis is that the form of 'self-maintenance' processes studied by psychologists in the West is culturally embedded and could therefore be otherwise (although she does not specify under what circumstances, if any, the concept of self would become untenable). In her view, then, much of the activity of social psychologists might readily be construed as a form of social anthropology.

REFERENCES

Eiser, J. R. (1980). *Cognitive Social Psychology*, McGraw-Hill, London.

Fiske, S. T. and Taylor, S. E. (1985). *Social Cognition*, Addison-Wesley, Reading, Massachusetts.

Goffman, E. (1957). *The Presentation of Self in Everyday Life*, Anchor Books, New York.

Hamlyn, D. (1974). 'Person-perception and our perception of others.' In T. Mischel (Ed.), *Understanding Other Persons*, Blackwell, Oxford.

Hamlyn, D. (1977). 'Self-knowledge.' In T. Mischel (Ed.), *The Self: Psychological and Philosophical Issues*, Blackwell, Oxford.

Honess, T. (1986). 'Mirroring and social metacognition.' In C. Antaki and A. Lewis (Eds), *Mental Mirrors*, Sage, London.

Jones, E. E. and Pittman, T. S. (1982). 'Toward a general theory of strategic self-presentation.' In J. Suls (Ed.), *Psychological Perspectives on the Self*, Erlbaum, New Jersey.

Price, G. (In press). 'Empathic relating and the structure of the self; Parallels in mother–infant and patient–therapist interaction.' In T. Honess and K. Yardley (Eds), *Self and Identity: Perspectives Across the Lifespan*, R.K.P., London.

Shotter, J. (1984). *Social Accountability and Selfhood*, Blackwell, Oxford.

Sullivan, H. S. (1953). *The Interpersonal Theory of Psychiatry*, Norton, New York.

Taylor, C. (1977). 'What is human agency?' In T. Mischell (Ed.), *The Self: Psychological and Philosophical Issues*, Blackwell, Oxford.

Toulmin, S. (1977). 'Self knowledge and knowledge of the self.' In T. Mischel (Ed.), *The Self: Psychological and Philosophical Issues*, Blackwell, Oxford.

Wegner, D. M. and Vallacher, R. (1980). *The Self in Social Psychology*, Oxford University Press, New York, London.

Self and Identity: Psychosocial Perspectives
Edited by K. Yardley and T. Honess
© 1987 John Wiley & Sons Ltd

13

Possible Selves: The Interface between Motivation and the Self-Concept

Hazel Markus and Paula Nurius

Possible selves represent individuals' ideas of what they might become, what they would like to become, and what they are afraid of becoming. They provide a conceptual link between the self-concept and motivation. Topics covered include: possible selves and motivation, possible selves and behaviour, the working self-concept, and the empirical study of possible selves.

INTRODUCTION

During the life-course most individuals develop a detailed and thorough understanding of themselves. They know what they like and do not like, what they can and cannot do, when they will react in certain ways and sometimes even why. Self-concept research in psychology, and identity research in sociology, has documented the diversity of this knowledge and has begun to examine its role in directing behaviour (e.g., Carver and Scheier, 1982; Kihlstrom and Cantor, 1984; Gergen, 1972; Greenwald and Pratkanis, 1985; Higgins *et al.*, 1984, and this volume; McGuire and McGuire, 1982). People appear to know a great deal about attributes of their personality, and about their demographics, roles, and habitual behaviours. They know what they have been like in the past and what they are like currently. But they also have a vision of what is *possible* for them. They know what they would like to become, what they could become, and what they are afraid of becoming. This domain of self-knowledge is seldom assessed by self-concept inventories. Yet it is critical for understanding how the self-system regulates behaviour because it reflects how individuals conceive of their potential and their future.

DEFINING THE POSSIBLE SELF

In this chapter we will focus on this neglected component of self-knowledge. Specifically we will examine the individual's *possible selves*. Possible selves are conceptions of the self in future states. The possible selves that are hoped for might include the powerful or leader self, the elegant and glamorous self, the revered and esteemed self, the rich and famous self, or the trim, toned, in-shape self. The dreaded possible selves may comprise an equally vivid and compelling set. One's fears and anxieties can be concretely manifest in visions of the alone and unwanted self, the addicted or dependent self, the violent or aggressive self, or the undervalued and unrecognized self. These constructions of potential selfhood are deft blendings of the representations of one's roles and social categorizations (self as worker, spouse, parent) with views of one's particular features, attributes or habits.

The repertoire of possible selves contained within an individual's self-system are the cognitive manifestations of enduring goals, aspirations, motives, fears, and threats. Possible selves provide specific cognitive form, organization, direction, and self-relevant meaning to these dynamics. As such they provide an essential link between the self-concept (or identity) and motivation (Markus and Nurius, 1986).

In surveys of the possible selves of college students, we find, for example, that the female student who fears she will not get married carries with her much more than a shadowy, undifferentiated fear of being unloved. Instead the fear is quite personalized and has a well-elaborated self associated with it. i.e., herself as uncared for and miserable, coming home from a dull job to an empty apartment, and watching others live exciting lives. Similarly, from a study of the possible selves of delinquents, we find that the boy who hopes to stop using drugs and to be different does not harbour this hope in vague abstraction but rather holds a vivid possible self, i.e. himself as clean, buying lots of clothes, having a car and lots of friends who admire him, and living a life rather like Michael Jackson's.

A COGNITIVE APPROACH

By focusing on the self-knowledge that accompanies an individual's goals, fears, and threats we are pursuing a cognitive approach to the self. In this approach the self-concept is not a unitary or monolithic entity but rather a system of salient identities or self-schemas (e.g., Markus, 1977; Stryker, this volume) that lend structure and meaning to one's self-relevant experiences. These self-schemas are generalizations about the self derived from past experience that help one integrate and explain one's own behaviour. Some of these structures derive from one's place in the social structure while others are constructed creatively and selectively from an individual's past thoughts, feelings, and behaviours in various domains. They might include, for example, the individual as independent, creative, shy, overweight, as a good athlete, a mother, a professor, an effective administrator, or a person with a sense of humour. While there is some overlap in the type of schemas individuals develop, one individual's *set* of self-schemas is likely to be quite different from another's.

Self-schemas are our unique and fundamental self-defining elements. They reflect personal concerns of enduring salience and investment, and they have been shown to have a systematic and pervasive influence on how information about the self is processed. Thus, for example, if a person has a self-schema about leadership or administrative ability, she will be sensitive to, and concerned with, issues relevant to leadership in both her own, and others, behaviour. She will interpret and respond to her social experiences according to the hypotheses and generalizations provided by this self-schema (see Greenwald and Pratkanis, 1985; Kihlstrom and Cantor, 1984; Markus, 1983; Markus and Sentis, 1982 for further detailed discussion of these ideas).

With the notion of possible selves, we are extending this approach to the self. A self-schema reflects a pervasive concern with a certain domain of behaviour, a sense that this particular identity has been, and will continue to be, an important way in which I can define myself and in which I can be differentiated from others. But it is not just an integration of past and present actions. It is most importantly a claim of responsibility for future behaviour in a particular domain. Thus self-schemas define a past and present self, but even more importantly they define a future, *possible* self. And it can be argued that this component is in fact the most significant aspect of the self-schema in shaping and fuelling behaviour.

Possible selves encompass within their scope visions of desired and undesired end states. Very often they also include some idea about the ways to achieve these ends and thereby provide the means–ends patterns for new behaviour. Represented within possible selves are the plans and strategies for approaching or avoiding personally significant possibilities (Cantor and Kihlstrom, 1985; Cantor et al., in press). Thus, it is the possible self that puts the self into action, that outlines the likely course of action. In sociological terms, possible selves are the link between salient identities and role performance (cf. Foote, 1951; Burke, 1980; Stryker, this volume). They are the cognitive bridges between the present and the future.

POSSIBLE SELVES AND BEHAVIOUR

Throughout the literature are accounts of unsuccessful attempts to link the self-concept to behaviour. Wylie (1979), for example, catalogues most of these failures. Recent efforts by cognitive behavioural psychologists have improved this track record by focusing on specific self-relevant thoughts as behavioural mediators (Arnkoff and Glass, 1982; Beck and Emery, 1985; Goldfried and Robins, 1983; Karoly and Kanfer, 1982; Mahoney and Arnkoff, 1978; Meichenbaum, 1977). Yet these researchers have yet to thoroughly explore the role of self-relevant thoughts about what is possible and how these expectancies and anticipations function within the self-system.

The vision of what might be—both what is hoped for and what is feared— can be linked with some of our most significant and individually distinctive behaviour. One has only to consider the vast range and diversity of our future oriented actions—dieting, setting up retirement plans, wearing seat belts, buying lottery tickets, jogging, taking karate lessons, reducing salt intake, giving up smoking, going to church—to be convinced that we must all have some very vivid and, in some cases, specific images and thoughts about our future selves and about what is possible for us. Some of these activities may be inherently pleasurable, of course, but many others are not, and one engages in them mostly because of the push and pull of one's personally significant hopes and fears for the future.

This reasoning is supported by empirical work on time perspectives. That is, while revealing large individual differences in degree of orientation to the future, this research shows quite conclusively that only a fraction of an individual's goals can be located within a time perspective of a week, or even a month (Nuttin, 1984). Instead, the majority of one's daily activities appear to be regulated by goals that are linked not to one's current view of self but instead to views of what might be possible for the self in the fairly distant future.

The unique behavioural power of certain positive possible selves is suggested by the impressive ability of some people to endure years of gruelling training for a future occupation, or to scrimp and save for an equally long time for a certain house or a special vacation. The resolve to deploy enormous effort or to suffer deprivation *now* for a goal that may not be attained for years must be sustained by enduring elements. These enduring elements that prompt people to persevere in pursuit of their aims and that remain as significant aspects of consciousness are their possible selves. Other actions seem to reveal the influence of negative possible selves. Some people, for instance, go from one relationship to another just to avoid being alone. Others engage in continual self-handicapping in an effort to ward off a direct test of their competence.

In our attempt to link possible selves to action, we are admittedly most concerned with information about the self that is available to consciousness or to working memory. This view does not deny the potential behavioural effects of uncommunicated desires and needs, and it does not ignore the influence of a diversity of social structural factors in producing behaviour. Rather, it suggests the following: in those situations that can be construed as self-relevant or self-revealing, an individual will be invested in his or her behaviour and attempt to regulate it, and it is then that behaviour that will be importantly controlled and regulated by possible selves. Whenever the situation is of a type that allows for flexibility in individual construction and interpretation (i.e., one that is not so highly constrained as to override all individuality) people will use their possible selves as blueprints for action. An intriguing question then becomes when will actions be in the service of realizing *positive* possible selves and when will they derive from efforts to avoid certain *negative* possible selves?

POSSIBLE SELVES AND MOTIVATION

In focusing on possible selves, we hope to better understand how the self works to regulate behaviour, both the overt and more covert forms of behaviour. A second, highly related intent of this approach is to personalize motivation. As astutely observed by Nuttin (1984), motivation for the large part has been analysed as if it were impersonal, instinctual, even unconscious. The important unanswered question of motivation theorizing is how the abstract, nebulous entity called a motive is transformed into the very personal activity of goal setting and into the concrete intentions and plans of which we are more or less aware.

Most theories of motivation do not speculate about the relations between the self and motivations and what shape this relation might take in self-knowledge. Several important questions need answering. How are motives, goals, and values cognitively represented and communicated within the self-system? What structures carry them? In what ways do they function? The contribution of the concept of possible selves to more traditional views of motivation is to suggest that some of the dynamic elements of personality may be carried in specific cognitive representations of the self in future states and that one's actions may be shaped by attempts to realize or avoid these states (see also Markus and Nurius, 1986). For example, goals are seldom held in total abstraction. It is not the abstract 'earning a degree' that is represented in the mind of a student. Instead, this goal is represented as the individual himself or herself achieving that goal. That is 'me getting a degree' or 'me having a degree' (cf. Guidano and Liotti, 1983).

Scattered attention to selves other than the present or actual self can be found throughout the psychological literature. Freud (1925) conceptualized the ego ideal as the child's conception of what the parents think is morally right. For Horney (1950) neurosis occurs when the idealized self becomes too powerful and takes the place of the real self as the focus of the individuals thoughts, feelings, and actions. Rogers (1951) building on James (1910) described the ideal self as what the individual thinks he or she should be and described one's level of self-regard as a function how far one was from the ideal self. James was also directly concerned with conceptions of the self beyond the here and now self. He wrote about the 'potential' social me and distinguished it from the 'immediate present me' and the 'me of the past' (see also Schutz, 1964 and Gordon, 1968, for reflections on tenses of the self).

More recently Rosenberg (1979) has theorized that there are important differences among desired selves and distinguished between fantasy or glorified idealized images of the self and the more realistic committed self-images which reflect what the individual actually believes he or she could become. Similarly, Levinson (1978) characterized 'the dream' as a single powerful construction that contains goals, aspirations, and values and that can be motivationally powerful. Neither Rosenberg nor Levinson, however, have analysed negative possibilities or nightmares as opposed to desired selves and dreams.

The link between the self-concept and action is implicit in the theorizing of Mead (1934) who argued that having a self implied the ability to rehearse possible courses of action depending on an evaluation of the other persons' reactions and then being able to adjust one's following actions accordingly.

This type of role-taking involves creating potential selves and occurs whenever one is the target of evaluation or expectation.

Other theorists directly approached the relation between identity and motivation. Foote (1951) believed that all motivation was a consequence of one's set of identities. Action, he wrote, is primarily an expression of one's identities and 'its products are ever-evolving self-conceptions' (p. 17). 'Thus, when doubt of identity creeps in, action is paralysed' (p. 18). These ideas are very similar to those of Erikson (1950) who, writing at about the same time, also viewed all important behaviour as shaped by the identity tasks. From these frameworks, most significant behaviour is in the service of meeting and resolving these identity tasks. Action is then largely controlled and regulated by one's set of identities. And Sartre (1956) described behaviour that was not self-defining and in the service of one's identities, but instead directed by someone else, as acting in 'bad faith'.

More recently, Stryker (1968 and this volume) contends that identities continually seek validation and that most important behaviour is in the service of confirming particular identities. And the more important the identity, the more it is in need of validation. The basic unit of the dynamic self then becomes not an attribute or a feature which is a summary or an integration of past behavioural regularity but rather a possible self which reveals the direction that action will take. Similarly, psychologists Gollwitzer and Wicklund (1985) have employed the notion of self-definitions to link the self-concept to motivation. Self-definitions are construed primarily as goals or ideals represented as conceptions of one's self as having a readiness to engage in certain behaviours.

The theories of Lewin (Lewin *et al.*, 1944), Atkinson (1958), and Bandura (e.g., Bandura and Schunk, 1981) are, of course, also very much concerned with the role of expectations and goal setting in motivation. But they are primarily concerned with task-specific goals and proximal goals as goads to behaviour. In contrast, the theories reviewed here have examined motivation not as a generalized disposition or as a set of specific goals but as a reflection of what individuals hope to accomplish with their lives and the kind of people they would like and not like to become.

THE WORKING SELF-CONCEPT

The self-concept is typically viewed as single, generalized or average view of the self. Such a view assumes that the self-concept is relatively constant and static. It does not allow for variability in self-perception, self-regard, and self-expectation. It does not explain, for example, how one can reflect on and experience one's self as mature, forthright, competent, and confident in the work setting, all of 10 years old when in the company of a favoured sibling during a visit with the family, and close to 110 when discovering that the next oldest person in the room was born when you were in high school. To examine the potential utility of the notion of possible selves, we have proposed thinking not in terms of *the* self-concept but instead in terms of the *working self-concept* (Markus and Nurius, 1986; Nurius and Markus, 1986). The working self-concept is that set of self-conceptions that are presently accessible in thought and memory. It can be viewed as a continually active, shifting array of available self-knowledge. Not all knowledge is equally accessible for thinking about the self at any one time. The array changes depending on the contents of the prior working self-concept, on what self-conceptions have been activated by the immediate social circumstances, and on those self-conceptions that have been wilfully invoked by the person in response to current experience (Markus and Nurius, 1986).

The self-concept is viewed as a collection of all of one's self-knowledge and self-conceptions. Each of us has a vast number of self-conceptions, i.e., the way we think about ourselves now, how we imagine ourselves in the future, the way we thought about ourselves in the past. This universe of self-conceptions includes the good selves, the bad selves, the hoped for selves, the feared selves, the ideal selves, the ought selves. Some of these self-conceptions qualify as self-schemas. That is, they define areas of expertise about the self, areas where one has a great deal of knowledge and involvement. These are the self-defining elements, the domains of investment and commitment. Such self-conceptions are likely to be chronically accessible for thinking about the self, that is, they are present whenever one thinks about the self. These may well be the selves most readily tapped by global self-concept inventories such as Twenty Statements Test (Kuhn and McPartland, 1954). Very often, the response to these scales reflects social categories, roles, and general attributes (e.g., female, black, mother, teacher, liberal, caring). Clearly, these types of self-conceptions or identities are related to a variety of important actions but they can be quite different from those self-conceptions that whether 'rational', 'accurate', or not are most keenly salient to the moment, and therefore most likely to influence interpretation of the situation and to colour affective responses to it (see Turner, this volume; Yardley, this volume).

The majority of our self-conceptions are of this more tentative variety. Self-conceptions like 'My paper is three weeks late', 'I made a fool of myself last night', 'I could win a fellowship'. 'I'm the only one who is dressed up' or 'No one will ever want to marry me' vary dramatically in their accessibility depending on the individual's affective or motivational state and on prevailing social conditions. In contrast to those self-conceptions which derive from self-schemas, not all of these self-conceptions are accessible for thinking about the self at any one time.

The working self-concept then is that *subset* of one's total repertoire of self-conceptions—including core, habitual views of self, the more episodic and domain-specific views of self, and the conceptions of possibility—that is active and 'working' at any given point in time. At two different situations, two very different sets of self-conceptions may be active. Notably, these two sets may well contain the same self-schemas or core self-conceptions. Yet these core self-conceptions may be accompanied by views of the past, current, or future self that derive primarily from the immediate social circumstances. And it is these latter self-conceptions that will often compete effectively with one's core self-conceptions for influence over the individual's prevailing affective and motivational states, current cognitive appraisals, and immediate actions.

THE ROLE OF POSSIBLE SELVES IN THE WORKING SELF-CONCEPT

When an individual experiences a defeat, a rejection, or a lapse in will power, the working self-concept will be configured with conceptions of negative possibility. The individual who is nearing a tenure decision and who receives word that a manuscript has been rejected has a working self-concept that includes not only some core self-conceptions but also a variety of negative possible selves (e.g., the failed self, the bitter self, the self as a mystery writer who cannot get her books published either, the self as undervalued, unrecognized clerk somewhere in a dull, grey office). In other instances, the working self-concept may contain largely positive possibilities. The working self-concept of the person who finally succeeds in losing ten pounds after six weeks of dieting is likely to be dominated by positive possibility (e.g., himself as 20 pounds lighter, the self as handsome, happy, sought after and as a model for the virtues of self-discipline).

Thoughts about what is possible allow the individual to develop a narrative of the self, to construct a self that is different from the present one. When some aspect of the current or now self is challenged, positive possible selves can be used as a protection against this challenge. Perhaps I am unsuccessful or unloved now, but I will not always be, nor have I always been. Such alternative conceptions of the self can be recruited into the working self-concept and, to the extent that they are well-elaborated, they may enable the individual to ward off, at least temporarily, threats to self-esteem and impulses to maladaptive actions. Such thinking is, in fact, quite central to some recently developed therapeutic cognitive restructuring paradigms. The goal of such programmes is to introduce alternative self-views into the individual's self-system and then attempt to modify the social environment so that these alternative self-views can be more frequently activated to enhance their strength (e.g., Beck *et al.*, 1979; McMullin and Giles, 1985).

Possible selves can have a powerful effect on functioning but they are also more vulnerable than other self-conceptions. Because they are often not anchored by overt social experience, and because they may not be evident to others and thus reinforced by others through social interaction, hoped for possibilities may be relatively easily threatened or challenged. Consequently, an assault on one's potential or one's dream is often far worse than an attack on one's performance or achievement. Unless these tentative positive self-views are particularly well-elaborated or deliberately invoked and reaffirmed, they may easily slip out of the working self-concept to be replaced by negative possibilities.

On the other hand, some possible selves may take firm root in the self-concept and become quite imprisoning. Fears that are held in place in consciousness by distinct negative possible selves may easily prevent growth and change. Some positive possibility may also have this quality. Some of our seemingly positive possible selves may be those that have not been fashioned personally but instead are those that have been imposed upon us by apparently well-meaning parents, mentors or lovers. These are what Higgins (Higgins *et al.*, 1984, and this volume) refers to as 'ought' selves, i.e., self-conceptions that have been created for us by others. Such possibilities, to the extent that they have been attended to by the individual, can represent a distinct burden.

THE EMPIRICAL STUDY OF POSSIBLE SELVES

In empirical work on possible selves we have conducted several types of studies: survey, experimental, and clinical. Two approaches have been used to assess possible selves. One has involved asking subjects to generate their own lists of possible selves, often related to a particular domain of functioning. Another has been to provide a list of possibilities generated by similar participants in previous studies. In some cases, the goal was purely descriptive: to examine the quantity and nature of possible selves generated. In other cases, the goal was to examine the relation of the self-concept as formulated here to various aspects of functioning. In these studies we first asked respondents to report whether each possibility described them now. We then assessed possible selves by asking:

1. whether the item had described them in the past;
2. whether the item was ever considered as a possible self;
3. how probable the possible self was for them;
4. how much they would like the item to be true for them.

We have discovered that all of the individuals we have studied have possible selves and that they are willing to describe them and reflect on them, both the positive and the negative. They do this easily and seem to enjoy the task. In developing a possible selves questionnaire we began by having small groups of students generate possibilities for themselves, both possibilities that were quite likely and those that were more the stuff of fantasy. We soon realized that there was a great deal of overlap in the selves generated by individuals of similar age and in similar social circumstances. For example, undergraduate students shared a great many possible selves, graduate students shared many possible selves, as did older women who were returning to school after a significant interruption in their education. There were important between-group differences in the nature of possible selves but within each group there was enough homogeneity among possible selves to justify creating a grid-type questionnaire which listed a number of positive and negative selves and then required respondents to respond to them.

Survey studies

An important goal of our research on possible selves is to survey individuals who are at different points in their life with respect to developing their potential. We hypothesize that *possible* selves will explain more of the variation in *current* affective and motivational states for younger people than they will for older people. Further, we expect that with increasing age negative possible selves will become relatively more important in explaining current affective and motivational state as well as overt actions. A major difficulty in interpreting this type of study, of course, is disentangling historical or cohort differences from actual differences due to age. Yet from preliminary analyses with just two age groups (20-year-olds and 30-year-olds) we find that the older group reports more possible selves and that this difference is primarily due to an increase in negative possible selves. Further, positive possible selves are strongly related to feelings of personal control while negative possible selves are related to feelings of a lack of control over ones' environment. It is reasonable to think that with increasing age, many individuals come to understand that they do not have complete control over their lives and that they are not completely invincible, as many undergraduates appear to believe. We also find a clear link between number of possible selves and amount of interpersonal responsibility. Thus those who report that a great many people depend on them endorse fewer positive possible selves.

We also hypothesized that possible selves will be the most developed in a domain of an individual's self-schemas. To explore this idea we (Wurf and Markus, 1985) selected individuals who had self-schemas for independence, outgoingness, and shyness (these were individuals who rated themselves extremely on these attributes and also thought these attributes were important for their overall self-evaluation). We compared these schematics with individuals who did not have schemas in these domains (aschematics). The schematics had many more selves, both positive and negative in the domain of their self-schemas than did the aschematics. The schematics could also supply a great deal of detail about the nature of their possible selves in the domain of their schemas that aschematics could not. The schematics and the aschematics did not differ in number or elaboration of possible selves in domains for which neither group had a schema. These findings support our reasoning that self-schemas are the result of a continuing investment in a particular domain of behaviour. As a result, they not only reflect past behaviour but very importantly contain goals and plans for future behaviour. Being schematic means that individuals think about certain features of their behaviour a great deal. It is likely that some important aspect of these thoughts will be about the potential for the self in this area. If self-schemas are thought to regulate actions it is because they contain possible selves which give substance and direction to certain end states and to the associated plans or strategies for achieving them. Without these clear, well-developed views of the self in particular futures, the self-concept cannot be expected to guide one's actions, and behaviour is likely to be determined by a variety of situational factors.

A central assumption of this expanded view of the self-concept is that dimensions of self other than the now self should make meaningful contributions to the explanation of variance in one's current affective and motivational states. We attempted to gain some general idea about these states by requiring respondents to complete the Affect Balance Scale (Derogatis, 1975), the Rotter Locus of Control Scale (Rotter, 1966), the Rosenberg Self-Esteem Scale (Rosenberg, 1965), and a Hopelessness Scale (Beck *et al.*, 1974). In one study with college students, for example, we attempted to explain current negative affect with both endorsements of now selves and endorsements of possible selves. We found that an individual's estimate of the probability of certain *possible* selves, both positive and negative, considerably augmented our ability to explain *current* affective and motivational states. That is, possible selves contributed significant additional variance to the explanation of these measures relative to what the here and now self-conceptions provided (see Markus and Nurius, 1986, for details).

In an on-going survey study we (Oyserman and Markus, 1986) are investigating the possible selves of delinquent youth. The study includes 100 adolescents aged 14–16 years of age who were either non-delinquent or were delinquent and residing in a group home or confined to a state training school. Using an open-ended format to elicit possible selves, the respondents were asked for their expected, hoped for, and feared selves. We found that delinquent youth were quite likely to score high on self-esteem and to report some positive possible selves. Yet they have a relatively constricted sense of possibility, both hoped for and feared possibility. These youths are being studied for a year following their release from the delinquency programme in an effort to determine how their systems of possibility may be related to consequent delinquent actions. It appears thus far that the delinquents who remain in school manage to create and sustain a larger array of positive possibility, and that measuring the probability of certain negative and positive possible selves significantly increases the size of relationship between the self-concept and behaviour.

Experimental studies

In an effort to examine the motivational consequences of possible selves, and to explore their role as incentives we (Ruvolo and Markus, 1986) carried out an experimental study with three groups of subjects. The first group was asked to imagine themselves in the future and to assume that everything had gone as well as it possibly could. They were told to imagine that they had worked very hard and that all of their goals and expectations, both social and career, had been realized. They were asked to describe this future in writing, indicating what was happening, what led up to it, who was there. A second group was asked to imagine themselves in the future but to assume that everything had gone as badly as it possibly could, that they had worked very hard but that none of their goals had been realized. A third group imagined themselves doing their laundry.

After several intervening tasks, members of each group were given two tasks to perform, each of which had clear performance criteria. In the first they were given a number of difficult mathematical problems: three digit multiplication and division problems, and asked to solve them in their heads. Their score was based on the number correct. In a second task, subjects were asked to copy a number of different figures but to do it with their left hand. Again they were told to complete as many as possible. In this case, the score was simply the number of figures attempted. These are two very different tasks, yet for both tasks, those who imagined themselves as having a very positive future significantly outperformed those who imagined themselves with a very negative future. This difference was primarily due to the fact that those in the failure imagery group performed very poorly.

In an attempt to determine what was mediating these performance differences we examined the responses of these subjects to a number of intervening tasks. One task which was performed immediately following the initial imagery involved showing the subjects a series of possible selves, both positive and negative and asking them to simply respond 'possible' or 'not possible'. As they responded, unbeknownst to them, their response latencies were recorded. Those in the success imagery group and those in the failure imagery group did not differ significantly in which possible selves they endorsed. Both endorsed more positive possibilities than negative possibilities. Yet when the response latencies for these endorsements were examined, we found that those in the success imagery group were significantly faster than the failure imagery group to endorse positive possibility. Those in the failure group were significantly faster to endorse negative possibility. On a measure of achievement motive the two groups did not differ.

This pattern of findings led us to speculate that those in the failure imagery group had recruited negative possible selves into their working self-concepts and consequently they could respond more quickly to negative possibility than positive possibility. Further this working self-concept dominated by negative possibility provided those in this condition with vivid negative end-states for themselves that functioned as deterrents to efficient performance. This may have occurred either by distracting these subjects from their performance on the task, or by creating a negative affective state which made views of self as successfully completing the tasks—views that are necessary for engaging the motivational cycle—temporarily inaccessible.

Clinical studies

Finally, we are exploring the value of possible selves for change-oriented, clinical purposes. Findings from both intensive single case study and from group treatment in a mental health setting have indicated considerable utility for the concept of possible selves. The single case study involved cognitive restructuring with a generally well-functioning white adult female around issues of confusion, self-deprecation, and dichotomous thinking associated with a recent major role transition. She had moved to a different part of the country and had entered graduate school. As with many individuals seeking treatment, this woman was functioning satisfactorily in many respects and in a variety of her life domains. Consequently, global measures of self-concept and self-esteem proved far less sensitive and therefore less useful for assessment than did efforts to assess the working self-concept in particularly troubling contexts.

Specifically, the woman was encouraged to articulate the self-conceptions that were most salient within the difficult contexts and that were the most funtionally relevant to the targeted problems. In school she felt inferior, lost, and inadequate. This included conceptions of both actual and possible selves. In addition, the client was aided in specifying her goals for treatment in terms of desirable possible selves. To evaluate progress toward her goals, Likert-type ratings of 'perceived actuality' (of these attributes being currently self-defining) of her alternative possible selves were monitored over the course of treatment. Statistically significant increases in perceived actuality of possible selves and in behavioural correlates were obtained (for more detail, see Nurius and Marjerus, 1985). In addition, the client found the working self-concept premise to be of substantial aid in resolving a sense of inauthenticity and dissonance stemming from an experience of 'different me's at different times', with some of these selves seemingly standing in contradiction to one another. Using a technique fashioned after Meichenbaum's (1977) self-instructional model, this client was trained to de-automatize her prior cognitive appraisal and response processes and to purposefully invoke, act upon, and reinforce her newly created possible selves.

A group study involved 15 women undergoing treatment for child abuse and neglect. These women were of diverse ethnic and economic backgrounds and, by and large, did not possess the abstraction skills of the client described above. Assessment with this group quickly revealed very few positive possible selves and a seeming inability to generate them. The procedure of each individual generating her own list of salient self-conceptions within contexts of high risk for abuse or neglect and of more funtional possible selves proved unmanageably difficult and time-consuming. An alternative approach was used which involved brainstorming exercises with the group to generate descriptors of good and poor parenting. Individuals were then aided to construct lists of descriptors that best described how they currently viewed themselves as parents and how they would like to view themselves as parents. Over the course of treatment, group members rated all items in both lists as to their current self-descriptiveness, their likelihood of being self-descriptive in the future, and how personally important it was to be this self.

The study is currently underway, yet initial results show evidence of greater cognitive elabortion of the positive parent possible selves. In modelling, role-playing, cognitive rehearsal, and discussion of events occurring at home, these women are demonstrating more varied, complex, and personalized ways of verbalizing and manifesting their possible selves. Furthermore, the women are demonstrating better understanding of the connection between their feeliings and their actions. As a result, efforts to invoke their positive possible selves in high-risk situations have increased, as have efforts to apply the same reasoning in other domains of their lives (Nurius and Lovell, 1985).

CONCLUSION

We have argued here for a more expansive view of the self-concept, one that includes individuals' conceptions of their potential and their future, both hoped for and feared. The concept of possible selves has been introduced to complement current conceptions of self-knowledge. Possible selves represent individuals' ideas of what they might become, what they would like to become and what they are afraid of becoming. They establish a conceptual bridge between the self-concept and motivation. They are the cognitive representations of hopes, fears, goals, and they provide the particular self-relevant, form, meaning, organization, and direction to these dynamics.

In research on possible selves, at least two difficult questions must be broached. The first is exactly how do possible selves relate to motivation? Does the thought of the self in a future state energize the self? Does thinking of the self achieving particular outcomes serve to channel one's energies and allow them to be deployed more efficiently? Is the individual's level of motivation some function of the degree of elaboration of the relevant possible self? And what is the relation between what might be termed unconscious motives and possible selves? The second broad question concerns whether it is our dreaded negative possible selves or our hoped for positive selves that will have the most influence on our actions? Are motives that are represented by negative possible selves of a different nature than motives that are given form in positive possible selves? As psychology returns again to an emphasis on motives and goals, the message of this chapter is that the nature of motivation and its link to action will not be fully understood without an emphasis on the self-concept and the elements of self-knowledge that carry motivation.

REFERENCES

Arnkoff, D. B. and Glass, C. R. (1982). 'Clinical cognition constructs: Examination, evaluation, elaboration.' In P. C. Kendall (Ed.), *Advances in Cognitive-Behavioral Research and Therapy*, Vol. 1, Academic Press, New York.

Atkinson, J. (Ed.) (1958). *Motives in Fantasy, Action and Society*, Van Nostrand, New York.

Bandura, A. and Schunk, D. H. (1981). 'Cultivating competence, self-efficacy and intrinsic interest through proximal self-motivation.' *Journal of Personality and Social Psychology*, **41**, 586–598.

Beck, A. T. and Emery, G. (1985). *Anxiety disorders and Phobias: A Cognitive Perspective*. Basic Books, New York.

Beck, A. T., Rush, A. J., Shaw, B. F. and Emery, G. (1979). *Cognitive Therapy of Depression*, Guilford, New York.

Beck, A. T., Weissman, H. W., Lester, D. and Trexler, L. (1974). 'The assessment of pessimism: The Hopelessness scale?' *Journal of Consulting and Clinical Psychology*, **42**, 861–865.

Burke, P. J. (1980). 'The self: Measurement requirements from an interactionist perspective.' *Social Psychology Quarterly*, **43**, 18–29.

Cantor, N. and Kihlstrom, J. F. (1985). *Social Intelligence: The Cognitive Basis of Personality*, (Tech. Rep. no. 60). University of Michigan, Ann Arbor.

Cantor, N., Markus, H., Niedenthal, P. and Nurius, P. (1986). 'On motivation and the self-concept.' In R. M. Sorrentino and E. T. Higgins (Eds), *Motivation and Cognition: Foundations of Social Behaviour*, Guilford, New York.

Carver, C. S. and Scheier, M. (1982). 'Control theory: A useful conceptual framework for personality-social, clinical, and health psychology.' *Psychological Bulletin*, **92**(1), 111–135.

Derogatis, L. R. (1975). *The Affect Balance Scale*. Clinical Psychometric Research, Baltimore.

Erikson, E. (1956). 'The problem of ego identity.' *Journal of American Psychoanalytic Association*, **4**, 56–121.

Foote, N. (1951). 'Identification as the basis for a theory of motivation.' *American Sociological Review*, **16**, 14–21.

Freud, S. (1925). *Collected Papers*, Hogarth, London.

Gergen, K. K. (1972). 'Multiple identity: The healthy, happy human being wears many masks.' *Psychology Today*, **5**, 31–35, 64–66.

Goldfried, M. R. and Robins, C. (1983). 'Self-schema, cognitive bias, and the processing of therapeutic experiences.' In P. C. Kendall (Ed.), *Advances in cognitive-behavioral research and therapy*, vol. 2, Academic Press, New York.

Gollwitzer, P. M. and Wicklund, R. A. (1985). 'The pursuit of self-defining goals.' In J. Kuhl and J. Beckmann (Eds), *Action Control: From Cognition to Behavior*, Springer-Verlag, New York.

Gordon, C. (1968). 'Self-conceptions: Configurations of content.' In C. Gordon and K. Gergen (Eds), *The Self in Social Interaction*, Wiley, New York.

Greenwald, A. G. and Pratkanis, A. R. (1985). 'The self.' In R. S. Wyer and T. K. Srull (Eds), *Handbook of Social Cognition*, Erlbaum, Hillsdale, New Jersey.

Guidano, V. F. and Liotti, G. (1983). *Cognitive Processes and Emotional Disorders*, Guilford, New York.

Higgins, E. T., Klein, R. and Strauman, T. (1984). 'Self-concept discrepancy theory: A psychological model for distinguishing among different aspects of depression and anxiety.' *Social Cognition*, in press.

Horney, K. (1950). *Neurosis and human growth*, Norton, New York.

James, W. (1910). *Psychology: The briefer course*, Henry Holt & Co., New York.

Karoly, P. and Kanfer, F. H. (Eds). (1982). *Self-management and behaviour change: From theory to practice*, Pergamon Press, New York.

Kihlstrom, J. F. and Cantor, N. (1984). 'Mental representations of the self.' In L. Berkowitz (Ed.), *Advances in Experimental Social Psychology*, vol. 15, Academic Press, New York.

Kuhn, M. H. and McPartland, T. (1954). 'An empirical investigation of self-attitudes.' *American Sociological Review*, **19**, 68–76.

Levinson, D. J. (1978). *The Seasons of a Man's Life*, Ballantine Books, New York.

Lewin, K., Dembo, T., Festinger, L. and Sears, P. S. (1944. 'Level of aspiration.' In J. McV. Hunt (Ed.), *Personality and the Behaviour Disorders*, Ronald Press, New York, vol. 1; Academic Press, New York.

Mahoney, M. J. and Arnkoff, K. (1978). 'Cognitive and self-control therapies.' In S. L. Garfield and A. E. Bergin (Eds), *Handbook of Psychotherapy and Behaviour Change*, 2nd edn, Wiley, New York.

Markus, H. (1977). 'Self-schemata and processing information about the self,' *Journal of Personality and Social Psychology*, 35(2), 63–78.

Markus, H. (1983). 'Self-knowledge: An expanded view.' *Journal of Personality*, 51(3), 543–565.

Markus, H. and Nurius, P. S. (1986). 'Possible selves.' *American Psychologist*, 41.

Markus, H. and Sentis, K. (1982). 'The self in social information processing.' In J. Suls (Ed.), *Psychological Perspectives on the Self*, Erlbaum, Hillsdale, New Jersey.

McGuire, W. J. and McGuire, C. V. (1982). 'Significant others in self space: sex differences and developmental trends in social self.' In J. Suls (Ed.), *Psychological Perspectives on the Self*, Erlbaum, Hillsdale, New Jersey.

McCullin, R. E. and Giles, T. R. (1985). *A Cognitive-Behaviour Therapy: A Restructuring Approach*, Grune and Strattan, New York.

Mead, G. H. (1934). *Mind, Self and Society*, University of Chicago Press, Chicago.

Meichenbaum, D. (1977). *Cognitive-Behavioral Modification: An Integrative Approach*, Plenum Press, New York.

Nurius, P. S. and Lovell, M. (1985). 'Self-concept change of abusive parents in treatment.' Unpublished paper, University of Washington.

Nurius, P. S. and Majerus, D. (In Press). 'Rethinking the self in self-talk: A theoretical note and case example.' *Journal of Clinical and Social Psychology*.

Nurius, P. S. and Markus, H. (1986). 'The working self-concept: contextual variability within a stable self-system.' Unpublished manuscript, University of Michigan.

Nuttin, J. R. (1984). *Motivation, Planning, and Action: A Relational Theory of Behavior Dynamics*, Erlbaum, Hillsdale, New Jersey.

Oyserman, D. and Markus, H. (1986). 'Delinquency and possible selves.' Unpublished, University of Michigan.

Rogers, C. (1951). *Client-centred Therapy: Its Current Practice, Implications, and Theory*, Houghton Mifflin, Boston.

Rosenberg, M. (1965). *Society and the Adolescent Self-image*, Princeton University Press, Princeton, New Jersey.

Rosenberg, M. (1979). *Conceiving the Self*, Basic Books, New York.

Rotter, J. B. (1966). 'Generalized expectancies for internal versus external control of reinforcement.' *Psychological Monographs*, 80, 1–28.

Ruvolo, A. and Markus, H. (1986). 'The motivational consequences of possible selves.' Unpublished manuscript, University of Michigan.

Sartre, J. P. (1956). *Being and Nothingness*, Philosophical Library, New York.

Schutz, A. (1964). 'On multiple realities.' In M. Natanson (Ed.), *Collected Papers of Alfred Schutz*, vol. 1, Martinus Nijhoff, The Hague.

Stryker, S. (1968). 'Identity salience and role performance.' *Journal of Marriage and the Family*, 30, 558–64.

Wurf, E. and Markus, H. (1986). 'Self-schemas and possible selves.' Unpublished manuscript, University of Michigan.

Wylie, R. C. (1979). *The Self-Concept*, vols. 1 and II, revised edn, University of Nebraska Press, Lincoln.

Self and Identity: Psychosocial Perspectives
Edited by K. Yardley and T. Honess
© 1987 John Wiley & Sons Ltd

14

Self-Discrepancies: Distinguishing Among Self-States, Self-State Conflicts, and Emotional Vulnerabilities

E. Tory Higgins, Ruth L. Klein, and Timothy J. Strauman

Self-discrepancy theory provides a general framework for understanding the emotional consequences of different types of self-inconsistencies. Evidence is presented to support the proposal that particular emotional vulnerabilities are associated with discrepancies between individuals' actual self-states and particular self-guides (or potential self-states). The intensity of discomfort also depends on individuals' beliefs about the interpersonal consequences of failing to meet their self-guides.

INTRODUCTION

What is the relation between self and affect? This has been a central question from the beginning of psychologists' interest in the self. The general answer most frequently given is that self-conflicts or self-inconsistencies produce emotional problems. But what precisely is the nature of the self-conflicts or self-inconsistencies that produce emotional problems? To this question psychologists have suggested a myriad of possibilities, such as James' (1890/ 1948) ratio of actualities to selected potentialities, Freud's (e.g., 1923/1961) conflicts among the Id, Ego, and Superego, Lecky's (1961) self-inconsistent environmental input, Allport's (1955) loss of inward unity, Roger's (1959, 1961) actual self versus ideal self-discrepancy and self versus experience incongruence, and Aronson's (e.g., 1969) disconfirmation of self-expectancies. Among the vast array of possibilities, three basic types of self-conflicts or self-inconsistencies can be identified.

1. conflicts or inconsistencies between an individual's self and external, behavioural feedback relevant to the self;
2. conflicts or contradictions among an individual's self-attributes or self-conceptions that impedes a coherent and unified self;
3. conflicts or discrepancies between an individual's actual self and his or her standards, values, or aspirations (i.e., James' potential selves).

Conflicts or inconsistencies between an individual's self and external behavioural feedback can occur from the individual's own responses or the responses of others. Aronson's (1969) version of cognitive dissonance theory (Festinger, 1957), with its emphasis on self-expectancies, focuses on the former case. The theory proposes that when people behave in a manner that is inconsistent with their self-concept, such as people who believe they are decent and truthful persuading another person to perform a task that they know is boring, they experience discomfort (see also Bramel, 1968; Rogers, 1959). Swann's (1983) self-verification theory is also concerned with conflicts between individual's self-concepts and external feedback, but it focuses on people's attempt to obtain responses from others that confirm their self-concept (see also Lecky, 1961). The theory states that people become upset when they receive social feedback that is inconsistent with their self-concept, even when the feedback disconfirms a negative self-conception. In fact, people will actively seek out self-consistent social feedback and avoid self-inconsistent social feedback in a manner reminiscent of the 'selective exposure' hypothesis of cognitive dissonance theory (see Olson and Zanna, 1979; Wicklund and Brehm, 1976).

In addition to the need for consistency between the self and external feedback, the need for consistency among an individual's different attributes and self-conceptions has been proposed by numerous scholars (e.g., Allport, 1955; Brim, 1976; Epstein, 1973; Lecky, 1961; Morse and Gergen, 1970). This unity principle (see Epstein, 1981) proposes that people have a basic need to maintain the unity and coherence of their self-attributes and ideas about the self. Indeed, Harter (in press) has found that adolescents are able to identify self-traits that they consider to be opposites and distinguish between those opposites that are in conflict with each other (e.g., 'smart' in school but 'fun-loving' with school friends) versus those that are not (e.g., 'outgoing' with friends and 'shy' with romantic interests). As suggested by theories proposing the need for self-consistency or unity, the adolescents were upset by their conflicting traits.

The third type of self-conflict discussed in the literature is discrepancies between an individual's actual self and his or her standards, values, or aspirations (e.g., Adler, 1964; Cooley, 1902; Freud, 1923; Horney, 1950; James, 1890/1948; Rogers, 1961; Sullivan, 1953). Many psychologists have stated that when individuals' actual self violates their own or society's moral standards, they feel guilty, fearful, and anxious (e.g., Freud, 1923/1961; Hoffman, 1971; Sullivan, 1953). And other psychologists have observed that individuals experience disappointment, dissatisfaction, and shame when their actual self fails to match their goals or wishes or others' goals or wishes for them (e.g., Cooley, 1902/1964; Duval and Wicklund, 1972; Rogers, 1961; see also Markus and Nurius, this volume).

These alternative theories of self-conflict or self-inconsistency provide a rich picture of how the self is related to affect. There are two limitations with this picture, however. First, there is no general conceptual system for fitting these various images into a single framework. Second, there is no general theory that predicts how different types of self-conflict or self-inconsistencies produce different types of emotional problems. It is even rare for a theory to discuss more than one kind of self-affect relation (e.g., James, 1890/1948). More typically, one theory will discuss how self-conflict relates to anxiety whereas another theory will discuss how self-inconsistency relates to disappointment or dissatisfaction. In fact, most theories simply propose that self-conflict or self-inconsistency produces general discomfort or tension without specifying the precise nature of the emotion involved. Recently, we have begun to develop and test a theory of the relation between self and affect—self-discrepancy theory (Higgins, 1984)—that attempts to overcome these limitations.

SELF-DISCREPANCY THEORY AS A GENERAL THEORY OF SELF-INCONSISTENCIES

Self-discrepancy theory (Higgins, 1984) proposes that people's representations of their self or self-states can be described in terms of two parameters: domain of self and standpoint on self.

Domains of the self

The theory distinguishes among three domains of the self:

1. the 'Actual' self;
2. the 'Ideal' self, which is a person's representation of the attributes that someone (self or other) would like the person, ideally, to possess, i.e., someone's hopes, goals, or wishes for the person;
3. the 'Ought' self, which is a person's representation of the attributes that someone (self or other) believes the person should or ought to possess, i.e., someone's sense of the person's duties, obligations or responsibilities.

James' (1890/1948) distinction among a person's actualities and his or her potential 'ideal social self' and 'spiritual self' resembles this distinction, as does Berne's (1964) distinction among Adult, Child, and Parent ego states, which in turn was derived from Freud's (1923/1961) classic distinction among the Ego, Id, and Superego (although the Id involved biological drives and the Superego contained an ego-Ideal component as well). Although explicit distinctions among these three domains of the self are rare, each of these domains have been frequently described in the literature (e.g., Allport, 1955; Cooley, 1902/1964; Duval and Wicklund, 1972; Rado, 1927/1956; Rogers, 1961; Sullivan, 1953; see also Markus and Nurius, this volume).

Standpoints on the self

A standpoint on the self is a point of view or position from which a person can be judged that reflects a set of attitudes or values, including her or his 'Own' standpoint and the standpoint of any significant 'Other' (e.g., mother, father, close sibling, close friend). Previous theories have not systematically considered the different domains of the self in terms of the different standpoints on those domains (e.g., individuals' own personal hopes and goals vs. their mother's hopes and goals for them). This has created some confusion in the literature, such as whether actual:ideal discrepancy measures of self-esteem refer to individuals' own ideals or others' ideals for them (see Wylie, 1979). The concept of different standpoints on the self is derived from Turner (1956) who distinguished between self-attitudes or self-viewpoint (i.e., Own Standpoint on self) and the attitudes or viewpoints of others (i.e., Other standpoint on self). Notions similar to 'standpoints on the self' appear, at least implicitly, in other theories of self-perception as well (e.g., Kelley, 1952; Lewin, 1935; Mead, 1934). Moreover, 'own' versus 'other' is a critical feature in various theories of the self (e.g., Scheier and Carver, 1983; Snyder, 1979). The notion of Own versus Other standpoints on the self, however, has not previously been used in conjunction with domains of the self to define different self-states.

By combining each of the domains of the self with each of the standpoints on the self, self-discrepancy theory distinguishes among six basic kinds of self-state representations: Actual/Own, Actual/Other, Ideal/Own, Ideal/Other, Ought/Own, and Ought/Other. The first two self-state representations, but especially Actual/Own, constitute what is commonly meant by a person's 'self-concept' (see Wylie, 1979). The four remaining self-state representations are self-directive standards or self-guides (see Higgins *et al.*, 1985d).

Self-discrepancy theory (Higgins, 1984) proposes that people are motivated to reach a condition where their Actual self-state matches their Ideal and Ought self-states (i.e., their self-concept matches their self-guides). This implies that discomfort will be induced by either chronic Actual:Self-guide discrepancies or momentary evaluative feedback on the self (by self or others) that is discrepant from a self-guide or disconfirms a non-discrepant, Actual-self attribute (see also Higgins *et al.*, 1985c). Most of the phenomena involving self-conflicts or self-inconsistencies described in the literature can be framed within this conceptual system. First, there are the cases of discomfort from inconsistencies between an individual's self and external behavioural feedback relevant to the self (Type 1 discussed earlier). These cases could reflect conditions where the feedback, whether from an individual's own evaluative response or from another person, implies that the individual possesses a novel attribute that would be discrepant from the individual's self-guides or does not possess an Actual self attribute that currently matches the individual's self-guides which, if the feedback were accepted, would create a discrepancy. Our analysis also suggests that under other conditions *consistency* between an individual's self and external, behavioural feedback could cause discomfort since feedback could confirm that the individual possesses an Actual self attribute that is discrepant from the individual's self-guides, thus increasing the accessibility of the discrepancy (see Higgins *et al.*, 1985c).

It should be noted that there is one case of discomfort induced by self-discrepant feedback described in the literature which self-discrepancy theory, as currently formulated, might not incorporate. This is the case where an individual who possesses negative Actual self-attributes is made uncomfortable by feedback disconfirming these attributes (see Swann, 1983). Such cases could be handled by self-discrepancy theory, however, if the negative attributes match one of the individual's self-guides. That is, the attributes may be discrepant from the individual's own desires (i.e., his or her Ideal/Own self-guide), which would make them 'negative', but nevertheless match some other self-guide that is important to the individual (i.e., Ought/Father or Ought/Mother). Disconfirming the 'negative' attributes, then, would produce discomfort because it would create a discrepancy with this other self-guide. As there is no conclusive evidence as yet available on this issue, it is not clear whether or not such cases can be incorporated within self-discrepancy theory.

Next, there are the cases of discomfort from contradictions among an individual's self-attributes or self-conceptions that impede a coherent and unified self (Type 2). Some of these cases may reflect discrepancies between the attributes individuals believe they possess and the attributes that significant others believe they possess (i.e., Actual/Own:Actual/Other) or discrepancies between attributes that different significant others believe they possess (i.e., Actual/Other$_1$:Actual/Other$_2$). Such discrepancies are often described as an 'identity crisis' and are especially common in adolescence (see Erikson, 1968; Harter, in press). Other cases of this general type may reflect discrepancies between different self-guides. Lecky (1961), for example, described how the need of unity is especially acute in adolescence because values associated with the adolescents' parents are challenged by values associated with their romantic partner, which probably reflects a discrepancy between the kind of person the parents believe the adolescent ought to be and the kind of person the romantic partner would like the adolescent to be (i.e., an Ought/Other$_1$:Ideal/Other$_2$ discrepancy). Another common discrepancy between different self-guides, and a frequent literary theme, is the conflict between an individual's personal desires and his or her sense of duty (i.e., an Ideal/Own:Ought/Own discrepancy). Given that self-unity theories usually contain the notion of a system operating in terms of a unified purpose or direction (e.g., Allport, 1955; Lecky, 1961), these theories and self-discrepancy theory would agree in predicting that discrepancy between different self-guides or directions would create tension and discomfort.

The third type of cases of discomfort involves discrepancies between an individual's actual self and his or her standards, values, or goals. Cases that involve individuals violating their own or society's moral standards reflect Actual:Ought discrepancies (i.e., Actual/Own:Ought/Own and Actual/Own:Ought/Other, respectively), and cases that involve individuals failing to match their goals or wishes or others' goals or wishes for them reflect Actual:Ideal discrepancies (i.e., Actual/Own:Ideal/Own and Actual/Own:Ideal/Other, respectively). These cases of Actual:Self-guide discrepancies, in fact, may also comprise some of the cases considered by self-unity theories as these theories do not distinguish among domains of the self, that is, all aspects of self need to be organized and integrated into a coherent and consistent whole.

TYPE OF SELF-DISCREPANCY AND TYPE OF EMOTIONAL PROBLEM

In addition to providing a general conceptual system that distinguishes among the various types of self-conflicts and self-inconsistencies that the literature describes as producing discomfort, self-discrepancy theory predicts how different types of self-discrepancies produce *different* types of discomfort. For the purpose of the present chapter, we will restrict our focus to the central distinction between Actual:Ideal discrepancies and Actual:Ought discrepancies.

Actual/Own:Ideal/Own discrepancy and Actual/Own:Ideal/Other discrepancy both involve a condition in which the current state of an individual's actual attributes, from the individual's own standpoint, does not match the ideal state that the individual believes someone (self or significant other) wishes him or her to attain, which means the non-obtainment of someone's hopes, goals, or desires. Actual:Ideal discrepancies, then, represent the general psychological situation of the absence (actual or expected) of positive outcomes (see Higgins, 1984). In contrast, Actual/Own:Ought/Own discrepancy and Actual/Own:Ought/Other discrepancy both involve a condition in which the current state of an individual's actual attributes, from the individual's own standpoint, violates the state that the individual believes someone (self or other) believes is the duty or obligation of the individual to fulfil, which is a condition associated with the application of sanctions (e.g., punishment). Actual:Ought discrepancies, then, represent the general psychological situation of the presence (actual or expected) of negative outcomes. Actual:Ideal discrepancies and Actual:Ought discrepancies, therefore, represent the two basic kinds of negative psychological situations that are associated with different types of discomfort: the absence (actual or expected) of positive outcomes, which is associated with dejection-related emotions (e.g., dissatisfaction, disappointment, sadness), and the presence (actual or expected) of negative outcomes, which is associated with agitation-related emotions (e.g., fear, apprehension, edginess) (see Higgins, 1984; Jacobs, 1971; Lazarus, 1968; Roseman, 1979). Thus, to the extent that there are individual differences in the magnitude and accessibility of Actual:Ideal discrepancies and Actual:Ought discrepancies, self-discrepancy theory predicts that there should be individual differences in vulnerability to dejection-related versus agitation-related emotions and emotional symptoms.

Although there is some indirect evidence consistent with these hypothesized relations (see Higgins, 1984), the most direct supporting evidence has come from our own recent studies. Higgins *et al.*, (1985b) measured New York University undergraduates' self-discrepancies and emotional problems as part of a general battery of personality tests. The measures of emotional problems included the Beck Depression Inventory (Beck *et al.*, 1961) and the

Hopkins Symptom Checklist (Derogatis *et al.*, 1974) as well as a list of negative emotions. The measure of self-discrepancy (see Higgins *et al.*, 1985b) asked subjects to list up to ten attributes associated with the Actual/ Own self-concept and each of the self-guides. To calculate the magnitude of discrepancy between the self-concept and each self-guide, the attributes in the self-concept were compared to the attributes in the self-guide (e.g., comparing the Actual/Own list of attributes to the Ideal/Own list of attributes), and the total number of attribute pairs that matched (i.e., synonyms) was subtracted from the total number of attribute pairs that mismatched (i.e., antonyms). Zero-order and partial correlations were then performed to examine the relation between emotional problems and both Actual:Ideal discrepancies and Actual:Ought discrepancies. These analyses revealed, as predicted, that Actual:Ideal discrepancies were more closely associated with dejection-related emotional problems (e.g., dissatisfied, shame, feeling blue) than with agitation-related emotional problems (e.g., guilt, panic, fear), whereas the reverse was true for Actual:Ought discrepancies.

In a couple of experiments, Higgins *et al.*, (1986) examined whether changing the accessibility of individuals' Actual:Self-guide discrepancies produces changes in different types of emotions, depending on the magnitude and type of discrepancy an individual possesses. New York University undergraduates' self-discrepancies were measured a few weeks prior to the experimental sessions in both studies. In the experimental session of the first study, subjects were asked to imagine either a positive event that matched a common standard (e.g., receiving a grade of 'A' in a course) or a negative event that failed to match a common standard (e.g., receiving a grade of 'D' in a course). In the former 'standard-match' condition, we expected that the manipulation of a non-discrepant active set would temporarily inhibit the chronic accessibility effect of any self-discrepancy that a subject might have (see Higgins and King, 1981). In the latter 'standard-mismatch' condition, we expected that the manipulation of focus on a discrepancy would temporarily 'prime' or increase the accessibility of any self-discrepancy that a subject may have (see Higgins *et al.*, 1985a). We also predicted that individuals whose predominant discrepancy was an Actual:Ideal discrepancy would experience a change in dejection-related emotions whereas individuals whose predominant discrepancy was an Actual:Ought discrepancy would experience a change in agitation-related emotions. Following the guided imagery task, subjects were given a mood measure and a writing-speed task (which they also performed prior to the imagery task). Consistent with our predictions, subjects with a predominant Actual:Ideal discrepancy felt more dejected and wrote slower in the standard-mismatch condition than in the standard-match condition, whereas subjects with a predominant Actual:Ought discrepancy, if anything, felt more agitated and wrote faster in the standard-mismatch condition than in the standard-match condition.

In the second study, New York University undergraduates were selected who either were high in *both* Actual:Ideal discrepancy and Actual:Ought discrepancy or were low in both. Half of the subjects in each of these groups were randomly assigned to a condition in which they discussed their own and their parents' hopes and goals for them (Ideal priming) and the other half were assigned to a condition in which they discussed their own and their parents' beliefs concerning their duty and obligations (Ought priming). Before and after this experimental manipulation subjects were given a mood measure. As predicted, Ideal priming increased high discrepancy subjects' dejection and slightly decreased low discrepancy subjects' dejection, whereas Ought priming increased high discrepancy subjects' agitation and slightly decreased low discrepancy subjects' agitation. Thus, both studies demonstrate that changing the accessibility of different types of self-discrepancies causes changes in different types of emotion. In addition, our second experiment shows that this is true even when individuals possess *both* types of discrepancies.

SELF-DISCREPANCIES AND INTERPERSONAL OUTCOME CONTINGENCIES

The results from these studies strongly support the hypothesis that different types of emotional vulnerability are associated with different types of self-discrepancies. But as we have pointed out elsewhere (Higgins *et al.*, 1985b), in order for the theory of self-discrepancy to be maximally useful as an approach for understanding and, eventually, treating emotional problems, the theory must be extended to include variables that reflect individuals' beliefs concerning the interpersonal implications of the discrepancy. Depressed individuals, for example, often grow up in families in which they receive the message that care, affection, and approval are contingent upon their living up to and pursuing their parents' high, if not grandiose, expectations for them (see Beck, 1967; Arieti and Bemporad, 1978). In our latest study, therefore, we included a measure of individuals' beliefs in such contingencies in addition to our measure of self-discrepancies.

As part of a Socialization Questionnaire, New York University undergraduates were asked the following questions:

1. Have you ever felt unloved because you didn't live up to your parents *ideals* for you? To what extent?
2. Have you ever felt you would be emotionally abandoned if you didn't live up to your parents' *ideals* for you? To what extent?
3. Did you ever believe that your parents would reject you if you didn't live up to their *ideals* for you? To what extent?

The same three questions were also asked with respect to their parents' *oughts* for them, where both *ideals* and *oughts* were previously defined for the subjects. These questions were answered on 5-point scales that ranged from 0 (not at all) to 5 (a great deal). Subjects' scores for the three Ideal questions were averaged to form an overall Ideal-Outcome Contingency score, and their scores for the three Ought questions were averaged to form an overall Ought-Outcome Contingency score.

The self-discrepancy measure used in this study was a modification of the measure described earlier. For each self-state, after the subjects listed the attributes for the self-state they were asked to rate the extent to which they or their significant other believed they actually possessed, ideally would like them to possess, or ought to possess (depending on the self-state) each attribute listed. The 4-point rating scale ranged from 1 (slightly) to 4 (extremely). These ratings permitted a new distinction to be made in calculating the magnitude of discrepancy between any pair of self-states, that is, between true 'matches' where synonymous attributes across the two self-states had a rating that varied by no more than one scale point versus synonymous 'mismatches' where synonymous attributes across the two self-states had a rating that varied by two or more scale points (e.g., Actual/Own: 'slightly attractive' versus Ideal/Own: 'extremely attractive'). Antonymous attributes across the two self-states continued to be coded as 'mismatches'. Antonymous 'mismatches' were given a weight of '2' whereas synonymous 'mismatches' and synonymous 'matches' were given a weight of '1' in the 'mismatches minus matches' calculation. This new measure of the magnitude of self-discrepancy takes into account the severity of the mismatch and reserves the 'match' classification to cases of true overlap. The reliability of this new scoring procedure was quite high (i.e., interrater correlation of 0.89).

In this study, as in our experimental studies described earlier, subjects' self-discrepancies were measured weeks before they answered the questionnaires measuring emotional problems (i.e., the Beck Depression Inventory and the Hopkins Symptom Checklist). Using tertiary splits, subjects were divided into three levels, high, medium, and low, with regard to both Actual:Ideal discrepancy (i.e., Actual/Own:Ideal/Own discrepancy and Actual/Own:Ideal/Other discrepancy combined) and Actual:Ought discrepancy (i.e., Actual/Own:Ought/Own discrepancy and Actual/Own:Ought/Other discrepancy combined). The subjects were also divided into two levels of Ideal-Outcome Contingency and two levels of Ought-Outcome Contingency using median splits. Separate Level of Actual:Ideal Discrepancy × Level of Ideal-Outcome Contingency ANOVAs and Level of Actual:Ought Discrepancy × Level of Ought-Outcome Contingency ANOVAs were then performed for each of the measures of emotional problems (i.e., the BDI measure of depression, the HSCL measure of depression, and the HSCL subscale measures of anxiety, paranoid ideation, and anger-hostility). The major prediction was that the intensity of individuals' emotional problems would be related to *both* their level of self-discrepancy and their level of outcome contingency, and that the quality or type of their emotional problems would depend on the type of self-guide involved (i.e., Ideal vs Ought).

The squared multiple correlation (R^2) for each ANOVA is a useful summary statistic of the amount of variance of the predicted (or dependent) variable that is accounted for by the main effects and interactions of the predictor (or independent) variables. The results for this summary statistic are presented in Table 1. As predicted, Actual:Ideal discrepancy combined with Ideal-Outcome Contingency were strongly associated with depressive (i.e., dejection-related) symptoms but had a relatively weak association with anxiety/paranoid (i.e., agitation-related) symptoms, whereas the reverse was true for Actual:Ought discrepancy combined with Ought-Outcome Contingency. The strong relation between Actual:Ideal discrepancy combined with Ideal-Outcome Contingency and depressive symptoms was due to significant ($p < 0.05$) main effects of both level of Actual:Ideal discrepancy and level of Ideal-Outcome Contingency, as well as a significant ($p < 0.05$) interaction between these variables. On the BDI, where the interaction was particularly strong ($p < 0.001$), subjects who were high in both Actual:Ideal discrepancy and Ideal-Outcome Contingency had a mean BDI score of 25.0 (which is moderately depressed), whereas the remaining groups of subjects all had mean BDI scores of less than 9 (i.e., non-depressed). In comparison, subjects who were high in both Actual:Ought discrepancy and Ought-Outcome Contingency also had a mean BDI score of only 9.0. The moderately strong relation between Actual:Ought discrepancy combined with Ought-Outcome Contingency and anxiety/paranoid symptoms was mostly due to a significant ($p < 0.01$) main effect of level of Actual:Ought discrepancy. For the paranoid ideation measure, there was also a borderline significant ($p = 0.06$) main effect of level of Ought-Outcome Contingency.

The results in Table 1 suggest that, although relatively weak, there was also some evidence of both a relation between the Ideal self-guide and anxiety and a relation between the Ought self-guide and depression. The implications of these results are unclear for a number of reasons. First, as predicted, the relation between the Ideal self-guide and paranoid ideation was non-significant, and the relation between the Ought self-guide and depression as measured by the BDI was non-significant. Second, the HSCL Anxiety subscale is not a pure measure of agitation-related symptoms nor is the HSCL Depression subscale a pure measure of dejection-related symptoms. Third,

Table 1. Squared multiple correlations between domain of self-concept discrepancy plus outcome contingency and type of emotional problem

Domain of self-concept discrepancy and outcome contingency	Depression		Anxiety HSCL R^2	Paranoid HSCL R^2
	BDI R^2	HSCL R^2		
Ideal	0.39‡	0.27‡	0.18*	0.11
Ought	0.11	0.17*	0.22†	0.24†

BDI: Beck Depression Inventory, HSCL: Hopkins Symptom Checklist.
$n = 70$.
*$p < 0.05$, †$p < 0.01$, ‡$p < 0.001$.

our previous studies have found that there is a significant positive correlation between the magnitude of subjects' Actual:Ideal discrepancies and the magnitude of their Actual:Ought discrepancies, which is why partial correlational analyses are a more appropriate test of the hypothesized unique relations (see Higgins *et al.*, 1985b). To control, at least statistically, for this problem in the present study, analyses of covariance were performed in which level of Actual:Ought discrepancy was the covariate for the Ideal self-guide analyses and level of Actual:Ideal discrepancy was the covariate for the Ought self-guide analyses. These analyses replicated the significant relation between Ideal self-guide and depressive symptoms, as well as the significant relation between Ought self-guide and anxiety/paranoid symptoms. Both the relation between Ideal self-guide and HSCL Anxiety and the relation between Ought self-guide and HSCL Depression, however, were no longer significant ($p > 0.20$).

One other finding of this study is worth noting. There was a significant ($p < 0.05$) Level of Actual:Ideal Discrepancy × Level of Ideal-Outcome Contingency interaction on the HSCL subscale measure of anger-hostility, reflecting the fact that subjects who were high in both Actual:Ideal discrepancy and Ideal-Outcome Contingency had relatively high anger-hostility scores ($M = 9.5$; approximately the level of clinical outpatients) compared to the rest of the subjects ($M = 3.1$; approximately the level of normal, non-patients). There was no similar interaction involving subjects' Ought self-guide. Higgins *et al.*, (1985b) also found that frustration-related emotions were more strongly related to individuals' Actual:Ideal discrepancies than their Actual:Ought discrepancies. This finding is consistent with our conceptual analysis since both Actual:Ideal discrepancies and 'frustration/anger' reflect the absence or non-obtainment of positive outcomes.

There is considerable evidence, then, to support our hypothesis that different types of emotional problems are associated with different types of self-discrepancies. The evidence described thus far has been restricted to differences associated with domain of self (i.e., Ideal vs Ought), but there are also differences associated with standpoints on self (i.e., Own vs Other). We have found, for example, that although both Actual/Own:Ideal/Own discrepancy and Actual/Own:Ideal/Other discrepancy are associated with dejection-related emotions and symptoms, as predicted, each of these types of discrepancy is associated with a particular kind of dejection (see Higgins, 1984). Actual/Own:Ideal/Own discrepancy is associated with dejection from perceived lack of mastery or self-fulfilment, which includes feelings of disappointment, dissatisfaction, frustration, ineffectiveness, and self-blame. In contrast, Actual/Own:Ideal/Other discrepancy is associated with dejection from perceived or anticipated loss of social affection or esteem, which includes feelings of dependency, helplessness, sensitivity to rejection, and lack of pride. Thus, a full understanding of emotional vulnerability from self-discrepancies must take 'standpoint on self' into account as well as 'domain of self' and 'outcome contingency'.

CONCLUDING REMARKS

Self-discrepancy theory provides a general framework for understanding the emotional consequences of a variety of different types of self-conflicts and self-inconsistencies. It also provides a conceptual system for predicting what types of emotional vulnerabilities are (or might be) associated with which types of self-inconsistencies. Indeed, the theory could guide research to discriminate among types of emotions that may be associated with different types of self-conflicts and self-inconsistencies that heretofore have been described only as inducing general states of tension or discomfort.

The first two types of self-conflicts and self-inconsistencies described earlier—inconsistencies between the self and behavioural feedback, and contradictions among aspects of the self—could, especially, benefit from such an analysis. For example, when individuals behave in a manner that they believe is inconsistent with their personal aspirations (i.e., an Actual/Own:Ideal/Own discrepancy) they should feel disappointed and dissatisfied, but when they receive social feedback that disconfirms an actual self-attribute that currently matches significant others' goals for them (i.e., creates an Actual/Own:Ideal/Other discrepancy) they should feel embarrassed. A contradiction between an aspect of self representing the kind of person individuals believe they are and an aspect of self representing the kind of person some significant other believes they are (i.e., an Actual/Own:Actual/Other discrepancy) could induce confusion (see Erikson, 1963). Alternatively, a contradiction between an aspect of self representing what one significant other wants an individual to be and an aspect of self representing what another significant other believes it is the individual's duty to be (i.e., an Ideal/Other:Ought/Other discrepancy) could induce indecisiveness and uncertainty. A major goal of future research is to investigate the implications of these differences in emotional vulnerability for clinical treatment of emotional disorders, emotional problems in interpersonal relationships, and performance in school and the workplace.

ACKNOWLEDGEMENTS

The research reported in this chapter was supported by Grant MH39429 from the National Institute of Mental Health to the first author.

REFERENCES

Adler, A. (1964). *Problems of Neurosis*, Harper and Row, New York.
Allport, G. W. (1955). *Becoming*, Yale University Press, New Haven.
Arieti, S. and Bemporad, J. (1978). *Severe and Mild Depression: The Psychotherapeutic Approach*, Basic Books, New York.
Aronson, E. (1969). 'The theory of cognitive dissonance: A current perspective.' In L. Berkowitz (Ed.), *Advances in Experimental Social Psychology*, vol. 4, Academic Press, New York.
Beck, A. T. (1967). *Depression: Causes and Treatment*, University of Pennsylvania Press, Philadelphia.

Beck, A. T., Ward, C. H., Mendelson, M., Mock, J. and Erbaugh, J. (1961). 'An inventory for measuring depression.' *Archives of General Psychiatry*, **4**, 561–571.
Berne, E. (1964). *Games People Play*, Ballantine Books, New York.
Bramel, D. (1968). 'Dissonance, expectation, and the self.' In R. P. Abelson, E. Aronson, W. J. McGuire, T. M. Newcomb, M. J. Rosenberg and P. H. Tannenbaum (Eds), *Theories of Cognitive Consistency: A Sourcebook*, Rand McNally, Chicago, pp. 355–365.
Brim, O. G. (1976). 'Theories of the male mid-life crisis.' *Counseling Psychologist: Counseling Adults*. Special Issue.
Cooley, C. H. (1964). *Human Nature and the Social Order*, Schocken Books, New York (Original publication, 1902).
Derogatis, L. R., Lipman, R. S., Rickels, K., Uhlenhuth, E. H. and Covi, L. (1974). 'The Hopkins Symptom Checklist (HSCL): a self-report symptom inventory.' *Behavioural Science*, **19**, 1–15.
Duval, S. and Wicklund, R. A. (1972). *A Theory of Objective Self-awareness*, Academic Press, New York.
Epstein, S. (1973). 'The self-concept revisited or a theory of a theory.' *American Psychologist*, **28**, 405–416.
Epstein, S. (1981). 'The unity principle versus the reality and pleasure principles, or the tale of the scorpion and the frog.' In M. D. Lynch, A. A. Norem-Hebeisen, and K. Gergen (Eds), *Self Concept: Advances in Theory and Research*, Ballinger, Cambridge, Massachusetts.
Erikson, E. H. (1963). *Childhood and Society*, 2nd edn, W. W. Norton, New York (Original publication, 1950).
Erikson, E. H. (1968). *Identity: Youth and Crisis*, W. W. Norton, New York.
Festinger, L. (1957). *A Theory of Cognitive Dissonance*, Row, Peterson, Evanston, Illinois.
Freud, S. (1961). 'The ego and the id.' In *Standard Edition of the Complete Psychological Works of Sigmund Freud*, vol. 19, Hogarth Press, London (Original publication, 1923).
Harter, S. (in press). 'Cognitive-developmental processes in the integration of concepts about emotions and the self.' *Social Cognition*.
Higgins, E. T. (1984). 'Self-discrepancy: A theory relating self and affect.' Unpublished manuscript, New York University.
Higgins, E. T. and King, G. (1981). 'Accessibility of social constructs: Information processing consequences of individual and contextual variability.' In N. Cantor and J. Kihlstrom (Eds), *Personality, Cognition, and Social Interaction*, Erlbaum, Hillsdale, New Jersey.
Higgins, E. T., Bargh, J. A. and Lombardi, W. (1985). 'The nature of priming effects on categorization.' *Journal of Experimental Psychology: Learning, Memory and Cognition*, **11**, 59–69.
Higgins, E. T., Klein, R. and Strauman, T. (1985b). 'Self-concept discrepancy theory: A psychological model for distinguishing among different aspects of depression and anxiety.' *Social Cognition*, **3**, 51–76.
Higgins, E. T., Strauman, T. and Klein, R. (1985c). 'Standards and the process of self-evaluation: Multiple affects from multiple stages.' In R. M. Sorrentino and E. T. Higgins (Eds), *Handbook of Motivation and Cognition: Foundations of Social Behaviour*, Guilford Press, New York.
Higgins, E. T., Bond, R., Klein, R. and Strauman, T. (1986). Self-discrepancies and emotional vulnerability: How magnitude, accessibility, and type of discrepancy influence affect. *Journal of Personality and Social Psychology*, **51**, 5–15.
Hoffman, M. L. (1971). 'Identification and conscience development.' *Child Development*, **42**, 1071–1082.
Horney, K. (1950). *Neurosis and Human Growth*, W. W. Norton, New York.

Jacobs, D. (1971). 'Moods-emotion-affect: the nature of and manipulation of affective states with particular reference to positive affective states and emotional illness.' In A. Jacobs and L. B. Sachs (Eds), *The Psychology of Private Events*, Academic Press, New York.

James, W. (1948). *Psychology*. The World Publishing Company, New York (Original publication, 1890).

Kelley, H. H. (1952). 'Two functions of reference groups.' In G. E. Swanson, T. M. Newcomb and E. L. Hartley (Eds), *Readings in Social Psychology*, 2nd edn, Holt, Rinehart and Winston, New York.

Lazarus, A. A. (1968). 'Learning theory and the treatment of depression.' *Behavior Research and Therapy*, **6**, 83–89.

Lecky, P. (1961). *Self-Consistency: A Theory of Personality*, Shoe String Press, New York.

Lewin, K. (1935). *A Dynamic Theory of Personality: Selected Papers*, McGraw-Hill, New York.

Mead, G. H. (1934). *Mind, Self, and Society*, University of Chicago Press, Chicago.

Morse, S. J. and Gergen, K. J. (1970). 'Social comparison, self-consistency, and the concept of self.' *Journal of Personality and Social Psychology*, **16**, 148–156.

Olson, J. M. and Zanna, M. P. (1979). A new look at selective exposure. *Journal of Experimental Social Psychology*, **15**, 1–15.

Rado, S. (1956). 'The problem of melancholia.' In S. Rado, *Collected papers*, vol. 1, Grune and Stratton, New York (Original publication, 1927).

Rogers, C. R. (1959). 'A theory of therapy, personality, and interpersonal relationships, as developed in the client-centered framework.' In S. Koch (Ed.), *Psychology: A study of a science*, vol. 3, *Formulations of the Person and the Social Context*, McGraw-Hill, New York, pp. 184–256.

Rogers, C. R. (1961). *On Becoming a Person*, Houghton Mifflin Company, Boston.

Roseman, I. (1979). 'Cognitive aspects of emotion and emotional behavior.' *87th Annual Convention of the American Psychological Association*, New York City.

Scheier, M. and Carver, C. (1983). 'Two sides of self: One for you and me for me.' In J. Suls and A. Greenwald (Eds), *Psychological Perspectives on the Self*, vol. 2, Erlbaum, Hillsdale, New Jersey.

Snyder, M. (1979). 'Self-monitoring processes.' In L. Berkowitz (Ed.), *Advances In Experimental Social Psychology*, vol. 12, Academic Press, New York. Sullivan, H. S. (1953). *The Collected Works of Harry Stack Sullivan*, vol. 1, H. S. Perry and M. L. Gawel (Eds), W. W. Norton, New York.

Swann, W. B., Jr. (1983). 'Self-verification: Bringing social reality into harmony with the self.' In J. Suls and A. G. Greenwald (Eds), *Social Psychological Perspectives on the Self*, vol. 2, Erlbaum, Hillsdale, New Jersey, pp. 33–66.

Turner, R. H. (1956). 'Role-taking, role standpoint, and reference-group behavior.' *American Journal of Sociology*, **61**, 316–328.

Wicklund, R. A. and Brehm, J. W. (1976). *Perspectives on Cognitive Dissonance*, Erlbaum, Hillsdale, New Jersey.

Wylie, C. C. (1979). *The Self-Concept*, University of Nebraska Press, Lincoln.

Self and Identity: Psychosocial Perspectives
Edited by K. Yardley and T. Honess
© 1987 John Wiley & Sons Ltd

15

Shyness and Self-Presentation

Robert M. Arkin

The shy individual, preoccupied with avoiding social disapproval, adopts a self-protective, self-presentational style. However, when the shy person has little to lose in a relationship an acquisitive self-presentational style is adopted. The consequence is little opportunity to diagnose self-worth; further, self-doubt (that characterizes the shy person) is sustained.

INTRODUCTION

Research on self-presentation has grown immensely in scope and sophistication during the past two decades. One can hardly scan a journal in social psychology without seeing some intriguing demonstration of the ways people behave to create impressions on others. Further, taxonomies, models, and analyses of the motivational basis of self-presentation have been offered (e.g., Arkin and Baumgardner, 1985; Jones and Pittman, 1982). Lengthy reviews of the process (Baumeister, 1982) and collections of perspectives on the topic (Tedeschi, 1981) have come fast and furious as well.

The term 'self-presentation' refers to the process by which individuals establish an identity by controlling the images of self available to others. The existence of self-presentation is the 'inevitable consequence of social perception' (Snyder, 1977); in short, people know that others are continuously forming impressions of them, and make use of these impressions to guide the course and outcome of social interaction. The particular image an actor is likely to convey depends on the specific interests, or goals, the presenter has in that social interaction (cf. Weary and Arkin, 1981). The goals are many and varied, of course (cf. Goffman, 1959, p. 3). To achieve certain audience reactions, quite diverse presentations of self are necessary (e.g., Jones and Pittman, 1982).

Interest in self-presentation has been sparked from time to time by various individual difference approaches. In the early 1970s, there was a flurry of activity among a group of social and personality psychologists studying the 'Machiavellian' personality. The Machiavellian was found to demonstrate awe-inspiring manipulative skill. Earlier, in the 1960s, the influential Marlowe-Crowne Social Desirability Scale was written. People scoring high in social desirability needs (i.e., need for approval) were found to engage in a wide range of socially desirable behaviours. Most recently, a scale was developed to identify the skilled impression manager (the 'high self-monitoring' individual).

Notably, each of these approaches has focused expressly on the successful, facile, smooth, and graceful among us. The polar opposite to the skill of the Machiavellian or the High Self-Monitor might be construed as the person unconcerned with social influence, or driven solely by the dictates of internal dispositions. However, the painfully shy individual, whom we have all met at one time or another, have read about in the popular press, and have recently seen analysed in the psychological literature (e.g., Jones *et al.*, 1985), presents another polar opposite to the skilled impression manager or facile Machiavellian.

SHYNESS: AN EXCEPTION TO THE RULE

There is some social risk inherent in all interpersonal relations. Failure, embarrassment, rejection, and losses in social status loom as potential outcomes of social relations right alongside the joys and pleasure of relating to others. The terms 'acquisitive self-presentation' and 'protective self-presentation' were coined to capture differences in reactions to this risk (Arkin, 1981). Acquisitive self-presentation refers to those instances in which an individual approaches and embraces this risk, treating the presentation of self as a challenge, by presenting an image of self that is the most favourable possible. By contrast, the term 'protective self-presentation' characterizes social conservatism. The 'protective' individual attempts to create an impression that is merely safe. The shy individual was posed as the prototypical sort of person inclined to adopt such a conservative social orientation (Arkin, 1981).

The term 'safe' seems particularly apt because of the unique motive system thought to underlie protective self-presentation: the motive to *avoid social disapproval*. Specifically, it was proposed that all people from time to time, and some people chronically, approach social situations intending merely to avoid social disapproval rather than to seek approval. Further, it was suggested that people accomplish this proactively by choosing, modifying, or creating social contexts so that social disapproval is unlikely to occur (cf. Arkin, 1981). In summary, despite the general preference to present oneself in socially desirable ways (in order to engender approval and liking, sustain an interaction, and maximize the likelihood that others will help meet one's social and material needs), the motive to sustain a sense of safety and security (e.g., Sullivan, 1953) often predominates.

For the shy individual, disapproval must be a most compelling experience; it would confirm self-doubts and damage an already precarious sense of self-worth. Because disapproval would diminish one's feelings of competence and self-worth, confirming the shy person's worst fears, it would also diminish the shy individual's sense of personal efficacy (Bandura, 1977) and perhaps have a paralysing impact on his or her future behaviour. To behave in ways that maximize pleasure and minimize pain, a person must have some measure of personal control over his or her own actions and the environment. Perhaps more importantly, an individual must *believe* in his or her own efficacy; if one does not, the likelihood of initiating potentially rewarding actions and continuing such actions to their completion may be diminished (e.g., Bandura, 1977). In the extreme, this may even lead to the sort of inaction associated with learned helplessness. Ironically, then, protective self-presentation may be a strategy for maintaining a sense of personal control.

The empirical link

Very little research has directly examined the self-presentational behaviour of shy individuals. Nevertheless, several studies shed some light on this issue. In particular, support for the self-presentation styles idea has been uncovered in the area of self-attribution.

The most direct way to establish a particular identity is to describe oneself to others. One self-description that has received a great deal of research attention is self-attribution for successful and unsuccessful task performance (cf. Arkin *et al.*, 1980b). It has been demonstrated time and again that individuals make greater self-attributions for their behaviour if it results in positive outcomes than if it results in negative outcomes. By taking credit for good acts and denying blame for bad ones, an individual is able to sustain or enhance his or her public image (cf. Weary and Arkin, 1981).

However, socially anxious individuals are more self-effacing than that. They report far more modest attributions (attributing greater causality to themselves for failure than for success), especially when they anticipate close scrutiny of their attributions and behaviour (Arkin *et al.*, 1980a). By contrast, persons low in social anxiety report more personally flattering attributions of responsibility under these very same conditions.

Modesty in one's attributions is safe and defensible. Nevertheless, while safe and defensible, modesty has its disadvantages. In particular, extreme modesty represents an unfavourable presentation of self, especially in the case of self-attribution for failure. While shy individuals may find themselves unable to be as aggrandizing as non-shy persons, modesty would not seem to be a perfect solution to the dilemma.

Jones and Berglas (1978) recently proposed a subtle behavioural strategem, called 'self-handicapping', that provides a viable means of regulating the threat of social disapproval. In self-handicapping an individual seeks out or creates a 'handicap' (an external, inhibitory factor that interferes with performance), and thereby obscures the link between performance and evaluation (at least in the case of failure). By asserting the presence of a persuasive external 'excuse' for poor performance one can mitigate the impact of the failure experience because the failure cannot be viewed as a clear reflection of low ability. Naturally, shy individuals should be reluctant to claim such an excuse unless the excuse is patently obvious to observers. Yet, if the handicap is quite clear, this would have some surprisingly desirable ramifications for the shy individual.

Two sets of findings support the idea that handicapping is a close cousin to protective self-presentation. First, there is mounting evidence that self-handicapping is found predominantly among individuals who harbour self-doubts and are plagued with concerns over social disapproval (Arkin and Baumgardner, 1985). Second, as mentioned above, there are surprisingly desirable ramifications of handicaps for the shy person. The presence of a persuasive handicap should free the shy individual to pursue acquisitive types of self-presentation because failure would no longer compromise one's public image. Indeed, there is evidence that shy persons stop worrying about failure, adopt an acquisitive self-presentation style, and perform much better in social relations when (ironically) there is a clear external reason why they should be unsuccessful!

Both Leary (1984) and Brodt and Zimbardo (1981) found that socially anxious individuals, exposed to a distracting noise that would supposedly interfere with an ability to interact with others, were less anxious during a social interaction than their counterparts not exposed to the 'handicap'. In a similar 'loud noise' condition, meant to be analogous to a noisy party or a nightclub with a loud band, we (Arkin and Baumgardner) recently found that high socially anxious individuals presented themselves more positively (in a variety of ways) than their low social anxiety counterparts. Further, they were rated by their interaction partners as having performed more successfully during the interaction. In the 'soft noise' condition, however, high social anxiety individuals were much more modest in their self-presentation than their low social anxiety counterparts. They were also less successful inter-personally.

In a related way, Arkin and Schumann (1983) found that shy individuals wrote less in defence of a decision (relative to non-shy individuals) when the experimental situation was rigged so that they could only lose social approval they had gained earlier (i.e., their essays might produce disapproval). Interestingly, when subjects could only gain approval, shy individuals wrote more than their non-shy counterparts! On another measure, shy persons took longer to get started writing a defence of a decision (i.e., were more cautious and hesitant) when they were facing the prospect of disapproval, but were quicker getting started than their non-shy counterparts when they could only gain approval.

These findings provide direct evidence for the link between fear of dis-approval and protective self-presentation. When fear of disapproval was experimentally eliminated, shy persons were even more 'acquisitive' in their presentation of self than were their non-shy counterparts.

THE MOTIVATIONAL BASIS OF PROTECTIVE SELF-PRESENTATION: THE ROLES OF 'STATE' AND 'TRAIT' SOCIAL ANXIETY

Having examined the initial empirical evidence concerning the self-presentation of the shy individual we are now in a position to expand our analysis to encompass both the antecedents and consequences of the protective presentation style. In between, speculations about the motivational basis of the protective presentation style, and the role of social anxiety in this approach, can be addressed.

Aetiology

The aetiology of the protective self-presentation style, when chronic, is thought to be associated with self-doubt and shaky self-confidence. To illustrate, in the course of one hour, children in one experiment were led to focus attention on potential losses as opposed to potential gains, or potential gains rather than losses; those focused on potential losses developed a conservative (e.g., hesitant and cautious) response style while those focused on gains were achievement-oriented (Canavan-Gumpert, 1977). Similarly, test-anxious individuals, who are known to worry about and doubt their own capabilities, tend to withhold their responses in a conservative and hesitant way (Geen, 1985) while non-anxious individuals are quick to respond.

Several authors have written the ideal prescription for producing chronic anxious uncertainty in an individual and, thus, an overriding concern with the question of self-worth (e.g., Jones and Berglas, 1978). Socialization conditions that foster such a concern may rest substantially with early family relationships (see Mollon, this volume). Yet, others have even argued that genetic predispositions play a role in shyness (e.g., Plomin and Daniels, 1985).

Regardless of its origins, the experience of shyness seems to be best characterized as feelings of a need for self-enhancement mixed with an overwhelming sense of self-doubt. For example, shy individuals are delighted at receiving positive interpersonal evaluations, yet they harbour doubt about the accuracy of such feedback and the insight of their benefactor (Lake and Arkin, 1985). Shy persons who can lose social approval behave quite protectively, yet they behave quite acquisitively (i.e., seek approval) when they could gain approval without the threat of disapproval (Arkin and Baumgardner, 1985; Arkin and Schumann, 1983).

Shy individuals must fulfil the requirements of the motive to avoid disapproval before turning to the job of seeking approval (Sullivan, 1953). For instance, the acquisitive self-presentation of socially anxious individuals (e.g., Arkin and Schumann, 1983; Leary, 1984) occurs only when features of the context suggest that disapproval is unlikely to ensue (i.e., when they feel safe). By contrast, people who are 'reward-oriented' generate little concern over disapproval. However, the shy individual, who is 'cost-oriented', must be very sensitive to situational factors that make disapproval more or less likely. The 'cost-oriented' shy person must always debate the choice between a protective and an acquisitive self-presentation style.

It may be that shy individuals tend to see most situations as potentially costly (i.e., disapproval is likely). This could account for the variety of findings that shy people spoil their social image through conservative and protective self-presentation tactics (e.g., modesty, conformity, social withdrawal, social reticence, attitudinal neutrality, and occasionally alcohol and drug abuse) so readily. If so, then shy persons may actually receive less social reinforcement from others than their non-shy peers. This would render social approval all the more powerful for them.

The regulation of 'state' social anxiety

Schlenker and Leary (1982) proposed that social anxiety arises when a person is motivated to make a particular impression on an audience, but doubts that he or she is able to do so. In short, if an unsatisfactory evaluative reaction from a subjectively important audience is likely, social anxiety should result.

Naturally, according to this viewpoint an individual must assess the likelihood of achieving a preferred self-presentation, or social anxiety should never occur. Schlenker and Leary (1982) therefore propose that an assessment process is triggered whenever a self-presentational goal is important to the individual, and when some signal indicates that the social performance underway may be undermined. If the assessment indicates that the desired image will be achieved, the initial presentation of self is reinaugurated. However, if the assessment indicates that the desired image will not be achieved, the individual must 'make the best of a bad situation' (p. 658). To cope with such a predicament, the individual will adopt a cautious, innocuous, or non-committal presentation (Schlenker and Leary, 1982).

In summary, then, Schlenker and Leary (1982) propose protective self-presentation as a way to deal with disapproval avoidance, and keep feelings of social anxiety in check. But they introduce a switch from acquisitive motives to protective motives rather than proposing protective motives as a separate end sought chronically by some individuals. They clearly focused on the average, non-shy individual's decision to switch from an acquisitive pattern to a protective pattern.

The self-presentation styles approach emphasizes that the shy individual is chronically engaged in an 'assessment' process, and therefore often opts for the protective style right from the outset in interpersonal relations. The shy individual readily sees disapproval as likely, and keeping feelings of social anxiety in check is therefore of paramount importance. Nevertheless, the two approaches are identical in asserting that protective self-presentation is designed to minimize feelings of social anxiety.

Consequences of protective self-presentation

The impact of self-presentational behaviour on self-concept is a topical concern of only recent vintage. Historically, most social psychologists have viewed the self as a '. . . product and reflection of social life' (Shrauger and Schoenemann, 1979, p. 549). Specifically, internalization is mediated by an individual's interpretation of others' responsive treatment of him or her. Unfortunately, the shy individual who adopts a protective stance is unable to gain this valuable social information. In an effort to protect a precarious sense of self-worth, and to avoid confirmation of self-doubts, the shy individual structures interpersonal encounters so that others are in a position to provide little, or at best ambiguous, evaluative feedback. The shy individual who 'plays it safe' may not receive disapproval, but is not likely to be highly regarded either. A vicious cycle ensues: to protect themselves from confirmation of self-doubts, shy persons avoid social evaluation, and this contributes to the uncertainty that fed their doubts about self-worth to begin with.

The impact of self-presentational behaviour on subsequent self-concept can follow two paths. The one described above might be called the social route. An audience reacts to a given behaviour; the presenter then interprets their reaction and sometimes internalizes the action as a reflection of self. As described above, the shy person precludes such a process through his or her protective actions.

Another, more individual or personal, route involves processes of self-perception and self-attribution. Individuals observe and interpret their own self-presentations and, as a result, sometimes internalize them through processes of self-perception or cognitive dissonance reduction. This would be particularly disadvantageous to shy individuals because, although shy persons may desire approbation even more than others, they rarely attempt to gain it. Thus, the presentation of self they are most likely to internalize is a modest and self-effacing one.

Interestingly, on the exceptional occasion when they seek positive evaluation acquisitively, shy individuals may do so with more effort and vigour than their non-shy counterparts. This effort may, ironically, sap the power of any positive evaluation received to increase feelings of self-worth; approval that is achieved through great efforts may be discounted as self-relevant (e.g., Arkin and Baumgardner, 1985; Jones and Pittman, 1982), and is unlikely to be incorporated into one's self-concept.

In sum, then, at least for the shy individual, self-conception is relatively resistant to change (cf. Wiley and Alexander, this volume). This is attributable, at least in part, to the sort of vicious cycle described above.

SUMMARY AND CONCLUSIONS

The shy person is preoccupied with avoiding social disapproval and, more often than not, adopts a protective self-presentation style (withdraws from social interaction, adopts neutral or conforming attitudes, is modest in attributions, and self-handicaps). The purpose of such an interpersonal style is to self-regulate feelings of social anxiety and perhaps to sustain a sense of personal efficacy, control, and therefore hope. Interestingly, the evidence also implies that when the shy person is highly confident that he or she has 'nothing to lose' in a social setting, he or she may adopt an acquisitive self-presentation style. By being protective whenever failure is possible, and acquisitive only when success is guaranteed, the shy individual has little opportunity to diagnose self-worth. As a consequence, the precarious sense of self-worth that characterizes the shy individual is sustained.

REFERENCES

Arkin, R. M. (1981). 'Self-presentation styles.' In J. T. Tedeschi (Ed.), *Impression Management Theory and Social Psychological Research*, Academic Press, New York, pp. 311–333.

Arkin, R. M. and Baumgardner, A. H. (1985). 'Self handicapping.' In J. H. Harvey and G. Weary (Eds), *Attribution: Basic Issues and Applications*, Academic Press, New York.

Arkin, R. M. and Schumann, D. (1983). 'Self-presentational styles: the roles of cost orientation and shyness.' *The American Psychological Association*, Anaheim, California.

Arkin, R. M., Appelman, A. J. and Burger, J. M. (1980a). 'Social anxiety, self-presentation, and the self-serving bias in causal attribution.' *Journal of Personality and Social Psychology*, **38**, 23–35.

Arkin, R. M., Cooper, H. M. and Kolditz, T. (1980b). 'A statistical review of the literature concerning the self-serving attribution bias in interpersonal influence situations.' *Journal of Personality*, **48**, 435–448.

Bandura, A. (1977). 'Self-efficacy: toward a unifying theory of behavioral change.' *Psychological Review*, **84**, 191–215.

Baumeister, R. F. (1982). 'A self-presentational view of social phenomena.' *Psychological Bulletin*, **91**, 3–26.

Brodt, S. E. and Zimbardo, P. G. (1981). 'Modifying shyness-related behavior through symptom misattribution.' *Journal of Personality and Social Psychology*, **41**, 437–449.

Canavan-Gumpert, D. (1977). 'Generating reward and cost orientations through praise and criticism.' *Journal of Personality and Social Psychology*, **35**, 501–513.

Geen, R. G. (1985). 'Test anxiety and visual vigilance.' *Journal of Personality and Social Psychology*, **49**, 963–970.

Goffman, E. (1959). *The Presentation of Self in Everyday Life*, Doubleday Anchor, Garden City, New York.

Jones, E. E. and Berglas, S. (1978). 'Control of attributions about the self through self-handicapping strategies: the appeal of alcohol and the role of underachievement.' *Personality and Social Psychology Bulletin*, **4**, 200–206.

Jones, E. E. and Pittman, T. S. (1982). 'Toward a general theory of strategic self-presentation.' In J. Suls (Ed.), *Psychological Perspectives on the Self*, Erlbaum, Hillsdale, New Jersey, pp. 231–262.

Jones, W., Cheek, J. and Briggs, S. (1985). *Shyness: Perspectives on Research and Treatment*, Plenum Press, New York.

Lake, E. A. and Arkin, R. M. (1985). 'Reactions to objective and subjective interpersonal evaluation: the influence of social anxiety.' *Journal of Social and Clinical Psychology*, **3**, 143–160.

Leary, M. R. (1984). *Social Anxiety and Interpersonal Concerns: Testing a Self-presentational Explanation*. Unpublished manuscript, University of Texas, Austin.

Plomin, R. and Daniels, D. (1985). 'Genetics and shyness.' In W. Jones, J. Cheek and S. Briggs (Eds), *Shyness: Perspectives on Research and Treatment*, Plenum Press, New York.

Schlenker, B. R. and Leary, M. R. (1982). 'Social anxiety and self-presentation: A conceptualization and model.' *Psychological Bulletin*, **92**, 641–669.

Shrauger, J. S. and Schoenemann, T. J. (1979). 'Symbolic interactionist view of the self-concept: Through the looking-glass darkly.' *Psychological Bulletin*, **86**, 549–573.

Snyder, M. (1977). 'Impression management: the self in social interaction.' In L. S. Wrightsman and K. Deaux (Eds), *Social Psychology in the Eighties*, Brooks/Cole Publishing, Monterey, California, pp. 90–121.

Sullivan, H. S. (1953). *The Interpersonal Theory of Psychiatry*, W. W. Norton, New York.

Tedeschi, J. T. (1981). *Impression Management and Social Psychological Research*, Academic Press, New York.

Weary, G. and Arkin, R. (1981). 'Attributional self-presentation.' In J. H. Harvey, W. Ickes and R. F. Kidd (Eds), *New Directions in Attributional Research*, vol. 3, Erlbaum, New York, pp. 223–246.

Self and Identity: Psychosocial Perspectives
Edited by K. Yardley and T. Honess
© 1987 John Wiley & Sons Ltd

16

Self-Awareness and Other-Awareness: The Use of Perspective in Everyday Life

Thomas J. Figurski

Whereas the allocentric perspective addresses one's own external image, it also addresses the other's internal experience. Conversely, the egocentric perspective addresses one's own experience, but the other's image. Experience Sampling data from 31 subjects revealed that patterns in the use of person-awareness were related to the differential use of these perspectives.

INTRODUCTION

The ability to take the perspective of the other has long been considered by symbolic interactionists and cognitive developmentalists as fundamental to the development of the self. Mead (1934) emphasized early social interaction as the context in which the child learns to take the role of the other and first perceive oneself as an object. Piaget (1926) and Flavell (1968) likewise pursued the significance of early communication for considering oneself from the perspective of the other.

Yet is is important to recognize that the ability to manipulate one's perspective is not only important to self-awareness but also has important implications for one's awareness of other people. As Flavell (1968) has pointed out in his work on role-taking, one must first become aware that other people have a different perspective before adopting that perspective in relation to the self. Furthermore, as Wegner (1982) has suggested, recognizing that others have a different point of view changes our understanding and awareness of them as well.

In this way, it is the manipulation of perspective that relates self-awareness to our awareness of other people, i.e., 'other-awareness', giving the study of self-awareness broader implications. What we learn about the use of perspective in self-awareness may teach us something about other-awareness and, even more fundamentally, about the nature of attention in general. Thus, while this chapter develops out of the study of self-awareness, it addresses a more comprehensive person-awareness, one that includes the awareness of others as well as oneself.

Of particular importance is the work in social psychology, spurred largely by Duval and Wicklund's (1972) self-awareness theory. Recent study in this area has distinguished between 'private' and 'public' forms of self-awareness, according to whether one is attending to internal or external aspects of the self. Private self-awareness has a more introspective quality and focuses on content that is considered unobservable to others, such as emotional feelings, bodily sensations, thoughts, and attitudes. Public self-awareness is defined as attention to the aspects of oneself that are relevant to one's status as a social object, primarily behaviour, expressions, and appearance (Buss, 1980; Carver and Scheier, 1981; Diener and Srull, 1979; Fenigstein *et al.*, 1975; Froming *et al.*, 1982). Although this distinction alludes to the significance of perspective, the relationship between this difference in content and the use of perspective has not been fully developed.

The purpose at hand is to reach a more precise understanding of the role that perspective plays, not only for the different kinds of self-awareness but for differences in other-awareness as well.

Wegner and Giuliano (1982) provide a thorough categorization of the different forms of social awareness, one that recognizes the significance of both the focus of attention (focal awareness) and the perspective that is used (tacit awareness). They discuss how these two features of awareness relate to what constitutes our attention, the meaning that is imparted to that content, and how it is evaluated.

The present chapter pursues the question of how such changes in focus and perspective are related to differences in the content of our awareness. Specifically, it addresses how changes in perspective can first explain the distinction made between private and public self-awareness, and second, account for related differences in our awareness of other people. This will be addressed both theoretically and empirically.

TOWARD A BROADER CONCEPTUALIZATION OF PERSON-AWARENESS

To understand the complexities of self-awareness and other-awarenesses, it is necessary to address the fundamentals. To that end, attention is defined as a relationship of perception or apprehension between a subject and an object. The subject is the source of the attention, that which does the perceiving or apprehending, and the object is the target of attention, that which is apprehended or perceived. The term 'awareness' is meant to indicate the subject's state of attending to something.

If the subject and object are the same entity or person, then the target of one's awareness is the self, and this creates the condition of self-awareness. If subject and object are not the same entity, then the target is not oneself but considered an aspect of the environment, and awareness is thus directed away from the self toward the environment. The present concern is specifically with the comparison of self-awareness to the awareness of one part of the environment, namely other people. While the self and other people are clearly different objects of attention, they are each capable of being subjects of attention as well. It is this shared capacity for awareness that renders our awareness of self and others all the more complex.

As for the more specific differentiation of private and public self-awareness, this distinction has rested on a determination of whether the given content is respectively unobservable or observable to others. What is intuitively understood by this difference in content is more precisely identified as a difference in the perspective one is using to apprehend the self.

Perspective is the attentional position or point of reference that is taken to attend to the target. Recognizing that other people have the capacity for awareness and are thus also subjects of attention, we have learned to vary our perspective by considering their point of reference as opposed to our own (Piaget, 1926; Mead, 1934; Flavell, 1968). Because taking the perspective of the other requires the assumption of a reference point outside the self, it is best referred to as other-centred or 'allocentric'. On the other hand, to anchor the point of reference in the self is to make use of a self-centred or 'egocentric' perspective (Piaget, 1926). These can be referred to as two different forms of 'tacit' awareness, as suggested by Wegner (1982).

The attentional 'orientation' is not the relationship beween the subject and target of attention but rather the relationship between the reference point that is used and the target. Specifically, if the reference point is separate from the object, as when one uses the perspective of the other to attend to the self, then the orientation is considered 'objective'. External self-aspects can be defined as the content of this objective self-awareness, i.e., those elements of the self that are accessible to the outside point of reference. This 'external' content will be referred to collectively as one's 'image'.

What is accessible to this perspective is often identified simply as that which is accessible to others. Yet it is important to understand that the essence of the criterion for external self-aspects is the use of an independent reference point to apprehend oneself, regardless of whether others actually perceive us in the same way or not.

On the other hand, if the reference point is not separate from the object, then the orientation is 'subjective'. By relying on the position of being the object and attending to the self-target from what is considered a reference point of 'privilege' (hence private self-awareness), one makes available a wealth of material that has been identified intuitively as internal self-content. Such internal aspects (e.g., affect, physical sensation) are generally referred to as 'experience'.

In this way, while private and public self-awareness are identifiable from their content, it is really the perspective of oneself that is differentiated.

However, the ability to manipulate perspective is not limited to self-awareness. If we can use these different perspectives to become aware of different aspects of ourselves, so we can also use them to attend to different aspects of other people.

It is obvious that we are capable of attending to others from our own physically separate point of reference, thereby adopting an objective orientation to others and focusing on external aspects of their presentation, whether appearance, behaviours, or expressions.

However, while we are physically separate from other people, we need not always maintain a separate reference point, as has often been assumed. Rather, we can manipulate our orientation and consider other people from what we generally think of as their own perspective. This is why the realization that others are similarly capable of awareness makes them more complex and intriguing objects of attention.

When we consider someone's own perspective of his or her own self, it is an attempt to attend to the other person as if from an unseparated reference point. We put ourselves in their shoes, so to speak, and assume an attentional orientation as if from the position of being them. In this way, our attention is sensitive to other people's experience by taking a subjective orientation toward them from their own perspective. This can be recognized as the means by which we empathize with others' experience, whether it is joy, anxiety or physical discomfort.

It is important to understand that the question of accuracy is an altogether different issue. The allocentric perspective, whether focusing on our own external image or the personal experience of other people, is essentially an 'as if' proposition. Just as we have questions about whether we can ever be truly objective toward ourselves, so we also question whether we can accurately assess other people's experience. Regardless of accuracy, the point is that we regularly try to do so. The allocentric perspective describes the attentional condition we use when we consider how we look or what other people feel.

To suggest that we can manipulate our perspective toward ourselves but not toward others would be an incomplete proposition. Indeed, it can be argued that adopting the perspective of the other toward ourselves is dependent upon the ability to first consider the other's internal experience, specifically the perception of ourselves from that perspective. In other words, if we can not consider the experience of the other, then we can never be objective toward ourselves. The ability to manipulate perspective toward the self is also the ability to manipulate perspective toward others.

This model identifies three main dimensions of person-awareness: target, perspective, and content. Perspective (egocentric or allocentric) interacts with target (self or other) to produce the specific orientation, and hence content (experience or image), of awareness. In this way, the ability to vary perspective is applicable to other-awareness as well as self-awareness, and allows us to focus our attention on different aspects of either target. Specifically, the perspective that addresses the experiential content of one target naturally focuses on the image content of the other. Using the two perspectives toward each of the two targets yields four categories of attention: self-experience awareness, self-image awareness, other-image awareness, and other-experience awareness, as illustrated in Figure 1.

TARGET

	Self	Other
Egocentric	SELF EXPERIENCE AWARENESS (INTERNAL)	OTHER IMAGE AWARENESS (EXTERNAL)
PERSPECTIVE		
Allocentric	SELF IMAGE AWARENESS (EXTERNAL)	OTHER EXPERIENCE AWARENESS (INTERNAL)

EMPIRICAL QUESTIONS

The theoretical focus of this chapter is to extend the study of self-awareness to address the more comprehensive phenomenon of person-awareness. On an empirical level, a secondary purpose is to explore this phenomenon specifically as it occurs in the natural context of everyday life. At this time, it is possible to present some preliminary data regarding the relationship among the four kinds of person-awareness. Two fundamental questions will be briefly addressed:

1. To what degree do self-image awareness, self-experience awareness, other-image awareness, and other-experience awareness each occur in everyday life; and how do they compare to one another in their overall level of usage?
2. To what extent are these four forms of person-awareness used together in everyday life? More specifically, do individuals differ in their tendencies to use certain kinds of attention together?

METHOD

Description of the sample

The sample consisted of 31 adult volunteers from undergraduate evening classes at Roosevelt University, a small private college located in the downtown business district of Chicago, Illinois. Sixteen males and 15 females ranged in age from 20 to 51 years, yielding a mean of 30.3 years. Thus they were older than the typical undergraduate population.

Most subjects maintained employment beside their student activities: twenty worked full-time and three worked part-time, while five were unemployed. (Three subjects failed to provide this information.) Occupations ranged from professional (teachers) to unskilled labour. Annual income was generally low to moderate, with a personal median of $15 500 and a household median of $26 900.

Materials and procedure

Data were collected using the Experience Sampling Method (ESM), a procedure that obtains self-reports at random moments in the participant's everyday life (Csikszentmihalyin and Figurski, 1982; Csikszentmihalyi and Graef, 1980; Csiszentmihalyi *et al.*, 1977; Larson *et al.*, 1980). Specifically, subjects were given an electronic paging device to carry for eight consecutive days: one practice day and a week of data collection. From 8:00 am to 10:00 pm, this instrument periodically emitted a signal (beep) according to a schedule randomized within two-hour segments. This schedule produced eight signals each day, allowing for a maximum of 56 self-reports over the seven days.

Subjects were also provided with a booklet of Random Activity Information Sheets (RAISs), which requested information regarding their attention, feelings, activities, and situational context as they were 'just before you were beeped'. Subjects' responses thus provide a description of the ongoing flow of events and of their moment-to-moment experience. Subjects were instructed to fill out the response form as soon as a signal was received, a task that required approximately one to five minutes. Their responses to the various items on this form provided the data. A minimum of 30 filled-out RAISs was required for inclusion in the sample.

At a follow-up session, subjects were asked for their general reaction to the procedure. Specific entries on the RAISs were reviewed for legibility and clarification. The possibility of bias from hypothesis-testing or discussion with others was addressed, and subjects were debriefed as to the specific nature of the investigation.

Among the questions regarding subjects' attention were four rating scales, each ranging from 0 ('not aware') to 3 ('very aware'), with which subjects indicated the level of their person-awareness. Each of these four items referred specifically to the content of a particular form of person-awareness:

1. aware of how someone else looked, sounded, or appeared' (other-image awareness);
2. 'aware of how you looked, sounded, or appeared' (self-image awareness);
3. 'aware of how you were personally experiencing something' (self-experience awareness);
4. 'aware of how someone else was personally experiencing something' (other-experience awareness).

Subjects' responses to these rating scales provided the data that will be discussed here.

By measuring each kind of person-awareness separately, these scales did not impose the dichotomies of self versus other, internal versus external, or egocentric versus allocentric. Rather each of the four kinds of awareness was free to vary independently, so that any relationship among them was possible. In this way, any consistent pattern to their use in everyday life would be revealed empirically rather than imposed artifactually.

RESULTS AND DISCUSSION

The everyday use of person-awareness

The 31 subjects provided a total of 1298 reports (mean = 41.9). Reasons for missing information included, as in past studies, the failure of the paging procedure or device; or the subject not being awake, not hearing the signal, not having the beeper, having the beeper turned off (e.g., during an exam) or being unable to respond immediately.

The first order of business was to determine the degree to which the subjects were aware of their own image, their own experience, other people's image, and other people's experience over the course of their daily lives. The rate at which each form of person-awareness occurred was indicated by the proportion of ratings on the designated scale that were at least 1 ('somewhat aware'). The mean intensity with which each subject used a particular form of awareness was determined from the given subject's mean rating on the appropriate scale. While the intensity score used the full range of the scale (0–3), it provided a more precise indication of the relative use of a particular form of awareness.

The four kinds of person-awareness were compared on both frequency rate and mean intensity by paired Student's t-test. Sample means of the subjects' frequency rates and intensity scores for each kind of awareness are presented for convenient reference in Table 1, while specific results of the paired t-test are presented in Table 2.

Differences among the frequency rates were all found to be statistically significant ($p < 0.05$) in the following descending order: self-experience awareness, self-image awareness, other-image awareness, and other-experience awareness. Likewise for differences in mean intensity, with the

Table 1. Person-awareness within individuals: the rate of frequency* and mean level of intensity† averaged across subjects‡ ($n = 31$)

Perspective percent > 0 mean	Target	
	Self	Other
Egocentric	88% 1.84 Self-experience awareness	69% 1.37 Other-image awareness
Allocentric	77% 1.39 Self-image awareness	49% 0.92 Other-experience awareness

* Percentage of beeps awareness rated > 0.
† Mean rating of awareness (range = 0–3).
‡ Figures were determined first for each subject and then averaged across the sample.

exception that the levels for self-image awareness and other-image awareness were not significantly different.

The staggering rate of occurrence for self-awareness (of experience: 88 per cent; of image: 77 per cent) indicated that this condition is not an isolated experience, but rather very much the rule. Recognizing this, it becomes more meaningful to speak of variations in the degree of self-awareness. Similarly other-awareness, although lower in frequency, still occurred to a substantial degree (of image: 69 per cent; of experience 49 per cent). That subjects reported being at least somewhat aware of other people's experience nearly half the time is particularly interesting, considering the argument that such content is difficult to access.

Of course, subjects may have simply been disinclined to indicate themselves at 'not aware' on any of the given scales. Yet, as long as subjects rated themselves aware of something, why would they feel the need to indicate themselves aware of everything? While these figures may be somewhat inflated, it is also possible that the non-dichotomous rating scales were more sensitive to legitimate levels of subsidiary or background awareness.

If these frequency rates are valid, then no two of the four kinds of attention are mutually exclusive. This in itself has important implications for studies that dichotomize self-awareness versus outward-directed attention or public versus private self-awareness, whether done with the ESM (as reviewed by Hormuth, 1985) or by experimental means. Obviously, the individual can be aware of the self and other targets at the same time and can likewise focus on external and internal aspects of the self simultaneously. Studies that fail to recognize this may be misconstruing the conditions of awareness and consequently misinterpreting their results.

Table 2. Comparing the four kinds of person-awareness on (a) frequency rates and (b) intensity

(a) $x = 88\%$	Self-experience awareness $x = 77\%$	Self-image awareness $x = 69\%$	Other-image awareness $x = 49\%$	Other-experience awareness
Self-image awareness	3.43†			
Other-image awareness	5.75‡	2.54*		
Other-experience awareness	11.01‡	6.76‡	5.66‡	

(b)	Self-experience awareness $x = 1.84$	Self-image awareness $x = 1.39$	Other-image awareness $x = 1.37$	Other-experience awareness $x = 0.42$
Self-image awareness	5.90‡			
Other-image awareness	4.91‡	0.23 (NS)		
Other-experience awareness	10.20‡	5.45‡	6.13‡	

*$p < 0.05$
†$p < 0.01$
‡$p < 0.001$

With regard to the differences among the four kinds of awareness, the results demonstrated, first, that subjects paid more attention to themselves than to other people and, second, that they relied on the egocentric perspective more than the allocentric with regard to both targets. Thus, the egocentric awareness of self—addressing one's own personal experience—was highest, while the allocentric awareness of others—addressing their experience—was lowest. These two preferences apparently offset one another. The egocentric awareness of others—addressing their external image—was equal in intensity to the allocentric awareness of oneself, which addresses one's own image.

That awareness of others' external aspects occurred less frequently but with just as much intensity overall as the awareness of one's own external aspects indicated that there must have been occasions when other-image awareness was more intense. Immediately, the significance of social context, beginning with the simplest distinction of whether one is alone or with others, suggests itself as a plausible explanation for this pattern. While other-image awareness is less likely to occur when alone, it is probably more intense when others are present. However, it is important to recognize that over the course of everyday life, the self was indicated to be the dominant focus of person-awareness.

Furthermore, that the egocentric perspective prevails whether attention is directed at the self or others was indicated by the findings that self-awareness focused on experience while other-awareness focused on image. While this may be common sense, the data provided an empirical demonstration that the egocentric perception of both oneself and others remains a vital part of adult person-awareness.

This is of particular importance to research on self-attention and the self-concept, which has emphasized the significance of adopting an external perspective to attend to one's public self-aspects. Apparently, such research assigns central status to those aspects of the self that receive significantly less attention. Conversely, by failing to give due consideration to the internal, experiential elements of the self, such research neglects those elements that were indicated by this data to be the major focus of self-awareness (Andersen, this volume).

Correlations among the four forms of person-awareness

Recognizing that the four kinds of person-awareness are not mutually exclusive, the degree to which they are used together is an important question for determining how person-awareness is structured. The moment-to-moment relationship among the four forms of awareness was addressed by the correlations among the four attention rating scales. These within-subject correlations allowed a determination of whether each subject's momentary awareness tended to correlate along the lines of target (e.g., self-experience with self-image) or content (e.g., self-image with other-image) or perspective (e.g., self-image with other-experience).

The question of individual differences focused on which subjects showed higher correlations between which kinds of person-awareness. However, rather than specific correlations emerging to characterize each individual, subjects tended to show consistently greater or lesser correlations among all four awareness ratings. If subjects showed a stronger positive relationship among any two forms of attention, they were likely to show it for any other two as well.

The consistency with which subjects showed this tendency for a higher correlation among all four kinds of awareness allowed an easy split of the sample into a group of 13 'attention-integrators' and a second group of 15 who showed no such pattern of integrating their attention. (Three subjects did not easily fit into either group.) An examination of the average attention-correlations for each of these two groups indicates that the differences were substantial and consistent (Table 3). The group of attention-integrators revealed a pattern indicative of a 'global' effect in their person-awareness: for them, there was a greater tendency for the four kinds of attention to rise and fall together.

Table 3. Correlations between attention-rating scales by group*

Attention ratings	Non-integrators	Attention-integrators
Self-image and self-experience	0.12	0.57
Self-image and other-image	0.21	0.53
Self-image and other-experience	0.15	0.46
Self-experience and other-image	0.07	0.36
Self-experience and other-experience	0.18	0.42
Other-image and other-experience	0.42	0.71

* Correlations calculated within individuals and then averaged across group.

What is especially interesting about these two groups is that this difference in the integrated use of person-awareness is related to the overall use of perspective. This was apparent from a set of *t*-tests that compared the two groups on their mean intensity for each of the four forms of person-awareness. Neither form of egocentric attention—self-experience awareness or other-image awareness—was significantly different between the two groups. However, both forms of allocentric attention—self-image awareness and other-experience awareness—were significantly lower in the non-integrators. Whereas the integrators made use of both perspectives, the non-integrators relied largely on the egocentric perspective and made little use of the perspective of the other (Table 4).

While this may be a legitimate effect, there is also the possibility of a response artefact. Perhaps some subjects merely rated the four kinds of

Table 4. Comparison of group mean awareness levels

Awareness	Non-integrators	Attention-integrators	t
Self-image	1.12	1.60	-2.56*
Self-experience	1.64	1.99	ns*
Other-image	1.30	1.47	ns
Other-experience	0.66	1.19	-2.64†

* Not significant.
† $p < 0.05$ for a two-tailed test.

awareness similarly because they did not make the conceptual distinction between them as carefully as the other group. However, further analyses suggested that this was not the case. The attention integrators demonstrated that they could and in fact did discriminate among the four kinds of attention under certain social conditions.

A second possibility is that the lower variance that would be expected to accompany lower levels of awareness simply lowers the possibility of correlation among the different ratings of attention. Yet this would not explain why it is specifically the two forms of allocentric attention that are lower in the non-integrators. What is especially interesting about this data is that the pattern of integrated person-awareness was associated specifically with a difference in the use of perspective, as opposed to a difference in all four kinds of attention or even in the awareness of a particular target or particular content. Why it was a greater use of the allocentric perspective in particular that was related to the higher correlations is not explained by simple differences in variance.

Rather, it would appear that the significance of perspective to this pattern is genuine. While use of the egocentric perspective is universal, taking the perspective of the other adds versatility to one's person-awareness. Apparently, this versatility leads people not to use each form of attention independently, but rather to take advantage of all the attentional tools at their disposal. They accumulate as much information as possible, perhaps comparing and validating across the different kinds of awareness, thereby maximizing the accuracy of their perception. It is the people with more versatile attention who need to integrate it more carefully.

In contrast, those who are less disposed to consider a second perspective have little need to integrate their attention. Their awareness of both self and others is more limited and one-dimensional. Quite simply, when aware of the self, they focus on experience; when aware of others, they focus on image. This discrepancy in the content of self-awareness and other-awareness has important implications for person-perception and interpersonal interaction.

If the two targets are consistently associated with different content, as in the non-integrators, then it is conceivable that the day-to-day differentiation of oneself from others may rely largely on what is essentially a content difference. In this way, identifying oneself primarily by experience while identifying others by external presentation would create an artifactual distinction that goes beyond real individual differences. In failing to adequately consider one's own image and the experience of others, one fails to recognize the similarity between self and others. This could interfere with effective communication and the development of understanding between people.

On the other hand, the integrators, who make considerably more use of the allocentric perspective, not only consider the image they present but are also more sensitive to the experience of other people. As a result, they would be expected to perceive a greater similarity between self and others, one that is likely to produce more effective communication.

Of course, it is the allocentric perspective that is generally understood to facilitate communication. Piaget (1926), Mead (1934), and Flavell (1968) maintained that the use of the allocentric perspective grows out of early interaction with others, specifically contributing to the development of a mature self. What needs to be recognized is that the same allocentric perspective is also instrumental to attaining a mature understanding of other people as experiencing human beings.

Finding that non-integrators show little use of either self-image awareness or other-experience awareness provides empirical support for the position that the same attentional skill is instrumental to both. The implication of this is, of course, that the trait of public self-consciousness (i.e., the tendency to be aware of one's own external aspects) is related to the ability to empathize (i.e., to understand the experience of others). This suggests further that empathy develops in conjunction with objective self-awareness, following a similar sequence of development steps, based on their common foundation of taking the perspective of the other.

Of course, such speculation needs to be addressed directly with further investigation. While the present data is exploratory and preliminary, subsequent research needs to more closely address the influence that other variables in everyday life, particularly social context, have on these patterns. However, it is suspected that as further research continues to uncover the nature of the various attentional styles, with their relevance to the awareness of others as well as oneself, perspective will emerge as a significant variable with important implications for the entire realm of interpersonal interaction.

ACKNOWLEDGEMENTS

The author wishes to thank Terry Honess, William J. McGuire, and Charles S. Carver for their helpful suggestions on an earlier draft.

REFERENCES

Buss, A. H. (1980). *Self-Consciousness and Social Anxiety*, W. H. Freeman, San Francisco.
Carver, C. S. and Scheier, M. F. (1981). *Attention and Self-Regulation: A Control Theory Approach to Human Behaviour*, Springer-Verlag, New York.
Csikszentmihalyi, M. and Figurski, T. J. (1982). 'Self-awareness and aversive experience in everyday life.' *Journal of Personality*, **50**, 14–26.
Csikszentmihalyi, M. and Graef, R. (1980). 'The experience of freedom in daily life.' *American Journal of Community Psychology*, **8**, 401–414.
Csikszentmihalyi, M., Larson, R. and Prescott, S. (1977). 'The ecology of adolescent activity and experience.' *Journal of Youth and Adolescence*, **6**, 281–294.
Diener, E. and Srull, T. K. (1979). 'Self-awareness, psychological perspective, and self-reinforcement in relation to personal and social standards.' *Journal of Personality and Social Psychology*, **37**, 413–423.
Duval, S. and Wicklund, R. A. (1972). *A Theory of Objective Self-Awareness*, Academic Press, New York.

Fenigstein, A., Scheier, M. F. and Buss, A. H. (1975). 'Public and private self-consciousness: Assessment and theory.' *Journal of Consulting and Clinical Psychology*, **43**, 522–527.

Flavell, J. (1968). *The Development of Role-taking and Communication Skills in Children*, Wiley and Sons, New York.

Froming, W. J., Walker, G. R. and Lopyan, K. J. (1982). 'Public and private self-awareness: when personal attitudes conflict with societal expectations.' *Journal of Experimental Social Psychology*, **18**, 476–487.

Hormuth, S. E. (1985). The random sampling of experience *in situ*. Manuscript under review, Universitat Heidelberg.

Larson, R., Csikszentmihalyi, M. and Graef, R. (1980). 'Mood variability and the psychological adjustment of adolescents.' *Journal of Youth and Adolescence*, **9**, 469–490.

Mead, G. H. (1934). *Mind, Self, and Society*, University of Chicago Press, Chicago.

Piaget, J. (1926). *The Language and Thought of the Child*, Harcourt, Brace, and Co., New York.

Wegner, D. M. (1982). 'Justice and the awareness of social entities.' In J. Greenberg and R. L. Cohen (Eds), *Equity and Justice in Social Behaviour*, Academic Press, New York.

Wegner, D. M. and Giuliano, T. (1982). 'The forms of social awareness.' In W. Ickes and E. S. Knowles (Eds), *Personality, Roles, and Social Behavior*, Springer-Verlag, New York.

Self and Identity: Psychosocial Perspectives
Edited by K. Yardley and T. Honess
© 1987 John Wiley & Sons Ltd

17

What do *you* mean 'Who am I?': Exploring the Implications of a Self-Concept Measurement with Subjects

Krysia Yardley

The fiction of 'context neutrality' in relation to self-concept and identity is challenged by extending 'Who Are You' methods. By negotiating with subjects the meaning of their own responses to self-concept questions and by using probes that examine subjects' experience of the total research situation it is demonstrated that the context of asking is a complex grounding that interacts with the very meaning of the concept of self.

INTRODUCTION

In the current critical climate the orthodoxy of objectivism is undermined on all sides. A generation of philosophical psychologists, social constructionists, and phenomenologists amongst us have challenged the view that knowledge can be equated with the accumulation of facts. It is also widely accepted that the traditional social psychological experiment distorts the meaning of phenomena occurring 'within' experiments by, among other factors:

1. isolating variables which are mundanely complexly and inextricably inter-related;
2. 'demanding' certain kinds of responses from subjects;
3. overdefining and overdetermining the possible ascribable meanings of events that have occurred.

(See Harré and Secord, 1972; Rychlak, 1977; McGuire, 1973; Romanyshyn, 1978; Mishler, 1979; and Yardley, 1982a.)

However, despite enormous strides in philosophical sophistication about the epistemological implications of such social psychological experiments, methodological developments have lagged behind. Exhortations to involve subjects more actively in research programmes and to involve subjects in the interpretation of data are in practice little heeded. Current self-concept research working within the realm of social psychology is open to the exact same criticisms.

We may not be surprised, therefore, that in the 1960s when the Twenty Statements Tests and other 'Who are You?' formats were being used to elicit self-concept, that this methodology did not reflect much sophisticated epistemological awareness. Although, it is of course of great interest that the degree of epistemological awareness that prompted the use of such measures gave rise to its own travesty.

Kuhn was the most influential proponent of such measures with his T.S.T. and has had a huge following (Spitzer *et al.*, 1971). He is important because he had hoped to create a test which would be consistent with a symbolic interactionist position and also avoid the problems of over-psychologizing Self. Specifically he held that Self was situationally and interactionally determined and that psychologists had over-stabilized and over-internalized Self by their reliance on trait concepts. Moreover, he argued that psychologists predetermined the nature of self-concept with their reactive assessment techniques. In providing subjects with a more open-ended written format where whole sentence responses were required to the question 'Who am I?' Kuhn hoped to avoid these problems. However (see also Tucker, 1966), that such procedures should arise from Kuhn's own theoretical position indicated an astounding lack of reflexivity. The test situation in which the Twenty Statements Test was given was deemed neutral and non-interactive. Subjects were no longer considered to actively construct meanings and identities for themselves in relation to the investigatory process in which they were engaged. Moreover, it was presumed that if this supposed neutrality was in any doubt, the simple expedient (well paralleled by their positivistic, meaning-decrying psychological colleagues) of instructing subjects to act as if they were only producing their responses for themselves would overcome any such agentic tendencies.

It is certainly the case that the self-concepts elicited in this manner were relatively de-psychologized. Countless studies since testify to the 'spontaneous' use of role concepts. However, the fact remains that there was no concern with subjects' active construction of the task or with the 'specialness' of such a research project. Indeed this has generally remained the case and even relatively radical psychologists such as the McGuires (1981) who have used a 'Tell us about yourself' oral format to enable subjects to respond less reactively, have unfortunately not concerned themselves with the context of the research enterprise itself. At a much more general level than we are shortly to consider, the importance of the apparently neutral context of asking has been demonstrated by Zurcher (1977) who has put forward the idea of the Mutable Self (see Turner, this volume) based on studies of generations of respondents answering the question Who are you/Who am I? Recent generations of respondents yield less role tags in identifying themselves than did their more 'sociologicalizing' predecessors. Here I want to consider what happens when subjects are asked 'Who are you?' but without being restricted by a written format or a time allocation. Second, I wish to consider what happens when the fiction of context neutrality is challenged by 'manipulating' the context of asking and by actively and directly engaging subjects in making sense of both the research event and their own responses within that event. The latter strategy is of particular importance and is, in Schutz's terms, '. . . the only but sufficient guarantee that the world of social reality will not be replaced by a fictional non-existing world constructed by the scientific observer (1971, p. 8)'. Last, the implications of all the above for self-concept research are considered.

PROCEDURE

Subjects were approached to take part in a research project 'in which their self-concepts would be explored'. These subjects aged between 25 and 55 were drawn from Open University and Extra-Mural courses together with their nominated associates. In the event 33 subjects were interviewed on two occasions. The first interviews were tape-recorded and later transcribed in preparation for the second interview.

The first interview

Three basic forms of the 'Who are you?' question were put to subjects: forms A, B, and C. The three WAY questions were given to subjects in three different orders, ABC/BCA/CAB, to militate against order effects. However, the statistical analysis indicated that there were no order effects (Yardley, 1984). On being asked a WAY question a second or third time subjects were explicitly directed not to be concerned about repetition and to repeat themselves or not as they felt appropriate and as arose spontaneously. All forms of the question were uttered by the questioner and an uttered response demanded of the respondent. The demand for an uttered response and its rationale was similar to the McGuires' (1981) use of 'Tell me about yourself' and was felt to offer the subject greater freedom of response than could be achieved through written semi-structured response formats such as the T.S.T. Furthermore, this 'freedom' was extended by allowing subjects to talk for as long as they wishes, explicitly without time constraints.

Form A of the WAY question

In this case the subject was merely asked to answer the question 'Who are you?' and reply within the general framing of the question, i.e., research concerned with self-concept. Subjects were free to say what they wanted in reply to the question, without time constraints.

Form B of the WAY question

This was a modification of C below and was intended as part of a different line of inquiry into role play methodology, and will not concern us here. *None* of the data emerging from this condition necessitates any qualification to be made concerning the results of A and C. (For fuller exposition, see Yardley, 1984.)

Form C of the WAY question

In this condition the subjects were first asked to identify a situation where they felt 'most free to be themselves'. Having done this subjects were then helped to become imaginatively engaged in this chosen setting and then the WAY question was asked of them. Imaginative induction consisted of particularizing and presencing the publicly observable aspects of their chosen context (see Yardley, 1982b, 1984, for details on induction techniques). The rationale behind the imaginative contextualization of a situation where subjects felt free to be themselves was twofold: first to create a situation which positively removed the subject from the immediate context of the investigation without any attempt to deny that the 'Who are you?' response is finally called for by the experimenter; second it was expected that situating self in a context where persons felt free to be themselves would facilitate the full disclosure of a fully experiencing self.

The second interview

Subjects were given their own transcripts and asked to describe and analyse the contents of the first interview particularly with respect to their own performance and presentation of self. (The experimenter had already studied the transcripts and drawn out key content themes and self-presentation themes for each subject.) After each subject had analysed their own scripts they were presented with the experimenter's analysis of themes and asked to validate or invalidate these. (In the event almost all the experimenter's themes were complementary to the subjects and if they were not complementary these themes were dropped from the analysis.)

Other questions and probes

It has already been stated that researchers in this area have totally failed to introduce procedures that allow subjects to actively contribute to the understanding of phenomena generated under self-concept probes. Thus, a deliberate attempt was made here to allow subjects to define what had occurred in the interview and to elaborate their understanding of what had occurred and also to inquire more generally into the quality of phenomena being elicited. Thus, within the first interview two sets of procedures were followed. First, following each completed WAY response general feedback questions were put to each subject: 'How did you feel about doing that? Do you have any thoughts or feelings?'. These questions were put to all subjects in order that they might reflect fairly immediately on the activity in which they had just been engaged.

Second, twelve other prompt questions were put to subjects after they had completed all three forms of the WAY questions. These questions, of various degrees of open-endedness, sought subjects' general thoughts about the whole procedure, their understanding of what had occurred, their assessment of the ease and involvement with which they had answered the questions, and their assessment of the fullness and adequacy of their communication with the interviewer about their self concepts.

THE DATA GENERATED

Overall responses to the WAY questions

There were extensive manifestations of individual differences in response to the WAY questions no matter what the condition. In terms of the crudest criterion of length of response differences were clearly manifest. The most prolific respondents produced more than ten times the amount than the most reticent responders produced. Although there was wide use of all types of categories by subjects (see content analysis below and Yardley, 1984) the qualitative differences in the extent of disclosure or in the expression of selfhood were considerable. These qualitative differences in depth and range are only fully apprehensible by descriptive analysis of individual transcripts as we shall see. Furthermore, there were enormous differences in the ways in which subjects differentially responded to conditions A and C, between subject differences which overrode the impact of the different experimental conditions of asking, with one important exception, which will be examined later. A content analysis system was used to provide an 'objective' comparison of conditions A and C and to also consider the range of content generated in both conditions and it is to this we now turn.

Content analysis

The extensive use of WAY and T.S.T. procedures to measure self-concept has given rise to various methods of analysing such content. Spitzer *et al.*, (1971) have provided a useful overview. In this instance Gordon's total domain analysis (1968) was initially chosen as it seemed to be the most thorough and discriminating with respect to psychological as well as sociological categories. However, like all other available systems of coding self-concept material, Gordon's system was designed to deal with a highly structured test such as the T.S.T. As we shall observe using a more open, less structured, form of asking the question 'Who are you?' led to more various forms of response and it was necessary to make major modifications to Gordon's content analysis system to account for 54.7 per cent of the data. This fact in itself is a clear demonstration of the extent to which T.S.T. and other such formats implicitly prescribe acceptable forms of response. The final set used retained only seven of Gordon's categories unmodified and necessitated creation of nineteen entirely new categories. Thus, it can be seen that given the freedom of such a response mode, as offered subjects here, subjects generate substantively different realms of reference than they do in response to a Twenty Statements format of a self-concept probe. These different areas most importantly concerned:

1. descriptions of others and explicit comparison of self with significant others;
2. descriptions of specific actions of self and others;
3. process statements that describe the self in flow and reflexive in-flow comments upon self.

These are of particular interest because they emphasize neither the static social nor psychological, neither roles nor traits but relationships, experiencing, and behaviour, all areas that are traditionally reified or excluded from academic conceptions of self. It also seems not unlikely that these ways of viewing self may be closer to mundane ways of viewing self inasmuch as they are expressed in a vital and spontaneous speech form.

These new domains of content occur across both conditions, both with the more direct form of the WAY question and with the WAY question introduced into the imagined context of 'Being free to be self'. This brings us on to consider what comparisons and contrasts may be made between the two conditions on the basis of the content analysis. In terms of the aggregate data the differences are minimal but for one interesting exception. We have already noted that in both conditions self-reference in terms of reflexive, processual, in-flow statements occurs with high frequency. Within the above superordinate category of 'process statements' one particular coding category occurs at a highly significant increased level in the imaginative condition ($p < 0.001$). This category concerns statements about self in an experiential and transitory state or mode of being (unrelated to the experimental task *per se*): statements such as, 'I'm feeling desolate at this moment'. This difference can best be illustrated by considering two subjects responses in both modes. In the first example, that of Elizabeth, not only does the style change dramatically in the imaginative condition but also the content expands considerably. By contrast, in the second example, Margaret, the style also changes qualitatively in the imaginative condition but conversely the content, objectively considered, suffers considerable retrenchment. This converse content relationship is interesting, as it is a feature of the data that is masked by considering aggregate data alone, and yet is highly visible when all the data is considered with respect to each individual subject. We will return to this later. For the sake of brevity a detailed descriptive analysis of Margaret's responses alone is offered.

Elizabeth's responses

Condition A

Well I see myself as an individual—not at this stage in my life—although I'm married and have three children I still always look upon myself as E.F.— which is my previous name, married to T.S., rather than Mrs. S. Oh who am I? Oh—I'm sort of lost. Now, who am I as a person? Mm, I'm an individual . . . I'm, mm I'm just . . . can we stop it a minute whilst I just collect myself?

Condition C: In a pub with husband and two close friends

Well I'm E. Mm—I feel I belong here. I think—I look back and I think of all the uncertainty that I've been through in the past and I think that this is the first time I feel safe and I really feel that I belong here . . . mm—certainly I feel happy, mm, despite all the things that are going on. Mm and I just think here . . . I am me, mm this is where I want to be as me, mm—and I want everybody to—that's around me, to er—look at me as a person and think about me and appreciate what I think and feel.

But I also like to think that I do have a lot of mutual understanding with my husband, so that . . . mm . . . though we're both individuals we've got lots of things, well we do feel things together. Mm, but mm the one thing that I'm feeling all the time is that, mm—who am I? I'm just me . . . I'm very much a person in my own right and er, I er, I love my family, you know, I love my children, but I don't—mm, don't ever see them as identity extensions of myself. I see them as three individuals, all with their own life and I hate to feel them to feel that they've got to look after me, mm. And I think while I think about myself I think about all the insecure things that have gone on. I think that its nice I do feel that I'm in a situation where I can feel that I am myself, where I feel safe. That's it.

Margaret's responses

Condition A

My name is M. A. I'm a Senior Lecturer at a College of Technology. I'm the daughter, the only remaining daughter living at home with my mother. Em my two brothers and my two sisters are all living away from the town. The one brother is in Connecticut and so I'm the remaining daughter of a widowed mother who's eighty-three and I'm a leader in the church, I mean I'm involved in church work as a Sunday School teacher and leader of the youth group or rather when I say youth group—not really—seven to fourteens—so

I'm quite involved in that. Em . . . perhaps that's enough at the moment . . . Well will things about relationships come up later? . . . Well perhaps I could expand it a bit about how I see myself in relation to my work.

Em I've already said I see myself as a Senior Lecturer—I guess that's partly because I've been in the right place at the right time and so I would say that I see myself as offering I suppose as a necessity some leadership but I don't really see myself as a leader. I much more need the support of other workers as well, em in any case that wouldn't be as far as I could see the better way of leading things. I prefer em a sort of more democratic approach but that also fits in with me. I don't think I'm a strong leader. Em I also act as a tutor so that I tutor for two courses em which I also like in that I think some other members of staff feel that they can't identify with the group and I feel that I am able to identify with the groups that I take. And gives you a personal relationship with students, I suppose a pastoral role as well. I probably quite like the idea of people being dependent that makes me feel that I'm more of a helpful role. Em I'm just trying to think of myself in relation to friends or whether that's . . . I tend I would say to make a very close relationship, a few close relationships rather than being much of an extrovert. I've got fairly high standards so I expect high standards from other people and probably from myself as well . . . bit of a perfectionist em so that I'm probably fairly selective about whom I make friends with although I think I get on quite well with the other people that I come into contact with but I would say that I tend to go for close relationships, not a lot of superficial relationships.

Condition C: Taking a Sunday School class

Storyteller—course quite enjoying, getting the satisfaction of having the control of having them all sat listening and the satisfaction of, by their response of um putting it over well. See them enjoying it and em if they are fidgety I see that as perhaps there is a lack of control and therefore not doing the job properly . . . Perhaps the missionary as well, in sense of in-putting over a message that I really feel is important . . . I think a little bit of the carer—but not perhaps when I'm telling the story that isn't in mind you know—because I have some concern for them as people as well . . . as children with backgrounds, but I suppose a little bit of the storyteller, enjoying having an audience.

Descriptive analysis of Margaret's response

In Condition A, Margaret produces a relatively straightforward, autobiographical, present-state description of herself. She names herself and gives her occupational status, describes her place in her immediate kinship network, and gives some minimal details about her kin. She then moves on to describe her church affiliations. For the first time she begins to declare her interests dynamically: 'So I'm quite involved in that' (line 08). She falters and looks for clarification from the interviewer and then moves on to expand her work identity, moving into a more personal disclosure of her social and inter-actional styles, needs, personality characteristics and moral values. We begin to get the sense of a person, but at no time do the disclosures blossom out into a full or really intimate sense of the person. One might characterize this response as efficient and moderately disclosing. The language is direct and there is little redundancy. The statements are couched as generalizations reflective about self. The auditor/interviewer is treated as a rational informa-tion gatherer. Quite unlike the former condition Margaret opens Condition C with a single-word, self-naming device, 'storyteller'. There is an intimacy and spontaneity here, in her locating her identity in that moment. Elaboration of this role follows and the verbs are noticeable in their present participle form 'enjoying', 'getting'. More 'correct' grammatical expression breaks down changing the emphasis from the self as object to the process itself 'See them enjoying it' rather than 'I see . . .'. It's as if there is less emphasis on consciously making sense of identity and more on the experiences, out-there, or in-here. Line 03 slightly breaks the mould here with the conditional form: '*if* they are fidgety . . .'. However, the immediacy returns with 'Perhaps the missionary' and the rest that follows combines immediacy with explanation to the auditor. In terms of objective disclosure of information in this condition there is relatively little, yet here in the immediacy of the piece we have a strong sense of the person and what makes them tick. The salient feelings of her life emerges—'The carer', the satisfaction and enjoyment the activities afford. There is a sense of catching this person in midstream, in activity, and seeing what there is in that activity for that person in her immediate experience.

Viewed generally the imaginative context responses of all respondents have a shared immediacy of experience and action that is quite lacking in Condition A. There are other common qualities. Foremost, there is an increase in experienced enjoyment. Generally speaking, the content does not otherwise 'improve' with respect to type or range. Indeed, at times the content appears to suffer retrenchment.

Above all, however, the style does change. The gap between post-hoc accounting for experience, and 'being' in that experience, seems to decrease. There is less sense of subjects constructing a plausible and summary picture (whatever the extent or restrictedness of that account) for another person, that identifies the speaker and is accessible to the observer which is the more typical response in A. There frequently seems to be less distinction between the self as knower and the self as object. At times these merge into an immediately apprehended state of being: for example, 'Who am I?'— 'Storyteller'; 'Who am I?'—'Someone without a care in the world'. This merging of subject and object has strong parallels with Czikszentmihalyi's (1975) findings on 'flow states' which he defines thus: '. . . Perhaps the clearest sign of flow is the merging of action and awareness. A person in flow has no dualistic perspective, he is aware of his actions but not of his awareness itself'. Although the subjects are reflecting on their awareness, there is also a sense in which they are *being* that awareness, through, and with their articulation of it. There is a sense in which saying, 'I am happy' does not distance the happiness but becomes part of the experience of happiness itself and not an analytic reflection of it. A different level of awareness occurs in the imaginative context than is usual in situations where self accounts are called for. Usually such reports amount to rather 'cold' reportage. They do not come close to the experience that may be the reference point for the question. It is interesting that subjects frequently produce less self-disclosure in the imaginative context of being free to be self than other conditions and this appears to be very much related to subjects' individual choice of context.

Choosing a context

It is not possible to deduce a one-to-one relationship between the type of situation chosen and the degree of fullness of response in that imaginative condition. Nevertheless, interesting communalities do arise between features of imaginative context and type of response generated. Subjects' choice of context can be roughly categorized into four groups:

1. subject alone,
2. subject at work,
3. subject in family situation,
4. subject in social situation.

Ten subjects chose 'being alone', six subjects chose 'work', nine subjects chose 'family', and ten subjects chose 'social'.

This choice of context and what follows, in terms of relationship between context and 'full' responding to the WAY question can be interestingly compared with the results of a fascinating study by Turner and Billings (1984). Although not directly concerned with self-concept Turner and Billings elicited student subjects' descriptions of contexts in which they had a 'real' or 'inauthentic' self experience. They found that both types of self experience are most frequently reported as occurring in casual (not work or formal) situations where the activity is predominantly conversation, but may less frequently be contemplation or a consummatory activity. They also found that in both cases a dyadic cast of characters was most typical comprising the subject together with a friend (rather than family) and that less typically but still frequently, particularly in 'real' self situations, the cast of characters was the subject alone. Moreover, great importance was attached to the expression of personal feelings and beliefs within conversations with respect to 'real' self experiences. This was not the case for 'inauthentic' experiences.

To return to our subjects, the clearest and most general factor with respect to the types of contexts chosen is that where full responses (in terms of 'objective' information about self) do occur in the imaginative condition—

none of these full responses occur in 'work' or 'alone' situations. These responses occur either in family or social situations where, without fail, that situation is characterized by having one other person only present, and the interaction with this one other person is intimate and self-revealing. Thus, feeling free to be self in this set of instances is almost dependent on the freedom to verbally reveal self. Moreover, subjects seem then to treat the interviewer as they would treat the close intimate other of their chosen situation. Other family and social contexts which do not give rise to such levels of disclosure (the majority) are very different in their internal structure. What seems to occur here is that a family or social situation is chosen which is extremely low-key, maintains relationships at a comfortable but not disclosive level, and may indeed highlight engulfment rather than individuation, i.e., the situation is safe or banal rather than existentially satisfying.

The contexts of 'being alone', as has already been stated, do not produce detailed self-revelation and are also very interesting in their structure. In these contexts typically 'being free to be self' is expressed as synonymous with not having to account for self to anyone. 'Being self', involved a high degree of salience for the position 'I'm just me' and is typified by the response of one subject 'I just don't think who the hell I am at nine o'clock in the evening, having a drink with J . . . I'm just me'. Another subject chose as her context 'Riding a horse cross-country in Tuscany'. The most salient and most frequently evoked aspect of this was the fact that she had escaped from the demands of others, and did not have to be any kind of person in particular. There was also a sense in which she immersed herself in the physical activity and in her perception of the surrounding countryside as if in a 'flow state' (see Czikszentmihalyi, 1975, on flow states).

With respect to the above relationships between context and responses it must still be reiterated that study of individual cases suggests much finer relationships between context and response as we shall shortly observe. However, even at the more general level, one confounding factor emerges that concerns subjects' total ability to respond well to the WAY questions. Of the 33 subjects only eleven were 'good' responders, and the vast remainder were poor responders generating very little information in any of the conditions. If one considers these two major groups separately in relation to context choice and general level of responding the following factors emerge. Of the good responders there was a tendency as in the rest of the sample to respond much more fully in one condition than another. However, rather differently from the rest of the sample the higher proportion of these 'fuller' responses occurred in the imaginative context (which, as has already been stated, always occurred in a one-person intimate situation). On the other hand, a substantial minority of these 'better' responses occurred in condition A and in these instances the chosen contexts for condition C, whether alone or social, were typified by the lack of need to account for self, and mostly featured the individual alone. Thus, with this group of high responders there is a suggestion that the choice of context of being free to be self is a 'genuine' choice not prompted in the main by a desire to escape answering the WAY question. As far as the poor responders are concerned, whatever their chosen context, it is typified by an ambience of low disclosiveness and seems to provide a deliberate refuge from the question, rather than providing an authentic self-experience. For example three of these subjects chose an escapist book for their situation where they felt free to be themselves, which hardly provided a self-reflexive or existential, flowing experience of self. More complex, however, and more difficult to characterize are subjects such as the man who found all the WAY conditions intrusive and chose as his context playing the organ by himself. He described the situation as one so engrossing that thoughts were not possible, let alone words and answers. Interestingly this man felt the whole interview was like having an argument with his wife where he was also asked impossible questions. He also disclosed that he only played the organ when his wife went out, as if he were metaphorically putting the interviewer outside as well.

In all the above cases and indeed throughout the whole group the choice of context and its meaning for the subject appear to relate to specific principles. On the one hand situations are chosen that extend or mimetically reflect what is held to be important about the self. For example, the essential self may be felt to be highly private and thus the intrusion of cognitive or sentient reflection is highly detrimental to that experience, or the essential self may be experienced in disclosure and revelation and thus be compatible with answering a self-concept question. On the other hand, there is a sense in which the context may be chosen strategically with respect to the interview. Some subjects may choose an 'alone' or 'work' context not so much because it reflects the 'real' self but because it reduces the likelihood that any distressing revelations will have to be made to the interviewer: the choice of context represents then a flight from the task.

Now, I want to consider the subjects' construction of the total WAY situation which emerged in response to the probe questions. This is important, not only because it allows further challenge to the idea that the interview situation can be neutral, but also provides us with valuable understandings of how subjects view the situation and the WAY questions.

CONSTRUCTION OF SITUATION

A systematic qualitative analysis of the data generated by the probe questions was undertaken (methods of analysis were derived from Kelly, 1955; Mullmerstadt-Helling, 1975; Glaser and Strauss, 1968).

A method was evolved, detailed elsewhere (Yardley, 1984), which I have named 'filtering and condensing'. The first target for analysis concerned the subjects' construction of the WAY interview situations. One hundred and twenty-two themes concerning construction of situation were generated by the thirty-three subjects. As can be seen by looking at Table 1, these themes were fairly evenly distributed amongst all the subjects. Although there was no

Table 1. Categorization of like-themes

Integrity

Need to be honest	7
Need to be responsible	1
Need for commitment	1
To be useful and helpful	1
Best of ability	1

Definitional

Defining question	2
Who/what?	2
What does she want?	6
Ulterior motive?	3
Incomprehensible	7
Unfamiliar	13

Awareness

Self-awareness	3
Deep	2
Philosophical	3

Threat

Difficult	12
Disturbing	2
Threatening/ controversial	6
Need to protect self	17
Restricting	3
Intrusive	1
Out of control	3
Concerned	1
Shock	4
Panic	1
Confusion	3
Alienating/ embarrassing	3

Other

Comfortable	4
Interesting	3
Not interesting	1
Normal familiar	3

Challenge/Provocative

	6

Like

Friends — intimate conversation	5
Friends — informal conversation	6
Job interview	9
Psychiatrists/ counsellor	8
Doctor's (medical)	4
Dentist	1
Inquisition	2
Tutorial	1
Church — being late	4
Not like	

Note:
1. The numbers represent the number of subjects expressing such a theme.
2. Key themes are listed in the boxes.
3. Superordinate categories appear separately at the top of the box.

Table 2. Case examples of key themes used by individual subjects in relation to construction of situation

Subject No.	1	2	3	4	5
Key themes	Confrontational Threatening Panic	Provide what wanted What wanted? Wish to be honest	Exercise in own Self-awareness Familiar but infrequent activity	What wanted? Wish to be helpful	Difficult Unfamiliar Wish to be helpful
Interview like?	Seeing a psychiatrist	Teacher-pupil situation	Self-awareness exercises	Conversation with friends at University	Psychiatrist's
Chosen context	With close friends and husband in a pub	Reading a book by self in the evening	Teaching Sunday School	Alone in cafe in Germany whilst studying	With family at home in evening

Subject No.	6	7	8	9	10
Key themes	Unfamiliar Difficult Deep/searching need for self preservation Concerned Threatening	Threatening Exploring self Provocation in the dark Comfortable Casual but with machinery Wish to be honest Need for self-protection	Unfamiliar Difficult What she up to? Out of ordinary	Difficult Threatening Intrusive Confrontational Provocative	Counselling training Challenging Provocative
Interview like?	Inquisition Dentist's	Therapy groups		Late for church and going to communion without wanting to	Counselling Training
Chosen context	With husband alone in evening	By self studying at home	Playing bridge	With husband and friends getting tipsy	Family and friends on holiday picnic

absolute identity of agreement about the construction of the interview, there was a surprisingly high degree of broad consensus. The degree of consensus is more remarkable given the variability in the actual responses to the WAY questions. The major communalities are easily apprehended inasmuch as many themes were easily assimilable into higher order categories. The strongest and most predominant superordinate themes are in order of magnitude (see Tables 1 and 2):

1. threat,
2. definitional,
3. integrity,
4. awareness.

Most subjects, whatever their willingness or ability to respond, found the overall experience highly threatening with many negative emotional accompaniments. For many there was a sense in which the subject had to protect the self against the intrusion of the question. Declaring *who one is* appears to be putting oneself at risk. Further, given the prominence of the category 'Definitional' the difficulty with which subjects understood the question—the risk increased in relation to the perceived open-endedness of the question. As Strauss has commented, 'In a problematic situation, a person must not only identify his current other, he must pari passu identify his current self. "Who am I?" in this situation is problematic just as long as the situation is problematic' (Mirrors and Masks, 1969, p. 47). Clearly, part of the problematic situation, in this case, was not merely identifying the other but identifying the realms of reference of the question.

Despite the degree of experienced threat it might be argued that it was the interviewers who made the situation threatening. However, the frequency of definitional problems together with the favourable comments made by subjects about the three interviewers make this an unlikely interpretation. At the second interview negotiation stage, the majority of subjects said they had found the interviewers themselves pleasant and non-threatening, although many added they were unhelpful. An important and influential construction for some subjects was based on the desire to be good subjects. This was not just in the sense of doing what the experimenter wanted, but in the more profound sense of being honest and responsible. Finally, the superordinate category of 'Awareness' is interesting. This category is a little looser than the other superordinate categories but it does pull together themes that allude to the task as somehow being special and possibly profound, although this is not necessarily a positive construction. At least one subject found it was a fault in the interview. More frequently, however, this type of thematic construction alludes to an almost enigmatic and magic status of the question related to its perceived depth.

Subjects were asked to describe a situation which for them felt similar to the interview situation. These comparisons were also very revealing about individuals' construction of situation and involved significant communalities. The major types of similar situation disclosed by subjects are:

1. friend/intimate conversation,
2. friend/informal conversation,
3. job interview,
4. psychiatric/counselling interview,
5. general practitioner consultation.

These five types seem to encapsulate aspects of the interview situation as actually constructed by the author. For those subjects who experienced the interview as similar to a conversation with a friend (either intimate or formal) it is likely that the intended informality and general supportiveness of the interviewer's style were most salient. On the other hand, for those who experienced the situation as like a job interview, the more formal aspects of the interview, arising from the standardization of format, together with the relatively neutral stance of the interviewer, were probably more significant. There is evidently an ambiguity in such an interview situation which arises from the disparity between the interviewer's general informality and the formality and rule boundedness of the interview structure. Moreover, this ambiguity is mirrored by those subjects who saw the situation as like a psychiatric counselling or medical situation. The latter situations may be characterized as having an almost identical ambiguity which is related to the demands for distance and relative detachment in the other. Other subjects compared the interview to the inquisition and the dentist's. These images speak for themselves.

Constructions of interview related to type of WAY responses, and to subjects' willingness and ability to respond

Considering the major thematic constructions of task as explored above, it does not seem possible to find any pattern of construction that is likely to lead to any particular type of response to the WAY questions. For example, although one may differentiate individuals who perceived the situation as highly threatening, from those who did not, the perception of threat does not appear to influence either subject's ability or indeed their willingness to respond. Looking qualitatively at the WAY responses, there seemed to be no relationship between the quality, or even the length of response, and any particular type of thematic construction. Only one factor emerged that had any generalizability. Those subjects (approximately one-third) who had had experience of seeking or giving professional psychological help (less in the latter category) expressed themselves more interested in the task, and appeared to find it more meaningful. This group also produced more disclosive material. However, they did not experience the task as any easier. It seems that where subjects have had previous 'psychological' experience, that the meaning and the acceptability of such a question approximates more closely that of the psychological enquirer.

We will complete this examination of the data here by detailing individual cases. This further enables one to understand both subjects' constructions of tasks and also the type of responses given to both WAY questions. This will be briefly considered in relation to selected subjects' utilizing material drawn from both interviews. The subjects' are not selected according to any particular or deliberate principle. Other subjects' would have served equally well as illustrations.

Specific illustrations

Jane felt particularly threatened by the whole interview procedure and was overtly upset at the end of the first WAY question, which was for her an imaginatively contextualized one. She specifically viewed the situation as one in which she felt compelled by the interviewer to talk although this did not lead to any lack of cooperation on her part. Indeed, she produced a great deal of relevant material, although this material was at times so egocentric that it seemed quite at odds with a commonsense understanding of the questions asked of her. It seemed that this lady had for a long period of time been sitting on a host of serious personal and marital conflicts. She chose a context which unwittingly threw her into absolute collision with these conflicts. In response to her own choice of context and in response to the WAY question she then poured out her feelings about her difficulties. In the second interview she expressed that she had been, and was, ashamed of such feelings, and, having given vent to these, experienced her outpouring as improper. Later in the second interview she also stated that she was an emotional person who needed to open up, but opening up was to be viewed as weakness particularly in the context of a husband and parental-in-laws who were strong on self-control. It appeared and she agreed that her own strong desire to 'ventilate', together with her sense of shame for 'letting the side down', led her to construe the situation as one in which she was externally compelled. Thus in the first interview she did not have to take responsibility for her 'lapse'.

One of the most dramatic constructions of situation was presented by John, the man who likened the interview context to a row with his wife. He was, in fact, interviewed by a woman and he stated that it was only women who seemed to put him in these impossible situations of demanding what he did not have to give. Not surprisingly, he generated very little material. Another subject, Mary, construed the situation as highly threatening and yet she produced a relatively full and disclosive set of responses, although devoid of any negative disclosures. Interestingly, she associated introspection with negative feelings and inextricably wound up with depression and she, therefore, rejected introspection as a way of being. However, she also presented herself as a strong 'coper', always active and positive. The major anomaly observed was the strength of her introspective and reflective skills as evidenced in her WAY responses. Such an anomaly opened many questions about the personal nature of depression, introspection, and coping. It emerged that such were the long-standing situational problems she was confronted with, that she had to cope or 'go under'. Reflecting on her experiences to any great degree inevitably led her to having to consider troublesome difficulties, or so she felt. Such reflection would then cause distress and disillusionment. The interview situation 'demanded' that she introspect. Because she was a cooperative and coping person she responded positively to these demands and demonstrated those skills but only in relation to positive disclosures. However, her imaginative context was interestingly one where she did not have to account for self but could merge comfortably and symbiotically with her husband.

There was only one interview which nearly 'went wrong' inasmuch as the subject became very hostile. This subject became very angry and confrontative with the interviewer. She seemed quite unable to produce any material at all in response to the WAY questions, and in this she became frustrated and disappointed. She chose as her context a family and social occasion where the most salient factor was that everybody was 'tipsy'. She at first said that she had expected to take part in an interesting exploration about herself and she had been let down because the task was boring and meaningless. Later at the negotiation stage when this matter was explored, the subject volunteered that much of her life to date might be viewed as failure, both socially and occupationally. She had tried various work activities but she had quickly become unable to cope and disillusioned. She would quit at the first obstacle while blaming others for the impossibility of the situation as she perceived it. Partly as a result of the interview she began to realize what she had been doing and was hoping to take a new job and approach it more realistically.

As can be inferred from the cases above, as well as from the more general thematic analysis in the section above, there is no sense in which subjects view the task as a neutral research project in which they can reflect on self with clinical and thorough detachment. The meaning of the research event and questions are pulled into a nexus of individual pre-existent meaning structures that relate to past experiences and current ways of being.

The aggregate generalizations made on the basis of extracting major themes, which give us some sense of the structure of the task, do not allow us to understand individual performance differences. It is only when one begins to consider individual constructions, in some detail, that an understanding of differences in performance begins to emerge.

CONCLUSIONS

It is difficult to wrap up this wealth of qualitative and quantitative data in any simple way, just as it is difficult to reduce the vast potential experience of Self to a self-concept. Nevertheless there arise from this study cautions we should heed in undertaking self-concept research. First, if it is the case that minor modifications of the form of asking of a self-concept question radically change the nature of response we receive, to the extent that radically different domains of response emerge, then we must pay very close attention to the questions we ask and the assumptions upon which we base those questions. It is not, however, sufficient for researchers to examine these assumptions in splendid isolation. For, as has been clearly demonstrated, subjects and researchers alike construct the meanings of research events. Individual subjects respond to a question only as it makes sense at a particular point in their individual lives. Moreover, if we listen to subjects, or more importantly, if we afford them the opportunity to comment upon our research proceedings and their own performance, we are forced to acknowledge that we usually gather only a fraction of what they understand to be relevant to the answering of our question.

If we must continue to 'raid' so briefly individual psychological lives we must be prepared to consider the temporal and relational nature of that contact and what it may achieve compared with, for example, the more painstaking and often tedious lengthy engagement of therapist and client. We may also wonder, reflecting on the above study, why it is that those subjects considered 'good' in terms of producing relevant self material are those subjects who have had previous experience of psychological or quasi-psychological situations. We may also wonder what it is to be a self if nobody asks the question 'Who are you?'

REFERENCES

Czikszentmihalyi, M. (1975). *Beyond Boredom and Anxiety: The Experience of Play in Work and Games*, Jossey Bass, London.

Glaser, B. G. and Strauss, A. L. (1968). *The Discovery of Grounded Theory*, Weidenfeld and Nicholson, London.

Gordon, C. (1968). 'Self-conceptions: configurations of content.' In C. Gordon and K. J. Gergen (Eds), *The Self in Social Interaction*, Wiley, New York.

Harré, R. and Secord, P. (1972). *The Explanation of Social Behaviour*, Blackwell, Oxford.

Kelly, G. (1955). *The Psychology of Personal Constructs*, vol. 1, *A Theory of Personality*, Norton, New York.

McGuire, W. J. (1973). 'The Yin and Yan of progress in social psychology.' *Journal of Personality and Social Psychology*, **26**, 446–456.

McGuire, W. J. and McGuire, C. V. (1981). 'The spontaneous self-concept as affected by personal distinctiveness.' In M. D. Lynch, A. A. Norem-Heberson and K. J. Gergen (Eds), *Self-concept: Advances in Theory and Research*, Bellinger, New York, chap. 11.

Mischler, E. G. (1979). 'Meaning in context: Is there any other kind?' *Harvard Educational Review*, **49**(1), 1–19.

Mullmerstadt-Helling, I. (1975). *First Order Constructs in Occupational Biography: An Attempt to Apply the Sociology of A. Schutz*, B.Phil. Thesis, Sociology, St. Anne's College, Oxford.

Romanyshyn, R. D. (1978). 'Psychology and the attitude of science.' In R. S. Valle and M. King (Eds), *Existential-Phenomenological Alternatives for Psychology*, OUP, New York, pp. 18–47.

Rychlak, J. F. (1977). *The Psychology of Rigorous Humanism*, Wiley, Chichester.

Schutz, A. (1971). *Collected Papers*, Nijhoff, Hague.

Spitzer, S., Couch, C. and Stratton, J. (1971). *The Assessment of Self*, Sernoll, Iowa City.

Strauss, A. L. (1969). *Mirrors and Masks*, The Sociology Press, San Francisco.

Tucker, C. W. (1966). 'Some methodological problems of Kuhn's self theory.' *Sociological Quarterly*, 7, pp. 345–358.

Turner, R. and Billings, V. (1984). 'The social contexts of self-feeling.' *International Conference on Self and Identity*, Cardiff.

Yardley, K. M. (1982a). 'On distinguishing role plays from conventional methodologies.' *Journal for the Theory of Social Behaviour*, 12(2), 125–139.

Yardley, K. M. (1982b). 'On engaging actors in as-if experiments.' *Journal for the Theory of Social Behaviour*, 12(3), 291–305.

Yardley, K. M. (1984). *The Individual and Contexts: A Generative Approach Towards the Understanding of Role Play Methodology*, Ph.D. Thesis, University of Wales.

Zurcher, J. L. A. (1977). *The Mutable Self: A Self-Concept for Social Change*, Sage Publishing, Beverley Hills.

Self and Identity: Psychosocial Perspectives
Edited by K. Yardley and T. Honess
© 1987 John Wiley & Sons Ltd

18

The Role of Cultural Assumptions in Self-Concept Development

Susan M. Andersen

Cultural assumptions affecting the perceived informativeness of self-manifestations are considered and their implications for self-development in Western culture explored. By way of illustration, a series of empirical investigations is presented that examine the inferential weight given to cognitions and affects relative to overt behaviours in self-knowledge.

Societies tend to provide people with various means of coming to 'know' themselves better, or further extend their identities. The 'tools' with which people may attempt to gain self-knowledge in a given culture, in fact, often span a rather wide range. Individuals may construct a sense of identity, for example, through conceptions such as the religious and political, on the one hand, and through more mundane social, occupational, and familial roles, on the other. The manner in which the various 'tools' of self-extension are construed and valued in a culture will undoubtedly determine, in large measure, the relative weight individuals allot to these sources of information in constructing self-knowledge. Cultural assumptions, then, can profoundly shape one's experience of self by dictating the degree to which various types of information about the self are seen as useful, important, and informative (see also Gergen, this volume; Paranjpe, this volume). Because of this, it becomes interesting to consider some of the assumptions about the self that people may make in Western culture, and the implications of these assumptions for the manner in which individuals experience and express self.

LAY ASSUMPTIONS ABOUT SELF-MANIFESTATIONS

In terms of the assumptions people may make about the various self-manifestations they experience, consider first the concept of intention. In Western culture, self-direction and self-control are highly valued commodities. Because of this, the ways in which we attempt to control ourselves may be seen as importantly reflective of self because these efforts appear to reflect our 'truest' values, aspirations, and preferences. Hence, we may

231

intentionally try to bring our personal reactions into harmony with our ideals about ourselves, and the *direction* of these attempts at self-control, that is, the direction of our 'acts of will', are seen as highly diagnostic of our own character and personality. The concept of personal agency, of course, constitutes a long-standing interest of philosophers and social scientists alike (e.g., the collection edited by T. Mischel, 1977) and is particularly relevant in cultures such as ours that emphasize individual self-development and achievement.

Given the role of self-control processes in self-conceptualization, the special credence that is also given to 'uncontrollable' self-manifestations in Western culture may seem contradictory or paradoxical. Yet the degree to which self-manifestations are seen as uncontrollable is also likely to be very important in the weight given to sources of evidence about the self. Spontaneous personal reactions—those that seem to be quite out of our own control—tend to be seen as reflective of our 'true' self (see also Turner, 1976). That is, those aspects of self that appear to be beyond our own will may seem to reflect our 'deepest' tendencies and dispositions precisely because we cannot, or feel we cannot, control them (see also Zajonc, 1980). In our culture, such reactions are considered to be diagnostic of self not only because nothing we do seems capable of changing them, but also because they seem to stem *directly* from the self. The pervasive influence of psychoanalytic theory in our culture, which directs attention to that which seethes invisibly and uncontrollably beneath the surface of consciousness, may also contribute to the impact of the concept of uncontrollability on the perceived informativeness of self-manifestations.

Beyond the twin notions of intentionality and uncontrollability in self-inference processes, one might also ask about the extent to which sources of self-inferences vary in their accessibility to other individuals, such as to family, friends, colleagues, acquaintances. That is, information about the self that cannot readily be known (and experienced) by others is 'private' and will probably be especially relevant in self-inference processes. Western culture places a great deal of weight on the notion of privacy and possession. As a result, it may be the case that those aspects of self that are not in the public eye, that are operative only within oneself, within one's primary relationship, or within one's family, are considered to be especially informative about the self. The distinction between private and public aspects of self, of course, is not a new one; it has been discussed at length in social psychology and is important in self-referrent processes (e.g., Fenigstein *et al.*, 1975; Scheier and Carver, 1983; Snyder, 1974; Tesser, 1984; Wicklund, 1982; Wicklund and Frey, 1980). This is not to say, of course, that consensual definitions of self are unimportant. Social roles and situated identities are, in fact, critical in self-perception (Alexander and Knight, 1971; McCall, 1977, this volume; McCall and Simmons, 1966; Tajfel, 1978; Turner, this volume). It is simply to say that exclusivity and privacy are highly valued in our culture and that self-manifestations that are assumed to fit this mould may come to play a profound role in self-conception.

Finally, although people frequently define themselves in terms of certain shared social 'fixtures' in society, people may give weight not only to the privacy of their self-relevant experiences but to the individuality of these experiences as well. That is, people may characterize their self-manifestations in terms of their apparent individuality and uniqueness with respect to the norms of the dominant culture or subculture (see also Harré, this volume; Snyder and Fromkin, 1980). In understanding self-inference processes, it may therefore be important to consider the degree to which people view their self-manifestations as distinctive *vis-à-vis* their primary social groups (see Andersen, 1984; Cronbach, 1955; McGuire and McGuire, 1981; Turner, 1976; Weiner, 1982; Wilson and Stone, 1985). There clearly are times, for example, when individuals attend to the ways in which they are similar to, and fit into, certain social groups, and times when they are more likely to focus on the way in which they are different from these groups (see also Tajfel, 1978; Tesser and Campbell, 1983). In our society, the notion of distinctiveness calls to mind that of individuality, which, like privacy, is one of the central tenets of Western Culture (Harré, this volume). Hence, one's most 'individualistic' or unique self-experiences might seem particularly diagnostic of self as compared with one's more 'typical' or normative responses.

In our culture, individuals may be particularly likely to perceive information about the self as important, accurate, and diagnostic if it is consistent with the above assumptions, i.e., if it is somehow intentional, uncontrollable, private, or distinctive. When these assumptions seem to apply, in some combination, to a set of self-experiences, these experiences may come to have an exalted status in self-inference processes and to receive more weight in people's self-conceptions. These beliefs about informativeness, of course, need not be 'accurate' to be influential. The 'truth' value of the assumptions made in Western culture, for example, is difficult to assess, as is the relative 'truth' of these assumptions as contrasted with others. Independent of 'accuracy', however, such assumptions are likely to influence the weight people give to various sources of information about the self when constructing self-knowledge. Thus, one could imagine a socially shared theory of self which suggested that the most diagnostic aspects of self are those that are socially controlled, rather than self-directed, predictable rather than spontaneous and uncontrolled, inherently public rather than private, and common rather than unique. Such a culture would undoubtedly be quite different from our own, but people in it would probably base their self-conceptions on sources of information that are characterized, in part, by these assumptions.

SOURCES OF SELF-INFORMATION

Clearly, people make inferences about themselves based on several different sources of information (Allport, 1955; Bandura, 1981; Bem, 1972; Cooley, 1902; Gergen, 1971; Hamlyn, 1977; McGuire and McGuire, 1981; Mead, 1934; Mischel, 1977; Rosenberg, 1979; Suls and Mullen, 1982; Swann, 1983;

Tesser and Campbell, 1983). These sources of information will play a role in self-inference processes as a function, in part, of their salience at the time of the judgment (Andersen and Williams, 1985; Andersen, Lazowski, and Donisi, 1986; Bandura, 1981; Figurski, this volume; Higgins, this volume; McGuire and McGuire, 1981; Tversky and Kahneman, 1974) and of the assumptions that people tend to make about these sources of information.

Consider first the concept of social feedback. People do seem to observe how significant others react to them and, in part, come to react toward themselves in this same way (Cooley, 1902; Kinch, 1963; Mead, 1934; Shrauger and Shoeneman, 1979; Sullivan, 1953). This is a relatively public source of knowledge about the self in the sense that it derives from other people's reactions. On the other hand, research suggests that the actual content of other peoples' opinions about us is far less relevant to our conceptions of self than is our *perception* of these opinions (Shrauger and Shoeneman, 1979), even when our perception is incorrect (see Lewinsohn *et al.*, 1980). Thus, the process of reflective self-appraisal is ultimately a rather 'private' and subjective one, based to a large degree on unspoken perceptions and expectations, rather than 'objective' feedback or actual social consensus.

In constructing their self-conceptions, people also compare their achievements and opinions with those of others, and utilize revealed similarities and differences in assessing themselves (Festinger, 1954; Suls and Mullen, 1982). In addition, people seem to surround and compare themselves with other individuals with whom they compare favourably (Epstein, 1973; Greenwald, 1980; Tesser and Campbell, 1983) and who, in fact, reaffirm their own self-conceptions (Swann, 1983). This suggests that social comparison processes are not passive and reactive ones, but are choreographed to a large extent by the individual so as to create positive self-feeling and the perception of excelling in relatively distinctive ways (cf. Tesser and Campbell, 1983). Hence, 'intentions' and 'private' feelings undoubtedly play a profound role in social comparison processes.

People also attend to their own overt behaviour in constructing self-knowledge. A long line of research in self-perception theory has shown that people make inferences about themselves based on their observations of their own behaviours and the situations in which these behaviours occur (Bem, 1967; 1972). Behavioural self-inferences are said to take place, for example, when people find themselves engaging in some new behaviour, such as smiling at someone, and then decide that they actually 'like' this person based on the observation that they have smiled at the person a number of times. Similarly, one might infer that one is a friendly or cheerful person because one notices oneself smiling a lot. On the other hand, individuals may make the assumption that they are responsible for most of their actions, either in the sense that they intended them in advance, that consistent thought and feelings accompanied the actions, or at the minimum that the actions were not ultimately prevented by the individual. Hence, the role of 'private' processes in traditional self-perception processes may typically be underestimated (with some exceptions, Chaiken and Baldwin, 1981; Taylor 1975).

Finally, it seems that, in a more general sense, people also make inferences about themselves based on subjective and covert reactions, such as their own wishes, goal states, evaluations, moods, and emotions. While some of these internal reactions undoubtedly derive, in part, from social comparisons, from observations of one's own behaviour, or from reflective self-appraisals, and thus are not entirely independent of these processes, cognitions and affects nevertheless contribute significantly to self-knowledge (Andersen, 1984, 1986; Andersen and Ross, 1984; Andersen and Williams, 1985, 1986). Overt behaviours, for example, also derive from social comparisons at times, from feelings and thoughts of various sorts, and from reflective self-appraisals; nonetheless, behavioural performances clearly contribute to self-knowledge. To further illustrate this point, both cognitive/affective reactions and behavioural reactions can be conditioned and are responsive to environmental contingencies. This does not imply, however, that these self-manifestations make no independent contribution to an individual's self-conception. Quite to the contrary: precisely because individuals are capable of characterizing the environmental contingencies surrounding a response as sufficient or insufficient to account for it, the response may come to play a role in the inferences people make about themselves (cf. Bem, 1972; Enzle, 1980; Jones and Davis, 1965).

Moreover, thoughts and feelings may be particularly likely to be attributed to self rather than to the environment because they appear, on the average, to derive from 'within' the person rather than from 'outside' the person. Thoughts and feelings are more 'private' than are overt behaviours in the sense that typically they are not visible to other people and may thus seem to derive from within us even when they do not. Goal states, feelings, and intentions are even important in social perception as shown by legal systems, which frequently base judgments about illegal actions on inferred motives, intentions, and feelings. It is through intention, conceptualization, and feeling, in fact, that 'behaviours' performed in a context become meaningful 'actions' (e.g., Gergen, 1984a; Vallacher, 1984; Wegner *et al.*, 1984; see also Markova, this volume). Hence, cognitive and affective reactions may be particularly relevant to self-inference processes.

THE ROLE OF COGNITIONS AND AFFECTS IN SELF-CONCEPTUALIZATION

Focusing specifically on the role of cognitions and affects in people's self-conceptions, it seems evident that people do make inferences about themselves based on their thoughts, feelings, preferences, goal states, desires, and other private perceptions. Further, it is intuitively obvious that people are quite willing, under certain circumstances, to ignore behavioural evidence about themselves in favour of their more private reactions (see Chaiken and Baldwin, 1981; Taylor, 1975), whether or not these private reactions hold them in a better light (see also Greenwald and Ronis, 1978; Rogers, 1951). It is easy to generate examples of this. For instance, individuals may behave badly toward someone 'by accident', that is, without intending any harm, and may then fail to attribute their actions to themselves because they did not intend them. Similarly, people may behave in a loving or friendly manner because they believe they 'should', even if they do not actually feel this way, then discounting their actions in favour of their feelings in their self-inferences. We may apologize when we are not sorry, profess beliefs that we do not hold, act aloof when we wish we were involved, and appear satisfied when feeling disappointed. In the end, our private reactions (e.g., perceptions, intentions, goals, affects) may often win out in our self-conceptions over and above our concrete behavioural responses, even though this will not always be the most useful, appropriate, or 'objective' means of integrating cognitive/affective and behavioural information.

These reactions differ, it should be noted, on each of the descriptive dimensions outlined earlier, that is, on the dimensions of intention, uncontrollability, privacy, and distinctiveness. Intentions, for example, are but one of the various types of thoughts and feelings one may have. When we intend to control our reactions, and thus attempt to do so, we are engaging in a cognitive and affective exercise that is critical to the definition of thinking and feeling. Beyond the potential exercise of agency, people also perceive their thoughts and feelings as emerging spontaneously and uncontrollably from the self. That is, they perceive their capacity to exert control over their thoughts and feelings as decidedly more limited than their capacity to control their actions even though this may not be true (e.g., Mahoney, 1974; Michenbaum, 1977). Further, people obviously experience their thoughts and feelings as occurring 'within' them and these manifestations of self are therefore inherently more private than are overt behaviours; in principle they are available to others only indirectly, e.g., when the individual chooses to communicate them to others. Thoughts and feelings, moreover, are frequently perceived as more idiosyncratic or distinctive than are behaviours, even though, actually, they may be no more unusual or distinctive (cf. Andersen, 1984; Wilson and Stone, 1985; see also Harré, this volume).

Each assumption is thus applicable to the distinction between cognitive/affective reactions and behavioural reactions. The assumptive differences between these self-manifestations, in fact, may play a role in their being differentially weighted in self-inference processes. In general, the research conducted in this area has provided support for the hypothesis that private thoughts and feelings have a profound impact on the self-concept: an impact quite beyond that of overt behaviours. The implications of this research suggest that certain assumptive differences between cognitive/affective reactions and overt behaviours are likely to exist. Overall, a number of studies have been conducted in this domain; each is described in turn.

The first set of investigations in this series showed that people seem to perceive their thoughts and feelings as far more informative and representative of the self than their overt actions—both when judging hypothetical samples of these personal reactions and when judging real samples of them (Andersen and Ross, 1984). In one study, for example, people were led to disclose their cognitive and affective reactions or their behavioural reactions in a spontaneous personal interview, by dealing with a series of interview topics such as 'my relationship with family and friends', 'my career and education', and 'experiences that shaped me as a person'. The results showed that participants came to view themselves more dispositionally and to see their disclosures as more informative about the self after they recounted their thoughts and feelings than after they recounted their behaviours. Thus, actors clearly perceive this source of information as highly valid and diagnostic. Observers, who observed each interview from behind a one-way mirror, seemed to share this perception, but gave considerably more inferential weight to actors' behaviours than did the actors themselves, a finding which has been discussed at great length in social psychology in recent years (Andersen and Ross, 1984; see also Jones, 1979; Jones and Nisbett, 1971; Monson and Snyder, 1977; Storms, 1973; Wegner and Finstuen, 1977).

One might wonder, however, whether thoughts and feelings actually are more diagnostic of actors' self-conceptions than are behaviours, or whether this is simply a misperception on the part of actors. That is, perhaps my thoughts and feelings play no greater a role in my self-conceptions than do my behaviours and therefore come to be no more diagnostic of me or reflective of my self-conception than are my overt behaviours. In a subsequent investigation, actors were again led to disclose their cognitive/affective reactions or their behavioural ones in a tape-recorded personal interview. This time, however, participants assessed themselves prior to their interview using a series of personality measures. During a later session, observers were exposed either to a cognitive/affective interview or to a behavioural interview via tape-recording and were then asked to assess the actor using the same personality measures. Results showed that observers came to assess actors more accurately after hearing the cognitive/affective interviews than after hearing the behavioural ones. That is, observers in the cognitive/affective, rather than the behavioural, condition came to assess the actors more as the actors had assessed themselves prior to their interviews (Andersen, 1984).

In spite of any actor-observer differences that may exist in the weight given to overt behaviours, then, gaining knowledge of a person's private thoughts and feelings—when there is little reason for intentional deception—may lead to more 'accurate' perceptions of this person's self-concept than gaining knowledge of the person's behaviour. This probably occurs, in fact, because cognitive/affective reactions are more primary than are behaviours in the inferences people actually make about themselves. As a result, when actors share with others the source of information that has been primary in their own self-inferences, these others come to know the actors as the actors know themselves. Interestingly, both actors and observers agreed that the thoughts and feelings expressed by actors were more rarely communicated (more 'private') than were the behaviours they expressed; further actors viewed their revealed thoughts and feelings as more rarely experienced (more 'distinctive') than their revealed behaviours.

The next study in this series examined more directly the notion that cognitive/affective reactions have more impact on self-inference processes than do behavioural reactions (Andersen, Lazowski, and Donisi,1986). In this research, participants were led to endorse a series of cognitive/affective or behavioural statements about themselves by agreeing that these statements were 'true' of them. Following their endorsements, participants made trait and attitude assessments about their own religiousness. The results showed that participants were significantly more influenced in their self-assessments by their cognitive/affective endorsements than by their behavioural endorsements. Hence, people's inferences about the self can be influenced by the mere salience of suggestive thoughts and feelings, just as other research has suggested that they can be influenced by salient past behaviours (e.g., Bem, 1967, 1972; Chaiken and Baldwin, 1981; Salancik, 1976; Salancik and Conway, 1975). Moreover, self-inferences made on the basis of overt behaviour may *require* the presence of compatible cognitive and affective content; hence, in the absence of such content, behaviours have little, if any, impact on self-inferences (see also Vallacher, 1984; Wegner *et al.*, 1984). Because potential differences in the abstractness and overall content of the cognitive/affective and behavioural reactions included in the research were controlled, revealed differences were not attributable to such differences. On the other hand, the inherent 'privacy' of thoughts and feelings (i.e., their lack of observability) and the fact that they tended to be perceived as more 'distinctive' than behaviours, even though they were not, may well have contributed to their greater impact in self-perceptions.

Another study in this series extended the question about the relative impact of cognitive/affective and behavioural information into the domain of more 'affective' self-evaluations (Andersen and Williams, 1985). This study explored the notion that, at least in some contexts, people may give more weight to their private cognitive/affective reactions than to their more public, behavioural reactions when making judgments about their self-esteem. In this research, the salience of these two sources of information was again manipulated, and subjects' subsequent self-evaluations were measured. Participants were asked to consider their positive past feelings or their positive past behaviours in response to probes such as, 'when I am alone I . . .', 'when interacting with the opposite sex I . . .', and 'when at a party I . . .'. Participants considered these positive past reactions in two very different contexts, by simply thinking about these experiences or by describing them aloud onto a tape-recording that they expected would be examined by trained judges at a later time. The results showed that participants evidenced significantly greater increases in self-esteem after thinking about their positive cognitions and affects than after thinking about their positive behaviours. This difference failed to emerge, however, when participants described their reactions aloud. One's public self-descriptions, of course, are likely to be more constrained by the perspective of outside observers than are one's experiences with private reverie, and the perspective of observers gives greater credence to overt behaviours than does the perspective of actors (Jones and Nisbett, 1971).

Private self-reflection may also enable greater expansion and elaboration in affects and cognitions than in 'objective' overt behaviours, in ways that public description does not. Private reflection, then, facilitates the process of giving greater inferential weight to thoughts and feelings than to behaviours.

The phenomenon of weighting cognitions and affects more heavily than behaviours in self-inference processes, it should be noted, is likely to vary not only across cultures as a function, perhaps, of cultural assumptions, but across cohorts and individual differences as well (see Turner, 1976). One mechanism likely to affect the manner in which people give weight to various sources of information about themselves when constructing self-knowledge is the degree to which they chronically attend to these sources of information. With regard to individual differences, evidence has suggested that they exist in the degree to which people attend to their internal states and to their public performances (cf. Fenigstein *et al.*, 1975; Scheier and Carver, 1983; see also Mollon, this volume; Pyszczynski and Greenberg, this volume). Little research, however, has examined the relationship between these chronic differences in self-attention and the quality of the inferences people make about themselves.

Participants in a final series of studies were preselected in terms of their scores on measures of *private and public self-consciousness* and also assessed themselves using a set of personality measures before participating in tape-recorded interviews that focused on cognitive/affective and behavioural information. These interviews were later presented to naive observers as in the studies described earlier and these observers then attempted to characterize the speakers using the same personality measures. The results revealed that individual differences do exist in the diagnosticity of cognitive/affective and behavioural information *vis*-à-vis the self-concept. Specifically, people who distinguished in their chronic patterns of self-attention between their internal reactions and their behavioural ones were assessed more 'accurately' by observers who had been exposed to cognitive/affective interviews rather than to behavioural interviews. That is, not only did high-private/low-public subjects show this effect, as expected, but low-private/high-public subjects showed the effect as well. Subjects who gave approximately equal attention both to their private and to their public aspects of self were assessed no more 'accurately' based on either source of information. Hence, these individuals appear to give greater weight to cognitions and affects than to behaviours in their self-conceptions, while people who are more even-handed in their chronic levels of self-attention (to that which is private and public) do not. In general, these data support the notion that one of the mechanisms underlying the phenomenon of cognitively based and affectively based self-inference processes is the experience of differentiating between that which is 'private' and that which is 'public' about the self (see also Figurski, this volume).

Returning now to cultural assumptions, Western culture, in particular, places a great deal of emphasis on the values of privacy and individuality, and this may facilitate the profound role that subjective reactions seem to play in the discourses about the self that people in our culture construct (cf. Gergen, 1984a, 1984b; Harré, this volume). All societies provide implicit rules as to the self-manifestations that are to be cherished and revered and those which, by contrast, should be considered contaminated, contrived or controlled. The assumptive principles of Western culture imbue that which is perceived as 'private' and 'distinctive' with considerably more profundity and 'reality', than that which is public or represented by agreed-upon social norms and institutions (see Andersen, 1984; Andersen and Williams, 1985; Turner, 1976; but see Tajfel, 1978). Although the degree to which most thoughts and feelings are socially common rather than distinctive is not entirely clear (see Andersen, 1984; Cronbach, 1955; Wilson and Stone, 1985), cognitive and affective responses tend to be perceived as more distinctive than behaviours in our culture, even when they are not (Andersen, Lazowski, and Donisi, 1986; see also McGuire and McGuire, 1981).

When considering the importance of the notion of individuality in Western culture, it also makes sense to take seriously the issues raised by Ralph Turner (1976) in the middle seventies (see also Turner, this volume). He argued that depending upon culture, one may recognize one's true self in the pursuit of institutionalized goals, that is, in an adherence to the norms of the dominant culture; one may also, by contrast, recognize this 'true' self more readily in the satisfaction of impulses that lie outside institutional frameworks, or in an adherence to what seems personal and unique, such as in one's own private values, feelings, and wishes. Not only does Western culture perpetrate the latter orientation by means of its emphasis on individuality and the notion of personal freedom, but certain cohorts, such as that composed of people who 'came of age' in 'the 1960s', for example, may accentuate this particular set of values.

STABILITY AND CHANGE IN THE SELF-CONCEPT

The present research is also importantly related to the problem of stability and change in the self-concept. Overall, this research suggests, for example, that private reactions, such as thoughts, feelings, wishes, and moods, can occur with sufficient frequency and vividness to induce changes in the self-concept that are more profound than those induced by comparable words and deeds. Such self-concept changes, like any others, will obviously become well-established when others can be convinced to believe in our changed self-conceptions (Swann, 1983; Webster and Sobieszek, 1974) and to provide us with social support for these changes (Snow and Machalek, 1983). Of course, changing one's environment and the people with whom one interacts can also facilitate self-concept change by opening up a variety of cognitive, emotional, and behavioural alternatives in one's life (Hormuth, 1984) in the form of new stimuli to which one may respond.

Although people probably oscillate between periods of stability and change in their self-conceptions throughout their lives, much bias in the service of self-concept maintenance does seem to exist. Empirical research involving the self suggests that internal states may guide, and bias, peoples' self-relevant behaviour (Greenwald, 1980; Markus, 1977; Swann, 1983), and that they may contribute to the subsequent self-inferences that people ultimately make (e.g., Andersen, 1984). For example, even though past research has shown that what we do and say has a great deal of impact on our general attitudes and evaluations (Bem, 1967, 1972; see also Jones and Davies, 1965; Shotter, 1981), other evidence has shown that one's private responses can overwhelm behavioural evidence about the self, preventing one from making correspondent inferences based on this behaviour (e.g., Chaiken and Baldwin, 1981; Taylor, 1975). Hence, while one's outer reactions change in response to situational or personal pressures, one's inner experiences may produce stability in the self-concept, in part by means of a number of self-maintaining cognitive strategies (e.g., Greenwald, 1980; Swann, 1983; Tesser and Campbell, 1983).

Thus, both theory and research suggests that the making of self-inferences is both an active process and one that is guided by cognitive and affective reactions. People maintain a stable sense of self, in part, by selectively affiliating with others who affirm their self-conceptions and by displaying various signs and symbols of this 'self' that are convincing (Goffman, 1957; McCall, 1977; Swann, 1983). People may even arrange their social lives, careers, marriages, and friendships in a way that verifies or further extends their self-conceptions (Markus and Nurius, this volume; see also Allport, 1955; James, 1910). Such consensual definitions of self undoubtedly help to stabilize peoples' self-conceptions (see Gergen, 1977; Goffman, 1957; McCall, 1977; Swann, 1983), just as other more private self-maintenance processes may serve this purpose (e.g., Greenwald, 1980).

CONCLUDING COMMENTS

Because self-maintenance processes exist, in part, as cognitive and affective processes, their implications for models of the self are worth considering. That is, the existence of self-maintenance strategies implies an active rather than a passive view of self-inference processes (see also Markus, 1983; Markus and Nurius, this volume). In contrast, a more Skinnerian or positivist view would suggest that people stabilize or change simply as a function of external contingencies, passively and reactively. In this latter view, people do not 'choose' the situations they enter so that these situations reflect well upon the self or are consistent with their own goals and intentions, but simply behave in accordance with available contingencies and acquire their particular sense of identity based on having done so (e.g., Bem, 1972; Enzle, 1980; Nisbett and Wilson, 1977; but see also McClure, 1983; Swann, 1983; White, 1980). This theory is very passive, of course, and suggests that people merely observe their own behaviours and dispassionately construct self-knowledge based on them. According to the present conceptualization, and a good deal of empirical research, there is a reciprocal interaction between the person and the environment (cf. Bandura, 1978; Mischel, 1973) and individuals have feelings, goals, and intentions that operate actively, affecting not only self-inferences, but overt behaviours, choices of situations to enter, and reactions to environmental contingencies (Mischel, 1977). Thus, a completely passive view of the acquisition of self-knowledge is likely to be quite deficient.

Finally, it should be noted that the differential weighting of cognitive/affective reactions relative to behavioural ones discussed here does not require that people have direct access to the 'truth' about themselves (cf. Gur and Sackheim, 1979; Morris, 1981; Nisbett and Ross, 1980; Nisbett and Wilson, 1977; Shotter, 1981; Wilson and Stone, 1985) nor does it require that such 'truth' even exists (cf. Gergen, 1977, 1984b, and this volume). It may, in fact, be that cognitive and affective responses can be more readily distorted than can overt behaviours (see Tesser, 1984) and they may therefore contribute more to the 'delusional systems' we frequently have about ourselves than do our overt behaviours (see Lewinsohn *et al.*, 1980). In the main, this research simply suggests that the categories one applies to oneself cannot be said to consist entirely of passive summations of overt behaviours and that, moreover, private emotional and cognitive reactions may have a profound impact on the self-inferences people make. Furthermore, because the assumptions we make in our culture, irrespective of their 'accuracy', contribute to self-inference processes, the 'accuracy' of these assumptions and the 'accuracy' of peoples' feelings and self-conceptions need not be the central issue in the study of the self. 'Accuracy' is unlikely to play a major role in self-inference processes unless the source of information in question happens to be equally vivid and 'cognitively available' (Tversky and Kahneman, 1973) as it is causally efficacious and applicable to the person and situation at hand (Nisbett and Ross, 1980). Cognitive and affective experiences are taken seriously by the individuals experiencing them, at least in this culture, and are thus given considerable credence not only in self-inference processes, but in the 'reasons' people construct for their actions (see Buss, 1978; Shotter, 1981), and in the assessments they make about the actions they ought to engage in or avoid in the future.

REFERENCES

Alexander, C. N. and Knight, G. W. (1971). 'Situated identities and social psychological experimentation.' *Sociometry*, **34**, 65–82.
Allport, G. W. (1955). *Becoming: Basic Considerations for a Psychology of Being*, Yale University Press, New Haven, Connecticut.
Andersen, S. M. (1984). 'Self-knowledge and social inference: II. The diagnosticity of cognitive/affective and behavioral data.' *Journal of Personality and Social Psychology*, **46**, 294–307.
Andersen, S. M. (1986). *Disparities in Chronic Self-Attention: Individual Differences in the Bases of Self-Knowledge*, Unpublished manuscript, University of California, Santa Barbara.

Andersen, S. M. and Ross, L. (1984), 'Self-knowledge and social inference: I. The impact of cognitive/affective and behavioural data.' *Journal of Personality and Social Psychology*, **46**, 280–293.

Andersen, S. M., Lazowski, L. E. and Donisi, M. (1986). 'Salience and self-inference: The role of biased recollections in self-inference processes.' *Social Cognition*, **4**, 75–95.

Andersen, S. M. and Williams, M. (1985). 'Cognitive/affective reactions in the improvement of self-esteem: When thoughts and feelings make a difference.' *Journal of Personality and Social Psychology*, **49**, 1086–1097.

Bandura, A. (1978). 'The self in reciprocal determinism.' *American Psychologist*, **33**, 344–358.

Bandura, A. (1981). 'Self-referent thought: The development of self-efficacy.' In J. H. Flavell and L. Ross (Eds), *Development of Social Cognition*, Cambridge University Press, New York, pp. 200–239.

Bem, D. J. (1967). 'Self-perception: An alternative interpretation of cognitive dissonance phenomenon.' *Journal of Experimental Social Psychology*, **1**, 199–218.

Bem, D. J. (1972). 'Self-perception theory.' In L. Berkowitz (Ed.), *Advances in Experimental Social Psychology*, vol. 6, Academic Press, New York, pp. 1–62.

Buss, A. R. (1978). 'Causes and reasons in attribution theory: A conceptual critique.' *Journal of Personality and Social Psychology*, **36**, 1311–1321.

Chaiken, S. and Baldwin, M. W. (1981). 'Affective-cognitive consistency and the effect of salient behavioral information on the self-perception of attitudes.' *Journal of Personality and Social Psychology*, **41**, 1–12.

Cooley, C. H. (1902). *Human Nature and the Social Order*. Scribner's, New York.

Cronbach, L. J. (1955). 'Processes affecting scores on "understanding of others" and "assumed similarity".' *Psychological Bulletin*, **5**, 177–193.

Enzle, M. (1980). 'Self-perception of emotion.' In D. M. Wegner and R. R. Vallacher (Eds), *The Self in Social Psychology*, Oxford University Press, New York, pp. 55–79.

Epstein, S. (1973). 'The self-concept revisited: Or a theory of a theory.' *American Psychologist*, **28**, 404–416.

Fenigstein, A., Scheier, M. F. and Buss, A. H. (1975). 'Public and private self-consciousness: Assessment and theory.' *Journal of Consulting and Clinical Psychology*, **43**, 522–527.

Festinger, L. (1954). 'A theory of social comparison processes.' *Human Relations*, **7**, 117–140.

Gergen, K. J. (1971). *The Concept of Self*, Holt, Rinehart and Winston, New York.

Gergen, K. J. (1977). 'The social construction of self-knowledge.' In T. Mischel (Ed.), *The self: Psychological and Philosophical Issues*, Basil Blackwell, Oxford, pp. 139–169.

Gergen, K. J. (1984a). 'Aggression as discourse.' In A. Mummendey (Ed.), *Social Psychology of Aggression: From an Individual to a Social Perspective*, Springer-Verlag, New York.

Gergen, K. J. (1984b). 'Narratives of the self.' In K. Scheibe and T. Sarbin (Eds), *Studies in Social Identity*, Praeger, New York.

Goffman, E. (1957). *The Presentation of Self in Everyday Life*, Doubleday, New York.

Greenwald, A. G. (1980). 'The totalitarian ego: fabrication and revision of personal history.' *American Psychologist*, **35**, 608–616.

Greenwald, A. and Ronis, D. (1978). 'Twenty years of cognitive dissonance.' *Psychological Review*, **85**, 53–57.

Gur, R. C. and Sackheim, H. A. (1979). 'Self-deception: A concept in search of a phenomenon.' *Journal of Personality and Social Psychology*, **37**, 147–169.

Hamlyn, D. (1977). 'Self-knowledge.' In T. Mischel (Ed.), *The Self: Psychological and Philosophical Issues*, Blackwell, Oxford, pp. 170–200.

Hormuth, S. E. (1984). 'Transitions in commitments to roles and self-concept change: Relocation as a paradigm.' In V. L. Allen and E. van de Vliert (Eds), *Role Transitions: Explorations and Explanations*, Plenum Press, New York.

James, W. (1910). *Psychology: The Briefer Course*, Holt, New York.

Jones, E. E. (1979). 'The rocky road from acts to dispositions.' *American Psychologist*, **34**, 107–117.

Jones, E. E. and Davis, K. E. (1965). 'From acts to dispositions.' In L. Berkowitz (Ed.), *Advances in Experimental Social Psychology*, vol. 2, Academic Press, New York, pp. 220–266.

Jones, E. E. and Nisbett, R. E. (1971). 'The actor and the observer: divergent perceptions of the causes of behavior.' In E. E. Jones *et al.* (Eds), *Attribution: Perceiving the Causes of Behavior*, General Learning Press, Morristown, New Jersey, pp. 79–94.

Kinch, J. W. (1963). 'A formalized theory of the self-concept.' *American Journal of Sociology*, **68**, 481–486.

Lewinsohn, P. M., Mischel, W., Chaplin, W. and Barton, R. (1980). 'Social competence and depression: the role of illusory self-perceptions.' *Journal of Abnormal Psychology*, **89**, 203–212.

McCall, G. J. (1977). 'The social looking-glass: A sociological perspective on self-development.' In T. Mischel (Ed.), *The Self: Psychological and Philosophical Issues*, Basil Blackwell, Oxford, pp. 274–287.

McCall, G. J. and Simmons, J. L. (1966). *Identities and Interactions*, Free Press, New York.

McClure, J. (1983). 'Telling more than they can know: the positivist account of verbal reports and mental processes.' *Journal for the Theory of Social Behaviour*, **13**, 111–127.

McGuire, W. J. and McGuire, C. V. (1981). In M. D. Lynch, A. A. Norem-Hebeisen and K. Gergen (Eds), *Self-concept: Advances in Theory and Research*, Ballinger, New York, pp. 147–171.

Mahoney, M. J. (1974). *Cognition and Behaviour Modification*, Ballinger, Cambridge, Massachusetts.

Markus, H. (1977). 'Self-schemata and processing information about the self.' *Journal of Personality and Social Psychology*, **35**, 63–78.

Markus, H. (1983). 'Self-knowledge: an expanded view.' *Journal of Personality*, **51**, 542–565.

Mead, G. H. (1934). *Mind, Self, and Society*, University of Chicago Press, Chicago.

Meichenbaum, D. (1977). *Cognitive-Behavior Modification*, Plenum Press, New York.

Mischel, T. (1977). 'Conceptual issues in the psychology of the self: an introduction.' In T. Mischel (Ed.), *The Self: Psychological and Philosophical Issues*, Basil Blackwell, Oxford, pp. 3–28.

Mischel, W. (1973). 'Toward a cognitive-social learning reconceptualization of personality.' *Psychological Review*, **80**, 252–283.

Monson, T. C. and Snyder, M. (1977). 'Actors, observers, and the attribution process: toward a reconceptualization.' *Journal of Experimental Social Psychology*, **13**, 89–111.

Morris, P. (1981). 'The cognitive psychology of self-reports.' In C. Antaki (Ed.), *The Psychology of Ordinary Explanations of Social Behaviour*. Academic Press, New York.

Nisbett, R. E. and Ross, L. (1980). *Human Inference: Strategies and Shortcomings of Social Judgment*, Prentice-Hall, Englewood Cliffs, New Jersey.

Nisbett, R. E. and Wilson, T. D. (1977). 'Telling more than we can know: verbal reports on mental processes.' *Psychological Review*, **84**, 231–259.

Rogers, C. R. (1951). *Client-centered Therapy*, Houghton Mifflin, Boston.

Rosenberg, M. (1979). *Conceiving the Self*, Basic Books, New York.

Salancik, G. R. (1976). 'Inference of one's attitudes from behavior recalled under linguistically manipulated cognitive sets.' *Journal of Experimental Social Psychology*, **10**, 415–427.

Salancik, G. R. and Conway, M. (1975). 'Attitude inferences from salient and relevant cognitive content about behavior.' *Journal of Personality and Social Psychology*, **32**, 829–840.

Scheier, M. F. and Carver, C. S. (1983). 'Two sides of the self: one for you and one for me.' In J. Suls and A. G. Greenwald (Eds), *Psychological Perspectives on the Self*, vol. 2, Erlbaum, Hillsdale, New Jersey, pp. 123–158.

Shotter, J. (1981). 'Telling and reporting: prospective and retrospective uses of self-ascriptions.' In C. Antaki (Ed.), *The psychology of Ordinary Explanations of Social Behaviour*, Academic Press, New York, pp. 157–182.

Shrauger, J. S. and Shoeneman, T. J. (1979). 'Symbolic interactionist view of self-concept: through the looking glass darkly.' *Psychological Bulletin*, **86**, 549–573.

Snow, P. A. and Machalek, R. (1983). 'The convert as a social type.' *Sociological Theory*, **1**, 259–289.

Snyder, M. (1974). 'The self-monitoring of expressive behavior.' *Journal of Personality and Social Psychology*, **30**, 526–537.

Snyder, C. R. and Fromkin, H. L. (1980). *Uniqueness: The Human Pursuit of Difference*, Plenum Press, New York.

Storms, M. D. (1973). 'Videotape and the attribution process: Reversing actors' and observers' point of view.' *Journal of Personality and Social Psychology*, **27**, 165–175.

Sullivan, H. S. (1953). *The Interpersonal Theory of Psychiatry*, Norton, New York.

Suls, J. and Mullen, B. (1982). 'From the cradle to the grave: comparison and self-evaluation across the lifespan.' In J. Suls (Ed.), *Psychological Perspectives on the Self*, vol. 1, Erlbaum, Hillsdale, New Jersey, pp. 97–125.

Swann, W. B. (1983). 'Self-verification: bringing social reality into harmony with the self.' In J. Suls and A. G. Greenwald (Eds), *Psychological Perspectives on the Self*, vol. 2, Erlbaum, Hillsdale, New Jersey, pp. 33–66.

Tajfel, H. (1978). *Differentiation between Social Groups*, Academic Press, London.

Taylor, S. E. (1975). 'On inferring one's attitudes from one's behavior: some delimiting conditions.' *Journal of Personality and Social Psychology*, **31**, 126–131.

Tesser, A. (1984). 'Public and private aspects of self-evaluation maintenance.' *International Interdisciplinary Conference on Self and Identity*, Cardiff, Wales.

Tesser, A. and Campbell, J. (1983). 'Self-definition and self-evaluation maintenance.' In J. Suls and A. G. Greenwald (Eds), *Psychological Perspectives on the Self*, vol. 2, Erlbaum, Hillsdale, New Jersey, pp. 1–31.

Turner, R. H. (1976). 'The real self: From institution to impulse.' *American Journal of Sociology*, **81**, 989–1016.

Tverskey, A. and Kahneman, D. (1973). 'Availability: a heuristic for judging frequency and probability.' *Cognitive Psychology*, **5**, 207–232.

Tverskey, A. and Kahneman, D. (1974). 'Judgement under uncertainty: heuristics and biases.' *Science*, **185**, 1124–1131.

Vallacher, R. R. (1984). 'Action identification and the emergence of self-conception.' *International Interdisciplinary Conference on Self and Identity*, Cardiff, Wales.

Webster, M. and Sobieszek, B. I. (1974). *Sources of Self-evaluation: A Formal Theory of Significant Others and Social Influence*, Wiley, New York.

Wegner, D. M. and Finstuen, K. (1977). 'Observers' focus of attention in the simulation of self-perception.' *Journal of Personality and Social Psychology*, **35**, 56–62.

Wegner, D. M. and Vallacher, R. R. (Eds) (1980). *The Self in Social Psychology*, Oxford University Press, New York.

Wegner, D. M., Vallacher, R. R., Macomber, G., Wood, R. and Arps, K. (1984). 'The emergence of action.' *Journal of Personality and Social Psychology*, **46**, 269–279.

Weiner, B. (1982). 'An attributional based theory of motivation and emotion: Focus, range, and issues.' In N. T. Feather (Ed.), *Expectations and Actions: Expectancy-value Models in Psychology*, Erlbaum, Hillsdale, New Jersey.

White, P. (1980). 'Limitations on verbal reports of internal events: A refutation of Nisbett and Wilson and of Bem.' *Psychological Review*, **87**, 105–112.

Wicklund, R. A. (1982). 'How society uses self-awareness.' In J. Suls (Ed.), *Psychological Perspectives on the Self*, vol. 1, Erlbaum, Hillsdale, New Jersey, pp. 209–230.

Wicklund, R. A. and Frey, D. (1980). 'Self-awareness theory: when the self makes a difference.' In D. M. Wegner and R. R. Vallacher (Eds), *The Self in Social Psychology*, Oxford University Press, New York, pp. 31–54.

Wilson, T. D. and Stone, J. I. (1985). 'More on telling more than we can know: the use of privileged information versus shared theories in self-attribution.' In P. Shaver (Ed.), *Review of Personality and Social Psychology*, vol. 6, Sage, Beverley Hills, pp. 124–135.

Zajonc, R. B. (1980). 'Feeling and thinking: preferences need no inferences.' *American Psychologist*, **35**, 151–175.

Section IV
Disordered and Precarious Selves

Self and Identity: Psychosocial Perspectives
Edited by K. Yardley and T. Honess
© 1987 John Wiley & Sons Ltd

19

Disordered and Precarious Selves: An Introductory Review

Krysia Yardley and Terry Honess

The committed systematic psychological treatment of subjective distress has a relatively recent history in the West compared with more general philosophical and psychological inquiry into the human condition. The former history undoubtedly significantly commences with the works of Sigmund Freud. It is therefore not surprising that some of the most interesting clinical work which aims to deal directly with problems of self should follow in the psychodynamic tradition, despite the radical and important departures that are necessitated by placing self at the centre of one's clinical and theoretical agenda.

The chapters by Wolf and Mollon exemplify these developments. Romanyshyn and Denzin can also be seen to be influenced by psychodynamic theory but they are primarily existential/phenomenologists, the former a psychologist and clinician, and the latter a sociologist. They both offer lucid accounts of problematic self experiences: Romanyshyn seeks to explore the metaphor of the mirror in therapy, where the self as image is seen to bring depth to what is otherwise lived on the surface, in a taken-for-granted manner. 'Mirror work' is, therefore, reflective of the self and yet disjunctive in relation to the person. Denzin seeks to elucidate the phenomena of alienation from self, an especially twentieth century condition earlier explored by existentialists such as Hegel, but neglected of late. The section is completed with a cognitive study by Pyszczynski and Greenberg. At first sight this contribution is quite different from those preceeding, however, in its emphasis upon 'lost objects' as the key factor in the development of inappropriate cognitive strategies, room is left for integrative understandings of self-experience. Moreover, the contributions by Arkin, Markus and Nurius, and Higgins *et al.* in the third section of this book broaden our view of the contributions of cognitive theorists to self orientated clinical issues. We now consider the chapters in this section in more detail.

Ernest Wolf presents us with a brief history of the emergence of the selfobject concept in psychoanalytic thinking to which he himself has contributed, following on from, and having collaborated with, the late Heinz Kohut. It was in the context of his own psychotherapeutic work that Kohut developed selfobject theory because he found extant psychoanalytic theories wanting in their explanatory power *vis-à-vis* the experiences that his clients reported. It has long been recognized that the highly specific monosymptomatic presentations of Freud and his contemporaries are rarely encountered in current analytic practice. Wolf points out that patients increasingly present with vague senses of depression, emptiness, meaningless, and alienation, that is, a catalogue of complaints of which the existential structure is described by Denzin, later in this section. Freud's increasingly technical theory left little room for any concept of self although Freud, Wolf states, was forced in later years to introduce the concept of 'narcissicism' to explain vulnerabilities in self experience. However, narcissicism, in the main, describes a pathologically rather than a normatively based state of affairs. The term becomes particularly perjorative in the context of Freud's treatment of the female psyche. (See Mendell, 1982 for a critical exposition of this concept.) Moreover, the introduction of 'narcissism' into the theory by no means signalled a recognition of either the relative salience of self, nor gave weight to the subjective experience of self in either therapy or everyday life. As Wolf is at pains to point out, selfobject theory gives primacy to this experience and most importantly throws emphasis upon the intersubjective context of experiencing individuals.

In considering the necessary conditions for an individual to be firmly and happily anchored in a positive experience of self, emphasis is thrown upon the adequacy of the caretaking environment with respect to the facilitativeness of such in rendering intelligible and acceptable the fragile emerging self of the child. This primarily intersubjective context is critical, and the implication is that both the child and the parent, particularly the mothering one, are mutually engaged in attuning to each other (see also Price, 1986; Harwood, 1986).

It is the parents/primary caretakers who provide the selfobject functions for the child and the key processes here are 'mirroring' (for extensive discussion of this concept in the context of child development see Pines, 1986), and 'idealization'. Wolf stresses that selfobjects are intersubjective, and are not to be confused with the internal objects of object relations theory (which are derived from the press of both instincts and external reality) nor with the relationship between the self and these objects. Similarly, selfobjects are not to be confused with the objective world of social relations. As other analytic theories, the severity of resultant pathological states and conditions is seen as bearing direct relationship to the pervasiveness and earliness of trauma in terms of selfobject functions. Such predisposing factors lead to conditions ranging from narcissistic behaviour and personality disorders to psychotic chaos.

The implications for psychotherapeutic practice are radical in comparison with classical analytic technique and have been the subject of a good deal of contention. The emphasis is upon the psychotherapist providing a positive and appropriate selfobject environment, empathically relating to the client rather than the emphasis being upon interpretation, confrontation, and therapist ambiguity. This emphasis upon the facilitating of the client is, of course, seen by conventional analysts as seriously interfering with transference.

Wolf touches upon the historical relationship between selfobject theory and other analytic theory, particularly object relations theory, however, as he himself acknowledges, the exact extent of Kohut's indebtedness to other analytic thinkers is not clear, despite there being a clear sense of legacy. In this matter it is to be remembered that Kohut's theoretical formulations were driven by his clinical experience and not by theoretical problems. The lack of explicit consideration of others' work is perhaps unfortunate as such consideration might have both increased the theoretical range of his observations by finding resonance in other works, for example, that of Guntrip. Moreover, consideration of the work of American analysts such as Horney, Fromm, and Sullivan might have led to some cultural adjustments to the theory. For example, some qualificatory statements about the content of the processes of mirroring and idealization might be apposite. There are questions about what it is exactly that must be mirrored within what kinds of culture for a healthy cohesive view of self. Additionally, in the selfobject framework, the child is clearly attributed with agentic powers, but it is not clear what these powers are or how much they contribute to the process of achieving cohesion. For example, what part do the child's developing cognitive powers play in the development of self and to what extent does the rationality, that Fromm so valued in human beings, play a part?

Despite these qualificatory remarks, selfobject theorists have succeeded in reasserting the primacy of the individual's experience within analytic therapy and have also succeeded in powerfully placing the experiential self within an analytic theoretical framework.

Mollon takes a more detailed look at the early stages of childhood development and integrates developmental, particularly cognitive, research into his descriptions while relying heavily upon the work of analytic writers such as Margaret Mahler for his account of separation, individuation, and the achievement of selfhood. In general, he approaches his subject matter influenced by selfobject theory but retains some allegiance to more mainstream British analytic thought. His particular concern in this chapter is one which he states has had little space in the literature and concerns the phenomenon of self-consciousness. Notwithstanding this lack of theoretical interest, self-consciousness is a phenomenon experienced mundanely and frequently by most of us and at its extremes can be profoundly disturbing, and an aspect of psychopathology.

Mollon differentiates between three types of self-awareness:

1. the ability to introspect and be conscious of one's self;
2. embarrassed self-consciousness;
3. compulsive hypochondriacal preoccupation with self.

The first type of self-awareness is presented as normal and one assumes desirable. The second type has mundane characteristics, but as it moves towards the extremes becomes pathological and the third type is characteristically pathological. There is a degree of disjunction between types of self-awareness which may be problematic for Mollon's theoretical position and we will return to this below. Both embarrassed self-consciousness and compulsive hypochondriacal preoccupation are very well illustrated by presentation of case material and phenomenological description. As with Wolf, we have the sensitive emphasis upon the experience of the client.

Mollon focuses a good deal upon the phenomenology of embarrassed self-consciousness and this is described as constituted phenomenally by the 'distinction between the background and the foreground of awareness collapsing'. Such self-consciousness arises from either the experience of an unempathic other or '. . . from an abrupt disruption of the relationship to the background' (of awareness). This background includes the empathic caretaker, experienced as part of the self: '. . . so that an abrupt disruption of the relationship to the background, especially any failure of the caretaker's empathy, is felt to be a wrenching away from the orienting framework resulting in disorientation'.

This distinction between background and foreground of awareness is evidently akin to that between the subjective 'I' and the objective 'me', and presumably the sustaining caretaking matrix is implicated ontologically in that subjective 'I'. However, given that there is an assumption that the sustaining matrix is essentially empathic, it is not altogether clear what the consequences of the background/foreground collapse would be if that original matrix was relatively unempathic. Hence, the relationship between the form of the primary caretaker/child matrix, and the division between 'normal' and 'pathological' self-consciousness merits further elaboration. Relatedly, one might posit that a disruption of the background of awareness might implicate a background 'false' self (as Mollon uses Winnicott's distinction between 'true' and 'false' self) in which case disruption might conceivably result in insight or liberation from the matrix. There are evidently some difficulties in trying to integrate 'false/true' self notions with selfobject theory and these difficulties are elsewhere tackled by Harwood (1986).

Essentially Mollon's work principally addresses, and is rooted in, models of pathological functioning. It might also be useful for the development of his thesis to consider in greater detail the normative, constitutive aspects of types of self-awareness. Although Mollon states that self-awareness is normal, it is not quite clear as to the exact constituents of this awareness or the extent to which they are implicated in more pathological forms of awareness. Mollon early on makes the claim that in order to function, the experiencing self has to focus on something which is not immediately itself. This view is very reminiscent of Hamlyn's (1977) view on self-consciousness, a view which is contested by Markova (this volume), but finds empirical support in the work of Pyszczynski and Greenberg (this volume). Further caution in holding this view in the extreme or without amplification of the theory, is indicated by the work of Figurski (this volume), who reports that individuals are commonly able to maintain high levels of self and other awareness from both internal and external positions. To risk reiteration, in Mollon's insightful phenomenological description of self-consciousness one gains a veridical sense of the experiential disjuncture and potential catastrophe of such states, but it is possible that the model would be strengthened by rigorous analysis of the nature of self-awareness itself.

It is interesting, in the context of Mollon's assertion that there has been little interest in self-consciousness within the analytic literature, that Denzin, who draws on existential phenomenology, should begin his account of the emotionally divided self with a Hegelian definition of the self-turned-against-itself as pivoted upon self-consciousness. 'Self', for Denzin '. . . is understood to refer to that process that unifies the stream of thoughts and experiences the person has about herself around a single pole, or point of reference'. Self is seen as a process, not a thing, and involves experienced identity over time, consciousness of consciousness itself, and moral feelings.

Denzin does not offer us an account of the aetiology of the disturbances of the alienated self although an integration of selfobject theory appears highly plausible. Nonetheless, Denzin's main purpose is to analyse the structure of alienated self experiences in terms of time, situation, and relationship. Self, for Denzin, is to be found in the world not in consciousness (see also Paranjpe, this volume). However, Denzin also suggests that the self that is divided and alienated from itself withdraws into its own subjectivity, so that self here, and indeed in the definition above, would seem to be within the person and within consciousness, as well as 'in the world'.

The self, as conceptualized by Denzin, has two levels: the surface level, that given to others, and the deep inner level which involves a feeling for the self as a distinct moral object/subject in the world. He is absolutely clear that self-feelings lie at the core of emotionality (contrast Gergen, this volume, but note similarities with some of the 'cognitive' contributions). Denzin further distinguishes four structures of the emotionally divided self and describes the phenomena associated with each.

It is not clear, however, in this present model, whether or not these structures might also be distinguished in relation to a non-divided self and a comparative analysis along these lines might be fruitful. These structures are defined as: Others, Self and Body, Situation, and Temporality. Denzin's description of the phenomenology of these is particularly evocative of psychotic phenomena with respect to his structure of 'Others' and that of 'Self and Body'. For example, consider the description of the self of those for whom meaningful engagement with others is experienced as damaging: '(such a self) . . . assigns a sense of moral superiority to this world and to itself. From that tremulous perch the subject directs a world that threatens to come apart at any moment. Its inwardness fears the fear that hovers on the borders of the barriers it has constructed around itself'. Such selves, Denzin states, are drawn to violence and continuously to 'ressentiment'. In such an analysis, Denzin reminds us of the darker side of human experience and behaviour that we are sometimes in danger of losing with overly benign theoretical approaches to human behaviour.

As already stated Denzin only touches upon the aetiology of the alienated self although he clearly implicates the caretaking experience (and one assumes that he would also, after Hegel, want to take in the larger social context into his understanding of aetiology). Evidently selfobject explanations of the development of disordered self experiences are highly compatible with much of Denzin's analysis and may be able to provide part of the aetiological picture. As the selfobject theorists, Denzin does attach great importance to the self in relationship although his emphasis is less upon intersubjectivity than the position of the alienated person in relationship. This emphasis reflects Denzin's interest in the adult rather than the developing child and even with the selfobject theorists, the interest in intersubjectivity is not developed with respect to adult relationships outside therapy. The concept of time in Denzin's analysis is also of much interest, and it is noteworthy that Denzin's 'divided selves' are unable to make full use of processual time (cf. the emphasis upon the future orientated aspects of 'normal' selves in Markus and Nurius' treatment of 'possible selves').

It is especially difficult to cogently summarize Denzin's work because of the density and richness of the description of phenomena. Moreover, it is, of course, the essence of phenomenological description to produce descriptive analysis that is essentially irreducible. In Glaser and Strauss' (1968) terminology such accounts sensitize us to phenomena rather than explaining these away.

Romanyshyn is also a phenomenologist and a practising psychotherapist. He presents an analysis of therapy around the idea of the mirror and the story wherein the self finds, constructs, and reconstructs itself, focusing the analysis upon one particular case, that of '. . . the fast rider on the dark plane and the shitty little boy'.

It is of note how pervasive the metaphor of the mirror is becoming. Within this volume we have McCall's dynamic use of the term to implicate the relationship between self, role, and society. We also have 'mirroring' used by the selfobject theorists to describe the intersubjective process of empathy. In Romanyshyn's case the metaphor extends from the highly specific and predominantly intrapsychic—between self and image—to the more general and exteropsychic where Romanyshyn talks of the world as the '. . . mirror of our subjectivity'. In all cases, for Romanyshyn, the individual sees *through* the mirror. The mirror does not offer us a duplicate self, but an image, and it is the perceiver's subjective experience of the self that is experiencing the image that enables the image to be a deepening of the person's experience.

Therapy is offered as 'self work' where a reconstruction of self, which involves the deepening of experience, can occur. Change for Romanyshyn lies not merely in experiencing through the mirror and experiencing the self that perceives the self (which adds an interesting dimension of subjectively based reflexivity to other models) but it also involves a standing back from the encounter. With respect to the latter, Romanyshyn adopts Wilshire's (1982) concept of 'thematizing' for the bringing into awareness the ways in which one is mundanely engaged in the world without awareness. This thematization does not appear to be simply a matter of objectifying nor seemingly can it involve 'false' dramatization. However, there is some ambiguity here that we will address below.

There is some contradiction between the idea of the mirror as a creative fictionalizing construction and mirror as the deepening of experience, especially *vis-à-vis* therapy. For, if the image is a construction limited only, but nevertheless limited, by the 'constructor' and if there is no absolute truth to the image, how is mere looking into the mirror to deepen experience and how is this deepening to be therapeutic? Clearly Romanyshyn does have very specific goals for therapy and in his examples of therapy one of the goals indicated is some veridical emotional experience. A clearer statement is needed here to resolve some of the apparent contradictions between the status of the image as a fiction that cannot be evaluated for its truthfulness and the status of the therapeutic act which holds truth values.

In Romanyshyn's description of the mirror experience particularly in his elucidation of the event as the experience of the familiar-stranger, we recognize the peculiar ambiguity of the experience. In that ambiguity Romanyshyn has convincingly communicated by image and metaphor that there is a depth. We need to know still more about that ambiguity to fully exploit the metaphor as a conceptual tool for dealing with the self.

Lastly in this section and quite distinct from the preceeding contributions is that of Pyszczynski and Greenberg who approach their subject matter from a cognitive perspective. This perspective together with the substantive matter of their argument has much in common with the other 'cognitive' contributions in this volume. However, we shall see there is a good deal of potential common ground between such contributions and the more dynamic contributions in this area, even though their respective metatheoretical positions are quite distinct with respect to the range of phenomena they will admit.

Pyszczynski and Greenberg develop the arguments of cognitive theorists such as those of Abramson *et al.*, (1978) and integrate these with the work of Carver and Scheier (1981) on self-focused attention. They propose, on the basis of empirical work that they have carried out, that a major distinction can be made between 'depressives' and 'normals' as to the strategy that each adopts with respect to self-focusing after failure. Carver and Scheier have already put forward a regulatory cybernetic view of self-focused attention where the latter is conceptualized as enabling desired goals and states to be achieved when there is a discrepancy between that which is desired and the present state. However, such self-focused attention becomes disruptive under certain conditions (see also Mollon, this volume). In particular, where success is increasingly unlikely, attention to self becomes self-defeating as it impedes progress to new achievements. The Depressives, it would seem, from Pyszczynski and Greenberg's evidence, maintain this self-focus in circumstances of likely defeat or actual defeat, and thus this style mediates the causal attributions depressives are likely to make. They go on to suggest that there may be several benefits for such persons, namely that they protect themselves from further failures and unrewarded strivings and from viewing the world as hostile and uncontrollable by an *acceptance* of a negative view of themselves. (Similar views are expressed by Arkin on shyness, this volume.) Such protective strategies could be viewed as secondary gain phenomena from a dynamic perspective.

Such a formulation although exclusively dealing with content available to consciousness, may, as already suggested, be made compatible with the more dynamic views of Mollon and Wolf. Thus this cognitive/awareness view of self can be seen as describing surface phenomena generated by underlying dynamic problems. Furthermore, Pyszczynski and Greenberg offer an aetiology for depression that is in relation to lost objects 'that provide a central source of self-esteem, value or meaning' for the person. If one were to take a dynamic developmental perspective these objects might be retermed self-objects. Unfortunately, Pyszczynski and Greenberg only explicitly concern themselves with unipolar reactive depression and thus do not address the aetiology of the so-called 'endogenous depressives' where it is even more likely that object loss if of great importance, particularly early loss (see Wolf, this volume).

The implications for therapy are not fully addressed here but one might extrapolate that a likely strategy commensurate with the authors' position would be to change clients' self-awareness patterns (e.g., through the strategies described by Markus and Nurius in their clinical studies). Other approaches might directly concern object loss and could be taken up as dynamic or rational-emotive issues. Combined approaches would seem to offer significant possibilities. One of the most interesting features of this chapter and others in this section, is that the formulation of problems within a particular paradigm does not seem to obstruct intervention at different levels and that each formulation throws light on some phenomenon that is recognizably an integrated part of a whole, notwithstanding that the phenomena occur at different levels.

REFERENCES

Abramson, L. Y., Seligman, M. E. and Teasdale, J. D. (1978). 'Learned helplessness in humans: critique and reformulation'. *Journal of Abnormal Psychology*, **87**, 49–74.

Carver, C. and Scheier, M. (1981). *Attention and Self Regulation*, Springer-Verlag, New York.

Glaser, B. G. and Strauss, A. L. (1968). *The Discovery of Grounded Theory*, Weidenfeld and Nicolson, London.

Hamlyn, D. W. (1977). 'Self-knowledge.' In T. Mischel (Ed.), *The Self: Psychological and Philosophical Issues*, Blackwell, Oxford.

Harwood, I. (1986). 'The evolution of the self: An integration of Winnicott's and Kohut's concepts.' In T. M. Honess and K. M. Yardley (Eds), *Self and Identity: Perspectives Across the Lifespan*, Routledge and Kegan Paul, London. (in press).

Mendell, D. (Ed.) (1982). *Early Female Development: Current Psychoanalytic Views*, Spectrum, New York.

Pines, M. (1986). 'Mirroring and child development.' In T. M. Honess and K. M. Yardley (Eds), *Self and Identity: Perspectives Across the Lifespan*, Routledge and Kegan Paul, London. (in press).

Price, G. (1986). 'Empathic relating and the structure of the self: Parallels in mother-infant and parent-therapist interactions.' In T. M. Honess and K. M. Yardley (Eds), *Self and Identity: Perspectives Across the Lifespan*, Routledge and Kegan Paul, London. (in press).

Wilshire, B. (1982). *Role Playing and Identity: The Limits of Theatre as Metaphor*, Indiana University Press, Bloomington.

Self and Identity: Psychosocial Perspectives
Edited by K. Yardley and T. Honess
© 1987 John Wiley & Sons Ltd

20

Some Comments on the Selfobject Concept

Ernest S. Wolf

Kohut's psychoanalytic psychology of the self is outlined and compared with traditional psychoanalysis. Special emphasis is placed on the central concept of the selfobject *and on clinical applications as well as on application to literature and art. Self development and its relation to self disorders are discussed.*

Since its creation during the waning days of the nineteenth century psychoanalysis has been dominated in its theories as well as in its major applications by the concepts that were introduced by Sigmund Freud. The idea of the mind as not just coextensive with consciousness but including also a vast unconscious has remained the *sine qua non* of any psychological theorizing that aims to be psychoanalytic. Indeed, the extent that the concept of the unconscious mind has become an accepted and integral though often unconscious, or at least unacknowledged part of popular culture in Western society is a measure of the penetration and permanent revolution set in motion by Freud. In common with all pioneering scientists Freud's achievements rest on the shoulders of his predecessors. He did not invent the unconscious nor was he the first to recognize it. Freud acknowledged that the credit for this discovery must go to the poets, especially Cervantes, Shakespeare, and Goethe, at whose feet Freud became a psychologist. Similarly, other fundamental Freudian ideas were as much a product of his immersion into tragedy and novel as they were the result of the systematic study of his patients, and, espcially, of himself. Freud's achievement was to take seriously these unconscious forces that had shaped the Western cultural tradition. He studied them systematically and built them into the theory and applications of psychoanalysis.

Psychoanalysis is not just a theory but also a method for probing into the depths of the human psyche. Freud did not enjoy being a physician and felt a greater kinship to his idealized mentors in the physiology and neurology laboratories. Reluctantly, and pressed by the need to support a growing family, he went into medical practice as a neurologist where he was confronted with the puzzling conditions that today we call the neuroses. Inspired by Charcot, the great French psychiatrist, and building on the 'talking cure' fortuitously discovered by the Viennese physician J. Breuer and his patient

'Anna O.' (real name: Bertha Pappenheim) he developed a method for the treatment of hysteria which he later extended to the other neuroses. Bringing together the analysis of symptoms, of dreams, and of parapraxes such as slips of the tongue, he proposed a basic model for the structure of psychoneurotic phenomena. In essence, the symptom is seen as a compromise structure consisting of an infantile sexual drive that had leaped across the repression barrier and then been contained through being modified and neutralized by a defence.

Let me illustrate with a simplified, somewhat schematic example. A naturally curious youngster will be intensely interested in the mysteries of sex and where babies come from. In a bourgeois family of *fin-de-siècle* Vienna such matters were not to be talked about directly and openly, especially with children. The boy's curiosity, however, got the better of him and when he was caught spying on his sister in the bath he was reprimanded severely. Some years later, as a young adult, he suddenly became blind but no organic-biological basis for his blindness was found. A diagnosis of hysterical blindness was confirmed when his sight returned during the course of psychological treatment. It also became evident that the blindness had occurred in the context of a sexually tempting situation where he feared his unacceptable sexual interest would be observed. According to the classical psychoanalytic model of symptom formation we would postulate that his voyeurism of early childhood represented infantile sexual wishes emerging from his *id* and that these had to be repressed into the unconscious because of the perceived threats of castration associated with the scolding he received for his boldness. When as a young adult a sexually stimulating situation provoked a renewed activity of the repressed impulses, the latter intruded into his *ego*. At the behest of his conscience, his *superego*, the ego was provoked into a defensive reaction of an inability to see, i.e., the blindness. Yet the compromise structure of the symptoms is evident in that he can now satisfy his impulse to look, albeit without seeing.

Psychoanalysis scored many successes in the treatment of such relatively simple symptom neuroses that expressed unconscious conflict focused on repressed infantile sexuality and aggression. The method of cure consists in making the unconscious conscious via interpretation. But the hope of curing all kinds of emotional and mental disturbances was soon disappointed as patients increasingly sought help with more complicated character and behaviour disorders where treatment was difficult and outcome often unsatisfactory. Many refinements in theory and technique were introduced. Still, a large group of so-called narcissistic and borderline conditions were generally thought to be unanalysable even though some modified forms of psychotherapy were deemed helpful. The therapeutic effectiveness of psychoanalytic treatment increased when attention began to be directed also to the development of object-relations in addition to the initial concentration on instinctual development. But it was especially the development of the concept of the self that has made contemporary psychoanalysis a much more powerfully therapeutic instrument. At the same time, contemporary psychoanalytic theory, particularly the theories of the psychology of the self, articulate more closely with other contiguous sciences of humankind than the classical theories.

Theory in psychoanalysis has been bedevilled from the very beginning by attempting an objective scientific discourse about concepts derived from 'inner', i.e., subjective experience. For the *essential* data of psychoanalysis are not the investigator's observations of behaviour alone—neither individual nor social nor verbal, neither that of statistics nor that of relationships—but it is through the analyst's assessment of subjective mental states by introspection into himself/herself in combination with empathy (defined as vicarious introspection) into others that psychological data become psychoanalytic. The psychoanalytic situation is set up to allow the controlled and systematic collection of introspective and empathic data. Not surprisingly, the conceptualization of these data into psychoanalytic theories always reflects the tension between the subjective origin and the goal of scientific objectivity. Freud's earliest theories exhibit this dilemma. He chose to use the German first person pronoun, 'das Ich', to designate both the concept person as well as the self without finding it necessary to distinguish these clearly. As theory became more elaborate and refined with the experience of some decades of analytic work 'das Ich', in English translation 'the ego', lost some of its subjective character and became a technical term for a system within a tri-partite mental apparatus consisting of id, ego, and superego (das Es, das Ich, das Ueberich). Theorizing became increasingly abstract and removed from the clinical origin of the data. Freud designated this theoretical superstructure a psychoanalytic metapsychology, thus hinting at its experience-distant status far from its subjective origins. The self had no place in it. The love of self, however, a phenomenon that could not be ignored, necessitated the introduction of the concept narcissism which was defined initially, by Freud, as the libidinal cathexis of the system ego. Hartmann (1950) clarified this by reintroducing the term self and redefined narcissism as the cathexis of the self rather than of the ego but retained the emphasis on libidinal cathexis, i.e., investment with quasi-biologic forces, the pleasure seeking instinctual drives, as the major motivating force in human development. Discrepant clinical experience and psychotherapeutic work with children, however, forced some psychoanalysts to begin a reconsideration of this experience—distant metapsychology. Melanie Klein, the most influential of the early object-relations theorists, continued to hold to Freud's emphasis on the instincts as the *primum mobile* for motivation but was able to accommodate the observations of important object-relations by enlarging the concept of unconscious fantasies about objects in her theories. Fairbairn (1944/1952) began to recast the instinct theory by proposing the drives to be primarily object-seeking. Object-relations moved into the centre of Fairbairn's concerns without dismissing the instinctual drives. At the centre of the personality he postulated a 'dynamic structure' with its own energy which manifests in the characteristic activity ascribed to instinctual drives. Guntrip (1961), in building on the contributions of both Fairbairn and Winnicott, acknowledged the essential importance of placing the self at the centre of psychoanalytic theory. In recognizing the fundamental need of all persons to possess a stable *experience* of themselves, Guntrip restated the subjective core of all psychoanalytic endeavours. Bacal (1985) calls Fairbairn's concept of dynamic structure an important step towards the evolution of a psychology of the strivings of a central self. Similarly, according to Bacal, for Guntrip (1961) '. . . the one fundamental thing that matters to human beings is to possess a stable experience of themselves as whole and significant persons.' Winnicott (1960/1965) introduced the concepts of a 'True Self' and a 'False Self' to distinguish normal from pathological aspects of the self-organization. His concept of the 'transitional object' began to call attention to the pivotal importance of neglected aspects of the developmental process while his concept of the 'holding environment' gave due recognition to the crucial role of the early caretakers. As a group, these British analysts by their focus on relations to objects were the first to begin correcting the imbalances that had crept into psychoanalytic metapsychology. They retained the term ego, using it interchangeably with self, and they did not free themselves completely from the old instinctual drive theories. They attempted to fit their conceptualizations into the framework of traditional psychoanalytic theory and refrained from systematizing their findings into a coherent psychology of the self. Their ground-breaking contributions prepared the way for Kohut's systematic conceptualization of self psychology though it is not easy to discern in detail the exact extent of their influence on Kohut's work.

Building thus on the contributions of his predecessors Heinz Kohut (1966) reformulated the psychoanalytic concept of narcissism and in a clinical paper outlined his evidence for the recognition and interpretation of what at that time he called the narcissistic transferences (1968). Without detailing the development of Kohut's thought I think it is important to keep in mind that his modifications of psychoanalytic theory and practice originally did not spring primarily from theoretical considerations but were forced upon him, so to speak, by clinical stalemates with patients who did not respond to the usual interpretations of unconscious conflict of a sexual drive versus defence emanating from an unresolved oedipus complex.

It was clear from the outset that these patients are characterized by a specific vulnerability: their self-esteem is unusually labile and, in particular, they are extremely sensitive to failures, disappointments and slights. It was, however, not the scrutiny of the symptomatology but the process of treatment that illuminated the nature of the disturbances of these patients. The analysis of the psychic conflicts of these patients did not result in either the expected amelioration or suffering or the hoped-for cessation of undesirable behavior; the discovery, however, that these patients reactivated certain specific narcissistic needs in the psychoanalytic situation, i.e., that they established 'narcissistic transferences', made effective psychoanalytic treatment possible . . .

As the understanding . . . increased . . . it became clear that the essence of the disturbance from which these patients suffered could not be adequately explained within the frame-work of classical drive-and-defence psychology . . .

The decisive steps forward in the understanding of these disorders, however, were made through the introduction of the concept of the selfobject . . . (Kohut and Wolf, 1978, pp. 413–414).

Kohut and a number of colleagues studied these narcissistic personality disorders and their treatment (Kohut, 1971, 1977, 1978; Kohut and Wolf, 1978; Goldberg *et al.*, 1978; Goldberg, 1980; Wolf, 1982; Goldberg, 1983; Lichtenberg and Kaplan, 1984). Increasing experience in the treatment of narcissistic personality disorders led to the recognition that mere minor modifications of classical psychoanalytic theory was not enough to encompass the mass of clinical data emerging from the treatment of these so-called narcissistic disorders. It was the introduction and elaboration of the new concept of the *selfobject* that allowed the formulation of a psychoanalytic psychology of the self. The remainder of this presentation will be focused on the selfobject and its central role in psychoanalytic self psychology.

The selfobject concept is a crucial departure from classical psychoanalytic concepts. To put it most simply, a selfobject is that function performed by an object that evokes in the subject the experience of selfhood. For example,

To begin with, it seems safe to assume that, strictly speaking, the neonate is still without a self. The new-born infant arrives physiologically pre-adapted for a specific physical environment—the presence of oxygen, of food, of a certain range of temperature—outside of which he cannot survive. Similarly, psychological survival requires a specific psychological environment—the presence of responsive-empathic selfobjects. It is in the matrix of a particular selfobject environment that, via a specific process of psychological structure formation called *transmuting internalization*, the *nuclear self* of the child will crystallize . . . The self arises thus as the result of the interplay between the new-born's innate equipment and the selective responses of the [caretakers as carriers of the] selfobject [functions] through which certain potentialities are encouraged in their development while others remain unencouraged or are even actively discouraged. Out of this selective process there emerges, probably during the second year of life, a nuclear self, . . . (Kohut and Wolf, 1978).

In this transaction, the selfobject is neither self nor object but a function of the relationship between self and object. Mistakenly, therefore, the selfobject is often taken to refer to interpersonal relationships or to interactions between self and object. Interpersonal and interactive relationships, however, are traditional concepts of social science that imply events taking place outside of an observer. Psychoanalytic data, in contrast, are derived from the observation of subjectively experienced complex mental states with the methods of introspection and empathy. They refer to the 'inner' experiences induced either by events 'inside', e.g., instincts, or by events 'outside', e.g., relationships with objects. The selfobject means the inner experience of those relationships that evoke and maintain the feeling of selfhood. Selfobject thus refers to the intersubjective context within which the self emerges as a psychological organization. I want to stress this easily overlooked distinction from object relations theory: selfobject relations refer only to the experience of relations between self and object. The psychoanalysts's field of observation is the analysand's subjective state, his/her inner experience, not his/her behaviour on the couch, not even the analysand's verbal behaviour. The latter merely are clues to the analysand's inner experience.

I will now survey briefly the consequences of the introduction of the self psychological point of view. The greatest impact has been on the clinical practice of psychoanalysis. For several decades it had been noted that the typical symptom neuroses that had been described by Freud were becoming rare among the patients that presented themselves for treatment. Instead, most of the patients who come for analysis these days complain of depressive states, of inability to maintain deep and meaningfully satisfying relationships with others, of incapacities in developing their full creative potentials, and in their symptoms one often finds a variety of uncontrolled behaviours such as addictions, perversions, and delinquencies. In other words, the classical psychoneurosis has been disappearing while the narcissistic personality disorder has become prominent among our patients. We cannot tell from the isolated vantage point among our relatively small practices whether this is just an apparent change due to factors of patient selection, or whether we are witnessing a true sociological change in patterns of morbidity, or whether we are just diagnosing with more discrimination. However, we are able to treat the narcissistic disorders much more effectively than it had been possible before Kohut introduced the self psychological concepts. Within the self psychological framework the strength and cohesion of the self depend on the patient's selfobject experience and the latter is accessible to the analyst only by vicarious introspection, i.e., by empathy. The analytic focus, therefore, shifts to understanding the patient's experiences, particularly on how in the transference he experiences the analyst as a selfobject (Wolf, 1983b). This emphasis on empathy and understanding the vicissitudes of the patient's selfobject experiences rather than on confronting the patient with his unacceptable instincts and defences in order to make them conscious has resulted in a therapeutic ambience that is experienced by the patients as more helpful and less adversarial. Consequently, even some of the more sensitive patients can now bear the emotional pain of being analysed and fewer therapeutic stalemates occur. Classical psychoanalysis had thought the narcissistic disorders mainly unanalysable. We are finding that this is not so.

Our view of psychological development has also changed. Our interest has shifted from the vicissitudes of instinctual development to the development of the self and its selfobject relations (Wolf, 1980). Here we find that our conceptualizations generally are in harmony with the findings of contemporary infant research based on the observations of mothers with infants (Lichtenberg, 1983).

At birth an infant has as yet no organized experience of selfhood though mothers invariably address their infants as if they were persons already. At approximately 18 months a sense of self emerges, at first very transiently, gradually more firmly and finally, by the age of 8 years, the self normally is fairly cohesive for life except for normally occurring periodic developmental crises such as adolescence, marriage, parenthood, midlife crisis, menopause, and old age. Of course, overwhelming traumas such as torture and concentration camps can also fragment a normally cohesive self. Psychological trauma before the emergence of the self, i.e., before the second year of life may result in perpetuating the prepsychological state of relative disorganization and can be recognized clinically as psychosis and borderline states. Trauma during the first 6–7 years of self development when the self is fragile and vulnerable to faulty selfobject responses, results in the narcissistic personality disorders.

> For example, to facilitate and strengthen the cohesion of his self, a child needs responses addressed to his whole self rather than to parts of him. A 7 yr. old comes into the kitchen and excitedly tells his mother about the beautiful castle he has built in the sand. He clutches at her apron to pull her outside to show off his achievement. Mother had just been washing the kitchen floor and she screams at him for tracking mud all over the clean floor, and, besides, 'look at you, you've got dirt and mud all over you.' With that she picks him up rather roughly and drags him into the bathroom for a quick wash-up.

By themselves, incidents such as this are not usually of great traumatic impact. But as typical expressions of a milieu that chronically deprives the child of needed responses to his wholeness and to his exhibitionistic pride in his budding self such incidents often become indicators of a characteristically humiliating and fragmenting ambience. Children who grow up in such chronically faulty selfobject environments will emerge with damaged and fragile self-structures that will probably manifest later in life as specific narcissistic vulnerabilities.

With the data we have been accumulating during the last decade and a half we are now beginning to develop a classification of the disorders of the self based on aetiological consideration of the vicissitudes of self-selfobject relations at various stages of psychological development (Kohut and Wolf, 1978; Wolf, 1983a). Let me briefly review our findings.

The *aetiology* of disorders of the self is to be found in faulty interaction between the child and his or her caretakers, especially during the early years when the self first emerges. These faulty interactions are experienced by the nascent self as inappropriate or even injurious selfobject responsiveness. The result is a diffusely damaged self or a self that is seriously damaged in one or the other of its constituents. To give firmness and cohesion to the child's fragile self the child needs two kinds of responses from the selfobject environment. Mirroring selfobjects provide confirmation for the child's innate sense of vigour, greatness, and perfection (Kohut, 1968, 1971). Idealized selfobjects are available to the child as images of calmness, infallibility, and omnipotence with whom the child can merge. Faulty interactions between the child and his or her selfobjects result in a damaged self which predisposes to the later outbreak of a disorder of the self. Depending on the nature of the damage, therefore, adult selfs exist in varying degrees of cohesion, have various levels of vigour, and are balanced in varying degrees of harmony.

The disorders of the self can be subdivided into a number of groups depending on the nature of the damage to the self. If the damage to the self is relatively permanent and the defect is not covered over by defences, then the resulting syndrome is like those that are traditionally referred to as the *psychoses*. Constitutional factors combine with the effects of deficient mirroring to produce the non-cohesive psychopathology of *schizophrenia*. In another category, inherent organic factors combine with the psychological depletion resulting from lack of joyful selfobject responses to leave a predisposition toward *empty depression*. Absence of structure building experiences attending the merger with calm idealized selfobjects is likely to result in insufficient self-soothing structures or self-supportive structures and, therefore, predispose to *mania* or *guilt depression*.

Borderline states are characterized by similar relatively permanent injuries to the self, except the damage is covered by complex defenses. A borderline self may protect its fragile structure against further serious damage from the rough and tumble as well as from the intimacy of social intercourse by using schizoid mechanisms to keep involvement shallow or by using paranoid mechanisms to surround itself with an aura of hostility and suspicion that will keep noxious selfobjects at bay.

Less severe and more temporary damage to the self is found in the *narcissistic behaviour disorders*. Characteristically these persons attempt to shore up their crumbling self-esteem through perverse, delinquent or addictive behaviour. In the *narcissistic personality disorders* we find even less severely damaged selves. Here the injured state of the self is experienced directly in the form of subjective symptomatology, such as hypochondria, depression, hypersensitivity to slights, lack of zest, inability to concentrate on tasks, irritability, insomnia.

In addition to its therapeutic dimension psychoanalysis has always been interested in the application of its theories to literature and other cultural artifacts. Self psychology has widened the scope of applicability and offered interpretive alternatives that often seem less reductionist. I will briefly mention three examples. Freud's and Ernest Jones' focus on Hamlet's oedipal tensions added important insights to the study of that great drama. Kohut added that 'the oedipal conflicts by themselves, however, cannot explain the extent and nature of the traumatic state from which Hamlet suffers' (1971, pp. 235–237). He then delineated the origin and fate of that traumatic state as, in essence, a temporary overburdenedness and fragmentation of a self injured in its central values or, to put it into more contemporary terminological usage, a bipolar self with a shattered pole of ideals. As for modern art, with which classical analysis has hardly grappled, Kohut has suggested that it deals with the problems of a crumbling or deeply injured self. Think of the dissonances of contemporary music and of Picasso's distorted and almost dismembered humans as a depiction of the world as experienced by a fragmented psyche. I have been particularly interested in Virginia Woolf who, in her sensitivity to self disorder, especially of her own self, and in her genius for subtle expression of self-experience, has expanded and enriched the world in which all of us live. Even more than Proust or Joyce, she wrote the modern novel of self-experience par excellence, forty years before psychoanalysts began to study this experience systematically (Wolf, 1981–81; Wolf and Wolf, 1978).

Selfobject psychology is concerned with the conflicts pertaining to the inexorable 'drive' of the organism to organize and order its chaotic prepsychological state into a cohesive self experience. The self seeks to achieve and maintain its integration, i.e., its coherence. Intense inner conflicts accompany these strivings. As an example, I would mention the conflict between the yearning for closeness to obtain the needed selfobject responsiveness from others and the fearful anticipation of a noxious and therefore fragmenting response.

A 30-year old professional colleague consulted me about her inability to establish lasting and intimate relationships. Though she enjoyed an active social life her friendships with both men and women appeared superficial and she never was free of feeling like an outsider. During the years of college and medical education she had become seriously and sexually involved with a number of apparently suitable prospective mates but in each case the liaison foundered when the young men withdrew for no apparent reason. Was there something wrong with her or was she just unlucky in her choices?

She was an exceptionally bright and intelligent woman, quite attractive in spite of a somewhat ponderously formal dress and manner that also found expression in her serious but all-too-reasoned approach to the analytic dialogue. She just couldn't let herself go and freely say anything that might come to mind. Nor did she have much awareness of how she really felt. When telling tensely about a colleague's interference with some research that she had meticulously planned she might acknowledge some frustration, perhaps, but was oblivious to the accumulated resentment and rage she harbored against this frequent disturber of the peace. Clarifying comments by me were often rejected coldly and contemptuously though I am sure she would have denied being aware of anything but the highest respect. It was only after I began to appreciate that she experienced anything I said—perhaps even the mere situation of patient with analyst—as an humiliating assault that I could cautiously begin to make her aware of this constant and terrible anxiety. It took some months before she could let herself really hear what I said about what was going on between me and her. Gradually, she began to relax and became more freely spontaneous and less guarded. The first major resistance in the analysis had been interpreted and weakened.

Much later in the analytic process enough material from her personal history had been gathered to explain both the complaint that had brought her into treatment and the fearful reluctance with which she engaged in the treatment process.

As the daughter of eastern European immigrants who had fled the Bolsheviks, she had been raised in a milieu of highly educated and somewhat aristocratic parents who were attempting to make a new life for themselves in the rough-and-tumble of American business. The children were overprotected against the vulgarizing aspects of popular culture with much love but scant affection. Not poverty but adherence to the old values created a climate of austerity against which the children rebelled each in their own way. Expression of anger, indeed, of any strong emotions, was not tolerated but proper behaviour without complaint was expected. My patient felt misunderstood, unloved and unlovable. She withdrew into herself, thus cutting herself off from the needed closeness to the parents as carriers of the self-sustaining selfobject responses. In a fantasy world of harmony and her own perfection she grew into an immature and emotionally deprived adult.

Her inner unconscious conflict between her yearning for loving and self-sustaining closeness and her fear of destructively disintegrating criticism became evident. So is her need to keep all comers at a safe distance to protect her vulnerable self structure from the injurious intrusions that comes in social intercourse with real people. We can understand the superficiality of her friendships, her apparent coldness under a cover of correct behaviour and rational attitudes. We can also recognize how she carried this self-saving—perhaps, even life-saving—armour into her relationship with me, a typical analytic transference of infantile experience into the present. And we can discern also how she could not help but resist, even against her better conscious judgment, the call to openly tell her mind. Such is the nature of unconscious resistance.

This small vignette from a long analysis has served me to demonstrate that conflict, transference, and resistance have not disappeared from psychoanalytic selfobject psychology. But they have assumed a new meaning. Conflict in selfobject psychology no longer refers primarily to conflict between unconscious sexual drives and defences against them to conflicts about relations between self and selfobjects. Transference no longer means the intrusion of unconscious drives and defences into the adult ego but the intrusion of the child's fears of loss of selfhood into the current psychoanalytic reality with the analyst. Resistance no longer means an unwillingness to give up the old neurotic satisfactions but a legitimate fear of being injured again. In short, the instincts and their vicissitudes have been recognized as peripheral to the central concerns of these patients, namely the cohesion of their selves.

This is indeed a major shift in psychoanalytic theory. You recall how I outlined the classical psychoanalytical conceptualization of symptom formation by using a hypothetical case of hysterical blindness. The symptom of blindness is formulated to be a compromise structure between the wish to see what's forbidden and the defence against it. In self psychology we would formulate this differently, with much more complexity and not nearly so elegantly. We would postulate that the childhood wish to peek was a healthy impulse originally, fed by natural curiosity, a curiosity about those people who are different, particularly whose anatomy is different. Especially there exists a near universal curiosity about where babies come from. Assuming a healthily sensuous parental couple without major neurotic sensitivity about infantile sexuality and aggression we would then postulate a response to the inquisitive and curious child that understands and accepts his sexual researches as part of his normal emotional development. At the same time the child could be made aware, gently and non-critically, of his sister's need for privacy as, indeed, the child wants his own privacy safeguarded also. But the parent confers legitimacy on the child's desire by offering explanations and even by showing some pleasure in the child's development having reached such a level of interest in others. As a result of such empathically tuned-in selfobject responsiveness by the parents the child's curiosity will find a measure of optimal affirmation for his self rather than deprivation of needed responses. The child's self will be strengthened by the experience of being understood, will probably act out to sneek a few more peeks at the forbidden fruit to satisfy his curiosity and to have the reassuring experience that he can go against the parents wishes without the walls crashing down on him. Then the issue will disappear without any harm having been done.

The scenario will develop differently when the child's needs to know and unravel the mysteries of sexuality and childbirth are blocked in a rejecting and derogatory manner by parents who have become upset by the child's precocious demands on its elders. Instead of receiving a supportive response to his courageous researches into the unknown the child is often made to feel he is bad, evil, beset with foul and dirty thoughts, and the adults may turn away in cold disgust. Or they may actively punish the child on the theory that he who spares the rod spoils the child and that the child's spirit must be crushed now to prevent worse, even criminal, actions, later on. Or, any variety of faulty selfobject response causes the child's self to disintegrate and the child's normal sensuality and healthy assertiveness are thus wrenched out of their integration into the whole self structure. Without being embedded in the restraining matrix of the intact self structure the sexuality and assertiveness become transformed into neurotic driveness and hostile aggression.

In the case of the peeping boy I don't know whether he was merely expressing any boy's natural voyeuristic tendencies or whether the peeping was already symptomatic of a fragmenting self in which the normally integrated sexual curiosity had already been transformed into the hyperactive disintegration product of a shattered self. Against these neuroticized impulses the ego brings the defences into action that psychoanalysis has studied so well over the last 100 years. But these constellations of drive and defence are not the result of inborn excessively strong drives or inborn weak defensive equipment of the ego. They are the result of overstimulation and distortions imposed by the weakening of the constraining self structure secondary to faulty selfobject responsiveness of the caretakers of early infancy and childhood. It is these end-products of the disintegration of a healthy self that remain active in the personality even into adulthood while being more or less repressed or disavowed until some intercurrent stimulus comes along and reactivates them into a full-blown symptom neurosis.

In this conceptualization the essential core of neurosis is not different from other disorders of the self. The variety of disorders of the self reflect the variety of developmental vicissitudes. The impact of the environmental ambience on the developing self depends on the nature of the traumatic insult to the self, on its severity and timing relative to the self's phase-appropriate strengths and vulnerabilities during successive developmental sequences.

An emergent self psychology has broadened the scope of psychoanalysis by moving from a too narrow biologic-mechanistic base and by making explicit the always implicit primacy of subjectivity in its conceptualizations. The time is now ripe for a new integration of the various streams of psychoanalytic thinking.

REFERENCES

Bacal, H. (1985). British Object Relations Theorists and Self Psychology: Some Critical Reflections. (in press).

Fairbairn, W. R. D. (1944). 'Endopsychic structure considered in terms of object-relationships.' In *An Object-Relations Theory of the Personality*, Basic Books, New York, 1952.

Goldberg, A. (Ed.) (1980). *Advances in Self Psychology*, International Universities Press, New York.

Goldberg, A. (Ed.) (1983). *The Future of Psychoanalysis*, International Universities Press, New York.

Goldberg, A. *et al.* (Ed.) (1978). *The Psychology of the Self: A Case Book*, International Universities Press, New York.

Guntrip, H. (1961). *Personality Structure and Human Interaction*, International Universities Press, New York.

Hartmann, H. (1950). 'Comments on the Psychoanalytic Theory of the Ego.' In *Essays on Ego Psychology*, International Universities Press, New York, 1964.

Kohut, H. (1966). 'Forms and transformations of narcissism.' In P. Ornstein (Ed.), *The Search for the Self*, International Universities Press, New York.

Kohut, H. (1968). 'The psychoanalytic treatment of narcissistic personality disorders: an outline of a systematic approach.' *The Psychoanalytic Study of the Child*, 23, 86–113.

Kohut, H. (1971). *The Analysis of the Self*, International Universities Press, New York.

Kohut, H. (1977). *The Restoration of the Self*, International Universities Press, New York.

Kohut, H. (1978). 'Remarks about the Formation of the Self (1974).' In P. Ornstein (Ed.), *The Search for the Self*, International Universities Press, New York.

Kohut, H. and Wolf, E. S. (1978). 'The disorders of the self and their treatment: an outline.' *International Journal of Psychoanalysis*, 63, 396–407.

Lichtenberg, J. (1983). *Psychoanalysis and Infant Research*, Analytic Press, Hillsdale, New Jersey.

Lichtenberg, J. and Kaplan, S. (Eds), (1984). *Reflections on Self Psychology*, Analytic Press, Hillsdale, New Jersey.

Winnicott, D. W. (1960). 'Ego distortion in terms of the true and false self.' In *The Maturational Processes and the Facilitating Environment*, International Universities Press, New York, (published 1965).

Wolf, E. S. (1980). 'On the developmental line of selfobject relations.' In A. Goldberg (Ed.), *Advances in Self Psychology*, International Universities Press, New York, pp. 117–130.

Wolf, E. S. (1980–81). 'Psychoanalytic psychology of the self and literature.' *New Literary History*, 12, 41–60.

Wolf, E. S. (1982). 'Comments on Heinz Kohut's conceptualization of a bipolar self.' In B. Lee (Ed.), *Psychosocial Theories of the Self*, Plenum, New York, pp. 23–42.

Wolf, E. S. (1983a). 'Selfobject relations disorders.' In M. Zales (Ed.), *Character Pathology: Theory and Treatment*, Bruner/Mazel, New York, pp. 23–38.

Wolf, E. S. (1983b). 'Empathy and countertransference.' In A. Goldberg (Ed.), *The Future of Psychoanalysis*, International Universities Press, New York, pp. 309–326.

Wolf, E. S. and Wolf, I. (1978). 'We perished, each alone: a psychoanalytic commentary on Virginia Woolf's "To the Lighthouse".' *The International Review of Psychoanalysis*, 3, 37–47.

Self and Identity: Psychosocial Perspectives
Edited by K. Yardley and T. Honess
© 1987 John Wiley & Sons Ltd

21

Self-Awareness, Self-Consciousness, and Preoccupation with Self

Phil Mollon

A psychoanalytic study of the distinction between normal self-awareness, embarrassed self-consciousness (as aspect of shame), and hypochondriacal preoccupation with the self is presented. Kohut's concept of the selfobject, self-consciousness as disturbance in relation of self to selfobject, self-consciousness as preserving sense of self, and the heightened needs for mirroring when sense of self is fragile are discussed. Clinical examples illustrating disturbances in the relation of self to selfobject are given.

In the last few years there has been a growing psychoanalytic literature on shame (Mollon, 1984). However, there has been very little focus on self-consciousness as a specific aspect of this experience. To the best of my knowledge, there has only ever been one psychoanalytic contribution (Amsterdam and Levitt, 1980) which takes this subject as its major focus. Even the literature on adolescence, on the whole, makes scant reference to either self-consciousness or shame. In this chapter I describe the phenomenology of self-consciousness and link it with psycho-dynamic and developmental aspects.

The theoretical framework here is broadly contemporary psychoanalytic. A predominant influence is the work of Kohut (1971, 1977) and his development of 'self-psychology' (see also Wolf, this volume), since it is he who most explicitly places the experience of self at the centre of his theorizing. The clinical material used as illustration is taken from psychoanalytic psychotherapy, employing the usual method of exploration of transference patterns enacted with the therapist as a means of reconstructing the early childhood pathogenic interactions with significant caretakers. While the clinical examples are of pathologically intensified disturbances of self experience, I believe they demonstrate vividly the processes involved in more everyday states of self-consciousness.

First it is important to distinguish three varieties of self-consciousness.

1. Self-awareness, the ability to introspect and be conscious of one's self.

2. Embarrassed self-consciousness, a painful and shameful awareness of the self as an object of other's unempathic attention.
3. A compulsive, and hypochondriacal preoccupation with the self: a compelling need to look in mirrors and to evoke mirroring responses from others.

Writing from a phenomenological base, Wilshire (1982) describes the normal state of mimetic engulfment one with another, in which we all exist to some extent much of the time. He discusses the way in which theatre and other arts can give us the means to reflect upon our position and thus become self-aware and more individuated. Speaking developmentally, the achievement of normal self-awareness may be described from various points of view. There is considerable evidence (summarized by Stern, 1983) that the infant can distinguish the self from other at birth and has a good deal of innate perceptual organization. Mahler's stages of separation and individuation describe the gradual development of a sense of self in parallel with the increasing ability to be physically separate from mother (Mahler *et al.*, 1975). However, the ability to take the self as an object, the emergence of a self that observes the self, must also depend on the beginnings of the representational thinking that is described by Piaget (e.g., 1951). There are a variety of indications that this development takes place in the second half of the second year (Kagan, 1981). Children at this time begin to show signs of concern over behaviour that violates adult standards. Kagan quotes observations which reveal major changes in children's reactions to the distress of others; at this stage they act is if they can infer a psychological state of the other, presumably based on their own experience, and give appropriate responses, such as a hug, a kiss, or a request for help from an adult. The most striking evidence is provided by Lewis and Brooks-Gunn (1979) using an experimental method in which a spot of rouge is placed on the child's nose and he or she is then held in front of a mirror; they report that between the ages of 18 and 21 months there occurs a large increase in the number of infants demonstrating self-recognition abilities.

So the development of self-awareness, and the emergence of an observing self, appears to take place according to a largely innately determined timetable interacting with social conditions. However, we might imagine that the appearance of an observing self might be enhanced by the following kind of incident. A child runs indoors, joyfully anticipating telling his mother what he has been up to but the mother's response is to remark 'look what a mess you are!' Here we enter my second category, that of embarrassed self-consciousness. This is much more determined by social conditions, the responses of the caretakers.

The phenomenology here is interesting. The normal situation of an experiencing self against an orienting background self (Spiegal, 1959) is disrupted. The background self is suddenly in the foreground of awareness. The distance between the object of awareness and the subject of awareness collapses, the self becomes as if two dimensional, and a spiralling feedback ensues, resulting in a panicky disorganization. An analogy can be drawn with the collapse of the distinction between signifier and signified in psychotic states, as described by Lacan (1959/1977): the normal tripartite structure of symbol, object symbolized, and user of the symbol break down, so that the word, the symbol, is confused with the object or action. Similarly, in states of embarrassed self-consciousness the distinction between the background and the foreground of awareness collapses, and indeed the experience does seem to have a rather psychotic quality to it. The coinciding of experiencing self and observed self creates a cybernetic problem. In order to function, the experiencing self has to focus on something which is not immediately itself (even if this be a memory or an anticipation of the self), it requires feedback from outside. Interestingly Yardley (1979) explains the efficacy of social skills therapy in relation to social anxiety in terms of the facilitating of other-awareness in place of self-preoccupation.

It is my impression that this kind of self-consciousness often arises when there is an experience or fantasy of an unempathic other observing the self; the more total this identification with the observing other, the more intense the self-consciousness. The presence of the other may be felt to be over-whelming, pushing the subjective self to the margin. Self-consciousness then emerges as a response to the threat to the self. Like the return of the repressed, the self refuses to be suppressed. One aspect of this experience is the sense of having to be something for the other—initially of having to play a role for the mother. Self-consciousness arises in the threat to this role, in the jarring between the collusive fitting in with the desire of the other and the actual separateness of the self.

A patient spoke of his surprise, pleasure, and relief whenever I seemed to be remembering details about him and his history correctly. He described his considerable anxiety that I might make a mistake and confuse him with another patient. The embarrassment he feared was actually *my* embarrass-ment: that he might turn out to be other than I expected, that his real self might embarrassingly emerge.

I have consistently found in patients who are prone to self-consciousness a background of a mother who required a child to function as an extension of herself, in such a way that there was no place for the child's separate self. Aspects of the child that were not consistent with the mother's expectations were not recognized. The mother reinforced separation only and ultimately in relation to herself, applauding only those achievements that confirmed *her*. To a significant extent, the child colluded with this need of the mother, often because the pay-off was the maintenance of the special or privileged position in relation to the mother. In these circumstances, the child's real rival for the mother's love is then the false image the mother has of the child. This is the dilemma portrayed in Oscar Wilde's novel, *The Picture of Dorian Gray* (Green, 1979). Here it is the picture, the image, that is loved and with whom Dorian wishes to swap places; the unseen and unmirrored self becomes increasingly degenerate and filled with envy, represented by the hideously deteriorating picture locked away in Dorian's attic. Often with these patients the father, denigrated by the mother, did not function effectively as an oedipal rival, or as a third person who could help separate mother and child. Thus, the child did not receive recognition of his or her own self. In each case, this resulted in strong needs for recognition and affirmation and a consequent vulnerability to the responses and opinions of others. Invariably I have found patients who are prone to self-consciousness to be compulsive accommodators, sensing what is required of them and presenting themselves accordingly.

Although embarrassed self-conscious reactions have been observed even during the first year of life, these become much more pronounced in the latter half of the second year. In terms of traditional psychoanalytic stages of development, the anal stage seems particularly important, with its attendant conflicts over autonomy and control of the body and its contents (Heimann, 1962; Oliner, 1982). The child's experience of sitting on the potty and being observed by the demanding mother may well be a prototype of self-consciousness in the presence of the overwhelming other. Sander (1983) has described how the child normally adopts a 'contrary position' in the second 18 months. Similarly, Spitz (1957) has pointed to the significance of the toddler's head shaking gesture and the use of the word 'no'. Winnicott (1963) has emphasized the significance of the toddler's option to 'not communicate', to protect an inviolate inner core. The child becomes aware that it has a self to protect. Thus it seems that these struggles for autonomy, the taking of a contrary position and so on, coincide with the emergence of increased self-consciousness.

Recognition by the parents that the child has a self which unfolds according to its own blueprint seems crucial. Alice Miller (1979), drawing on the work of Mahler, Kohut and Winnicott states, 'the child has a primary need to be seen, noticed and taken seriously as being that which it is at any given time, and as the hub of its own activity. In contra-distinction to drive wishes, we are here dealing with a need which is narcissistic, but nevertheless equally legitimate, and whose fulfillment is essential for the development of a healthy self-esteem'.

THE SELFOBJECT MATRIX

Kohut has described how a coherent sense of self is dependent, particularly in childhood, upon the presence of empathic responsive figures. As children we need these others to be there not as separate and autonomous beings, but to be there reliably, predictably, and responsively. We need them there as a background for our own self. Hence Kohut termed such figures selfobjects, to indicate that their presence is experienced as part of the self. Kohut has postulated two separate, albeit intertwining, lines of development: first, the relationship of self to object and, second, the relation of self to selfobject. The prime roles of selfobjects are in terms of their mirroring (empathically responsive) functions, and their availability for idealization. Tolpin (1983) describes it thus: 'by merger of self and selfobject we mean psychological connectedness—for instance, between delighted child and mirroring audience, between cranky tired child and idealized, uplifting pillars of strength and support; between the child who wants company and the lively partners who lend their presence'. The notion of the selfobject matrix may be compared to similar concepts, such as Sandler's (1960) 'background of safety', Winnicott's (1963) 'environment mother', Grotstein's (1981) 'background object of primary identification', and Bion's (1962) 'container and contained' and maternal reverie. Kohut emphasizes that we never outgrow the need for selfobjects, although their form changes. Similarly, Kegan (1982), a neo-Piagetian, has described a model of a helix of development, a succession of holding environments that support us while we individuate and differentiate. One implication of these formulations is that the background including the empathic caretaker is experienced as part of the self so that an abrupt disruption of the relationship to the background, especially any failure of the caretaker's empathy, is felt to be a wrenching away from the orienting framework, resulting in disorientation.

Earlier I referred to Spiegel's notion of an experiencing self against a background self. Here I would postulate that normally the experiencing self is held between a background inside mirrored by a background outside. A similar point is made from a Jungian perspective by Schwartz-Salant (1982, p. 46), who writes 'The need for mirroring from another is lifelong, and represents the inevitable incompleteness that accompanies growth. For mirroring is an externalization of an internal psychic reality. It is based upon the fact that consciousness and the unconscious exist in a relationship of mirror symmetry . . . The ego's stability is dependent upon an inner sense of being mirrored by the Self'.

CLINICAL ILLUSTRATIONS

In the following I describe three clinical examples, illustrating disturbances in the relation of self to selfobject.

During one of her sessions, Mrs L was describing how she was increasingly able to be with her small daughter, Lucy, in a much more relaxed kind of way. She talked of how the two of them might play together, or be busy with some activity together, such as re-potting a plant, and how Lucy might play quietly and privately, secure but alone in the presence of her mother in the background (Winnicott, 1958). She contrasted this with her own experience as a child, of activities with her mother always being focused on *achieving*, and her sense of her mother as an intrusive presence. As she went on to relate this new way of being to her experience in therapy, she suddenly complained of feeling acutely self-conscious and of a sense of being observed. This reminded her of her mother's behaviour with Lucy, how she would tend to talk *about* her grand-daughter rather than simply being with her; she would make comments such as 'Isn't she wonderful! Look what she's doing now!' and so on, in a way which Mrs L felt turned Lucy into an object. It seemed that in talking *about* her experience in therapy, as opposed to simply living it, she felt she had colluded with an intrusive mother version of me (in the transference), who objectified her. Mrs L would often describe feeling self-conscious in her sessions at moments when she felt treated as an object to be made sense of rather than a person to be empathically understood. She drew a distinction between being understood from inside, from her subjective position, and being made sense of from a more outside position, which she felt was like being slotted into an interpretation. She found the latter experience to be fragmenting, like being a piece on a chess board; she indicated her wish to be grasped in her totality or, as she put it, to be 'understood as the whole chessboard'. On the other hand, she was very prone to fit in with my interpretations in such a way that we created something false together. She displayed a tension between acting as if she had no separate self—assuming whatever role a situation seemed to require of her—and, on the other hand, an acute and painful awareness of her self as an object for the other.

Much of the time Mrs L appeared to feel that she had either to be there solely as a selfobject for the other, an echo with no self of her own, or else the other had to be there just as a selfobject for her. She sometimes indicated that she felt compelled to accommodate to my 'atmosphere', but on other occasions she would so fill the room with her words and her atmosphere that I would feel that there was hardly any room for me. She described how she tended to feel either in the centre of *her* world, into which others could be invited, or else she felt pushed to the margin of someone else's world. In this way she described the tension, discussed by Bach (1980), between what he termed 'subjective awareness', the feeling that the world is 'all me', and 'objective self awareness', the sense of being there for someone else. One of the gains of Mrs L's therapy was that she became more capable of sharing, a meeting of worlds, without either party needing to be diminished or taken over.

Mrs L experienced her mother as an extremely needy and demanding woman, unsatisfied by the father, and exploiting her daughter emotionally; it was as if Mrs L was required to fill the void left in her mother by the missing paternal function. From seeing her mother's manner with her own daughter, Mrs L observed how she was affectionate and caring, but at the same time intrusive and controlling. We gradually came to understand a very pervasive pattern in which any aspect of Mrs L of which her mother disapproved was simply not recognized by her mother; sometimes this would amount to quite gross distortions of reality. During her life Mrs L had colluded with this to deny aspects of herself. As a result she experienced a deep sense of shame at the surrender of her integrity. However, her acute self-consciousness insured that she was not successful in this denial of herself; at times of greatest dishonesty she would feel the greatest self-consciousness. As I have emphasized in a previous study (Mollon, 1984), shame and self-consciousness are the preservers of the sense of self. Persons whose sense of self is fragile or under threat are particularly prone to self-consciousness. Optimally of course, a secure sense of self, which can be taken for granted, removes the need for painful self-consciousness.

Mrs L was brought up in accord with stern ideals of always putting the other first. She considered, accurately I think, that she tended to be over empathic with others, unable to assert her own point of view because she always felt so aware of the other person's position. She was so afraid of seeming selfish that she would end up selfless. In this way she felt compelled to diminish herself, to get rid of aggressive or assertive parts of herself and present herself as small, passively accommodating and sweetly smiling. Periodically she would rebel against this position and engage in violent rows in which the important thing for her was to stand her ground. Mrs L seemed to exist in two distinct states of mind, partially split from each other. On the one hand was a state of happy merger in which her needs matched those of the other, a marvellous feeling of being 'in the same atmosphere'; on the other hand, there was the state of enraged suffocation. Her dilemma was how to have the background selfobject support without the engulfment.

Although tending to be so accommodating, Mrs L was far from subdued. Her clothes were always colourful and striking, and recognition and admiration were very important to her. From one point of view, she might have been described as exhibitionistic. However I think it is quite typical that the more the self is suppressed, paradoxically, the greater the wish to display the self and have it recognized. Essentially this is the point made by Kohut (1971) in his discussion of the natural grandiose self and its need for a mirroring response. A related common phenomenon is the fear sometimes experienced by children in school assemblies or in church of doing or shouting something shocking. I think this reflects the mobilization of intense exhibitionistic wishes at times of enforced anonymity. Sometimes this expression of the suppressed self may take on a sadistic quality, and then the associated fantasies are of doing something highly disturbing, aggressive or violent, reflecting again the anal stage (Heimann, 1962; Oliner, 1982). For example, Mrs L often imagined wrecking my room and creating a big mess.

I have worked with a number of patients who experience self-consciousness when feeling their communications are not immediately understood. This seems analagous to the baby's disturbance when the mother's face appears mask-like and unresponsive, as described in studies by Brazelton *et al.*, (1974) and Tronick *et al.*, (1978). Another clinical observation is that a number of patients who seem particularly prone to self-consciousness have suffered the loss of a parent in early life, or some similar experience of an early arbitrary catastrophe. Such early losses cannot easily be mourned by the young child, especially if the remaining caretakers are less than optimally responsive. The experience then seems to be one of a sudden tearing from the empathic matrix, leaving a frightened self at the centre of a cold and hostile world. These people seem to have internalized the absence of an empathic response in the form of the *presence* of an unempathic internal object.

Another patient, Miss B, of much more severe disturbance, would complain of feeling disturbed and self-conscious if I did not immediately respond to her and indicate a correct understanding of what she was trying to communicate. There was some evidence that Miss B's mother may not have been able to easily receive and comprehend her daughter's emotional communications. For example, Miss B recalled that once as a little girl she had a tantrum, which in retrospect she viewed as an attempt to get her mother's attention. Her mother's response was to take her to the casualty department of a local hospital, assuming that she must be ill!

Often Miss B would attempt to communicate in a very flat, intellectual, and unemotional way, as if fearing to convey her fears. Although hoping that I could understand and make sense of her anxiety, she seemed convinced that I would regard her in a completely non-comprehending way and judge her mad. In terms of Bion's (1962) model of primitive communication between baby and mother, whereby the baby evokes an anxiety in the mother who can then make sense of this and respond in an appropriate manner which restores order to the baby, my impression was that Miss B had internalized a maternal imago (an internal object) felt to be hostile to empathic communication. As we explored this issue, she actually stated that she did not believe she could be understood other than in terms of 'a psychiatrist's textbook', i.e., a psychiatric diagnosis. She went on to say that she worked very hard to try to express herself clearly in words since she was sure that if she really were to convey her feelings, there would come a point when I would stop trying to understand her and would dismiss her as mad. The alternative seemed equally horrifying, that I might become completely overwhelmed and as confused and anxious as she felt herself to be. She explained that because of her fear of the impact on the other person she was always acutely conscious of herself, constantly observing and monitoring herself. I think that in this continual monitoring of herself she was attempting to take the place of the other, to exclude the other, with the basic motive of warding off the danger of an unempathic and uncontaining response. (The typical counter-transference reaction in the therapist to this warding off is a feeling of sleepiness and boredom.) In this instance of a young woman who felt herself to be constantly on the edge of a breakdown, can be seen the link between the absence of an empathic selfobject in early life, and false self development in which the person compulsively attempts to accommodate to the other, in such a way as to ward off the other and the danger of further unempathic responses.

A related pattern has been described by Lewis (1963) where she describes the role of watching in a four-year-old psychotic child. The child showed a peculiar, precocious embarrassed self-conciousness whilst her mother demonstrated a kind of total involvement with the child, constantly present and anxiously watching. Lewis suggested that the child seemed to have identified with the mother's watching, and in this way maintained a link to the mother, while at the same time she affirmed her own sense of self and warded off the terror of engulfment. Issues of self-consciousness are often intimately bound up with looking. Merleau-Ponty (1964) has described an abrupt change in the small child's reactions to the look of the other. Prior to a certain point, the other's look is encouraging, but after this it becomes an embarrassment—'everything happens as though when he is looked at, his attention is displaced from the task he is carrying out to a representation of himself in the process of carrying it through.'

I have described how embarrassed self-consciousness arises in the gap, in the sudden break up of a selfobject relationship—in a jarring in the fitting in between self and other. This may arise either because the other fails to respond as expected, or because the self no longer fits the other's expectations. Just as self-awareness emerges through the gradual process of separation and individuation, embarrassed self-consciousness seems to arise in the sudden jarring awareness of separateness, in the shuddering loss of the sustaining matrix. The small child may experience this, for example, on its first day at school, or when confronted with a stranger whose manner and speech is unfamiliar. A new environment is experienced as unknown, unknowing, and unempathic. The child is deprived of the familiar matrix which mirrors, precisely because of its familiarity. In the presence of the stranger, whether this be another person or a newly emerging part of the self, the child feels awkward and disjointed. A previous harmony is disrupted and the self emerges precipitously from its embeddedness. Similarly, the adolescent may feel gauche and disoriented in response to the rapid and sometimes disconcerting changes in his or her bodily and mental self.

A final example also illustrates my third category: hypochondriacal preoccupation with the self. Miss J, an art photographer, sought therapy some months after the break up of a relationship. At this time she complained of feeling that her appearance had changed, she felt old and ugly and found herself compulsively looking in mirrors and seeking her reflection in shop windows. She was afraid that she might not be seen, that she might become invisible. Constantly preoccupied with her appearance, she told me she felt continually compelled to take photos of herself. She was particularly concerned with what she felt to be changes in the appearance of her eyes (I's), since she had always regarded these as a constant feature against her ever-changing inner state. All these sensations reminded her of similar feelings at the age of five, when she and her family had moved from Italy, where she was born. She quickly settled into a selfobject transference in which I was required to be responsive as a reflective mirroring presence, and to be constantly so as a background for her changing and contradictory states of mind. Any evidence of inattention or boredom on my part was extremely disturbing to her. At one point she went on holiday on her own, feeling very alone. She described looking out of her small room and seeing happy and beautiful people, and then looking in her mirror and seeing an old lady; she felt that she did not fit with her surroundings, she did not belong. She experienced a similar panic and depersonalization when she had to leave the studio in which she had worked for many years, and which she clearly experienced as part of her. The importance of her studio, she explained, was that wherever she went within it, it reflected *her*. In both instances, and also in the early experience of leaving Italy, she felt wrenched from an environment or person in which she had felt embedded. She then found herself lost and alone in an alien context which did not mirror her in a familiar way. Her sense of self was then considerably disturbed.

Like Mrs L, Miss J tended to sense automatically what the other required of her, subtly responding to cues so efficiently that it was not usually at all apparent that she was doing this. She was acutely sensitive to my response to her and would become panicky if she felt I was not interested. She would constantly look at me during the session, and indeed seemed to be always seeking the right kind of look from others. She recalled how when she was young her mother would look at her, and be preoccupied with her appearance; at one time she had felt this to be flattering, but now it seemed to her to have been more controlling. The picture that emerged was that her mother had unrealistically praised her, maintaining an idealized image of her. Although gratifying, this had left her trapped, locked into the look of her mother as Narcissus at the pool, dreading to move away from her mother's orbit. In the world at large she appeared to experience a kind of chronic embarrassed self-consciousness.

What she had not received from her mother, it seemed, was recognition of herself as a separate autonomous being. In the transference she was continually afraid that I would withdraw my support and enviously undermine her attempts to express herself. She described a sense of always having had to be merely an echo, a stooge, for her mother, who indeed may well have been undermining her daughter's attempts to separate and individuate. The corresponding internal object almost certainly consisted of aspects of her mother's actual personality, combined with projections of Miss J's own envy and jealousy of her parents' relationship with each other. It appeared that she had longed for, but never felt she got, an admiring and affirming look from her father. Her conscious attitude towards him was one of defensive scorn, but behind this we found a deeper love for him as an idealized figure. It became clear that what she had sought was the look from her father that would release her from the grip of the look of her mother, and allow her to be herself. Her father was the oedipal third term whom she longed for to free her from her prison of narcissism.

A brief consideration of the nature of mirroring is appropriate here. Pines (1982) has explored the concept in a wide-ranging discussion of clinical and historical aspects. The term has been popularized by Kohut (1971), whose concept of mirroring is based on the model of the 'gleam in the mother's eye' in response to the child's natural exhibitionism. However it is clear throughout his writings that really what he is referring to is the caretaker's general empathic availability (Mollon, 1985). Zinkin (1983), in discussing benevolent and malignant aspects of mirroring, points to the way in which it is through the empathic responsiveness of the other than one comes to know who one is—the original mirror being the mother's face (Winnicott, 1971)—and that an unempathic response will lead to alienation from the self. Lichtenstein (1977) talks of mirroring in terms of the mother's selective responsiveness to the infant, whereby she picks out only certain aspects of the infant's potential to recognize and encourage, and thereby imparts an 'identity theme'. This is a view which also emphasizes the mother's role in facilitating or impeding the development of the sense of self. In the present study I have argued that a familiar environment, including the non-human environment, can have a mirroring function, affirming the sense of self: the environment is experienced as a selfobject. I have also postulated that mirroring is an internal function, the experiencing self against a background self, a relationship which like any other relationship can be disrupted. Another type of internal mirroring is described by Pyszczynski and Greenberg (this volume). He reports that certain depressives may selectively focus upon their failings and inadequacies, protecting themselves from disappointment. (A similar view is proposed by Mollon and Parry, 1984.)

In the case of Miss J, the loss of her previous relationship, functioning as a selfobject background, had led to the emergence of a grandiose self, shoring up a disintegrating self representation, and combined with an imperious demand for mirroring. In the absence of a human mirroring partner, she had turned to actual mirrors and to photographing herself. The use of mirrors to restore the sense of self in lieu of a human mirroring response seems very common. Mrs L, for example, spoke of a compelling need to look attractive. She explained that when she felt chaotic internally she would look in a mirror and feel both amazed and reassured that her outer appearance was still organized. Her body image was actually rather unstable and she often described a feeling that her body was changing shape in some way. She was able to talk to me about this only after she had reached the point of feeling more confident that she could be recognized by others—that she could come to her therapy in different moods and states of mind and still be recognized as the same person. I am aware of the link here with Lacan's (1937/1977) mirror stage, wherein the fragmented body image is jubilantly replaced by the new coherence of the image of the self in the mirror—a process which Lacan sees as involving a fundamental alienation; the lived self is confused with the image out there. However, the glass mirror is a poor substitute for the kind of mirroring that is really needed—which is a more active responsive one, the human empathic response that sees and understands in depth, and goes beyond the surface images to the living, experiencing, and communicating self.

SUMMARY

A distinction can be made between self-awareness, self-consciousness, and preoccupation with the self. *Self-awareness* seems to unfold according to an innately determined timetable in interaction with the early social environment. In the case of patients prone to embarrassed *self-consciousness* a frequent background is one in which the normal situation of the parent being a selfobject for the child is reversed to that the child becomes a selfobject to the mother. The child is not recognized for who she really is, but is captured by a projected image from the mother's psyche. The father does not effectively intervene in such a way as to break this spell and allow the child her own identity. Because of this the child becomes prone to embarrassed self-consciousness in the discrepancy between who she is experienced to be by the other and who she experiences herself to be, and will develop an abnormally intense need for a mirroring selfobject to sustain the sense of self. In the absence of appropriate mirroring responsiveness the person falls into the state I have called *hypochondriacal preoccupation with the self.*

REFERENCES

Amsterdam, B. K. and Levitt, M. (1980). 'Consciousness of self and painful self-consciousness.' *Psychoanalytic Study of the Child*, **35**, 67–83.
Bach, S. (1980). 'Self-love and object love: some problems of self and object-constancy, differentiation and integration.' In R. F. Lax, S. Bach and J. A. Burland (Eds), *Rapprochement. The Critical Subphase of Separation-Individuation*, Aronson, New York, pp. 171–179.
Bion, W. R. (1962). *Learning from Experience*, Heinemann, London.
Brazelton, T. B., Koslowski, B. and Main, M. (1974). 'The early mother-infant interaction.' In M. Lewis and L. Rosenblum (Eds), *The Effect of the Infant on its Caretaker*, Wiley, New York, pp. 49–77.
Green, B. A. (1979). 'The effect of distortions of the self: A study of The Picture of Dorian Gray.' *Annual of Psychoanalysis*, **VII**, 391–410.
Grotstein, J. S. (1981). *Splitting and Projective Identification*, Aronson, New York.
Heimann, P. (1962). 'Notes on the anal stage.' *International Journal of Psycho-Analysis*, **43**, 406–414.
Kagan, J. (1981). *The Second Year. The Emergence of Self-Awareness*, Harvard University Press, Cambridge, Massachusetts.
Kegan, R. (1982). *The Evolving Self*, Harvard University Press, Cambridge, Massachusetts.
Kohut, H. (1971). *The Analysis of the Self*, International Universities Press, New York.
Kohut, H. (1977). *The Restoration of the Self*, International Universities Press, New York.
Lacan, J. (1937). 'The mirror-stage as formative of the function of the I as revealed in psychoanalytic experience.' *Ecrits*, 1977, Tavistock Press, London, pp. 1–7.
Lacan, J. (1959). 'On a question preliminary to any possible treatment of psychosis.' *Ecrits*, 1977, Tavistock, London, pp. 179–225.
Lewis, H. B. (1963). 'A case of watching as defense against an oral incorporation fantasy.' *Psychoanalytic Review*, **V 50**, 68–80.
Lewis, M. and Brooks-Gunn, J. (1979). *Social Cognition and the Acquisition of Self*, Plenum, New York.
Lichtenstein, H. (1977). 'Identity configuration and developmental alternatives.' *The Dilemma of Human Identity*, Aronson, New York.
Mahler, M., Pine, F. and Bergman, A. (1975). *The Psychological Birth of the Human Infant*, Basic Books, New York.
Merleau-Ponty, M. (1964). *The Primacy of Perception*, Northwestern University Press, Evanston, Illinois.

Miller, A. (1979). 'The drama of the gifted child and the psycho-analyst's narcissistic disturbance.' *International Review of Psycho-Analysis*, **60**, 47–58.

Mollon, P. and Parry, G. (1984). 'The fragile self, narcissism and the protective function of depressive states.' *British Journal of Medical Psychology*, **57**, 137–145.

Mollon, P. (1984). 'Shame in relation to narcissistic disturbance.' *British Journal of Medical Psychology*, **57**, 207–214.

Mollon, P. (1985). 'The non-mirroring mother and the missing paternal dimension in a case of narcissistic disturbance.' *Psychoanalytic Psychotherapy*, **1**, 35–47.

Oliner, M. (1982). 'The anal phase.' In D. Mendell (Ed.), *Early Female Development*, MTP, Lancaster, pp. 25–60.

Piaget, J. (1951). *Play, Dreams and Imitation in Childhood*, Routledge and Kegan Paul, London.

Pines, M. (1982). 'Reflections on mirroring.' *Group Analysis*, **15**, suppl, 1–26.

Sander, L. W. (1983). 'To begin with: reflections on ontogeny.' In L. Lichtenberg and S. Kaplan (Eds), *Reflections on Self Psychology*, The Analytic Press, Hillsdale, New Jersey, pp. 85–104.

Sandler, J. (1960). 'The background of safety.' *International Journal of Psycho-Analysis*, **41**, 352–356.

Schwartz-Salant, N. (1982). *Narcissism and Character Transformation*, Inner City Books, Toronto.

Spiegal, L. (1959). 'The self, the sense of self and perception.' *Psychoanalytic Study of the Child*, **14**, 81–109.

Spitz, R. (1957). *No and Yes in the Genesis of Human Communication*, International Universities Press, New York.

Stern, D. N. (1983). 'The early development of schemas of self, other and "self with other".' In J. Lichtenberg and S. Kaplan (Eds), *Reflections on Self Psychology*, The Analytic Press, Hillsdale, New Jersey, pp. 49–84.

Toplin, M. (1983). 'Discussion of papers by Drs Stern and Sander.' In J. Lichtenberg and S. Kaplan (Eds), *Reflections of Self Psychology*, The Analytic Press, Hillsdale, New Jersey, pp. 113–123.

Tronick, E., Als, H., Adamson, L., Wise, S. and Brazelton, T. (1978). 'The infant's response to entrapment between contradictory messages in face-to-face interaction.' *Journal of the American Academy of Child Psychiatry*, **17**, 1–13.

Wilshire, B. (1982). *Role Playing and Identity: The Limits of Theatre as Metaphor*, Indiana University Press, Bloomington.

Winnicott, D. W. (1958). 'The capacity to be alone.' In *The Maturational Processes and the Facilitating Environment*, Hogarth, London, 1965, pp. 29–36.

Winnicott, D. W. (1963). 'Communicating and not communicating leading to a study of certain opposites.' In *The Maturational Processes and the Facilitating Environment*, Hogarth, London, 1965, pp. 179–192.

Winnicott, D. W. (1971). 'Mirror role of the mother and family in child development.' In *Playing and Reality*, Tavistock, London.

Yardley, K. M. (1979) 'Social skills training: A critique.' *British Journal of Medical Psychology*, **52**, 55–62.

Zinkin, L. (1983). 'Malignant mirroring.' *Group Analysis*, **16**, 113–126.

Self and Identity: Psychosocial Perspectives
Edited by K. Yardley and T. Honess
© 1987 John Wiley & Sons Ltd

22

A Phenomenology of the Emotionally Divided Self

Norman K. Denzin

A phenomenological case study of the emotionally divided self, or the belle âme *(beautiful soul) is presented. The works of G. Hegel, H. S. Sullivan, J. Lacan. H. Kohut, R. D. Laing, M. Scheler, M. Heidegger, and J. Sartre are drawn upon and elaborated, as the temporal, situational, and relational structures of experience of the emotionally divided self are examined. The emotionally divided self continually experiences what Scheler termed* ressentiment, *a cluster of emotional experiences, including anger, wrath, envy, jealousy, and fear, directed towards the other, or the 'They-selves' of the everyday world.*

'Self-consciousness withdrawn into the inmost retreats of its being . . . Doubled, divided and at variance with itself . . . it lives in dread of action and existence . . . it is a hollow object which it fills with the feeling of emptiness . . .' (Hegel, 1807).

The phenomenology of the emotionally divided self requires analysis. Since Hegel's (1807/1931) pioneering analysis of the self turned against itself and the world, sunk in inwardness and retreat, philosophical and psychological concern with the divided self has received little attention in the literature. Hegel's location of the divided self in the historical transition between feudalism, the reformation, the renaissance, and the modern world has lost favour in critical circles. The self of the modern post-structuralist period is a figment of the imagination. In Foucault's (1970) words man is 'like a face drawn in sand at the edge of the sea,' to be erased by the forces of science, rationality, technology, repression, and capitalist economies. While William James (1904/1961), and Scheler (1912/1961) devoted considerable attention, as did Goethe, Neitzsche, Kierkegaard, Freud, and Marx, to the divided selves of the modern individual, only recently has concern returned to the topic. Laing (1965), Lacan (1968), Laing and Cooper (1964), Sartre (1963), Wilden (1968), Kohut (1984), Deleuze and Guattari (1977), have succeeded in making the divided self and the *belle âme* (beautiful soul) problematic once again in our discourse. The present analysis builds on this tradition.

The emotionally divided self has been described as a self against itself, as a false-self system, as a self trapped within its own bad faith, as a self without objective existence, as a self that is torn apart internally, as a self that feels emptiness and nothing. The emotionally divided self is a disembodied self (Lacan, 1968, p. 44; Laing, 1965, pp. 65–119; Wilden, 1968, pp. 284–292; James, 1904/1961, pp. 143–159). Self-estrangement, contradiction, a withdrawal of emotional life into itself, the reckless pursuit of desire and/or labour, deep feelings of unhappiness, brooding, hollowness, emptiness, longing for fulfillment, self-loathing, and self-destructiveness are key features of the emotionally divided self (Hegel, 1807/1931, pp. 250, 259, 263–264, 666–667). The divided self becomes a 'sorrow-ladden "beautiful soul"' (Hegel, 1807/1931, p. 667). It turns back upon itself and destroys itself. It refuses to engage its own alienation, remaining locked instead within its own subjectivity. Conscious of the contradictions within itself, it becomes 'unhinged, disordered and runs to madness' (Hegel, 1807/1931, p. 676), wasting itself in yearning, while being drawn all the while to negative, guilt-provoking experiences and what Hegel (1807/1931, p. 667) termed 'evil'. The self is divided between its 'subjectivity and its own existential poverty' (Wilden, 1968, p. 289). The cleavage, or split that is felt spurns a joining with the world. A negative dialectic turns back against the self, refusing to affirm out of the negativities that are experienced a positive association in the world of others. The dialectical reason (Sartre, 1976) that operates within the structures of the divided self negates the possibilities of a totalization of experience. Such a totalization would bring the self out of its divisions into positive, emotional experiences with others. Crushed under the weight of its own negativity, the divided self risks its own annihilation.

The divided self, or beautiful soul, cultivates a particular moral individualism that sets it above and apart from others, thereby cutting itself off from society. It nurtures its goodness and its divisions in solitude and isolation, running away from people, as it disengages itself from the world. Rejecting objective experiences with others, the divided self lives within its own insulated, private world of madness and the uncanny. It assigns a sense of moral superiority to this world and to itself. From that tremulous perch the subject directs a world that threatens to come apart at any moment. Its inwardness fears the fear that hovers just on the borders of the barriers it has constructed around itself.*

---

* Lacan (1977) has argued that the mirror stage of self genesis in early childhood prefigures alienation, narcissism, aggressivity, neurosis, and madness in adulthood. This is so because no firm and steady centre to the self can be located. Indeed Lacan's subject is caught in a dialectical confusion between ego-ideals and ideal egos and finds its unstable location in the shifting signifiers of language; in particular the personal pronouns. Hence the realm of the 'real' for Lacan is always illusive. A different view of the 'mirror' and the inner psychology of the self is given in Romanyshyn (this volume).

Lacan's arguments concerning narcissism extend Freud's classic formulations (see Wolf, this volume), and suggest certain parallels with Kohut's (1984) concept of selfobject. The aetiology of the disorders of the self that Wolf discusses, following Kohut, turn on the fragility of the self, on idealized selfobject experiences, and on the emergence of bipolar self experiences which shatter

The feelings of guilt, anger, anxiety, fear, dreading, trepidation, suspicion, self-despair, self-irritation, exasperation, a loss of self-hope, a splitting of the self from the body, and an inability to communicate with others exist alongside these feelings of moral superiority. Suicidal thoughts are not uncommon. *Ressentiment* (Scheler, 1912/1961, pp. 39–40) towards the past, towards others, and a fear of the past and the present are overwhelming temporal orientations. The present is experienced as oppressive. The subject withdraws from the present into himself. A temporal vacuum engulfs him.

Ressentiment, or negative, hostile relations with himself and with others is experienced over and over again. The subject drawn to ressentiment is also drawn to violence, both physical and emotional; whether it be inward violence, or outward aggression and hostility towards others. The self of the emotionally divided individual is violent (Denzin, 1984a, chap. 6). The emotionally divided self feels her emotions through the structures of the self that are resentful, and turned against her. *The analysis of the emotionally divided self advances the thesis that self-feelings lie at the core of emotionality* (Denzin, 1983, 1984a, chap. 3).

THE STRUCTURES OF THE EMOTIONALLY DIVIDED SELF

Self is understood to refer to that process that unifies the stream of thoughts and experiences the person has about herself around a single pole, or point of reference. Not a thing, but a process, the self is consciousness conscious of itself, referring always to the sameness and steadiness of something continuously present to the person in her thoughts, as in 'I am here, now in the world, present before and to myself.' The self involves moral feelings for self, including all the subject calls hers at a particular moment in time, such as material possessions, self-feelings, and relations to others. The self is *not in* consciousness, but in the world, in front of the person. Its presence in the world haunts the subject, and draws her forward, in *a circuit of selfness* (Sartre, 1943/1956, pp. 102–105), into the world. As she turns back on herself, in reflection, giving meaning to herself, the subject catches a glimpse of herself. It is these meanings that she draws inward, to her self. Two levels to

---

self ideals. The borderline self, like the divided self, experiences the three varieties of self-consciousness that Mollon (this volume) has discussed. That is the divided self experiences itself (1) through ordinary, introspective self-consciousness, (2) through shame and embarrassing interactional experiences, and (3) through compulsive, hypochondrical, preoccupations with itself.

Following Kohut and Wolf it is apparent that the selfobject experiences of the divided self turn on the inner relations the subject has with those contexts that evoke and maintain a feeling of inadequate selfhood (Wolf, this volume). The nuclear self of the subject is grounded in an unstable structure of selfobject experiences that continually evoke narcissism, self-alienation, fear, and ressentiment. Injurious selfobject experiences in childhood perhaps lie at the basis of the divided self in adulthood. While Kohut locates narcissism in selfobject experiences, Lacan posits the primacy of language as the foundation of this experience. These two psychoanalytic formulations of narcissism require more attention than I am able to give them in this chapter.

the self, surface and deep, may be distinguished. The surface, public self is given to others through the subject's communicative acts (Goffman, 1959). The deep, inner self is revealed to the subject through self-feelings which involve a feeling for the self as a distinct moral object and subject in the world. In self-feelings, a feeling for self, a feeling of this feeling and a revealing of the moral self to the person through these feelings is given (Heidegger, 1982, p. 137). These feelings and disclosures radiate through the person's inner stream of consciousness.

THE STRUCTURES OF THE EMOTIONALLY DIVIDED SELF

Four structures of the emotionally divided self may be distinguished:

1. others,
2. self and body,
3. situations,
4. temporality.

Each one will be treated in turn.

Others

The following features of the Others who populate the world of the divided self may be noted. *First*, they are near to the subject, as intimate, warm points of reference, even sources of stability, yet also distant, as vague, unnamed 'Others'. *Second*, they are threats because they are so near. *Third*, the other's perceived 'normality' or stability is threatening. *Fourth*, the other is a source of ressentiment, anger, and guilt. Feelings from the past are directed to the other. An aversion to the other is felt and sensed, yet the subject cannot be free of them. He or she feels a debt of emotion towards them. If they die before the debt is repaid, ressentiment is added to guilt as a feeling that binds him to them. *Fifth*, feelings are 'emptied-out' on or at the other, often through violence, withdrawals of affection, or inward obsessive dwellings on the other's emotions and expectations for the person.

Sixth, feelings of 'they-self' are drawn from the other (Heidegger, 1962, p. 154). The subject *'fails to hear* its own Self in listening to the theyself' (Heidegger 1962, p. 315). The self feels, sees, and hears itself through the voices and the eyes of the other. It stands stripped of clothing, naked to the eyes and gaze of the other (Sartre, 1956). The other sees through the subject. He is hollow inside. He has 'fallen' in his own eyes and in the eyes of the 'they-other'. The subject becomes indistinguishable from the 'they-self'. These others are indefinite. They haunt the subject with their presence in the world. The 'they-other' is given the qualities of emotional solidity, calmness, serenity, security, and a sense of superiority that makes him feel inferior to them. The subject attempts to take on the moods of the other and fails. This failure places a double wedge between the subject and himself, and between the subject and the others of the world. Such persons are driven, in their own eyes, which are the appropriated eyes of the other, further into the empty interiority of the self. Acts of violence draw them out into the world. The use of chemical substances such as prescription drugs and alcohol is sought as a source of strength. Elevated moods fill the emptiness the subject feels on the inner sides of his self. The other is resented and ressentiment is an overwhelming emotional attitude toward them (see Scheler, 1961).

Seventh, the other or others who dominate the world of the emotionally divided self may be from the immediate situation of the subject (an employer, interactional associate, family member, spouse, etc.), or they may reside in the distant past (see Lemert, 1962). Laing (1965, p. 98) insists that the 'other . . . must in the first instance always be the mother, that is, the 'mothering one'. This is not necessarily so, for the other may be a vague undifferentiated 'they-other'. Regardless of biographical origin, the other overwhelms the subject, setting (in the eyes of the subject) standards that are impossible to attain. The subject attempts to win the approval of the other: to be a 'good' self in their eyes, but finds this impossible.

The other may be imitated, or copied. Their mannerisms are interiorized. They are in H. S. Sullivan's terms (1953, pp. 167–168) 'personifications' who become part of the subject's false self-system. This false-self system interiorizes the other as a negative significant other. The subject hates the persons he imitates, yet he complies with their perceived wishes. One of Laing's patients (1965, p. 98) observed that 'he was a response to what other people say I am'. Emotionally divided selves translate into action other people's definitions of who they are. They seem unable or unwilling to move forward in terms of their own self-definitions. The self that complies with the wishes of the other is perceived as a false or inauthentic self.

A basic split in the self-system of the subject occurs. Outwardly she complies with the wishes of others. Inwardly she rebels. Outwardly the behaviour of her false self appears normal. Yet this is a facade (Laing, 1965, p. 99). She perceives herself as living a lie. Inwardly she feels intense anxiety, hatred, and fear. (These emotions will be elaborated below). There may be momentary liftings of the veil of normality. In an emotional outburst her 'truer' inner self is exposed to the world and to those others who dominate her. Such outbursts may take the form of violence towards herself and others. She feels captured within the very skin of her body. She feels that she is a captive of the other. In an insane outburst she will pour out accusations of persecution, directing her vengeance toward the other who has forced the compliance of her false self. She will declare that the 'alien' other has been trying to destroy her. She will claim that the other makes her do things she does not want to do. She may argue that the other is driving her insane. (The other makes similar claims).

As more features of the other are interiorized into the false self, the subject's hatred for them increases. The secret, inner self of the person hates the public, normal self of the other that has come to inhabit her body. She also hates her inner self.

Paraphrasing Cooley (1956, p. 184), a 'negative looking-glass-self' relationship is established between the subject and the other. Positive attributions from the other are interiorized negatively, thereby contributing to the negative inner view of self held by the subject. A hatred of the other is 'focused on the features of him which the individual has built into his own being' (Laing, 1965, p. 104). Still, the assumption of another person's personality gives the inner self a sense of security. The subject has a way of not being himself publicly. Thus the other is both a shield and a sword for the divided self. The subject can hide inside this identity of the other.

Self and body

It can be argued that the emotionally divided self is fractured into multiple selves which add up to nothing. The subject may become a mass of quivering fear. He has no centre, only a sense of massive insecurity. A pit of emptiness lies at the base of his stomach. The acute sense that an older, more normal embodied self has been lost is felt. The new self has no pieces that can be fitted together. It is not a new self. It is nothing. The 'bulging inner life' that wants out has no point of reference. Laughter may keep the self intact.

The emotionally divided self lives two lives, one that is inner and perhaps fantasy and one that is outer and perhaps real. The imaginary self is an inner, hidden self. It lives in fantasy. It may be, as Sartre observes, violent, and inwardly self-destructive towards others, perhaps killing them in fantasy. The imaginary self dissolves and disappears when it has contact with reality. The subject withdraws from his imaginary self; allowing others to define who he is and who he will be. The real and the imaginary cannot coexist in the same moment.

Sartre and Laing suggest that the emotionally divided self lives an imaginary life that is *split*, or dissociated from the *real* world of *real* others. In the world of imagination and inner fantasy, the subject perhaps lives a full, rich life of embodied feelings, pleasures and desires. She escapes from a harsh world of impoverished frustrated emotionality. In her imagination she may dare to take chances which she cannot or is not willing to take in the outer world. *For the emotionally divided self the world of emotion and the world of fantasy merge into one.* These two worlds gather strength in the inner world of the divided self and crowd out the demands and exigencies of the demanding external world. In this inner world he or she can be anything. They are free to control people, places and things. They are, as Laing notes, omnipotent and that omnipotence may be indulged and over-extended (Laing, 1965, p. 84).

For analytic purposes the self-system of the emotionally divided subject may initially be divided into three categories: the good-me, the bad me, and the not-me (Sullivan, 1953, pp. 161–162). The *good-me* refers to those self-personifications 'which organize an experience in which satisfactions have been enhanced by rewarding increments of tenderness . . .'. Good-me, as it ultimately develops, is the ordinary topic of discussion about I (Sullivan, 1953, pp. 161–162). The good-me refers to those things about the self that the subject takes pride in, cherishes, and values highly. The *bad-me* is the 'beginning personification which organizes experiences in which increasing degrees of anxiety are associated with behaviour involving the mothering one . . . bad-me is based on this increasing gradient of anxiety' (Sullivan, 1953, p. 162). The bad-me describes those features of the self which cause the subject guilt and anxiety. The mothering one may be replaced by any emotional associate of the subject in later life. *Violence may be a part of the bad-me.* The *not-me* references those personifications characterized by the *uncanny emotions* of awe, dread, loathing, and horror (Sullivan, 1953, p. 72). The not-me elements of the self may reference sexual acts which are taboo in the culture of the subject (see Lindesmith *et al.*, 1977, p. 473). These emotions of the not-me persist throughout life, often erupting in nightmares in adulthood. The not-me elements of the self refer to a 'private mode of living' (Sullivan, 1953, p. 164).

Situations

The emotional situations of the divided self have a threatening transparency that makes action within them nearly impossible. The subject can see through the situation to its other side. The situation acts back on him. It drives him out. He is pushed, or forced into a corner. From that vantage point he may or may not gaze out and around himself, into the situation that he is afraid to enter. He may even turn his back on the situation. Thereby turning his back on himself. Situations move towards him with a compelling force that cannot be stopped. The subject is literally unable to enter the situation. Yet, he is the situation. It is this fact that overwhelms him or her. He is trapped in the situation. He can neither enter nor leave. The reflective self-awareness of the emotionally divided self makes action in the situation problematic, if not impossible. However, inaction is action, for not to act is to act. The divided self knows this. By not acting in the situation the subject is acting in the situation.

The situations of the emotionally divided self are alien. While they appear to be filled with projects that need to be undertaken, the subject is unable to either move forward or backward. Divided selves attempt, then, to distance themselves from the situations that surround them. They are locked into an unyielding present, for any movement through the situation would be a movement through time and space. Unable to accomplish such an action they are forced to remain still, thereby stopping both time and space.

Temporality

Heidegger's *Thesis of the Temporality of Moods* states 'that *except* on the basis of temporality *moods are not possible* . . .' (Heidegger, 1962, p. 391).

The thesis assumes that 'moods temporalize themselves, that is, their specific ecstasis belongs to a future and a present in such a way, indeed, that these equiprimordial ecstases are modified by having been' (Heidegger, 1962, p. 390). The thesis of the temporality of moods is applied by Heidegger to the analysis of anxiety and fear (Heidegger, 1962, p. 395).

The thesis suggests that persons may experience time in three reflective modes, or three *ecstases*. The future is what moves towards them. The *present* is what they are alongside. The *past* is what has just been accomplished. If, as has been argued elsewhere (Denzin, 1983, 1984a) emotions are temporal phenomenona, then it is possible to see how the emotions of the emotionally divided self are, in part, temporally static phenomena. That is, the subject can neither move forward or backward in the situation that confronts him. If he attempts to stop the passage of time by remaining immobile, then his emotions are dead and lifeless. His emotions are stripped of any of the liveliness that comes from the infusion of time into feeling and thinking.

Heidegger further argues that the person experiences time within two modes: the *authentic* and the *inauthentic*. Emotionally divided selves experience time both authentically and inauthentically. *Authentic temporality* is self-reflective and processual. Authentically the subject stands outside time as a static phenomenon. She is processually in time and in the world, confronting time and the meaning of her being within the three ecstases of the future, present, and past. *Inauthentic temporality* is chronological time, cut into bits and pieces. The past, the present, and the future are regarded as discretely different temporal spheres. Inauthentic time locates emotions in the subject's past, in the far-off threatening future or in the hostile present.

Emotionally divided selves are caught reflectively between the edges of authentic and inauthentic time. Authentically they are able to view and grasp time processually. The past, the future, and the present come against them, as overpowering forces. Inauthentically, they feel trapped in the past and in the present. The future seems unapproachable. They hold to a double vision of time. On the one hand, time is reflectively understood as a process. On the other hand, they are rooted in an unreflective, inauthentic view of the past, the present, and the future as discrete temporal entities. To the extent that they are overwhelmed by the situations that confront them, they are driven deeper into an inauthentic view of themselves, their emotions, and temporality. *They are the reflective victims of their own inauthentic temporality.* They are trapped in the past and in the present. They cannot move forward. Every step backward is a step further into the past. The inability to enter the situation, which lies in the present, in front of them, drives them further back into the past. By being driven into the past, emotionally divided selves find that their emotions are in the past. They live and feel in the past. Their emotional attachments are in the past. The selves they attach on to are in the past. The others and the experiences they dwell upon are in the past. Any liveliness they find in their world comes from and out of the past. They battle the past. They symbolically kill significant emotional others. They may even attempt to kill themselves. By killing themselves they kill the other who has killed them. Since they make the decision to attempt to kill themselves and the other, they are the victors, for they have killed first. Such is the inner temporal logic of emotionally divided selves.

CONCLUSIONS

Self-feelings lie at the core of emotionality. The following points deserve highlighting:

1. The lived-body is central to the feelings of the self.
2. The Other figures centrally in the self-feelings of the person.
3. The inner thematic structures of the self divide and work against one another.
4. Temporality, in all its forms, is basic to emotionality.
5. Negative emotionality destroys positive emotionality.
6. Repair of the self is an interpersonal process involving meta-communication and the location of the self outside itself.

The violent self is a divided self. Violence becomes one mode of striking out at the 'false' world that surrounds the subject. In violence the self attempts to regain support for its faltering inner self-system. The divided self, like the violent self, is an interpersonal process, subject to the same schismogenic forces that destroy families of violence (Denzin, 1984a, chap. 6, 1984b).

The processes that produce persons, families, selves, self-feeling, and emotionality are interactional and governed by their own inner dialectical logic and force. A part of the very process that they produced, persons often find that they are trapped by their own creations. Not wishing to take responsibility for these creations, they retreat into a divided self; one part of the self wants credit for what it has created, the other part wants to destroy it. Such is the fate of the violent self and the emotionally divided self (Denzin, 1984a, p. 238, 1985).

REFERENCES

Cooley, C. H. (1956). *The Two Major Works of Charles H. Cooley. Social Organization and Human Nature and the Social Order*, The Free Press, Glencoe, Illinois (Originally published 1902, 1909, 1922).

Deleuze, G. and Guattari, F. (1977). *Anti-Oedipus: Capitalism and Schizophrenia*, The Viking Press, New York.

Denzin, N. K. (1983). 'A note on emotionality, self and interaction.' *American Journal of Sociology*, **89**(2), pp. 402–409.

Denzin, N. K. (1984a). *On Understanding Emotion: A Social Phenomenological and Interactionist Inquiry*, Jossey-Bass, San Francisco.

Denzin, N. K. (1984b). 'Toward a phenomenology of domestic, family violence.' *American Journal of Sociology*, **90**, 483–513.

Denzin, N. K. (1985). 'Violence, emotionality and the alcoholically divided self.' *The*

1985 Annual Meetings of the American Sociological Association, 27 August 1985, Washington, D.C.

Foucault, M. (1970). *The Order of Things: An Archeology of the Human Sciences*, Random House, New York.

Goffman, E. (1959). *The Presentation of Self in Everyday Life*, Doubleday, New York.

Hegel, G. W. F. (1807, 1931). *The Phenomenology of Mind* (transl. and intro. J. B. Baillie), Allen and Unwin Ltd, London.

Heidegger, M. (1982). *The Basic Problems of Phenomenology*, Indiana University Press, Bloomington.

Heidegger, M. (1962). *Being and Time*, Harper, New York (Originally published 1927).

James, W. (1961). *The Varieties of Religious Experience: A Study in Human Nature*, Collier Books, New York (Originally published 1904).

Kohut, H. (1984). *How Does Psychoanalysis Cure?* The University of Chicago Press, Chicago.

Lacan, J. (1977). *Ecrits: A Selection* (transl. A. Sheridan), Norton, New York.

Lacan, J. S. (1968). *Speech and Language in Psychoanalysis* (transl. and notes A. Wilden), The John Hopkins University Press, Baltimore.

Laing, R. D. (1965). *The Divided Self: An Existential Study in Sanity and Madness*, Penguin, Middlesex, England.

Laing, R. D. and Cooper, D. G. (1964). *Reason and Violence: A Decade of Sartre's Philosophy, 1950–1960*, Tavistock Publications, London.

Lemert, E. M. (1962). 'Paranoia and the dynamics of exclusion.' *Sociometry*, 24, 2–20.

Lindesmith, A., Strauss, A., and Denzin, N. K. *Social Psychology*, 5th edition, Holt Rinehart and Winston, New York, 1978.

Sartre, J. P. (1956). *Being and Nothingness*, Philosophical Library, New York (Originally published 1943).

Sartre, J. P. (1963). *Saint Genet, Comedian and Martyr*, Knopf, New York (Originally published 1952).

Sartre, J. P. (1976). *Critique of Dialectical Reason*, NLP, London.

Scheler, M. (1961). *Ressentiment* (Ed. L. A. Coser and transl. W. W. Holdeim), The Free Press of Glencoe, New York (Originally published 1912).

Sullivan, H. S. (1953). *The Interpersonal Theory of Psychiatry*, Norton, New York.

Sullivan, H. S. (1956). *Clinical Studies in Psychiatry*, Norton, New York.

Wilden, A. (1968). 'Lacan and the discourse of the other.' In J. Lacan (Ed.), *Speech and Language in Psychoanalysis* (transl. and notes A. Wilden), The John Hopkins University Press, Baltimore.

Self and Identity: Psychosocial Perspectives
Edited by K. Yardley and T. Honess
© 1987 John Wiley & Sons Ltd

23

Mirror as Metaphor of Psychological Life

Robert D. Romanyshyn

Psychological work is mirror work which re-members self as image, as a configuration of characters in a story. Self is a poetic history, a process of fictionalizing the factual, of making the past real as much as discovering a real past.

INTRODUCTION: AN OPENING EXAMPLE

The chapter begins with a brief account of a recent experience reported by a patient. First I will give a short description of who the patient is and then I will recount the experience which he described. Finally, an implication is drawn from that experience which forms the theme of this chapter.

The patient

The patient is a 26-year-old, single male, who is a graduate student in psychology. I mention this last fact because this young man, whom I have been seeing for several months now, is not only very knowledgeable about psychological dynamics, but also quite apt at using his knowledge as an intellectual defence against his emotions. More specifically, he has conducted himself in the sessions in a way that allows him to present and to interpret his life as a heroic tragedy. He is and has always been the neglected and misunderstood genius, destined to be surrounded by lesser mortals, and thus condemned to be eternally alone. At his best he is articulate and charming, and indeed he values these abilities precisely because they allow him to fascinate others, especially women, while simultaneously keeping them at a distance. In conjunction with this self image, he often describes himself as a runner or as a rider on a dark plane. The key element here is *motion* because, as he says, were he to stop he would die, that is, he would be found by others to be ordinary.

The horizontal polarity of motion and rest has, moreover, a vertical counterpart. The one who is in motion, the fast rider on a dark plane, is a brilliant figure who looks upon life and upon others from above. He is brilliant in thought, brilliant in word, brilliant in action. But opposite this brilliant figure lurks the 'shitty little boy'. He is stupid, needy, vulnerable, and always sad and suffering.

Between motion and rest; between fascination and ordinariness; between brilliance and shit, my patient lives out his life in the world with others. He is as terrified of falling as he is of stopping the motion, because to do either is to fall from the position above life into the shittiness, the messiness of ordinary daily living. So my patient struggles to keep moving. He struggles to be brilliant. And in this context he has constructed his life as if it were a tragedy because the tragic pose has allowed him to avoid experiencing the sadness of an ordinary human life. In making his life into tragedy, he has raised himself above mere mortal suffering.

Psychotherapists will recognize that much of what I have just described exists between me and my patient as much on the level of mood as it does on the level of speech. To be sure, in the several months which we have been together these images have been spoken. But I have done very little interpretation, preferring to leave them as *his* creations. And in this process I have seen that *how* my patient tells his story is as important as *what* he says. In the telling he is living out with me his brilliance and fascination. He is re-making the tragedy right before me. But in doing so he feels little if any of the emotions, and he displays less. He is, as he said recently, an actor. But he is an actor quite removed from the part which he plays. He knows the lines and the story, but he is singularly unmoved by them. Theatre is, in this instance, a defence against life.

The reported incident

A recent hour began with the patient telling me the following memory. It was the first time he had spoken of it in our sessions, and it occurred following one hour in which he had talked about himself in terms of the metaphor of brilliance and shit. He had said in that hour that he now understood himself. I had had the impression, however, that he was running again, that he was fleeing toward health, that he was putting himself above the shitty, suffering, sad, little boy. But I said nothing of this impression. Instead I simply remained silent in the face of his assertions about how good he was feeling. It was within this context, then, that he spoke this memory.

I was about six years old. It was the night before Christmas and my father had just come home. He had been selling Christmas trees with his friend. He came in the house and he told my mother about a family which had come to the tree lot looking for a Christmas tree. There was a father and his two small sons. They seemed to be very poor and as the father looked through the trees, it became clear that he could not afford to buy one for his family. Then my father told my mother that he picked out a tree and gave it to the man.

I could not believe it. I began to tremble and I started to cry. My parents were confused and they could not console me. I kept thinking about the father and his sons, about how poor they were. It was painful to imagine them, to see them looking at the trees. I could not bear it. I had to run, and I did. Twice I ran as hard as I could into a wall. It hurt, but it hurt less than the pain I was feeling in thinking about that family. I did not know that there was so much suffering and pain in the world. No one had ever told me. It hurt and it continued to hurt even on Christmas day. I could not open any of the presents which my parents and grandparents had given to me. I did not want them. I felt so sad. I wanted only to cry.

Implication: world as mirror of self

It is a dramatic episode which my patient remembered, and in recounting it he seemed somewhat awed by it. His voice was noticeably different. He spoke not as if he was above the incident but more as if he was in the midst of it. In telling it he seemed stunned or shocked by the memory.

Apart from any interpretations which might be made of this memory, I want to suggest that the psychological significance of this incident lies in its functioning as a mirror through which a configuration of my patient's self is reflected. The shitty, suffering little boy is *seen through* the figures of this event, as he imagined it through the words of his father and as he remembered his imagining of it. He was *moved* by this event, by his imagining of it, because it is an image of his own self. He was moved by it because through those figures and that story he encountered something of himself. He never *knew* there was suffering and pain in the world. No one had ever told him. But he heard his father's words and he trembled and he cried. He heard his father's words and they moved him. He ran. He ran away. No one ever told him there was suffering and pain in the world, and yet 'he' knew. His shaking, his tears, and his running, so incomprehensible to others, showed that 'he' knew. 'He', the shitty, suffering little boy, knew. The shitty, suffering, and sad little boy saw himself through the events described by his father.

The event, imagined and remembered, is, then, a mirror. And the world, in which this and all other events take place, is itself a mirror through which a person encounters the multiple figures of his/her life, figures who enact a story.

The theme of my paper, hopefully illustrated in this introduction, is that *psychological work is mirror work*. The elaboration of this theme has two parts. First, I want to show that mirror work is a deepening of self which recovers the world and its events as the landscape of self, the person as a multitude of figures, and the factual history of one's life as a creative story. Second, I want to show that this work of recovery is a work of imaginatively *re-membering* one's life. Psychological work as mirror work is a *making*, a *poesis*. The history of one's life is psychologically a *poetic history*. The making of one's life, as in psychotherapy, is a work of fictionalizing the factual.

PSYCHOLOGICAL WORK: MIRRORING AS DEEPENING

The world is a mirror of self, and the events which take place within the world reflect humanity's psychological life. The way in which an age paints its paintings and builds its buildings; the way in which it does its science and constructs its laws; the way in which it fashions its clothes and worships its gods incarnate the human self. We see ourselves, individually and typically, *through* the world. As the Dutch phenomenological psychiatrist J. H. Van den Berg (1955), to whose work I am greatly indebted, says, 'The world is our home, our habitat, the materialization of our subjectivity', and he who would understand the other must learn to read the 'landscape within which he demonstrates, explains and reveals himself'.

The world as a mirror of self is a metaphor of human psychological life. To understand how this metaphor elucidates human psychological life, it is necessary to understand the experience of mirroring. Limitations of space, however, do not allow me more than a brief summary here. For a fuller treatment of this issue I refer readers to a recent book, *Psychological Life: From Science to Metaphor* (Romanyshyn, 1982), where a phenomenology of the mirror experience is elaborated.

The phenomenology of the mirror experience opens up the space of the *image* as a *depth* which is neither real nor unreal. The image, the reflection, which one encounters 'in' the mirror lies as far on that side of the mirror as the one who is looking is on this side of the mirror. From the viewpoint of physics and optics, however, that depth is an illusion. The image lies in a virtual space, a space which only appears to be real. With empirical eyes attuned to the physical facts we would discount the depth of the image, and the image itself, as unreal.

The lived experience of the situation, however, affirms what is otherwise denied. The living eye, as opposed to the eye of physiology which belongs to the physics and optics of the mirror, focuses on the depth of the image. It looks beyond the mirror to that point in space which the image haunts. The living eye does not look *in* the mirror. On the contrary it sees *through* it. The depth of the image, the reflection as it appears, is real. True, it is *not* factually, empirically real. Nevertheless it is not unreal in the sense of an illusion. The depth of the image is a depth that we live.

The mirror reflection, the image and the depth which it opens up, mixes up the categories of the real and the unreal. It confuses them and in this sense undercuts the dichotomy of the real, circumscribed as the material, and the unreal, circumscribed as immaterial. The image and its depth, we might say, is *surreal*, recalling here the marvellous words of Andre Breton (Wilshire, 1982):

> Everything tends to make us believe that there exists a certain point at which life and death, the real and the imagined, past and future . . . cease to be perceived as contradictions. Now, search as one may one will never find any other motivating force in the activities of the Surrealists than the hope of finding and fixing this point.

The first conclusion which I draw from the mirror experience is that the *image matters*. It matters in the sense that it counts in the conduct of human life, and it matters in the sense that it presents us with a reality which is incarnated in and visible through the world, without, however, that incarnation being reduced to *physical* materiality. Moreover, insofar as the image matters, I also conclude that the mirror experience teaches us that the *image is a deepening of human experience*. If mirror work is psychological work, then the self as image, as psychological reality, *is* this function of deepening human experience, of bringing depth to what is otherwise lived on the surface, that is forgetfully or in a taken for granted manner.

But what precisely is deepened in this experience of mirroring? The mirror experience gives two replies.

First, the one who looks is deepened in the sense that the mirror reflection is never merely a double or duplicate of the person on this side of the mirror. On the contrary, the one who looks is *re-figured* as this or that type of character. Mirror, mirror on the wall does reveal the fairest of them all. Sometimes! For it is equally possible that the mirror reveals a figure one does not wish to be. The anorexic, for example, sees through the reflection an image of one too heavily weighted down by life. But lest from this example we erroneously restrict the image to the realm of psychopathology, consider how each of us in daily life encounters through the reflection only the self he or she is *able* to see. We see, in other words, only what we can *believe*, and we believe what we see in this fashion.

It is, therefore, not simply my-self whom I encounter in the depths of the reflection, but rather my-self re-figured as *familiar-stranger*. Between my-self and the reflection, between the person who looks and the figure who is seen, there is a relation of identity and difference. Indeed that relation is not unlike the one between the actor and the character he portrays. Wilshire (1982) in his recent book dealing with role playing and identity within the context of theatre has discussed this issue brilliantly and in great detail. For our purposes I note here only that the actor as person *is* the character and it is this identity which makes this piece of make-believe believable. But the actor as person also *is not* the character, and it is this difference which keeps the believable a piece of make-believe.

We may suggest, then, that the mirror reflection is a *re-figuring* of the person which displays a *believable fiction*. In the depth of the image one encounters an enactment of oneself, and in that depth and through the figure the empirical life of the person is deepened as a dramatic fiction. And herein lies the second sense in which self as image deepens human life. The deepening is not only a *re-figuring* of the person, it is also a transformation of history into story, fact into fiction, event into drama, and knowledge into belief. The person who looks into the mirror meets, therefore, not only a character but also a character within a tale, and through the image the historical and factual events of one's life are gathered together, woven we should say, into a story. In this regard, the mirror image suggests that the self is much more a matter of the stories which one believes than it is a matter of the facts which one knows.

The brief summary of the mirror experience has led to three conclusions concerning the character of the human self. Two of them we have already stated. First, self is *a matter of image which matters*. Second, self as image is a *deepening* of human experience. The third conclusion is that this deepening concerns a *re-figuring of person as character and history as story*.

We should not forget, however, that this deepening and re-figuring proceeds through and with the things of the world. My patient listened to his father's words which described an event *in the world*; the person encounters a figure *through a mirror*; the character is enacted by *the person of an actor*. If the life of self is characterized by such terms as *image, fiction, drama, belief*, and *make-believe*, then nevertheless all of these terms which characterize the self belong to and remain in the world. The self is not on the other side of the world, merely mental or subjective. It is a *psychological* reality, which means that it is given *through* the materiality of the world, the world as it is touched, deepended and trans-formed by self. We can demonstrate this point by considering how mirror work is also a work of re-membering.

PSYCHOLOGICAL WORK: MIRRORING AS RE/MEMBERING

On one obvious level the mirror experience as a re-figuring of person as character and as a deepening of history into story needs to be remembered. It needs to be remembered because it is lived forgetfully. Just as we *see through* the mirror in order to see the image, we *live through* the story which is encountered in that depth. The story is not in us; we are in the story, and in such a way that it unfolds itself through our typical habits, routines, gestures, relations, etc. Looking through the mirror I encounter a reflection, which is much more than a duplicate of myself. That reflection which I encounter, however, requires an act of reflection if it is to become explicit in my life. For a moment, and for whatever motive, the habitual encounter between the one on this side of the mirror and the image has to be disrupted if the reality of the image is to enter one's life thematically.

There is, however, another sense of remembering which matters here, another moment of remembering. It is the moment of remembering as *re-membering*, the moment in which re-membering displays itself as a creative act, a *making*. Re-membering is, in this respect, not simply the opposite of forgetting. Rather, it is the other pole of remembering as a discovery, the pole of remembering as creation. The story which I encounter through the mirror is not only a *discovery of a real past*. It is also a way of *making the past real*. The image re-membered through the mirror, like the images of the past remembered (re-membered) by the patient in psychotherapy, are as much creations as they are discoveries. In short, *psychological work is image making*. *Psychologically* the past is not merely the already made. It is also, and most importantly, something to be made.*

---

* Not only is the past something to be made, so too is the human body a reality to be made. The human body is a biological, cultural, *and* psychological reality. It is organism, history, and flesh of self. The historical gestures which mark a character, which define a style, are, like bodily symptoms, habitats of figures. The work of psychotherapy is, at least in part, a sculpting of the

Evidence for this view lies quite close to the heart of one's life. Now at 41 a man re-members his parents' house where he was a child in a way which radically differs from his memory of it at 20. That childhood home, his re-membering of it, the past change. However, just as we would discount the reality of the image we would discount a past which changes. We would insist that we change while *it* has remained the same.

Such a past, fixed and factual, exists however for *no-one* because time does not sediment in the human self the way in which it does in the earth. Thus when Freud likened psychotherapy to archaeology, he may have been accurately describing events and processes as they occur in the physical and perhaps even in the biological world. But he thereby proposed for us a metaphor which is erroneous with respect to events and processes in the psychological world. It is erroneous *unless* we realize that therapist and patient in digging up the past are as archaeologists simultaneously engaged in making it. Indeed even the archaeologist works in this way, because the old bones which lie beneath the earth, like the facts of one's historical life, are simply there. Without a creative vision the empirical eye of the archaeologist sees nothing but the bare bones, the outline or the skeleton perhaps, of a story.

Facts! That is where and how we become stuck. The facts of the past: we cannot quite believe that anything so solid as a fact can change. And counterposed to this solidity of the fact, all this talk of remembering as a work of making and creation seems little more than a fiction. We trust the fact and at best we tolerate the fiction. We believe, empirical minded people that we are and living as we do in an empirically minded world; we believe, because we need to believe, that remembering, at its best, unearths what truly was. We resist (again out of need?) the notion that re-membering can also create what might be.*

But are facts as solid as they seem, and is fiction merely something we make up, a mental creation, an idea of mind which lacks the weight of the world? Here we are helped by the etymology of the terms which, as all etymologies do, preserves the word as an experience of the world, the word as a means of engaging reality.

Fiction! It derives from the Latin *fingere* and it means a making and/or a shaping of a clay pot. As a way of engaging the world, fiction in its root sense is the producing of something real, but it is a producing, a making, which

---

* Do we resist the creative aspect of re-membering because it would face us with a responsibility for the past? If re-membering is as much a creation as it is a discovery of the past, then *how* we remember matters. And if what one remembers influences what one will be, then our responsibility is doubled. In re-membering we become responsible for what we become.

---

flesh, the making of the body into a psychological reality. What the patient carries as a symptom is a figure needing to be incarnated as a posture, a story needing to be enacted. In short, bodily symptoms are figures needing to be formed and they are formed in the enactment of psychotherapy, in creating the figure's posture which gives flesh to a story.

makes use of something already given, the clay of the earth which is already made.

The clay of the earth is already made. *That* is a fact. Fact is *factum* which means what is already done, finished, and complete. But fact as what is already *done* derives from *facio* which means what I make and/or do. And in this respect, fact, like fiction, betrays the connection between making and the already made. What we would live out as a dichotomy, then, reveals itself as convergence. What we would separate, fact as what is made and fiction as what we make (up), betrays a fusion which finds us inextricably involved in the work of real-izing reality. The poet Rilke (1939) understood this fusion in the relation between humanity and the Earth:

> Earth, isn't this what you want:
> An invisible re-arising in us?

There on the ground is the clay of the earth. There, inert, lifeless it seems, but also seeming to pulse with a pregnancy of possibilities! And next to it there is the clay pot, fashioned and shaped, standing there upon the ground of earth. Between them we recognize the same relation of identity and difference which we have encountered between the person and the image, and the actor and the character he portrays. The clay vessel *preserves* the earth out of which it has been fashioned, even while it *transforms* it. It *remembers* the earth out of which it has been made, even while it *re-members* it. It *discovers* the earth out of which it has arisen, even while it *creates* the earth as a cultural world.

To re-member is to engage in this kind of fiction. To re-member is to engage in this work of fictionalizing the factual, making what is already made, real-izing the real. It is to transform the past, even while preserving it. Indeed it is to preserve the past precisely because it is transformed, because the past as already made is re-made. What would the earth be without the fiction of clay pots? Whatever we say, it seems certain that it would not be the human earth, the earth re-membered in and through the images of our cultural worlds. And, in like manner, what would a human life be *without* the work of re-membering? Would it also *not* be human, or less than human? Our presence as a species on the planet has meant nothing less than the earth re-membered as world. Are we not equally imposed upon to *re-member* ourselves—the persons and the histories which we are—in the same way?

Whether with respect to the earth or to ourselves in time, it seems that the human self is destined to *participate* in its own creation and in the creation of its world.* Psychological work, it seems, is this work of remembering, a re-membering which we have seen involves the making (the fashioning and the reshaping) of the history of one's life into a story. It is a work which

---

*Of course, the danger here is to forget that the self one is, is already made, already created. The temptation is to father one self, to take up the task of making, of creation, ex-nihilo, forgetfully. *This* is the Oedipal struggle, the denial of the father. It was a temptation well understood in Greek tragic drama.

proceeds through the mirror of the world where the image of self, the self as image, opens up as a depth which is real and which matters.

CONCLUSION

There is one final point I wish to make in this contribution. It is also an acknowledgement of indebtedness. I am alluding here to the remarks on fiction, specifically the remarks with respect to the clay pot and its re-membering of earth. The language there of earth and world is, of course, Heidegger's (1971), and specifically his wonderfully rich essay entitled 'The Origin of the Work of Art'. What I said there of fiction as a re-membering of earth as world is the manner in which Heidegger understands the *work of art*. To be sure he does not situate the strife of earth and world which is the work of art within the context of re-membering. But he does say that within this strife the art work does give humanity its outlook on itself. In other words, there is in the work of art something of a discovery through creation. In discovering who we are, the work of art, the work of making, matters.

I take this final remark, then, as a suggestion about the character of the human self. If the self is the work of image making, then it is, in the root sense of the term, a *poetic* reality. Recalling here the opening illustration of my patient, I would now say that through the mirror of the world's events he has been involved in poeticizing the history of his life. He has been engaged in *poetic history*.*

REFERENCES

Heidegger, M. (1971). 'The origin of the work of art.' In A. Hofstadter (Ed.), *Poetry, Language, Thought*, Harper, New York.
Rilke, R. M. (1939). *Duino Elegies* (transl. J. B. Leishman and Stephen Spender), W. W. Norton, New York, p. 77.
Romanyshyn, R. (1982). *Psychological Life: From Science to Metaphor*, University of Texas Press, Austin.
Ven den Berg, J. H. (1955). *The Phenomenological Approach to Psychiatry*, Charles C. Thomas, Springfield, p. 32.
Wilshire, B. (1982). *Role Playing and Identity: The Limits of Theatre as Metaphor*, Indiana University Press, Bloomington, p. 105.

---

* That the consequences of making one's life are not always positive, as is suggested in my remarks about my patient's tragic pose as a defense against the experiences of sadness, does not fault the argument advanced here. The problem is not that my patient has engaged in fictionalizing the facts of his life. The problem lies in the fiction made, *and* most importantly in his unawareness of the making, in his unawareness that he does participate in the making of his life. The task of therapy, then, is to face him with his participation, to help him to see that he does create his life, and *how* he does it. The task is to transform what he would live out *only* as an event (as fate) into a responsibility, into an ability to respond.

Self and Identity: Psychosocial Perspectives
Edited by K. Yardley and T. Honess
© 1987 John Wiley & Sons Ltd

24

The Role of Self-Focused Attention in the Development, Maintenance, and Exacerbation of Depression

Tom Pyszczynski and Jeff Greenberg

A theory of the role of self-focused attention and self-regulatory processes is presented and supporting evidence is discussed. We propose that depression is instigated when a person is unable to exit a self-regulatory cycle after the loss of a central source of self-worth and that such episodes are maintained and exacerbated by a maladaptive deployment of self-focused attention.

INTRODUCTION

Since the publication of Beck's (1967) influential book, interest in the role of cognitive factors in depression has grown considerably. Current theoretical work on depression gives prominent roles to such concepts as attributions, expectancies, and self-schemata (cf. Abramson *et al.*, 1978; Beck, 1967; Kuiper *et al.*, 1983). However, the role of attentional factors, and particularly self-focused attention, in the aetiology and maintenance of depression has been largely ignored. The present chapter employs recent research and theory on the cognitive and motivational consequences of self-focused attention to develop a theory of the development, maintenance, and exacerbation of unipolar reactive depression. The theory is an attempt to specify relationships among a variety of processes that are believed to play a central role in depressive episodes. In essence, we argue that depression is the result of an inability or unwillingness to exit a self-regulatory cycle after the loss of a significant source of self-worth and that it is maintained and exacerbated by a maladaptive deployment of self-focused attention that we refer to as the depressive self-focusing style.

Interest in the effects of focusing attention on the self was first stimulated by Duval and Wicklund's (1972) theory of objective self-awareness. According to their formulation, conscious attention can be focused either inwards, on the self, or outwards, on the environment. Focusing attention on the self leads to the instigation of a self-evaluative process, by which one's current standing on a currently salient dimension is compared with whatever standard for that dimension is most salient at the time. If one exceeds the standard, self-focus produces positive affect and a tendency to maintain the self-focused state. However, if one falls short of the standard, self-focus produces negative affect and results in attempts to either reduce the discrepancy between one's current state and the standard or to escape self-focus. Duval and Wicklund's (1972) formulation, along with their clever use of a mirror to manipulate self-focus, led to a large number of empirical investigations, most of which have been generally supportive of the theory.

Recently, Carver and Scheier (1981) have proposed a cybernetic model of self-awareness processes. While retaining most of the central aspects of Duval and Wicklund's theory, they emphasize the adaptive self-regulatory function served by self-focus. They conceptualize self-focus as part of a self-regulatory cycle that keeps individuals 'on track' in their pursuit of important goals. According to their model, the disruption of ongoing activities leads to the instigation of a self-regulatory cycle (test–operate–test–exit), in which the individual alternates between engaging in self-focus (and the resulting comparison of current and desired states) and behaviour aimed at reducing any perceived discrepancies. This cycle continues until either the discrepancy is eliminated or the individual begins to perceive that the probability of successful discrepancy reduction is below some critical value; when either of the above occurs, the self-regulatory cycle is exited and self-focus is decreased. Thus, from Carver and Scheier's perspective, the function of self-focused attention and the resulting comparison of current and desired states is to provide the individual with information useful in regulating his/her behaviour in the direction of obtaining important goal objects. Our self-regulatory perseveration theory of depression builds on this more general approach to self-regulatory processes.

A number of very striking parallels exist between the behaviour of non-depressed individuals under conditions of enhanced self-focus and that of depressed individuals under normal conditions. As Smith and Greenberg (1981) and others (e.g., Lewinsohn *et al.*, 1984) have pointed out, both self-focused 'normals' and depressives show: an intensification of affective states (e.g., Beck 1967; Scheier and Carver, 1977); an increased tendency to take personal responsibility for negative outcomes (e.g., Duval and Wicklund, 1973; Fenigstein and Levine, 1984; Kuiper, 1978; Rizley, 1978); an increased self-evaluative tendency and lowered self-esteem (e.g., Beck, 1967; Duval and Wicklund, 1972; Ickes *et al.*, 1973; Laxer, 1964); and an increased tendency to withdraw from tasks after an initial failure experience (e.g., Carver *et al.*, 1979; Miller, 1957).

Based on the above similarities, Smith and Greenberg (1981) hypothesized and found that depressed individuals are especially prone to self-focus; specifically, a small but significant positive correlation was found between scores on the D-30 Depression Inventory and the private self-consciousness scale (a measure of the dispositional tendency to self-focus, developed by

Fenigstein *et al.*, 1975). Recent research (Ingram and Smith, 1984; Smith *et al.*, in press) has replicated this finding with different measures of both self-focus (the Exner Self-Focus Sentence Completion Task) and depression (the Beck Depression Inventory). Thus, it seems fairly clear that self-focused attention and depression are positively associated. Based on this relationship, and the parallels between the symptoms of depression and the effects of self-focus, the present theory attempts to explicate the role of self-focused attention in the onset, maintenance, and exacerbation of depression.

THE ROLE OF SELF-FOCUS IN THE ONSET OF DEPRESSION

Theory and research support the notion that depression is usually preceded by extremely stressful life events (e.g., Beck, 1967; Brown and Harris, 1978; Freud, 1917/1953; Lewinsohn *et al.*, 1984; Paykel *et al.*, 1969). Generally, these events involve losses in the personal, social, or work spheres. Thus, many theorists consider depression to be an extreme, distorted version of how individuals generally react to such losses (e.g., Freud, 1917/1953; Klinger, 1975; Lewinsohn *et al.*, 1984). Consistent with a variety of other theorists (e.g., Arieti and Bemporad, 1978; Brown and Harris, 1978; Oatley and Bolton, 1985), we suggest that it is the loss of objects that provide a central source of self-esteem, value, or meaning in life that instigates the occurrence of a depressive episode.

Insight into the mechanisms underlying reactions to such losses is provided by Carver and Scheier's (1981) cybernetic model of self-focused attention and self-regulation. From this perspective, contact with the object that functions as a source of self-esteem is conceptualized as a goal or standard that the individual strives to maintain. When a negative discrepancy between one's current and desired state with respect to the object becomes salient, the individual alternates between self-focusing, to compare the current and desired states, and engaging in behaviour directed toward reducing the perceived discrepancy, until that discrepancy is greatly reduced or eliminated. Of course the greater the dependency of the individual's sense of self-worth on the object, the greater the tendency to engage a self-regulatory cycle in the hope of returning to the desired state. This will be especially true to the extent that the loss engenders extreme negative affect and interrupts the individual's daily routine (Carver and Scheier, 1981; Wegner and Giuliano, 1980). Therefore, after an impactful loss, self-focus will occur as part of a negative feedback loop that directs behaviour toward discrepancy reduction. Thus, self-focus after negative events serves an adaptive function by providing information essential to goal attainment.

However, in formulating a model of self-regulation that accounts for adaptive behaviour, Carver and Scheier (1981) proposed that when the individual assesses the probability of discrepancy reduction to be very low, further self-focus is avoided, and the individual withdraws from behaviour directed toward reducing the discrepancy. Steenbarger and Aderman (1979) provided support for this proposition by demonstrating that self-focus is avoided after negative discrepancies are made salient when there are no options available for reducing the discrepancy. Further support comes from a number of studies that have shown that when the perceived probability of goal attainment is low, heightened self-focus discourages goal-directed behaviour (Carver *et al.*, 1979; Carver and Scheier, 1981). Although the self-regulatory cycle normally functions to facilitate discrepancy reduction (or goal attainment), when faced with an irrevocable loss, disengagement from the self-regulatory cycle, which in part consists of reducing self-focus, becomes an adaptive response. We propose that depression occurs when the individual who experiences such a loss fails to disengage the self-regulatory cycle. As a result, the person continues to self-focus in the absence of any way to regain what was lost. Essentially, the individual becomes stuck in a self-regulatory cycle in which successful discrepancy reduction is impossible.

We suggest that such fruitless persistence is likely to occur when what is lost was of central importance to the individual. To the extent that the lost object had previously functioned as a major source of emotional security and provided the individual with a sense of identity and self-worth, withdrawal from the self-regulatory cycle is greatly inhibited. In essense, we are suggesting that to the extent that the individual has centred his or her life around his/her relationship with the lost object he or she may fail to exit the self-regulatory cycle because of an inability or unwillingness to tolerate the absence of the object. Because of the intense attachment to and dependence on the lost object, normal mechanisms for coping with the loss, such as the pursuit of alternate objects or the denial of the importance of the loss are both unappealing and ineffective. Perseverance in such a self-regulatory cycle may also be encouraged to the extent that cues that remind the individual of the lost object remain (Klinger, 1975). We suggest that this perseveration in focusing on the discrepancy between current and desired states sets off a spiral of events that produce many of the affective, cognitive, behavioural, and social characteristics symptomatic of depression.

When the self-regulatory cycle following a significant loss is greatly protracted, the resulting constant confrontation of the discrepancy between current and desired states greatly exacerbates the negative affect that is experienced in response to the loss. As Scheier and Carver (1977) and others have demonstrated, the increased awareness of one's internal state that is produced by self-focus increases the intensity of subjective affective reactions to a variety of stimuli. In the case of the individual who is perseverating on an irreducible negative discrepancy, this negative affect is further intensified by the individual's continual awareness of his/her inability to reduce the discrepancy between current and desired states.

Perseveration in focusing attention on the loss is also likely to increase the individual's tendency to blame him or herself for his/her unfortunate circumstances. Given that self-focus increases the salience of the self and that the attributions that individuals make are heavily influenced by the salience and availability of various potential causal factors (cf. Taylor and Fiske, 1978; Tversky and Kahneman, 1973), it follows that self-focus will increase the extent to which one's behaviour and outcomes are attributed to internal factors. Duval and Wicklund (1973), Fenigstein and Levine (1984), and many others have provided evidence consistent with this proposition, demonstrating that self-focus increases the internality of the attributions that individuals make for their behaviour and outcomes. Thus the tendency to perseverate on the lost object may contribute greatly to the individual's tendency to blame him or herself for the loss. Consistent with this reasoning, a wide variety of theorists and researchers have observed that depressives often blame themselves for their negative experiences (e.g., Abramson *et al.*, 1978; Beck, 1967; Freud, 1917/1953).

So far, it has been proposed that the individual's preoccupation with dealing with the initial loss results in a chronic state of self-focus that creates a spiral of negative affect and self-blame. As a direct result of this spiral, the individual may begin to adopt a negative self-image. Recall that the perseveration in focusing on the loss was set in motion by the loss of a central source of self-worth. Consequently, the individual's self-image is likely to be especially malleable at this point. Given the individual's high level of self-focus and emerging negative self-image, she/he is also likely to accept blame for other negative outcomes that occur. Because the individual is perseverating on the lost object, he or she is unlikely to be able to attend sufficiently to other concerns. As a result, such additional negative experiences are likely to become increasingly frequent. The mounting negative affect and self-criticism is also likely to interfere with effective behaviour in other areas, especially the social realm (cf. Coyne 1976). This proliferation of negative outcomes then further exacerbates the individual's negative affect and self-blame and provides substantiation of the negative self-image that has been developing.

THE DEPRESSIVE SELF-FOCUSING STYLE AND THE EXACERBATION OF DEPRESSION

At this point, a negative self-image may be firmly established. As Beck (1967) points out, this negative self-image will then contribute to a continued exacerbation of the depressed state. To a large extent, this deleterious influence may result from a depressive self-focusing style that emerges as a result of the individual's self-regulatory perseveration on the lost object. In three recent experiments (Greenberg and Pyszczynski, 1986; Pyszczynski and Greenberg, 1985, 1986) we have obtained evidence that, in sharp contrast to the pattern typically exhibited by non-depressed individuals, depressed persons engage in high levels of self-focus after negative outcomes and low levels of self-focus after positive outcomes. It is important to note that this pattern of self-focus allocation was observed following outcomes unlikely to be directly related to the initial depression-instigating loss; thus we suspect that it represents a fairly general tendency. We propose that this depressive self-focusing style is one of the principal mechanisms that maintains and exacerbates the depressive state.

Previous research on self-focusing tendencies in non-depressed samples has demonstrated that self-focus after negative outcomes is generally aversive, especially when the discrepancy created by the negative outcomes is perceived as irreducible (Duval *et al.*, cited in Duval and Wicklund, 1972; Gibbons and Wicklund, 1976; Steenbarger and Aderman, 1979). To assess the possibility that a unique depressive self-focusing style exists, we induced either a success or failure experience in mild to moderately depressed and non-depressed college students (as assessed by scores on the Beck (1967) Depression Inventory, BDI). In all of these experiments, subjects were randomly assigned to succeed or fail a supposedly well-respected test of verbal intelligence (consisting of either solvable or unsolvable anagrams) and their self-focusing tendencies were then assessed.

In our first study (Pyszczynski and Greenberg, 1985), subjects' self-reported preference for working on a task in the presence versus absence of a mirror was used as an indication of preference for self-focus. Presumably, the affect induced by the self-focused attention brought by subjects' confrontation with their mirror images would affect subjects' reports of liking for the puzzle that they worked on in the presence of the mirror (for a review of evidence concerning the self-focus enhancing effect of mirrors, see Carver and Scheier, 1981). If self-focus produced positive affect, the mirror-associated puzzle would be preferred; if self-focus produced negative affect the puzzle worked on in the absence of the mirror would be preferred. The data indicated that although non-depressed subjects liked the puzzles worked on in front of a mirror more after success than after failure, depressed subjects clearly did not. In fact, the depressed subjects exhibited a weak tendency to like the mirror-associated task more after failure than after success. It appears, then, that depressed and non-depressed subjects differ in their affective responses to self-focus after positive and negative outcomes.

In our second study (Pyszczynski and Greenberg, 1986), a behavioural measure of time spent on the mirror-associated puzzle during a ten-minute free choice period was used as the measure of subjects' self-focusing preferences. This study also differed from the first in that it included a no-outcome control condition; thus the question of whether depressed subjects avoid self-focus after success, seek self-focus after failure, or both, could be addressed. In this study depressed subjects spent significantly more time with the mirror-associated task after failure than after success. When compared with depressed subjects in the no-outcome control condition, depressed success subjects spent significantly less time with the mirror-associated task, while depressed failure subjects tended to spend more time ($p < 0.10$). Thus this study provided clear support for the hypothesis that depressed individuals avoid self-focus after success and hinted at the possibility that they may also seek self-focus after failure.

Admittedly, responses to self-focus enhancing stimuli such as mirrors are rather indirect ways of assessing an individual's self-focusing tendencies. The self-regulatory perseveration theory of depression applies not only to individual's responses to such stimuli, but also to their spontaneous allocation of attention to the self. Thus in our next two studies (Greenberg and Pyszczynski, 1986) we attempted to assess depressed and non-depressed subjects' self-focusing tendencies in a more direct way.

In a preliminary study (Greenberg and Pyszczynski, 1986, Study 1), in which we used the Exner (1973) Self-focus Sentence Completion Task as a measure of self-focus, we found that the spontaneous self-focusing tendencies of non-depressed subjects are quite different from those that are typically observed in studies of mirror avoidance behaviour; both depressed and non-depressed subjects *spontaneously* self-focused more after failure than after success. Although initially unexpected, these findings are actually quite consistent with Carver and Scheier's (1981) cybernetic model of self-awareness processes. From this perspective, a self-regulatory cycle (of which self-focus is a component) is instigated by disruptions of ongoing behaviour because such disruptions signal the possibility that adjustments in that behaviour may be necessary. Because failure certainly provides such a disruption, it follows that the initial response to failure should be an increase in one's level of self-focus. This, of course, is precisely what our data suggest.

What, then, accounts for the pattern of self-focus avoidance after failure that is typically found in studies of responses to self-focus enhancing stimuli? Because of the adaptive self-regulatory function served by self-focus, people are undoubtedly willing to tolerate a certain amount of negative affect produced by their initial self-focusing response to failure. We suggest, however, that self-focus enhancing stimuli are avoided after such outcomes because they increase an already elevated level of self-focus beyond a tolerable and useful level. This line of reasoning suggests that if the utility of self-focus is reduced or eliminated, even spontaneous self-focus will be avoided after negative outcomes because of the negative affect that it entails. Thus after a delay or distraction, subjects' spontaneous self-focusing tendencies may 'mirror' those that are typically observed in studies of responses to self-focus enhancing stimuli.

To assess this possibility, we conducted a second study of spontaneous self-focusing in which self-focus was assessed by simply asking subjects at various points in the experimental session to list whatever thoughts occurred to them. These thought-listings were taken immediately before taking the verbal intelligence test, immediately after the test, and after a delay period during which they read ten pages of involving fiction, and were later coded for extent of self-focus. The data from subjects' thought-listings immediately after the test replicated those from the previous study: both depressed and non-depressed subjects were more self-focused after failure than after success. However, after the delay and distraction, the pattern of data was highly consistent with that from studies of responses to self-focus enhancing stimuli. Depressed subjects continued to engage in higher levels of self-focus in the failure than in the success condition; non-depressed subjects, on the other hand, had switched to the more hedonically pleasing pattern of higher levels of self-focus after success than after failure.

Taken together, these four studies provide support for the notion that there is a unique depressive self-focusing style. It appears that depressed persons prefer self-focus after negative outcomes to self-focus after positive outcomes and persist in spontaneously self-focusing after negative outcomes past the point at which non-depressed persons exit the self-regulatory cycle, even when the outcome is unrelated to the loss that instigated their depressive episode. We should also point out that this persistence in self-focusing is consistent with the theory's central proposition that depression is associated with an inability or unwillingness to exit self-regulatory cycles after negative outcomes. Of course these findings cannot be used as direct support for the causal role of self-regulatory perseveration after an impactful loss in the onset of depression because the subjects in these studies were already depressed. They do, however, clearly support the proposition that the tendency to perseverate in self-focus generalizes to negative outcomes beyond the initial instigating event. We turn now to a consideration of the consequences of this generalized depressive self-focusing style for the depressed individual's affect, attributions, self-esteem, and motivation.

THE ROLE OF SELF-FOCUS IN THE MAINTENANCE AND EXACERBATION OF DEPRESSION

If depressives do indeed have a unique self-focusing style, the majority of the laboratory evidence (and a great deal of clinical evidence as well) concerning the characteristics or 'symptoms' of the depressive state could be explained as the result of this tendency. We argue that the depressive self-focusing style plays a central role in the maintenance and exacerbation of these characteristics. Previous research has demonstrated clear effects of self-focus manipulations on subjects' affect, attributions, self-esteem, and performance. Given these findings, the typical non-depressive pattern of high levels of self-focus after positive outcomes and low levels of self-focus after negative outcomes appears to be quite adaptive in that it produces beneficial effects for the individual on all of these dimensions. More interestingly for the present purposes, the depressive self-focusing style appears to be precisely the pattern that would create the most detrimental effects possible on these dimensions.

Specifically, research has demonstrated that self-focus leads to:

1. an intensification of affective states (e.g., Scheier and Carver, 1977; Scheier *et al.*, 1981);
2. an increase in the internality of attributions (e.g., Duval and Wicklund, 1973; Fenigstein and Levine, 1984);
3. an increase in self-evaluative tendencies and comparison of self with

standards and a decrease in self-esteem after negative outcomes (e.g., Ickes *et al.*, 1973; Scheier and Carver, 1983);
4. an increase in the tendency to persist at tasks when the subjective probability of success is high and withdraw from tasks when the subjective probability of success is low (e.g., Brockner, 1979; Carver, *et al.*, 1979).

Consequently, depressed individuals' tendency to engage in high levels of self-focus after negative outcomes and low levels of self-focus after positive outcomes would be expected to:

1. increase the intensity of the negative affect they experience after failures and decrease the intensity of the positive affect they experience after successes;
2. increase the internality of the attributions they make for their failures and decrease the internality of the attributions that they make for their successes;
3. intensify the self-criticism and loss of self-esteem that results from their failures and minimize the self-praise and increase in self-esteem that could (but usually does not) result from their successes;
4. increase their tendency to withdraw from tasks after initial failures and decrease their tendency to persist at tasks after initial successes, thereby producing performance deficits in both cases.

In general, then, the depressive self-focusing style is posited to increase the negative psychological consequences associated with failures and decrease the positive psychological consequences associated with successes.

Although prior research on the consequences of self-focused attention among non-depressed samples suggests that the depressive self-focusing style is likely to produce serious negative consequences, research with depressed samples that investigates this possibility directly is needed. We have just recently begun to conduct such studies. Our first such experiment was an attempt to examine the effect of the depressive self-focusing style on the attributions depressed individuals make for performance outcomes.

Previous research on depressed persons' causal attributions suggests that, unlike their non-depressed counterparts, depressed individuals do not exhibit a self-serving attributional bias (e.g., Kuiper, 1978; Rizley, 1978). That is, although non-depressed individuals exhibit a strong and consistent bias toward making internal attributions for their positive outcomes and external attributions for their negative outcomes, depressed individuals appear to be relatively even-handed in their attributions, i.e., their attributions do not seem to vary as a function of performance outcome. From the present perspective, this absence of attributional egotism on the part of depressives is a consequence of their self-focusing tendencies after positive and negative outcomes. As suggested above, because self-focus increases the internality of attributions, a depressive self-focusing style would be expected to decrease the internality of their attributions for positive outcomes and increase the internality of their attributions for negative outcomes. Our initial study of the consequences of the depressive self-focusing style was designed to investigate this possibility.

In this study (Greenberg *et al*., 1986), mild to moderately depressed and non-depressed college students (as measured by the BDI) succeeded or failed on a supposed test of verbal ability and were induced to focus their attention either on themselves or externally. Their attributions for their performance on the test were then assessed. In consistency with prior research (e.g., Duval and Wicklund, 1973; Fenigstein and Levine, 1984), a general tendency for self-focus to increase the internality of subjects' attributions was observed. More importantly for present purposes, the data suggested that the differences between depressed and non-depressed persons' self-focusing tendencies that have been observed in previous research (e.g., Greenberg and Pyszczynski, 1986; Pyszczynski and Greenberg, 1985, 1986) may mediate the attributions they make for positive and negative outcomes. Specifically, for depressed subjects, the conditions analogous to the depressive self-focusing style (external-focus-success versus internal-focus-failure) yielded the same absence of self-serving bias that has been reported in other research on depressed persons' attributions. However, in the conditions that reversed this style (internal-focus-success versus external-focus-failure), a strong self-serving bias emerged. Likewise, for non-depressed subjects, the conditions analogous to their typical self-focusing preferences (internal-focus-success versus external-focus-failure) produced the usual pattern of self-serving bias that is observed with such subjects. However, the conditions analogous to the depressive self-focusing style (external-focus-success versus internal-focus-failure) led to the absence of bias normally associated with depressives. These data suggest that the tendency toward realistic, unbiased attributions that has previously been observed among depressed persons is at least partially mediated by the manner in which they focus attention after positive and negative outcomes.

It seems clear that this style of self-focus allocation is likely to have severe negative consequences for the depressed individual. Why, then, does the depressive persist in such a maladaptive pattern? We suggest that the depressive self-focusing style emerges as a direct result of the individual's self-regulatory perseveration on the lost object and the spiral of events that this perseveration sets in motion. After the loss the individual is desperately trying to recover the lost object. Unfortunately, the individual's high level of dependence on the object as a source of self-worth and well-being, coupled with the unavailability of alternative sources of these commodities, has made it impossible for the individual to effectively cope with the loss. The intense desire to regain the lost object leads the individual to persist in focusing on the loss in spite of the fact the chances of recovering the lost object are extremely low or even non-existant. Due to this perseveration, he or she may begin to find self-focus after positive outcomes aversive because dwelling on such outcomes would interrupt his or her attempts to regain the lost object. Thus self-focus after positive outcomes may be actively avoided because such outcomes are viewed as annoying distractions that seem trivial in comparison to the more important problems upon which the person is dwelling. On the other hand, the individual may engage in high levels of self-focus after other negative outcomes that occur because such outcomes are quite consistent with the problems he or she is facing; they may be seen as symptoms of and/or contributors to his or her unfortunate circumstances. Thus the depressive's preoccupation with the precipitating loss and lack of concern with other more positive events occurring around him/her may generalize to other negative and positive outcomes because of the effect such outcomes have on his or her perseverated attempts to regain the lost object.

We also suspect, however, that, at least in more severe cases of depression, the depressive self-focusing style persists because it serves a function for the individual. As suggested above, self-regulatory perseveration and the depressive self-focusing style are likely to push the individual's self-image in a negative direction. We suggest that, once a negative self-image is firmly established, it may begin to provide benefits for the individual. Thus the depressive self-focusing style may persist and become resistant to change because it helps to maintain this negative self-image.

Although the assertion that depressed individuals become motivated to maintain a negative self-image may seem rather paradoxical, a variety of other theorists have proposed very similar interpretations of the persistent self-deprecating behaviour commonly observed among depressives (e.g., Arieti and Bemporad, 1978; Becker, 1973; Freud, 1917/1963; Mollon this volume). We are not, however, suggesting that depressed individuals take masochistic pleasure in their misery. Rather, we propose that there are liabilities associated with a positive self-image and assets associated with a negative self-image, and that, given the negative spiral set off by the individual's self-regulatory perseveration, these factors become especially powerful and influential for the depressed person (cf. Arkin, this volume).

As we have suggested, maintaining a positive self-image while perseverating in one's attempts to reduce an irreducible negative discrepancy is unlikely to be successful. In addition, persisting in attempts to maintain a positive self-image in the face of all the difficulties with which the depressed person is faced must certainly require a great deal of cognitive effort (cf., Pyszczynski and Greenberg, in press). Thus the initial benefit of adopting a negative self-image is likely to be that it provides relief from the individual's increasingly futile attempts to maintain a positive self-image. Given all of the negative experiences with which the individual is faced, the distortions in information processing that we all must employ to maintain a positive self-image may become increasingly transparent; it may thus begin to appear to the individual that accepting a negative view of the self reflects a parsimonious, honest, and perhaps even noble, acceptance of the rather painful reality of his or her lot in life.

In addition, as a number of theorists have suggested (e.g., Becker, 1973; Lerner *et al.*, 1976) blaming the victim of misfortune may sometimes be preferred to the alternative of concluding that the world is a cruel and unjust place in which to live. Believing that one is deserving of his or her misfortune may thus shield the individual from the more threatening prospect of viewing the world as unjust and hostile. Given the aversive nature of the depressed individual's recent life experiences, buying into a negative self-image may, in some cases, be more endurable than accepting the possibility that tragic events can occur in an unpredictable and uncontrollable fashion.

Finally, depressed individuals may become motivated to maintain a negative self-image because such a perspective provides a buffer against additional pain and disappointment in the future. Rothbaum *et al.* (1982) have recently argued that self-deprecating attributions and pessimism regarding the future are often attempts to achieve what they refer to as 'secondary control' over an otherwise uncontrollable outcome. Rather than attempting to control the occurrence of the outcome itself, the individual works to control his or her emotional reaction to it. In this case the individual strives to minimize disappointment by keeping expectancies for positive outcomes low. Recall that the tremendous emotional devastation that followed the initial loss of the object was made possible by the individual's optimistic investment in the object as a source of self-esteem and meaning. Consequently, depressed individuals may find any event that implies optimism concerning anything related to the self a source of great anxiety. Conversely, events that reinforce a pessimistic outlook may be less threatening and even comforting. Thus depressed individuals may actively seek to maintain a negative self-image because it minimizes the potential for devastating losses in the future.

CONCLUSION

To summarize, a depressive episode is instigated when an individual is unable to exit a self-regulatory cycle after the loss of a central source of self-worth, emotional security, or meaning in life. This self-regulatory perseveration sets off a spiral of events, including intensification of negative affect, self-blame, loss of self-esteem, and decrements in motivation and performance that culminates in the state of depression. As a result of this self-regulatory perseveration, a depressive self-focusing style emerges in which the individual engages in high levels of self-focus after negative outcomes and low levels of self-focus after positive outcomes. This depressive self-focusing style then maintains and exacerbates the depression.

The self-regulatory perseveration theory is generally consistent with a broad range of clinical observations and research findings. The research that has been conducted to directly test the theory has thus far been supportive. However, many components of the theory have not yet been directly tested. A great deal of additional research will be needed to assess the theory's ultimate validity.

In most respects our theory is not in conflict with other contemporary theories of depression. We agree with other theorists that attributions, self-esteem, self-schemata, affect, and expectancies all play a major role in the depressive syndrome. Self-regulatory perseveration theory is an attempt to use the conceptual framework provided by theory and research on self-awareness and self-regulatory processes to integrate the roles played by a variety of the processes emphasized by other contemporary theories of depression. Although in this sense, the theory is complementary to many other perspectives on depression, there are some important points of divergence with other perspectives that merit consideration.

Although a thorough discussion of the relationship of self-regulatory perseveration theory to other theories of depression would be beyond the scope of this paper, a brief look at how the theory relates to one other very influential theory might be informative. Abramson *et al.*'s (1978) revised learned helplessness theory of depression has had a major impact on the field and has generated a great deal of very useful empirical research. According to this theory, the attributions a person makes for an inability to obtain desired outcomes (determined largely by his/her dispositional attributional style) influences his or her expectancies concerning the possibility of obtaining other outcomes in the future. These expectancies, in turn, affect the person's motivation and performance in future social and performance settings. Internal, stable, and global attributions are posited to have the most detrimental effects on self-esteem, and to produce the most chronic and generalized deficits. In essence, Abramson *et al.* (1978) argue that depression occurs when people are unable to control desirable outcomes, give up in their attempts to do so, and generalize this giving up to a broad range of other situations.

Although Abramson *et al.*, argue that the individual's attributions play a causal role in the onset of a depressive episode, the literature on the relationship between attributions and depression is inconsistent with respect to whether attributions interact with loss to produce depression (cf. Peterson and Seligman 1984) or whether depressive attributional tendencies emerge as a consequence of being depressed (cf. Lewinsohn *et al.*, 1981). Furthermore, the revised helplessness model offers no explanation of what determines the occurence of a dispositional tendency to make depressogenic attributions in the first place. From the present perspective, depressive attributions emerge as a consequence of the self-focusing tendencies that result from the individual's inability to let go of a lost source of self-esteem. Greenberg *et al.*'s (1986) recent finding that depressive attributional tendencies can be reversed by controlling their self-focusing tendencies is highly consistent with such a position. Thus, although we acknowledge the possibility that dispositional attributional tendencies may play some role in the instigation of depression, we argue that the major determinant of the depressed individual's pattern of attributions lies in his or her inability to give up on a lost source of self-regard and the pattern of self-focus allocation that results from such perseveration.

There is one other important way in which self-regulatory perseveration theory diverges from the learned helplessness model and most other cognitively oriented theories of depression. It is widely assumed that depression occurs when an individual encounters a highly important but uncontrollable outcome, gives up his or her attempts to control the outcome, and then generalizes this loss of motivation to other domains (e.g., Abramson *et al.*, 1978; Bowlby, 1980; Kanfer and Hagerman, 1981). In contrast, according to self-regulatory perseveration theory, depression occurs when a person is *unable or unwilling to give up* on an unattainable goal when it would be adaptive to do so. The affective, cognitive, and motivational consequences of persisting in the self-regulatory cycle would normally be quite adaptive in that they facilitate the individual's attempts to reduce the discrepancy between current and desired states. However, in the absence of any way to reduce the discrepancy, this failure to give up the unattainable object sets into motion a spiral of events that culminates in a state of depression.

REFERENCES

Abramson, L. Y., Seligman, M. E. P. and Teasdale, J. D. (1978). 'Learned helplessness in humans: critique and reformulation.' *Journal of Abnormal Psychology*, **87**, 49–74.

Arieti, S. and Bemporad, J. (1978). *Severe and Mild Depression: The Psychotherapeutic Approach*, Basic Books, New York.

Beck, A. T. (1967). *Depression: Clinical, Experimental, and Theoretical Aspects*, Hoeber, New York.

Becker, E. (1973). *The Denial of Death*, The Free Press, New York.

Bowlby, J. (1980). *Loss, Sadness and Depression*, Hogarth, London.

Brockner, J. (1979). 'The effects of self-esteem, success-failure, and self-consciousness of task performance.' *Journal of Personality and Social Psychology*, **37**, 1732–1741.

Brown, G. W. and Harris, T. (1978). *Social Origins of Depression: A Study of Psychiatric Disorder in Women*, Free Press, New York.

Carver, C. and Scheier, M. (1981). *Attention and Self-Regulation*, Springer-Verlag, New York.

Carver, C. S., Blaney, P. H. and Scheier, M. F. (1979). 'Reassertion and giving up: The interactive role of self-directed attention and outcome expectancy.' *Journal of Personality and Social Psychology*, **37**, 1859–1870.

Coyne, J. C. (1976). 'Depression and the responses of others.' *Journal of Abnormal Psychology*, **85**, 186–193.

Duval, S. and Wicklund, R. (1972). *A Theory of Objective Self-Awareness*, Academic Press, New York.

Duval, S. and Wicklund, R. (1973). 'Effects of objective self-awareness on attributions of causality.' *Journal of Experimental Social Psychology*, **9**, 17–31.

Exner, J. E. (1973). 'The self-focus sentence completion: a study of egocentricity.' *Journal of Personality Assessment*, **37**, 437–455.

Fenigstein, A. and Levine, M. P. (1984). 'Self-attention, concept activation and the causal self.' *Journal of Experimental Social Psychology*, **20**, 231–245.

Fenigstein, A., Scheier, M. and Buss, A. (1975). 'Public and private self-consciousness: assessment and theory.' *Journal of Consulting and Clinical Psychology*, **43**, 522–527.

Freud, S. (1963). 'Mourning and melancholia.' In J. Strachey (transl. and Ed.), *The Complete Psychological Works of Sigmund Freud*, vol. 14, Hogarth Press, London (originally published in 1917).

Gibbons, F. X. and Wicklund, R. (1976). 'Selective exposure to self.' *Journal of Research in Personality*, **10**, 98–106.

Greenberg, J. and Pyszczynski, T. (1986). 'Persistent high self-focus after failure and low self-focus after success: the depressive self-focusing style.' *Journal of Personality and Social Psychology*, **50**, 1039–1044.

Greenberg, J., Pyszczynski, T., Kelly, C., Burling J., Byler, E. and Tibbs, K. (1986). *Depression, self-focused attention and the self-serving attributional bias*. Unpublished manuscript, University of Arizona.

Ickes, J., Wicklund, R. and Ferris, C. (1973). Objective self-awareness and self-esteem. *Journal of Experimental Social Psychology*, **9**, 202–219.

Ingram, R. E. and Smith, T. S. (1984). 'Depression and internal versus external locus of attention.' *Cognitive Therapy and research*, **8**, 139–152.

Kanfer, F. H. and Hagerman, S. (1981). 'The role of self-regulation.' In L. Rehm (Ed.), *Behavior Therapy for Depression: Present Status and Future Directions*, Academic Press, New York, chap. 4.

Klinger, E. (1975). 'Consequences of commitment to and disengagement from incentives.' *Psychological Review*, **82**, 1–25.

Kuiper, N. (1978). 'Depression and causal attributions for success and failure.' *Journal of Personality and Social Psychology*, **36**, 236–246.

Kuiper, N. A., McDonald, M. R. and Derry, P. A. (1983). 'Parameters of a depressive self-schema.' In J. Suls and A. Greenwald (Eds), *Psychological Perspectives on the Self*, vol. 2, Erlbaum, Hillsdale, New Jersey.

Laxer, R. (1964). 'Self-concept changes of depressed patients in general hospital treatment.' *Journal of Consulting Psychology*, **28**, 214–219.

Lerner, M. J., Miller, D. T. and Holmes, J. G. (1976). 'Deserving and the emergence of forms of justice.' In L. Berkowitz and E. Walster (Eds), *Advances in Experimental Social Psychology*, vol. 9, Academic Press, New York, pp. 133–162.

Lewinsohn, P. M., Hoberman, H., Teri, L. and Hautzinger, M. (1984). 'An integrative theory of depression.' In S. Reiss and R. Bootzin (Eds), *Theoretical Issues in Behavior Therapy*, Academic Press, New York.

Lewinsohn, P. M., Steinmetz, J. L., Larson, D. W. and Franklin, J. (1981). 'Depression-related cognitions: Antecendent or consequence?' *Journal of Abnormal Psychology*, **90**, 213–219.

Miller, W. R. (1975). 'Psychological deficit in depression.' *Psychological Bulletin*, **82**, 238–260.

Oatley, K. and Bolton, W. (1985). 'A social cognitive theory of depression in reaction to life events.' *Psychological Review*, **92**, 372–388.

Paykel, E. S., Myers, J. K., Dienelt, M. N., Klerman, G. L., Lindenthal, J. L. and Pepper, M. P. (1969). 'Life events and depression: a controlled study.' *Archives of General Psychiatry*, **21**, 753–760.

Peterson, C. and Seligman, M. E. P. (1984). 'Causal explanations as a risk factor for depression: theory and research.' *Psychological Review*, **91**, 347–374.

Pyszczynski, T. and Greenberg, J. (1985). 'Depression and preference for self-focusing stimuli following success and failure.' *Journal of Personality and Social Psychology*, **49**, 1066–1075.

Pyszczynski, T. and Greenberg, J. (1986). 'Evidence for a depressive self-focusing style.' *Journal of Research in Personality*, **20**, 95–106.

Pyszczynski, T. and Greenberg, J. (in press). 'Toward an integration of cognitive and motivational perspectives on social inference: A biased hypothesis testing model.' In L. Berkowitz (Ed.), *Advances in Experimental Social Psychology*, vol. 20, Academic Press, New York.

Rizley, R. (1978). 'Depression and distortion in the attribution of causality.' *Journal of Abnormal Psychology*, **87**, 32–48.

Rothbaum, F., Weisz, J. R. and Snyder, S. S. (1982). 'Changing the world and changing the self: a two-process model of perceived control.' *Journal of Personality and Social Psychology*, **42**, 5–37.

Scheier, M. F. and Carver, C. (1977). 'Self-focused attention and the experience of emotion: attraction, repulsion, elation, and depression.' *Journal of Personality and Social Psychology*, **35**, 625–636.

Scheier, M. F. and Carver, C. S. (1983). 'Self-directed attention and the comparison of self with standards.' *Journal of Experimental Social Psychology*, **19**, 205–222.

Scheier, M. F., Carver, C. S. and Gibbons, F. X. (1981). 'Self-focused attention and reactions to fear.' *Journal of Research in Personality*, **15**, 1–15.

Smith, T. W. and Greenberg, J. (1981). 'Depression and self-focused attention.' *Motivation and Emotion*, **5**, 323–331.

Smith, T. W., Ingram, R. E. and Roth, D. L. (in press). 'Self-focused attention and depression: self-evaluation, affect, and life-stress.' *Motivation and Emotion*.

Steenbarger, B. N. and Aderman, D. (1979). 'Objective self-awareness as a nonaversive state: effect of anticipating discrepancy reduction.' *Journal of Personality*, **47**, 330–339.

Taylor, S. E. and Fiske, S. T. (1978). 'Salience, attention and attribution: top of the head phenomena.' In L. Berkowitz (Ed.), *Advances in Experimental Social Psychology*, vol. 10, Academic Press, New York.

Tversky, A. and Kahneman, D. (1973). 'Availability: a heuristic for judging frequency and probability.' *Cognitive Psychology*, **5**, 207–232.

Wegner, D. N. and Giuliano, T. (1980). 'Arousal-induced attention to self.' *Journal of Personality and Social Psychology*, **38**, 719–726.

Author Index

Subject Index

329